YOUTH CRISIS

Growing Up in the High-Risk Society

Nanette J. Davis
Foreword by David Matza

Westport, Connecticut
London

Library of Congress Cataloging-in-Publication Data

Davis, Nanette J.
   Youth crisis : growing up in the high-risk society / Nanette J.
Davis ; foreword by David Matza.
     p. cm.
   Includes bibliographical references and index.
   ISBN 0–275–95939–2 (alk. paper). — ISBN 0–275–96443–4 (pbk. :
alk. paper)
    1. Youth—Social conditions.   2. Juvenile delinquency—Prevention.
I. Title.
HQ796.D335   1999
305.235—dc21   98–24558

British Library Cataloguing in Publication Data is available.

Library of Congress Catalog Card Number: 98–24558
ISBN: 0–275–95939–2
     0–275–96443–4 (pbk.)

First published in 1999

Praeger Publishers, 88 Post Road West, Westport, CT 06881
An imprint of Greenwood Publishing Group, Inc.

Printed in the United States of America

The paper used in this book complies with the
Permanent Paper Standard issued by the National
Information Standards Organization (Z39.48–1984).

10 9 8 7 6 5 4 3 2

Contents

Foreword

Nanette Davis proposes that youth in contemporary society are in crisis, and that the crisis is of "great scope and magnitude." The crisis of this generation of youth includes, too, the younger children. The character and detail of this crisis is social and derives its characteristics from these two basic properties: a high-risk environment and negative justice system; and thus the main thesis of this book can be neatly summarized, though, of course, oversimplified.

Youth in crisis occurs in the context of a high-risk environment in a low-justice society. That this context exists differentially and throughout the world is detailed, illustrated, shown, documented and mapped in various ways by Nanette Davis. To develop and argue her highly original, well-argued, and revealing thesis, Davis utilizes several new theoretical discourses and research literatures. She devises a postmodern theory for the postmodern era. Environmental Risk theory and Social Justice theory are relatively new, rapidly developing, postmodern, academic modes of analysis. Davis presents the background and methods of risk and justice models of environment and society, explains the development of these frameworks, and begins the application of a postmodern mode of analysis to the everyday worlds of real youth in actual crisis.

Davis begins her book by exhorting the reader "CONSIDER: Every year, an estimated two million juvenile prostitutes between the ages of five and fifteen in the United States enter the sex market." Where, one asks, can such a terrible thing be happening? In the world, Davis explains: There is an international sex market for juveniles. Beginning on page 1 and throughout the book, Davis documents and analyzes the various ways in which youth increasingly become statistics. Becoming a statistic is the postmodern expression for being a victim in an accidental society. Whether it is being killed by a stray bullet, sitting in the wrong car-seat or without a buckled seat belt, getting maimed or killed going down a long slide with too many classmates in a commercial swimming pool, HIV and AIDS, drug and/or alcohol addiction, or being murdered or raped by parents and friends, kids have become the prototypical victim.

Nanette Davis proposes that we reconceive our thinking about and methods of collecting delinquency statistics and drug-using rates in the manner of the disciplines of public health or ecology and environmental studies. The statistics can portray clearly the victims and only dimly or misleadingly the suspected perpetrators of willful action. Someone happened to exist at the wrong time and the wrong place and then someone no longer existed. This is the postmodern perception from the university to the barrio and from literature to the ghetto. Life is harsh. Danger is imminent. Force, competition, greed, and pollution are unrelenting. Chaos becomes a theoretical perspective, though clearly one that leads nowhere.

In truth, there is a structure around the accident of being murdered, dying in a car crash, or contracting AIDS or HIV. The structure is detailed carefully and patiently by Nanette Davis, for she is aware that she is suggesting a new language of social analysis of crime, delinquency, deviant behavior, social problems. The analysis of high environmental risk and low social justice are relatively recent ways of reformulating older ways of approaching and organizing the study of social life.

Developed in a variety of disciplines and standpoints, the critical environmental risk and critical social justice models provide the conceptual framework. Nanette Davis does an admirable job of the difficult task of bringing together fresh ideas from diverse sources in the multicultural university. These ideas grew from the abandonment and reconstruction of older modes of discourse, and apply new concepts and techniques of measuring and assessing the systematic dimensions of technological environment and political and economic power. At the beginning and throughout the book, Davis explains the relevance of these new standpoints and applies the concepts associated with the environmental risk and social justice models to the description of the postmodern predicament of childhood and youth.

Her descriptions of youth and children are derived from a variety of sources, including United Nations statistics and reports, surveys of youth, ethnographic studies, journalistic and literary descriptions. These descriptions are well organized into analytic and imaginative chapters moving from the general predicament of endangered youth (which refers to all youth) through chapters on homelessness among the young, the pseudo-community of gangs, the worlds of drugs and alcohol addiction, the inner-city war zones of barrio and ghetto, and a final substantive chapter on the current predicament of black America. Each chapter deals with an aspect of the general crisis of the social problem as it impinges upon the mass of endangered youth. Her history or genealogy of youth is written with a firm grasp of the new history and summarizes an entire generation of scholarship developed after Aries, Duby, and Foucault. Her chapter on schooling is a gem of radical analysis of education. Her analysis culminates in the suggestion that we adapt a progressive, social, environmental, kind of critical pedagogy to teach and enliven the oppressed youth inhabiting the public school and much of the private-school sectors.

The logic of the substantive chapters proceeds unremittingly to demonstrate the depth and breadth of the crisis. As the reader is moved to consider the predicament of youth, it becomes clear by the final chapter that the fundamental solution—if there is to be one in a democratic society—must be structural and be framed in a manner and method different from the tried and failed panaceas of the premodern and modern eras. The twentieth-century romances of modern ideology and revolution ended in terror, and the revival of premodern religious fundamentalisms begins in terror.

The restructuring of justice provides Davis with a basic orientation toward beginning a consideration of saving youth from the morass of a contemporary wasteland, which ranges from suburban meaninglessness to inner-city war zones. Beginning with a radical and critical reading of Emile Durkheim, Nanette Davis concludes her book by proposing an organic solidarity of postmodern society, which necessitates divesting inequities and investing equalities, so as to create an actual society of interdependent individuals. In other words, a society predicated on the basis of individuality must—in order to exist on its own terms—create each individual's capacities and skills and self and soul. Only by enlarging the real reservoir of individuality is the framework of society able to reproduce itself or improve. This conclusion is quite provocative and challenges American ingenuity to face up to the severe challenge of an endangered youth. She asks that we cease and desist from feigning a collective irresponsibility, and instead provide a spiritual guidance to the arduous process of growing up in a material and complex world.

Postmodern youth need an holistic education that values and teaches emotional and relational skills instead of what passes for current schooling. Juveniles need a restorative justice to replace the defunct models of punishment and bureaucratic treatment. The restoration of peace and goodwill between offenders and victims and innocent or guilty community bystanders is a matter of far greater urgency in many cities and neighborhoods than whether to raise the prison sentence for one or another crime. Davis appeals to the basic ideals of a civil society and mobilizes a deep vein of rich and creative social-psychological-educational theory on behalf of reform. From Durkheim and William James and G. H. Mead through Habermas and Giddens, Nanette Davis infers a new strategy for coping with the breakdown of the current society's capacity to raise the next generation of youth. This strategy is postmodern in the critical sense of being post-socialist as well as postindustrial. The solution, according to Nanette Davis, is in the direction pointed to by our own structuralist sociologist, Emile Durkheim: reintegration into a community, restorative justice, holistic education, soul creation.

Building an actual society of individuals—Nanette Davis proposes we attempt a rescue of individual youths from the mechanical bureaucracies of the mass society. In the imminent years of the new millennium, it may well turn out that the organic, ecofeminist approach developed and presented by Nanette Davis is the coming paradigm for a new age and a new criminology. An ecofeminist standpoint provides a beacon for people of diverse genders, races, and classes. Ecofeminism is organic; Durkheim, as well. Many thanks to Nanette Davis for this critical reminder of a neglected point in social theory and for an excellent, challenging, and original book on the predicament of postmodern youth.

DAVID MATZA
Emeritus Professor of Sociology
University of California, Berkeley

Preface

Why write a youth book, especially a book about the youth crisis? It may be part of the nature of social change for adults to perpetually bewail the condition of the younger generation. Is this younger generation different, and how is it different? And why is it different? These are the questions I posed when I launched this study nearly three and one-half years ago, after spending some considerable time interviewing homeless teenagers in Portland, Oregon, and Sydney, Australia.

My initial answer to these questions was that the youngsters who landed on the streets or in the institutions, detention centers, shelters, and other makeshift living arrangements came from "unusual" families—those that were dysfunctional, disturbed, terminally disorganized. It took intensive research and a newly expanded awareness that "troubled youth" were not exceptional. Rather, over the last twenty years or so our culture has shifted dramatically its focus away from families and children/young people to a preoccupation with grown-up needs and wants, best understood in terms of the logic and language of the marketplace.

Another reason for writing a youth book is in response to the treatment of young people in criminology. This discipline has long been preoccupied with adolescent deviance, as any perusal of juvenile delinquency textbooks reveals (see Krisberg and Austin 1993). More recently, a wide range of topics on youth has surfaced, including the traditional concerns of legal definitions and behavior patterns of delinquency and child dependency, but also other youth concerns as well: studies of abused children, African American families, high school drop outs, teen employment, differential arrest rates of minority youth, drugs, violence, gangs, poor laws, teenage pregnancy, juvenile victims, juvenile justice, incarceration trends, and a host of other topics related to youth problems. In all instances the disciplinary rubric is "juvenile delinquency" rather than youth studies.

The delinquency approach, though, lends itself to the pathologization of young people and to control-over models, because analysis of delinquency and juvenile justice (with significant exceptions) tends to be confined to status quo, nonstructural interpretations. Instead, the analytical model I propose in this book revolves around the "youth crisis in postmodern society," a significantly different rubric than classical delinquency models offer. This suggests that for many young people, growing up in America can be a harrowing, dispiriting experience.

The main thesis of this book is this: Youth problems are not an American aberration but a reflection of fundamental features of American society. In this book, we explicate and illustrate the structural forces that contribute to the high rates of child and youth victimization and offending behavior. American adolescents today are at higher risk than any other age cohort. Children growing up in the pre-industrial period had to contend with serious diseases and early death; young people in our contemporary society are more likely to be seriously injured or die from accidents, gunshot wounds, and suicide—all preventable occurrences.

Destructive forces have been unleashed among a large cohort of adolescents. The FBI reports that juveniles (seventeen years old or younger) were responsible for 30 percent of the growth in violent crimes between 1988 and 1992. Within a four-year period, juveniles were responsible for 26 percent of the increase in murders, 41 percent of the increase in forcible rapes, 39 percent of the increase in robberies, and 27 percent of the increase in aggravated assaults (Snyder and Sickmund 1995). Such violence may be one way disadvantaged groups make a statement, however distorted the message.

Reflecting on American society reveals a paradoxical social order, in which the features of American culture that adults cherish so greatly for themselves are virtually denied for many of our children. Take individualism, for example. Americans are deeply committed to individual rights and individual autonomy. The sociologist Robert Bellah and his associates (1985) describe the centrality of individualism to the American identity in these terms:

Americans believe in the dignity, indeed the sacredness, of the individual. Anything that would violate our right to think for ourselves, judge for ourselves, make our own decisions, live our lives as we see fit, is not only morally wrong, it is sacrilegious.

Yet how many young people in our country are virtually denied all rights of personhood and self because they are born poor, black, female, physically challenged, mentally disabled, or otherwise fall short of the ideal. Barry Krisberg and James Austin (1993) observe that so callous have we become as a nation that many propose that we "write off" the current generation of underclass youth. The dangers of this option are only too apparent. The practice of genocide means losing a generation; in effect, forfeiting the future of a whole segment of the population.

I use the term "risk" throughout this book to imply not merely a chancy situation; the normal run of unpredictability and instability that characterizes human life. Rather, we should refer to "surplus risk," "excessive risk," an "extreme risk" condition that plagues American adolescents. The high risk conditions stem from many sources—dysfunctional families, poor schools, lack of rights, drastic cutbacks in funds for education and welfare; poor physical and dental health; insensitive and brutal caregivers; and simply the levels of stress and aggravation of living in a society that provides little direction or values for youth outside of materialistic success goals (that exclude the largest proportion of American teenagers).

The term "manufactured risk" best distills the reality of the current youth crisis. American institutions—our economy, political order, schools, families, communities, and even churches—have made life more difficult, often impossible, much less welcoming, and certainly far less nurturing for those growing up today. Young people are not suffering because it is in the nature of the age group—their biology or stage of life. Instead, the extraordinarily large numbers of young people in America succumbing to permanent social and economic disadvantage, victimhood, deviance, or criminal lifestyles mark the end of the American Dream, as generations of us have known it. Add to this, the unproductive punitive "warehousing" approach to juvenile delinquents, and the trends take on greater clarity. Without transformative changes, the American public appears to be settling in for a debilitating epoch of increased numbers of wasted lives.

The vision of a lost generation should be taken as a timely warning rather than as a finished act. The book addresses not only the youth crisis, but the kind of society we have created for young people that now and even more in the future will be mirrored back to us. As we shift gears into the twenty-first century, it is time to pay attention to the next generation and confront those parts of the culture and institutions that simply are not working any longer. It is also time to stop blaming youth for problems that originate in adult-driven motives and lifestyles. And most timely of all, as we face the new epoch, it is essential that we strengthen social institutions and rethink the American Dream if we are to develop creative solutions to the youth crisis.

Accumulating intellectual debts is all in the course of writing a book. I want to thank especially friends and colleagues who looked at parts or all of the manuscript, or gave me advice and support during the writing. Australia proved to be a great stimulus to reflecting about the condition of youth, and I have the Fulbright Commission, University of Sydney, Flinders University, and Southern Cross University to thank for sponsoring me over a three-year period to interview displaced youth and their caregivers, as well as attend to the superb research and lecture opportunities. My gratitude to Professors Elaine Martin and Suzanne Hatty, and to all my other Australian friends and colleagues, who provided insights and critical observations of life and youth in that society.

Thanks to Annette Jolin and Peter Nelson who were there when I needed them. David Matza (1990), an original and critical voice in the early years of youth studies, not only consented to write the Foreword but also served as a greatly appreciated reminder of "high sociology," the kind of reflexive sociology that casts a broad and unremitting light on the darkest cultural corners. Katherine Davis-Delaney was instrumental in compiling and skillfully sorting out the research on gangs. Barbara and the late David Washburn were very helpful with graphs. Thank you, Jim, as always, a good reader and editor, as well as life partner, who took time out of his own book preparation to massage my work. To daughter, Patricia, computer luminary, you saved my work, as well as my sanity, on numerous occasions.

YOUTH CRISIS

"Don't Tell Us about It"—The Social Condition of Youth

I believe that our civilization, far from honoring our youth and celebrating them, consumes and devours them. . . . In this failure to honor our children and the child within lies one of the most critical dangers of our epoch—and, ironically, one of the most powerful sources for a global renaissance [because] in fifteen years . . . over 50 percent of the human race will be under fifteen years of age.

Matthew Fox, *The Coming of the Cosmic Christ*

CONSIDER

Every year, an estimated two million juvenile prostitutes between the ages of five and fifteen in the United States enter the sex market. According to the U.N. Children's Fund, there are tens of millions of children in the international sex market.

Two of every three teen mothers in a Washington State study were victims of child sexual abuse, including rape and molestation—nearly half of them by someone in their family.

In one weekend in August 1995, twenty-nine people were shot dead in Los Angeles County as a result of gang violence alone.

The nation's two million Indians, whose children are the poorest in the nation, experienced severe cuts in welfare, food stamps, and Federal housing subsidies. According to the 1990 census, 31 percent of Indians earned incomes below the poverty line.

More than thirteen million children under the age of thirteen have no adult supervision either before or after school. Paying for day care would use up all or most of a mother's wages.

These and other grim statistics stress the critical importance of understanding the social condition of the younger generation, an age cohort that confronts perhaps the least sympathetic political environment in history.

CRISIS AND COMPASSION

The question—What is the social condition of youth in our time?—has never been more urgent. Because the survival of the next generation lies in the capacity of a society to sacrifice time and energy in a spirit of charity, not only for their own family or generation, but for generations to follow, most societies demand a dutiful commitment to the young. Ours may be among the first of modern societies to withdraw from this collective obligation.

Instead of resolving chronic social problems of race, poverty, violence, child abuse, war, and other destructions, ours is an age of crisis, much of it invisible—neither publicly acknowledged nor privately examined. At the trivial level, we hear people speaking of their identity crisis, midlife crisis, job crisis, and crises in their families. Often, what is taken for the crisis are really temporary indispositions, psychological shifts or transitions to a different status group (e.g., midlife crisis). The systemic problem that generated the crisis in the first place tends to be ignored (e.g., ageism, corporate oligopolies, addictions, violence in the family, and others). The media succeed in generating situations that "identify, substantiate, bypass or create crisis" (Gerbner, Mowlana, and Schiller 1996, 2). But such media events are short-lived, and have relatively little impact on stabilizing the system or of generating new initiatives to solve the crisis.

As defined by George Gerbner and associates (1996, 2), crisis derives from the Greek *krinein*, which is to judge. Hence crisis implies the decisive moment, the time of judgment. It is in this sense that I use the term in this book.

As we prepare to enter the new millennium, we must ask ourselves a collective question: What kind of a world order are we creating, and for whose benefit? At this juncture, it seems only too apparent that democratic principles and spiritually informed policies of care and concern for others have been severely eroded; some would say that they have been erased altogether. In their place are mega corporations, big politics, and centralized media that not only control information but also shape our very existences on a daily basis. The siege mentality of our cities continues uninterrupted by political shifts in mayors or parties; the savage inequalities of income and opportunities contribute to virtual wholesale exclusion from mainstream society millions of persons because they are young, old, poor, illiterate, disabled, displaced, and discarded.

Under the guise of a "free market" economy, we have generated a global system of capitalist production and distribution that is ecologically, economically, and socially unsustainable. Depending upon the specific country, we have a food crisis, ecological crisis, health crisis, an education crisis, an economic crisis, a crisis of political legitimacy, an immigrant crisis, a crisis of violence, a crisis for survival, and significantly, a crisis in common understandings. In the United States, all these crises exist simultaneously but definitely do not impact equally on the population. Children and adolescents are most likely to be adversely affected by these interconnected crises because of their greater vulnerability, dependency, and little or no coping skills (depending upon their age and circumstances).

The youth crisis assumes many forms. These range from the personal to the global, from the specific to the general, and from the material to the symbolic levels. To speak of any youth crisis, say, gangs or homelessness, is to confront an array of interconnected crises, stemming from what the sociologist recognizes as "structural" arrangements: gender, race, culture of violence, poverty, ethnicity, and other divisive features that are an everyday, hence unnoticed, state of affairs.

The important feature of the contemporary crisis is that much of it is invisible. The invisible crisis implies that for many Americans it lurks beneath the surface of our everyday lives. If Caucasian, we are not conscious of racism until our daughter, for example, marries an African American, and we observe firsthand the everyday humiliations and fear that our loved one faces at the job or on the street. All these responses are a normal part of race relations in this country. In our middle class cocoons, we rarely confront the hazards of the single mother unless she works for us and must absent herself because of a sick child, or who must borrow from next month's pay because her childcare payments are late, or more likely, have stopped altogether.

Most Americans are amazed to discover that our city streets are home to nearly two million homeless young persons, thousands of whom must prostitute or steal to stay alive. For example, a Seattle-based study shows that the streets in this city of a half million persons contain over two thousand homeless youth; yet shelter space is available for only sixty young people (*Seattle Post Intelligencer*, November 23, 1997, A1).

How many of us consider the implications of the now-standard school policy of expulsion (for weeks or months) for minor infractions that affect thousands of students? How many of us have written our congressperson an outraged letter because of drop-out rates of 50 percent in inner-city schools? At the end of the twentieth century, there is little public protest left; little energy to look beneath the surface of things. As a society, we appear absorbed in our own smallness—too busy, anxious, confused, fearful, angry, and cynical—to address our collective problems. Above all, our current epoch has erased the one quality that bonds human to human, that of compassion.

Compassion—as mother love; as unconditional love; as a feeling of deep sympathy for the young and helpless, or sorrow for another human who may be stricken with suffering or misfortune—is out of vogue. Matthew Fox (1988, 31) says that the Hebrew word for compassion is derived from the word for womb. Womb love, mother love, and creative love are all part of the power we know. This places compassion as the source for our basic energy force, essentially a connection with self and others. The social-spiritual idea that we are all connected, despite differences in culture, family of origin, class, race, gender, or personal taste, and therefore have obligations to one another, has never been very popular in our highly individualistic society.

Today, compassion is a dying virtue. Two thirds of Americans say it is important not to get too involved in the problems of others. You have to take care of yourself first (Zeldin 1994, 249). In an era of "tough love," where people are expected to suffer for their wrongdoing, where children are ostracized and institutionalized for their parents' failures, and where we cross the street to avoid the homeless beggar, love of neighbor does not figure significantly in the social calculus.

M. Scott Peck (1993) argues that ours is a deeply ailing society. Our illness is *incivility*, which he claims goes far beyond mere impoliteness and goes back much further in time than the blatantly self-centered "me" generation of the 1980s. The morally destructive patterns of self-absorption, callousness, manipulativeness, and materialism, that are so deeply ingrained in our everyday behavior, have become routine ways of being in the world. In multiple ways, Peck says, we engage in subtle forms of unconscious injury toward ourselves and others—ways that have become accepted as the norm in American society.

Compassion did not really expire in one day, nor in one year. Rather it is more like a process, a shift from one level of consciousness to another, which means that it can be revived and reborn. In fact, there is recent evidence of its rebirth in small and large matters: from random acts of kindness by anonymous donors, to the sacrificial efforts of helping individuals in times of crisis or to save the environment, to a presidential summit on renewing volunteerism. The origins for the attack on compassion lie in industrialization and technology, where things, not people, take center stage.

Compassion is the ingredient that gives our relationships and work life their ultimate meaning and satisfaction. Its absence creates profound disadvantages and uncertainties with ramifications throughout all our personal and social relationships. Without a sense of deep connection to others, we use people for our temporary convenience or as stepping stones to personal or corporate goals. The incredible "downsizing" efforts by corporations to cut workers and expand profits is part of this dearth of compassion. So is the foster care system that locks children into caregiving systems that are oppressive and loveless (Craig 1995). Exploitation, manipulation, indifference, and violence have become commonplace images of public life; for many individuals this negative state characterizes their marriage, family, and social life as well.

For children, the absence of adult compassion and the political denigration of their needs has contributed to a growing tide of social disorder. A world waiting to explode is how some observers perceive the youth scene. Because of their size and inadequate strength, small children pose few threats to the social order. Adolescents, however, offer a different scenario. The potential for anarchy, self- and other destruction, and protracted alienation are genuine. As we careen toward the twenty-first century, these negative conditions have become more pervasive for growing numbers of young people. The social situation plays a critical role in shaping youthful behavior. For example, some neighborhoods are organized in ways that produce crime and delinquency (Reiss 1986; Reiss and Roth 1993).

This book reports on the youth crisis as an outcome of a twofold process: the general state of social crisis and the decline of compassion as a core principle of culture. As a social scientist, I draw on the concept of *compassion* as a metaphor to account for the severity of cultural absences: the absence of love, faith, hope, justice, civility, certainty, and continuity in our public and private relations with one another, but especially with children and young people. Most of us work very hard to deny the reality of what this culture is doing to children. We identify losers or punish offenders, but rarely do we acknowledge the social condition of youth as itself very problematical because of the nature and organization of our society.

The book draws on a variety of trends and scholarly research to articulate one major proposition: To be young today is a very risky enterprise in which many will fail or succumb to early death, destruction of others, or oblivion.

DENYING THE REALITY

"Why Are Kids Killing?" asks *People* magazine (June 23, 1997). Could this be "coincidence or a scary trend?" During the past decade, the number of murders committed by teenagers has leaped from around one thousand a year to nearly four thousand. Media surveillance of casual violence ranges from stories of infanticide to killing on a whim—killing for the thrill of it.

They entail a variety of lurid episodes: One horrific incidence involves a New Jersey girl, eighteen years old, dressed up for her senior prom, who excused herself at the dance to go to the ladies room, and while there, gave birth in the stall to a 6 lb., 6 oz. boy. She then asphyxiated her live newborn with a plastic bag, placed him in a trash can, and then returned smiling to continue dancing at the prom. Two Bellevue, Washington youth, followers of the gothic subculture, killed an entire family—a mother, father and two daughters—"for the sheer experience of killing." A fifteen-year-old daughter of a millionaire businessman, accustomed to hanging out in Manhattan's Central Park, stands accused with her fifteen-year-old friend, of stabbing a forty-four-year-old real estate agent, then heaving his body into a lake. Two boys, ages eleven and thirteen, dressed in camouflage clothing, masterminded an ambush during a fake fire drill at an Arkansas middle school. Four girls and one teacher died from this gruesome outburst; eleven other children were seriously wounded. It was the third mass killing in a public school within a six-month period.

The list goes on. Most of these and the other youngsters depicted in the various media stories are not psychopathological. They are typically reported to be normal kids from a variety of backgrounds engaged in crimes of incredible callousness. Experts are pointing to the flaws of the socialization process, where families emphasize comfort and intellectual achievement, but ignore or dishonor moral excellence.

Yet, public outrage fizzles out. It rarely lasts long enough to examine what is really going on beyond the veneer of the latest media report. Once the official decision to severely punish the offenders has been made, the public response is passivity and indifference. "Don't tell me about the youth problem!" means that the public not only does not want to know about the social conditions confronting contemporary youth but also collectively feels helpless to do anything about it.

As a society we are fascinated with violence, saturating ourselves with the images and acts of cruelty and death so readily available on television. The print media is not far behind. Consider how many readers are exposed to thriller stories, murder reports, and other newspaper/magazine dissections of homicide. In a country where the murder rate exceeds that of Lebanon, and around twenty-five thousand people die of gunshot wounds every year, young Americans are faced with a cultural tradition where violence is "as American as apple pie." In effect, high rates of murder and assault can be explained in terms of a "culture of violence," in which threats to honor require a violent response (Luckenbill and Doyle 1996). When adolescents act out the violent scenarios, however, the public mood shifts. Punishment after the fact becomes the unreflected policy of choice; juveniles charged with violent acts are more likely to be incarcerated or placed on formal probation, compared with adults charged with similar crimes (Irwin and Austin 1997).

Blaming the child is a misguided policy. Instead, I suggest we consider children who act out in destructive ways as analogous to the canary bird, which acts as an alarm system in underground coal mines. When the canary is exposed to deadly methane gas (which is invisible, tasteless, and odorless), it quickly dies, thereby alerting the crew to vacate the mine immediately. The canary bird thesis points to both the greater vulnerability of children to our toxic society, and a warning that we ignore children and youth problems at our ultimate peril.

This book challenges our understanding about growing up in America. It confronts our collective denial about the real conditions experienced by young people, especially among the more vulnerable. Also, it exposes the everyday pitfalls and dangers youngsters experience. Finally, this book invites you to rethink the youth issue as a social-spiritual phenomenon.

WHY STUDY YOUTH?

Youth—the age group between twelve and nineteen, but sometimes including young adults up to twenty-five years old—presents a puzzle. The adolescent cohort, usually referred to as "teenagers," often behaves in mysterious, typically awkward, invariably embarrassing, and sometimes dangerous ways relative to adult standards of conduct. And even though every adult has experienced being in this age group, a generalized notion prevails that no adult can really understand what his or her teenager really thinks about the world that makes much sense to a grown-up mind. The music, the clothing, the street argot, the gangs (in some neighborhoods), erratic moods, and other insignia of youth appear foreign to the adult mind. The official tendency is to label differences as "deviant," and punish accordingly. Especially in high-risk settings, such as those found among physically and emotionally absentee or abusive families and violent neighborhoods, nonattachment and disengagement among youth is one measure of this generation fallout (Commission on Behavioral and Social Sciences and Education 1993).

The pervasive power of the media, and, for more-advantaged families, computer ownership offering the high-speed global "information superhighway" or cyberspace, have transformed consumption, entertainment, information, and socializing. By the time they reach age 18, adolescents as a group will have logged more hours in front of the television set than they will have spent in the classroom (Strasburger 1995). During this viewing time, the average child or adolescent will see about one thousand murders, rapes, or aggravated assaults each year (Huston et al. 1992). Overall, adolescents who have the poorest life chances, because of poverty, minority status, and learning problems, watch more television than typical adolescent groups (Huston et al. 1992).

The current adolescent cohort—the so-called Generation X—is said to be cynical and apolitical, self-centered and withdrawn, overly preoccupied by material acquisitions, undermotivated for creative expression, and unforgiving of adult insensitivities and arcane expectations (Howe and Strauss 1993). At its worst, this generation of youth has been said to facilitate the loss of the American Dream, because with them will die progressive ideas about America as the land of opportunity, and of middle-class home ownership as a basic right. How far this rather dismal depiction of youth captures the reality of young people's experience may never be definitely known. One thing, however, is certain. Being an adolescent today is a high-risk activity from a wide range of perspectives and, as such, deserves our special attention. So, why study youth? Here are some compelling reasons to do so.

The first, and most obvious, reason to study youth is that youth represent the future; as we sow, so shall we reap. How well are we providing for our children's well-being? The data on child poverty, child abuse and neglect, nonlearning in schools, community disorganization, and massive disappearance of family-wage jobs strongly indicate that young people can be only as strong as the society that raises them. In this case, a weakened society produces a fragmented population. Globalization trends have changed the face of society more than any other single factor. If it takes a village to rear a child, as the adage has it, we must confront the fact that in the postmodern world we have lost the village, a once unified, cohesive community, and replaced it with a far more diffuse sense of place. The global village is a world of blurred boundaries.

A second compelling reason for studying this age cohort is that children and youth comprise a significant proportion of the population. The 1990 census reveals that about 25 percent of the U.S. population, or over sixty-three million persons, are under eighteen. Leaving out the preschool child, over fifty-seven million Americans are between the ages of five and twenty years old. Infants and small children account for another eighteen million (see Table 1.1). Because the child/youth population are necessarily dependent upon parents, guardians, communities, and local, state, and federal governments for their well-being, they represent the heaviest resource-consuming group in the country.

Social, emotional, economic, and political dependency marks their status. As such, youth receive only conditional rights and liberties, as defined by adults. Rules, imposed from above by adult caregivers and managers, are rarely devised in consultation with the youth status. The resulting youthful efforts at self-expression along with strong peer identification often take the form of rebellion and acting out. For a growing proportion of youth, this acting out behavior may eventuate in delinquency, and for some, adult criminal careers. For still other youth, problem behavior severely impacts on psychosocial development rendering the young person incompetent for fulfilling adult roles (Jessor and Jessor 1977).

Highlighting the study of youth is intergenerational conflict. Adolescents as a whole are considered to be a problem population, but one in which the problems are said to reside with the age cohort, rather than with the society or individual ("What do you expect; she's a teenager"). We expect young people to "mature out" of their problems, whether it be simple rebellion, drug addiction, delinquency, or gang behavior (Haggerty et al. 1994). In a significant number of cases, though, the deviance persists as a lifestyle and can be life-threatening. Depression and a deep sense of futility are commonly experienced by adolescents (Garber, Robinsonk, and Valentiner 1997).

Table 1.1
Number of Persons and Percent of Child/
Youth Population, 1970–2020 (numbers in thousands)

Age in Years	1970 N	%	1980 N	%	1990 N	%	2000 N	%	2010 N	%	2020 N	%
Under 5	17,166	8.4	16,458	7.2	18,408	7.4	16,898	6.3	16,899	6.0	17,095	5.8
5-13	36,672	17.9	31,095	13.7	32,393	12.9	33,483	12.5	31,001	11.0	31,697	10.8
14-17	15,924	7.8	16,142	7.1	13,237	5.3	15,332	5.7	14,746	5.2	14,074	4.8
18-24	24,712	12.1	30,350	13.3	26,140	10.4	25,231	9.4	27,155	9.6	25,018	8.5
Total Percent Of Population	46.2		41.3		36.0		33.9		31.8		29.9	

Sources: U.S. Bureau of the Census. Projections of the Population of the United States by Age, Sex, and Race 1988 to 2040 (1989), and Statistical Abstract of the United States (1993).

One of ten young people in America has attempted suicide. Among Native Americans, that figure leaps to one out of ten who has actually succeeded in committing suicide. The suicide rate for fifteen- to nineteen-year-olds has tripled in the last three decades from 2.6 per 100,000 in 1955 to 8.5 per 100,000 in 1980 (Doyle 1987). Firearms account for the majority of teenage suicides, and the rate of suicide by firearms has more than doubled in the last twenty years (*Seattle Times*, June 2, 1996).

Issues of economic and political inequality among youth are paramount reasons for studying this population. Poverty and minority status mean that many young Americans will face serious risks and hardships. Children and youth comprise the largest proportion of poor people in America today. Among young adolescents (ten to fourteen years old), approximately 20 percent are living below the poverty line, which in 1993 was $14,763 for a family of four (Carnegie Council on Adolescent Development 1995, 24).

By the year 2000, nearly 40 percent of all young people will be members of racial or ethnic minorities: African Americans (16 percent), American Indian, Eskimo, and Aleut (1 percent), Asian/Pacific Americans (5 percent), and Hispanic/Latino (14 percent). From a futurist perspective, it could be said that the future generation is being ransomed for the well-being of today's affluent generation. What is the fate of poor children? Have we as a society abandoned the needy and most vulnerable among us? Policymakers and citizens continue to evade this question, even as the evidence of our collective neglect mounts.

Youth constitute a significant proportion of index crime offenders—a situation that requires our immediate attention. Young males, including juveniles and young adults, steal, fight, rape, rob, and murder at rates that are beginning to approximate adult criminal involvement (Rojek and Jensen 1996). Once believed to be a problem limited to adult minority or marginal populations, crime has surfaced as a young person's activity as well, possibly linked to the youth culture and certainly connected to neighborhood and community disorganization (Reiss 1986). Do youth crime rates also reflect the growing disenchantment of the young about the outmoded social and political values of their elders? How do we explain the growing popularity of gang membership? When youth join gangs, the likelihood of criminal involvement is even higher than for those not gang-involved. In American cities and towns, gangs have become criminal organizations that both attract the lawless and teach the innocent criminal behavior (Whitehead and Lab 1996).

Gender differences and how they play out among young people offers a significant reason for examining this group. In adult society, gender role conflicts are often concealed behind traditional rhetoric and practices. In adolescence, however, the gender disparities are rampant and ill-disguised. From everyday harassment of female students in school, to "gang bangs" against vulnerable girls, to creating victims among younger or nonathletic boys, young men exert dominance behavior in a variety of ways. No place is really safe for young women—not home, school, or street. Excessively high rates of coercive sex testify to this reality. The Carnegie Council on Adolescent Development (1995) reported that in a national representative sample of adolescents ten to sixteen years old, one fourth of respondents reported having experienced sexual assault or abuse in the previous year.

Another concern is that child abuse does not stop when the youngster enters adolescence. Approximately 20 percent of the documented child abuse and neglect cases in 1992 involved young adolescents between the ages of ten and thirteen years. Pagelow's (1989) research on family violence shows shockingly high abuse prevalence rates among adolescents. Her data demonstrate that although adolescents constitute about half of the population of abused children, they are unlikely to report their abuse; when they do, they are often disbelieved or blamed. Sibling violence, including sexual exploitation, occurs more frequently than any other form of family violence, yet it is the least likely to be reported to authorities (Pagelow 1989; Finklehor and Dziuba-Leatherman 1995).

Added to the social and psychological woes of being adolescent are the physical deprivations that often accompany this age. Dietary deficiencies are commonplace, and sleep deprivation so ordinary that educational reformers are talking of delaying the start of the school day to accommodate the "walking zombies," whose sleep patterns are grossly out of sync with their learning curve. Most middle and high school students are overprogrammed, recent studies show (Richardson 1995). Starting school at 7:30 A.M., a typical school routine, appears to satisfy the educational bureaucrat's need for effectively utilizing space, rather than to meet growing children's physiological requirements for rest.

Finally, we study youth to transform losses into gains, to keep the flame of hope alive. Americans are among the world's most innovative people. Yet through denial and neglect we are abandoning large segments of an entire generation. Stuffing ever larger numbers of youthful miscreants into adult prisons is not the answer to our youthful crime problem. Nor is the laissez-faire attitude that "the kids will take care of themselves"—often expressed among adults who have already given up the dream—a solution to these problems and others identified in this book.

THREEFOLD ANALYSIS

We take up the issue of youth as a threefold analysis. The first aim is to clarify the status of youth as a high-risk population; and, conversely, how certain segments of the youth population are at very high risk to the degree that some behavior is actually life-threatening for self or others—for example, gang membership, substance abuse, and use of handguns. The second purpose is to show the social and political sources of youth's structural disadvantages by focusing on the problem of social justice. It is not only the inherent lack of justice for youth, but also the paucity of scholarly attention to youth as a problematic social and legal category that tends to perpetuate the injustice. The third objective is to provide a global perspective on youth issues by citing some relevant literature from international sources. By no means does this constitute a comparative approach. Instead, the global perspective generally shows significant cultural continuities and discontinuities to better clarify the contemporary youth status in the United States.

This book takes issue with narrow psychological and educationalist views that affix pathological attributes to individual offending young people. Instead, I argue that youth issues are structural, which is to say, that youth problems, deprivations, aggravations, and contradictions have their source in social, political, legal, and economic institutions. In today's global society, such social conditions foster rootlessness, alienation, and violence.

THEORETICAL PERSPECTIVE

Risk taking is one of the keys to understand the youth crisis. The theoretical perspective entails a **risk model** that contains both value laden and analytical components. These components underlie how we assess the social condition of youth, the social control processes that are built into adult-youth relationships, and the youth policies that contribute to either rule compliance or deviance.

The book is built around an analytical perspective that posits the potential for risk behavior among youth throughout all facets of institutional life. The idea of "risk behavior" among adolescents is tantamount to describing everyday existence for the vast number of the youth cohort. "Risk" is popularly associated with that which is emotionally edgy, dangerous, exciting, hazardous, challenging, volatile, possibly disreputable, potentially costly (emotionally, socially, and financially), life-threatening, and invariably opposed to security and established ways of being in the world (Bell and Bell 1993; Lyng 1993). Youth and youthful activities that embody elements of risk run the gamut from learning to drive a vehicle—practically a rite of passage for most fifteen- and sixteen-year-olds—to negotiating the hurdles of developing appropriate drinking comportment, to establishing a personal and sexual identity, to adapting to the labor market, and to evolving conscious patterns of relating and living, while moving at a normative pace through the most tumultuous period of the life cycle. At the foundation of risk is social, emotional, economic, and political dependency. Their status is created by others; their roles are defined by others; their selfhood is constructed for the interests, needs, and conveniences of others.

According to David Hamburg (1992), president of the Carnegie Corporation of New York and child advocate, adolescence is a "fateful time," and needs to be taken seriously.

The problems of adolescence deal with deep and moving human experiences. They center on a fateful time in the life course when poorly informed decisions can have lifelong consequences. The tortuous passage from childhood to adolescence requires our highest attention, our understanding, and a new level of thoughtful commitment.

Ulrich Beck (1992) has extended the risk idea to include the notion of a high-risk society; a society with such severe steering problems that it threatens the survival of the planet. Beck's concept of the "risk society" depicts social disaster: "We are living on the edge of a volcano."

Conduct that entails risk or danger for youth typically constitutes a burden for adults and all of society. For example, inexperienced drivers have higher accident rates; teenage sexuality may lead to pregnancy and venereal disease; peer interaction can result in drug use or gang formation; after-school and weekend jobs often reduce students' grade point or contribute to early school withdrawal; alcohol and drug addiction generates runaway behavior, criminal involvement, and, for thousands of youth annually, homelessness.

Youth and youth issues clearly have an image problem in the United States and around the world. The dismissive phrase, "They're just kids, what do they know?," is intended to disparage the maturing process or person with negative traits. The aloof, judgmental attitude undermines mutuality, acceptance, equality, or humanity, virtues that connect us despite our differences. At best, youth are tolerated or endured, but rarely treated as viable partners or creative contributors to the social fabric (T. Bernard 1996, 31). The popular press may go further, castigating young people as the worst kind of criminals. For example, *Time* magazine in 1989 described the "beast that has broken loose in some of America's young people."

Adults, in effect, have marginalized young people. Much of the recent empirical and analytical literature underscores the precarious status of youth (Carnegie Council on Adolescent Development 1995; Dryfoos 1993; Bell and Bell 1993). At best, every young person enters adolescence unprepared for the open-ended risk situations that await them. It is essential that we recognize the range of ordinary interactions between adults and youth and between peers that carry implicit risk.

The risk model points to structural arrangements that have exacerbated the normal risks of growing up for all children, but especially poor, minority youngsters, and contributed to highly deleterious conditions for families and entire communities. Importantly, these risks are outside of individuals' or their families' control. Think about some of the everyday social arrangements that we have come to take for granted, and reconsider how these generate risky circumstances for families and children.

1. Structured uncertainty comprises the nature of contemporary social life. Planning a future in this context is rife with liabilities. Job "deskilling," which reduces skill level and pay; elimination or loss of jobs; divorce and newly constituted families; lack of relational continuity because of frequent job shifts and geographical mobility are only some of the commonplace events that make planning and a stable life difficult.

2. Rational choice-making, the basis for a democratic society and personal integration, is severely undermined when political, economic, and educational institutions opt for short-term advantages while ignoring long-term consequences. For example, lack of a living wage for many working poor families undermines the American Dream that hard work results in economic success.

3. A consumer society has replaced worker identification as the most salient basis for social interaction. Although many Americans lack the financial capacity to participate broadly in these activities, the consumer mentality with its artificially induced needs and impulse buying affects nearly all of us. You can see it in the suburban high school, where competition for peer acceptability depends upon family income and the material goods to show it. Ghetto youth play out the status game as well, not by affluent family scripts, but by participation in illegal markets that allow them to engage in conspicuous consumption.

4. As costs and benefits of social participation are increasingly unbalanced because of class, race, ethnicity, and age inequalities, it is more and more difficult for people to assess realistic benefits from finite choices that extend beyond oneself or one's immediate family.

5. Child care has become a national emergency. Low-income families are in many ways the forgotten class in the national debate over child care. They make too little to afford the choices of professional women— whether to use a nanny or a licensed child care facility. Often, they must sacrifice quality for substandard, non-nurturing arrangements, that may entail little more than setting children in front of a television set for hours on end. For millions of Americans, the new welfare law that demands that single mothers work throws ever larger numbers of children into a high-risk situation. Studies show that children in low-quality care can have delayed cognitive and language development, behave more aggressively toward others, and react poorly to stress.

6. Risk reduction practices rarely reflect social justice considerations. Ability to pay and access to dominant institutions and authority persons, based on social class and occupational advantages, usually determine how risk will be managed. This leaves many vulnerable persons at very high risk.

7. Much of our current impasse has to do with the cult of individualism that has preempted collective and group identities. Lasch (1977) refers to this condition as the "narcissistic self," capturing the notion of the overly self-involved individual doomed to drown in his/her own reflection. We teach our children as a matter of course to put their own interests above those of others. Obviously, collectively managing our high risk society becomes a sheer impossibility if each

person simply makes choices based on a very narrowly construed conception of society, as singular individuals occupying private worlds.

The risk model can also account for extreme risk takers, who calculate (perhaps not in adult fashion) their options, often choosing to take on very risky endeavors. For example, joining a gang is very risky. As a subculture, it exposes the youth to a variety of unknown dangers, drug use and street violence among them. But not to join a gang in certain inner-city neighborhoods is even riskier. Joining means *protection*, the safety of numbers. Concerned adults know that protracted drug use among adolescents is linked to a variety of consequences: dropping out of school, delinquency, troubled home life, relationship difficulties, personality changes, addictive reactions, and homelessness. Yet, the youth culture has normalized drugs; prohibition has had little or no impact on current youth drug patterns. Today, cannabis is widely distributed among youth groups, as are other psychoactive drugs: Ecstasy, LSD, and "speed." When taken with alcohol (polydrug use), street drug use can produce severe physiological reactions for some young people.

The risk model is particularly persuasive in providing frameworks for the study of long-term consequences of early familial risk structures. For instance, physical, emotional, and sexual abuse against children and adolescents set the stage for risk participation in later adolescence and adulthood (e.g., delinquency, crime, mental illness, divorce, intergenerational family violence).

The model of risk that I propose runs counter to most economic, administrative, and educational theories. The "rational man" or "rational actor" argument portrays individuals as making sound choices once presented with an array of alternatives. In classic economic theory, people are supposed to enter the market seeking to maximize "utilities," that is to buy the best goods or services at the lowest possible prices. This premise also holds for social behavior. The "economic man" optimizes choices by deciding in favor of highest benefits, lowest cost options.

Administrative theory likewise proposes that organizations act efficiently to maximize "net value achievement" to the benefit of the organization or the entire society (Dye 1978, 28). This calls for the "sacrifice" of one or more values no longer deemed relevant in a particular situation. Similarly, educational theories draw increasingly on sociological, market, and administrative analysis to discern future distributions of students along with their purported interests and needs.

In the case of adolescents, what is the "best choice/least cost" alternative may be irrelevant, because of family or community or traditions that dictate particular choices. Again, many young people assign greater significance to peer norms, which may emphasize impulsive and irrational behavior (Bell and Bell 1993). Even among seemingly very rational young people, lack of experience and the desire to experiment are twin factors that undermine the "rational actor" argument.

The risk approach is not a theoretical panacea to grasping the social condition of youth. However, it may offer the most fruitful overarching perspective that can give coherence and discipline to my description and analysis of youth as a social process and as an inherently problematic social group.

SOCIAL JUSTICE

If the entire focus were restricted to risk elements and their negative influence on youth, I could be accused of perpetuating the youth problem. Without a vision of other possibilities, we tend to be part of the problem; hence, the urgency of actively pursuing the solution. I have been deeply involved with youth as a parent, grandparent, and teacher, as well as being a close student of the youth scene, especially since the cultural eruptions of the 1960s. I clearly recognize the limits of a risk analysis, which analytically takes us only as far as the machinations of modern society and its ills. We clearly need a visionary paradigm—presented here as a **social justice model**—to offset the burden of social facts that risk analysis yields.

Social justice, couched in terms of a critical ecology paradigm, offers a second analytical and policy-oriented approach. Over the course of the book, I expand on the philosophical and policy limitations inherent in current justice theories. I also invite you to engage in some critical and transcendent thinking to envision a new paradigm of social justice as compassion making—celebrating children and youth, healing our intergenerational wounds, and esteem building for the vulnerable among us.

The old paradigm—an elitist and reductionist version of social life— barely speaks to the contemporary social scene where population diversity, rapid and unpredictable social change, and globalization are transforming societies. Elitist versions of justice, moreover, contribute little to our understanding of youth and its peculiar and tortuous passage from childhood through adolescence and eventually to adulthood. Nor do existing models offer guides to peacefully and positively tracking young persons into prosocial behaviors and relationships. Justice, as a predominant metaphor for the political process, offers an image of balanced scales. But there is little balance in adult institutions that have control over youth. The justice model totally fails to capture the current expressions of adult power that ranges from moral indifference to draconian levels of wrongdoing. The old paradigm not only lacks credibility; when it comes to youth, it lacks compassion and any sense of how to restore the human connection.

Social justice, as a concept and social vision, is counterposed to risk theory. The book argues that as we introduce principles and policies of social justice into troubled arenas or those areas where youth are locked into structured jeopardy, we can expect different results. For example, as Chapter 8 details, the old justice model claims to deal with the drug problem by having a "war on drugs." This has actually opened up economic opportunities for very young drug sellers, because they rarely are prosecuted. It has also fostered more highly organized gangs, who increasingly run their organizations like businesses. The "war" is really a war on youth, poor people, and deviants; and it deserves to be lost.

Social justice has a visionary quality. It invites us to reconsider our current social relations in favor of more life-enhancing ones. But it also offers a significantly different approach to crime, delinquency, and behavior problems among youth. Unlike the old paradigm that extols marginalization and punishment for young offenders, a social justice perspective takes into account the seductive attraction of various deviant activities, such as gang membership and drug selling, or other illegal conduct, and considers alternative activities that generate more-benign youth alliances. After all, most gang members seek companionship and structure; the criminal activities follow. Pro-social intervention requires attending to the needs and interests of youth; not in adult terms, but on their own ground.

Finally, social justice as a new paradigm enables us to critically assess the entire array of social practices that contributes to a risk society, as this affects youth. The proposed paradigm eschews fragmentary analysis of specific policies in favor of an ecological model that focuses on the interactive effects of various institutional arrangements. The book examines both theories and practices of injustice and mistreatment, as well as proposes new ways of thinking and acting to create regimes and practices of social justice. As a start, we need new definitions of justice, which begin with a simple prescription: full social participation and socially supported self-determination for all young people, regardless of gender, class, race, ethnicity, or conditions of parenting.

OVERALL THEMES OF THE BOOK

To recapitulate: The risk perspective allows us to describe and analyze how a youth crisis has emerged in our epoch, including the scope, dimensions and consequences of the crisis (Hamburg 1992; Lyng 1993; Bell and Bell 1993). A number of themes will be pursued that provides a conjunction between risk analysis that exposes the social conditions of youth, and a vision of social justice that clarifies the degradation of adult institutions in their management and treatment of young people. These themes are as follows:

• The youth crisis is worldwide and recognizes no national borders. It is both analogous to, and part of the general pattern of, ecological decay, the now accelerating pattern of destruction of the natural environment, traditional cultures, and nonindustrial ways of life.

- An historical perspective reveals that children and youth are cultural constructs, convenient social inventions, related to the changing nature of work and adult-child relations. At one level, childhood/youth is a product of a more complex society, one in which small children, and more recently, adolescents are set aside as a distinct social and legal category with a distinctive set of rights, obligations, and social rituals. At another level, childhood/youth as a subjugated population stand for the disadvantages of powerlessness—all decisions, choices, and futures determined by adult others. From the latter perspective, children and youth must forge their own means of survival, which invariably entails uncertainties. Risk inheres in the child or youth status itself, as well as within the larger social context.

- Social injustice prevails insofar as inequality is taken for granted as part of the nature of things. This implies that gross inequalities among youth in health, education, economic opportunity, social power, and happiness are not chance occurrences. Rather they reflect structured outcomes of racial, ethnic, gender, and other social differences. Race matters on nearly every social measure; so do class and gender. Laws and policies made by affluent and professional adults often run counter to the needs and interests of poor and working class families. Sexual dominance threatens all children, but is particularly oppressive for adolescent females, who are commonly exposed to sexual assault, rape, and pregnancy from older male companions.

- Danger or the threat of danger pervades young people's lives. Not all youth are equally affected, of course, but the growing number of young people who are risking their lives and futures on drugs, eating disorders, suicide attempts (or successful completion), becoming homeless, involvement in serious delinquency or criminal pursuits impacts an ever larger number of this age cohort. Additionally, many juveniles have been victimized by parents, older siblings, school mates, acquaintances, and strangers. Abuse/neglect victimization contributes to juvenile offending, which may continue into adult offending (Maxfield and Widom 1995).

- Social policy efforts to ameliorate the turmoil and uncertainty of the adolescent transition are often fragmentary, overly selective, and ineffective. For example, drug education and treatment seek to abolish all drug/alcohol use. Such prohibition may have counterproductive results for young people. Moreover, drug-alcohol-focused intervention often ignores social and familial conditions that gave rise to the addiction pattern in the first place.

CONCLUSION

This chapter examined the social condition of youth as a twofold problem: the rising incidence of unresolvable social problems that have reached a crisis state, and that impact directly on the moral, social, psychological, economic, and spiritual well-being of youth; and the lack of public compassion for young people as they confront the dilemmas of contemporary life. The fact that youth comprise a significant proportion of the population at the same time that their role in society has measurably declined exacerbates the problems of growing up. Adolescents, as an age cohort, are an endangered group. The next chapter considers in detail how social change has impacted on young people, creating a crisis of great scope and magnitude.

2

"It Isn't Easy Being Young": Youth and the Risk Society

I have learned that whenever a community is threatened, all are affected. Whenever a single human being is humiliated, the human image
is cheapened. Whenever a person suffers for whatever the reason and
no one is there to offer a hand, a smile, a present, a gift, a memory, a
smile again. What happens, something is wrong with society at large.
Elie Wiesel

WHAT HAS CHANGED?

It's tough being a kid in the 1990s. Since the aftermath of World War II,
and the emergence of adolescence as a definable period in the life cycle,
teenagers, along with their parents, experienced a rush of freedom and
opportunity. From the early 1950s to 1980, the economy was expanding
and the need for technocrats abounded. University and college enrollments
were up, because students expected to develop and did achieve the necessary level of job skills that translated into employment opportunities paying
at least entry-level wages, and eventually a family wage income. Young
people presumed, along with most Americans, that hard work pays off, the
rewards go to the deserving, and the promise of the good life was theirs.
What has happened to change this rosy picture?

Society itself has changed. The electronic revolution combined with a
global economy has decentered our familiar social order. The 1990s are
marked by increased economic insecurity for middle, even highly trained
professionals, as well as working class groups; the growing disparity between rich and poor; a world population explosion, and subsequent rise in
immigration; the flourishing of Asian economies (until recently) leading to
increased competitiveness and decline of American industry; and the dis-
mantling of the welfare "safety net" for low-income and disabled groups.

Globalization trends have created a new term, *postmodernism*, that points to a process of cultural fragmentation and collapse of the symbolic power and cultural capital in Western societies. In a word, postmodernism points to the decentering of culture and the introduction of cultural complexity (Featherstone 1995, 13). Whereas globalization makes us aware of the "sheer volume, diversity, and the manysidedness of culture," drawing on Featherstone's analysis, the outcome for young people has often been deleterious with increased levels of uncertainty and risk.

According to recent surveys, adolescents face challenges that were unknown, or at least, far less severe than their parents experienced growing up. Heavy emphasis on violence in film and television, ready availability of handguns, easy access to drugs, high rates of teen pregnancy, the ever-present threat of AIDS, gang involvement, and the breakdown of the nuclear family are among the high-risk situations that led one survey group to observe that "as young people move through teen years, their level of exposure to health and safety threats increased" (Morin 1995, 34).

A new national survey of one thousand randomly selected young people age eleven through seventeen conducted for Kaiser Permanente and Children Now, a California-based advocacy group, emphasized that youth today are exposed to a myriad of threats that did not exist in their parents' or grandparents' generation—and that these exposures begin at an ominously early age. Contrary to popular belief, these high-risk youngsters are not confined to stereotypical poor, minority males from broken homes. Instead, they are more likely to be white (64 percent), female (62 percent), and live in two-parent households (68 percent) (cited in Morin 1995).

A Report by the Carnegie Council on Adolescent Development (1995) outlined the new risks faced by adolescents, and continues the theme introduced in Chapter 1 of a society that devours its own children (Fox 1988; see also Takanishi 1993).

- One third of eighth graders use illicit drugs; nearly 50 percent of twelfth graders use them.
- Binge drinking is a serious drug problem in the eighth grade; and rises to nearly 28 percent among twelfth graders.
- Births to young adolescents are rising, while births to older adolescents remain high with over a half million births per annum to mothers fifteen to nineteen years old.
- Among young girls the first act of intercourse is usually forced. Among girls thirteen years and younger, 60 percent had experienced involuntary sex (incest, molestation, rape, coercive sexuality).
- Twenty percent of adolescents ten to fourteen years are living below the poverty line, a figure that exceeds 40 percent among African American youth.
- As communicable diseases decline through biomedical research and public health advances, new behavior-based morbidities have arisen. Suicide and gun-related

Table 2.1
Reported Rates of Child Abuse, 1976–1992

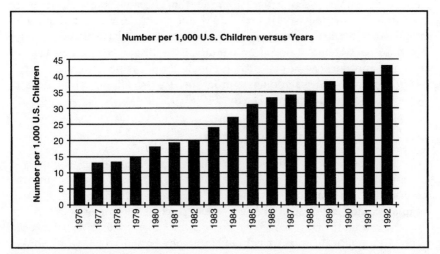

Source: U.S. Department of Health and Human Services, National Center on Child Abuse and Neglect. *Child Maltreatment 1992: Reports from the States to the National Center on Child Abuse and Neglect.* Washington, D.C.: U.S. Government Printing Office, 1994, p. 9.

homicides are at record-high levels; injury, homicide, and suicide taken together account for most adolescent deaths.

• The firearm homicide rate for ten- to fourteen-year-olds more than doubled between 1985 and 1992 (from 0.8 to 1.9 per 100,000). For black males, the rate increased from 3.0 to 8.4 per 100,000 during the same period.

• Destructive and health-damaging behaviors in adolescence tend to cluster. Thus, substance abuse, reckless driving, and unsafe sex, to provide an example, tend to occur together.

Even more damaging are the alarming increases in adult crimes against children. According to national estimates of violence toward children, as many as 5,000 children died, and more than 160,000 were seriously harmed as a result of violence (Reiss and Roth 1993, 228–29). The U.S. Advisory Board on Child Abuse and Neglect indicates that many of the deaths caused by child abuse and neglect are wrongly identified as accidents or erroneously attributed to natural causes because police, physicians, and coroners are mainly untrained in identifying evidence of inflicted trauma and extreme neglect in children (Clement 1996, 202) (see Table 2.1).

This catalog of adolescent risks, and others to be explored in this book, points to the failure of community. In the breakdown of community and the nuclear family, children and adolescents have lost out. Young people seek—but perhaps the overwhelming majority are unable to find—a coherent, plausible social order. I argue that because the culture is in transition, a coherent social order does not exist, despite status quo ideologies that insist that it does. The youth crisis, as I have defined it, is a response to systematic social and political exclusion, as well as lack of meaning and purpose of our current epoch. At the same time, social intervention by way of legislation and programs are "small, uncertain, distant, and poorly communicated" (Dryfoos 1993, 152).

SOCIAL CRISIS AND THE RISK SOCIETY

The contemporary condition of youth signals a *crisis* of great scope and magnitude. We are, after all, talking about the survival—physical, mental, emotional, and spiritual—of the next generation. Its Greek root *krisis* points to a decisive or separating moment, as when the patient goes through an indeterminate state of recovery or death. Crisis releases social, moral, economic, political forces of unpredictable power and scope, which makes a return to a status quo condition impossible (Strauss and Howe 1998). It is indeed a judgment time.

But whose crisis is it? Adults tend to point the finger at young people, demanding that *they* shape up, "take responsibility," "quit acting like teenagers" (i.e., volatile, disorderly), and other admonitions of disapproval. Politicians blame the disappearing family, especially working moms. When adults wake up to their delusion of invincibility, they often respond to the youth crisis as "something out there" that is out of control, but "kids will just have to deal with it." But children neither created this particular social crisis, nor are they likely to have the power or know-how to change the course of social events. The social crisis reflects a world out of synch, an unpeeling of the dense layers of understandings and practices that we refer to as "culture." This crisis also reflects the dissolution of our most cherished institutions, an irrevocable rupture of the sociocultural "container" that provides the boundaries defining our individual selves as well as the relationships among those selves.

Rather than a "blame structure," new thinking about crisis and change employs the risk-taking perspective. The sociology of risk is a relatively new but growing specialty area within sociology (Heimer 1988; Short 1984; Beck 1992; Douglas and Wildavsky 1982). The risk-taking perspective, as it pertains to youth, provides an understanding of self and socially destructive behavior—whether substance abuse, unprotected sex, crime, or homelessness—as a global orientation to the problem of dysfunctional, dangerous, and sometimes life-threatening environments (Bell and Bell 1993; Beck 1992).

The concept of risk-taking encompasses much more than choices to engage in dysfunctional behaviors, that is, behaviors that seem to have little or no long-term benefits for the individual. It also includes consideration of decisions to embark upon a variety of risky activities or occupations, where sensation seeking is the primary motive for action. Street crime and mountain climbing appear to be worlds apart. Yet both activities call for a level of daring, perseverance, and intensity that places the individual out of the ordinary, or "on the edge" (Lyng 1993).

Adolescents engage in many behaviors with a high probability of negative outcomes. Early in adolescence, teenagers make differential assessments of risk behaviors, and with age tend to reduce their assessments of danger or threat associated with these actions. As opportunities expand with age, there is a predictable shift toward engaging in higher levels of risk behaviors. Charles Irwin's (1993, 17) data on middle school and high school students clarifies adolescents' increased risk behavior by identifying three sets of factors.

Biopsychosocial factors. Conditions that reside within the individual or are ascribed, such as affective states, aggression, race and ethnicity, gender, genetics, hormonal levels, and internalization of role models serve as predisposing factors. Gender has also been identified by other researchers as highly significant in risk decisions, although few people acknowledge gender differences as a reason for taking or avoiding risks (Wilson and Daly 1993). What young men see as ordinary behavior—cruising the streets at night, picking up strangers, hitchhiking—may be perceived by young women as potentially dangerous behavior.

Environmental factors. The role of the social environment remains an important predictor in the onset of risk behavior, including family situations, school, peer behavior, and societal denial and unresponsiveness. Social denial is particularly apparent in the arena of child poverty, where the United States is the most backward country among all Western industrial nations in having the highest child poverty rates (see Table 2.2). Parental involvement in risk behaviors, such as addictive drinking, and low socioeconomic status contribute to a maladaptive family situation. Such family factors serve as predisposing conditions that contribute to the likelihood of an adolescent engaging in risk behaviors.

Precipitating factors. One set of precipitating factors flow from the biopsychosocial factors, resulting in increased vulnerability and/or risk situation, and include lack of experience/knowledge, lack of skills to resist peer pressure, and substance use/multiple substance use. From the risk-taking perspective, self-esteem, gender, and race may be equally involved in placing a youngster in a potentially vulnerable situation. Another set of precipitating factors derives from the environment, and includes such components as type of peer initiation, multiple school transitions, social pressure, and

Table 2.2
Child Poverty: Poor Marks for U.S.

The percentage of those under 18 living in poverty, before and after government assistance. Data, the most recent available, are for various years.

Still in poverty after receiving government assistance: ▇

Lifted out of poverty by government aid: ☐

Country	0%	5%	10%	15%	20%	25%	30%

United States

Australia

Canada

Ireland

Israel

Britain

Italy

Germany

France

Netherlands

Norway

Luxembourg

Belgium

Denmark

Switzerland

Sweden

Finland

Note: In this study, a child is defined as poor if he or she lives in a family with income less than half the national median.

Source: Luxembourg Income Study, reprinted in the *New York Times,* June 1, 1996, p. A-10. Copyright © 1996 by the New York Times Co. Reprinted by permission.

substance use availability. Adolescent male culture, especially gang membership, is frequently defined by the preponderance of risk activities: heavy drinking and drug use, violence, and failure to resist peer pressure.

Rational theory models purport to explain decisions on the basis of individual calculation of benefits and costs, but this approach fails to answer significant questions about adolescent risk taking. What constitutes risk for individuals or social groups is subject to local definitions, opportunities, and expectations. Much behavior that appears highly risky from a middle-class adult perspective may actually be a mode of coping for young inner-city adolescents. For example, joining a gang, selling drugs, having unprotected sex, and living off your girlfriend's welfare check, if male, and working as a prostitute, if female, carry potentially serious consequences for young people. But these actions may be the "normal" risks inner-city youngsters take to participate in the local scene. To appreciate the localism as well as the variety of factors associated with risk taking, an ecological perspective is required. This examines the social context as a set of historical and social relationships and their meanings to participants. From this perspective many social dangers are perceived by large sectors of the public as outside the individual's or group's control.

Awareness of environmental danger, so long denied, has become increasingly difficult to avoid. According to Douglas and Wildavsky (1982), at the level of public policy the main dangers may be grouped into four kinds:

1. Foreign affairs—including war; risk of foreign attack; loss of power, influence, and prestige
2. Crime—including failure of law and order, collapse of the social order, and violence
3. Pollution—including fears for the environment, abuse of technology, dangerous chemicals, radioactive materials
4. Economic failure—including loss of prosperity; and most recently, dramatic collapse of white collar jobs as a result of corporate downsizing. Wage stagnation plagues working class families, whose incomes have actually declined over the last twenty years in real money terms.

Fear is a characteristic response to the increased risks that have accompanied the technological society and that appear to be out of political, economic, and social control. At the same time, a *cultural* definition of risk is essential for understanding our changing perception of what constitutes risk in the first place. After all, people are living longer; our health standards have risen; and technology in Western societies has certainly enhanced people's lives. An argument can certainly be made that higher educational levels have raised public consciousness about potential threats and dangers. But other factors intrude to raise our overall risk level. In our more densely populated society, our degree of tolerance appears to have declined. Additionally, in a hyperindividualistic society, there certainly seems to be less forgiveness, more festering of conflict and animosity between individuals and groups. In a word, we are as a population demanding higher standards of health and well-being; at the same time, we are assigning a larger arena of action and events to the risk category.

The quest for equality and justice also factors into the risk equation. When research demonstrates that life for African American males throughout the life cycle is a great deal more tenuous, considerably less safer, far less healthier, and more likely to be cut short with incarceration, murder, or debilitating disease than for whites, these data point to socially induced cause and effect. When we discover that recent immigrants from Asia, Africa, and developing countries generally use physical punishment when disciplining their children—action that could constitute child abuse by most American parents—we recognize how cultural our interpretations of risk actually are (see Dugger 1996). Risk is not a flat definition, therefore, that applies to all time and places, but one that shifts with the changing culture and circumstances of living (Douglas and Wildavsky 1982).

FROM MODERN TO POSTMODERN SOCIETY

Modern society, founded in the nineteenth century, was based on rationality and positive beliefs about the world as having the possibility of being created and shaped by humans, not distant and rejecting gods. This new era, signaled by the Enlightenment, offered a new paradigm: a citizen-centered society to replace the tyranny of church and king—liberation in thought and deed for the average "man" (women and children were excluded from freedom's call). In canceling the organic society of fixed statuses, where compassion was an obligation, as well as a set of expectations, modernists also ruptured the mutual obligations between classes that held this highly stratified society together. Replacing the old order with the concept of social contract, society was now to be transformed into a consensual, voluntary enterprise dominated by individuals with rights. The sociocultural "container" was thus changed from a theocentric to a homocentric one, thereby handing us direct control over the mythosymbolic structures that define us. We have moved from being held by the container to becoming its engineers with license to remake both self and society.

Postmodernism is associated with a host of steering problems. A century of global conflicts and wars; excessive capital accumulation; racial, class, and gender discrimination; massive state and corporate bureaucracies; and effective denial of citizenship to millions of the "undeserving" have all tarnished the myth of a homocentric world that responds to mechanistic control. The postmodern consciousness is characterized by a crucial loss of meanings and a form of self-reflection that casts doubts on previously held absolutes (e.g., God, Science, State, and the like). This altered self-awareness has led to disenchantment with technical rationality and the view of science it expounds—it cannot balance the federal budget, hold down inflation, or restrain juvenile crime. From the postmodern perspective, we confront a world of indeterminacy and relativity. It is also a world of immense diversity that refuses to be denied by the now outmoded linear, mechanical way of thinking. Modernism, with its singular project of scientific progress operating for the benefit of dominant groups, has exhausted itself.

As we move into this postmodern world, we detect the signs of fragmentation and dissolution throughout all of our social, economic, and political institutions. Our collective flight of progress, hinged as it was on technology and human dominance over the earth, has been profoundly shattered by a loss of vision and direction. Youth, among all population groups, is the most severely affected by this crisis, and is the least prepared age cohort to deal with it. Reflecting on young people and social change, Furlong and Cartmel (1997) argue that the greater array of risks and opportunities faced by young people as they transition from childhood to adulthood frequently obscures the fact that existing social divisions—class, race, gender, educational attainment—are really only being reproduced in different ways.

This book addresses the youth crisis as an outcome of an outmoded technological-industrial worldview and life-threatening set of social practices. The techno-industrial society offers mechanistic solutions to social problems that fail to mitigate the increasing natural and human costs. More and more, the "development-at-any-cost" principle that now dominates worldwide, generates a risk society, one that has become increasingly disconnected from nature and human need.

Historically, social control within this rubric has stressed adult hierarchies and centralized power that leads to youth containment policies. Such policies focus on their status as social and economic dependents. Issues of justice and empowerment for youth are either ignored or translated into "control talk"—apolitical and commercial strategies that transform youth expression into adult profit and foster bureaucratic monopolies over pleasure and punishment. Family, school, labor market, welfare, justice, military, and leisure institutions have worked together to diminish, if not extinguish, self-determination among young people. Of course, the adult controllers attempt to place youth in the social "container" the adult world created. However, fundamental to the definition of that sociocultural form is the imperative to make yourself into "something"—keyed to this message is the notion that the "container" can be made according to one's will. What the older generation ignores is that each succeeding generation perceives different needs and finds different ways of defining the container as well as the type of risks necessary to maintain it.

The modern era of social control is coming to an end. The dominant classes may never have had much use for the children of the poor or struggling classes. Ruling elites are interested in power, not children and their problems; in the system of control of youth conduct, not in the behavior itself. They appear less interested in the human problems of delinquency or community chaos. Elites are concerned above all else with the mechanisms by which delinquency and crime are controlled, punished, reformed, or contained. From the 1960s "war on poverty" to the current "war on drugs," techniques and tactics of domination have driven every effort to ameliorate community disorganization and youth marginalization. It was a war that could not be won.

Over the last two decades or so we have had a growing awareness of the increasing vulnerability to criticism of all manner of things that relate to our understanding of youth: their bodies, emotions, and everyday behavior. Traditional institutions, control practices, and discourses have become precarious. They are said to be unworkable, or they are observed to be subject to fragmentation and dissolution. Established regimes of thought and action increasingly are accused as the source for a variety of hostile encounters between young people and established society, whether within the family or the school, community, and larger society. To maintain the old paradigm as though it were "working" appears to border on collective insanity.

An alternative model is offered—a **critical ecology of justice** perspective—that rejects hierarchy and dominance modes of relationship in favor of ecological principles of diversity and interdependence (Bookchin 1991; Merchant 1992; E. Wilson 1994). The model specifies the urgency of paying attention to "subjugated knowledges" (Foucault 1990), local discourses about justice by young people and their advocates.

The argument may be briefly summarized as follows:

1. The youth crisis is an accumulation of social problems created by a technological world system that benefits elites and whose fundamental premise is a frontier without containment boundaries waiting for the strong to take the riches.

2. Youth problems on a global level are increasingly magnified as the technological order loses its legitimacy.

3. Justice as the foundation for a revitalized social order must be reconceptualized as social justice based on a "justice of multiplicities" (Lyotard 1992). The approach rejects the outmoded discourse of justice, based on corporate and dominant class claims of property, demands for public order, and punishment. A new consciousness takes account of the experiences, feelings, language, and symbol systems of young people regarding their social condition and their local, even naïve, claims for justice.

4. Only critical ecology, among macro theoretical models, offers a holistic paradigm that addresses necessary changes in the ethics and practices of human

collectivities and their organization of resources and peoples, and thereby suggests a path to reestablishing a cohesive sociocultural container.

5. Drawing on the critical ecology model allows us to consider how social control over youth can be radically redesigned from power-over strategies that strangle self-determination to dispersed power approaches that allow full participation of youth in the larger society.

THE YOUTH CRISIS

As depicted in Chapter 1, the youth crisis is a condition wherein larger numbers of children and adolescents are exposed to risks over which they lack the power or knowledge to resist. The risk society, by definition, throws up problems that are insurmountable by individuals or even communities—for example, corporate closings and downsizing, crime, family breakdown, and homelessness. Chapter 1 also delineated the social crisis as a time of decision, a judgment call. Each of the three levels of crisis examined here calls for an immediate social and policy response.

At the first level of analysis, we study crisis as social and psychological problems that afflict youth throughout industrial and developed societies. For example, the World Health Organization reported in 1993 that nearly one hundred million homeless children lived on city streets; these figures were updated three years later to two hundred million (1996). The homeless situation exposes young people to maximum risk of suffering from substance abuse, malnutrition, sexual victimization, physical violence, suicide, criminality, and early death (see also Alder 1991a; Davis 1993a; Davis, Hatty, and Burke 1994; McCarthy and Hagan 1991). At the same time, these youth are not under the hierarchical orders of school or work regimes and are often able to elude local authority systems.

In the United States, the youth crisis is especially pronounced in "inner-urban war zones" (Garbarino et al. 1992). Many inner-city children are growing up amidst worsening problems of community violence and degradation—shootings and stabbings on the street, domestic violence that spills out of households into public view, widespread awareness of murders and serious assault within local communities, evident gang activity, unsafe schools, dangerous streets, profoundly dilapidated housing, and defunct community organizations (Garbarino et al. 1992; Prothrow-Stith 1993; W. J. Wilson 1987; Kozol 1992). In this highly touted "century of the child," critical observers are showing us the reverse side of the myth, as in the analysis of "endangered children" (Regoli and Hewitt 1991), "the erosion of childhood" (Suransky 1982), the "troubled adolescent" (White 1989; Leone 1990), "children in danger" or "children under siege" (Garbarino et al. 1992), "children without childhoods" (Winn 1984); and the "rise and fall of childhood" (Sommerville 1982). Given the current political environment of indifference or superficial "fix-it" programs, there is little possibility of resolving any of these entrenched social problems.

The second level of crisis has to do with the breakdown of traditional structures of control. The family has been a declining institution since the post-Reformation period under the dual impact of industrialization and the loss of extended family and community containers. When fathers ruled in Reformation Europe, the nuclear family rose to a position of importance. Its subjugation of women and production of children paralleled the political absolutism and rigid economic order of the day, as political and domestic subjects alike were effectively stifled (Ozment 1983). Late eighteenth century Europe confronted libertarian impulses that shattered the cohesive forces of king and patriarchy. Women and children remained outside these new political relations.

The nineteenth-century family was little more than a remnant of its former patriarchal glory. Rule of the father had become little more than a myth. The real family experienced father loss and emotional abandonment, as men were driven into urban offices and factories, and women, however mute and powerless, remained the dominant—if unacknowledged and husband-tyrannized—influence in the domestic sphere (J. Bernard 1981; Pleck 1987). Additionally, child labor in casual, dead-end jobs consigned increasing numbers of working class youth to a culture of poverty.

In many parts of the Third World, child labor persists. As many as forty-six million children around the globe make goods for the U.S. market (Herbert 1995a). In Pakistan, despite laws that limit child labor and indentured servitude, both practices flourish, and some eleven million children, aged four to fourteen, keep that country's factories operating, often working in squalid and brutal conditions (Silvers 1996) (see Box 2-A).

Economic pressures and divorce have now moved women, as well as men, into full-time employment, severely reducing adult supervision and care over children, diminishing further the boundaries that define the social container. Arlie Hochschild (1997) proposes that women, similar to men, are now seeking work as the "great escape" from needy children, housework, and messy family emotions. A parent deficit clearly marks the postmodern family.

At the same time, women's wages lack global parity with men's, and for millions of children around the world, especially those with single mothers, growing up poor has become a way of life (L. Mead 1992; Edelman and Ladner 1991; Edelman 1987). In the United States, poverty is especially pervasive for African American families, where single parent status, lack of resources, and severe community demoralization drastically undermine the already fragile parental authority (Taylor 1992) (refer to Table 2.1). At the same time, we know that the failure of caregivers to protect and socialize children—and this occurs across all social classes—exposes children to a

---

Box 2-A
A Global Perspective

At least half of the 11–12 million children who work in Pakistan are under ten, according to a report on child labor in that country by Jonathan Silvers. The average age for entering this labor market is 7. Children now constitute one quarter of the unskilled work force, and earn overall a third of the adult income. Some industries virtually depend upon child labor, such as carpet making and brick making, where children do the work of machines. In addition to depressing the already very low adult wage, child labor prevents normal family life, as children work up to 14 hours a day, 7 days a week, often geographically far from home. The child worker remains one of the most exploited workers in the newly developing countries; wholly unprotected by minimum wage laws, occupational safety regulations, trade union activity, or minimal health standards. In the lowest castes, children become workers almost as soon as they can walk. By the year 2000 less than one third of Pakistani children will be attending school. The remaining two thirds will enter the labor force or become beggars. Reform groups, such as the Bonded Labor Liberation Front, have led the fight against bonded and child labor. In a recent carpet factory visit, one reformer from the BLLF found that:

Of the twelve weavers, five were eleven to fourteen, and four were under ten. The two youngest were brothers named Akbar and Ashraf, aged eight and nine. They had been bonded to the carpet master at age five, and now worked six days a week at the shop. Their workday started at 6:00 a.m. and ended at 8:00 p.m., except, they said, when the master was behind on his quotas and forced them to work around the clock. They were small, thin, malnourished, their spines curved from lack of exercise and from squatting before the loom. Their hands were covered with calluses and scars, their fingers gnarled from repetitive work. Their breathing was labored, suggestive of tuberculosis. Collectively, these ailments, which pathologists call captive-child syndrome, kill half of Pakistan's working children by age twelve.

Jonathan Silvers. 1996. "Child Labor in Pakistan." *Atlantic Monthly* (February): 87.

---

variety of psychosocial disruptions, among which childhood victimization, suicide, eating disorders, substance abuse, criminality, and pseudomaturity are commonly attributed (Snyder and Huntley 1990).

Child maltreatment is endemic to the nuclear family structure (A. Miller 1984; 1990; 1993). Millions of children are beaten, starved, raped, and killed by parents or surrogates every year (Finklehor 1979). Family and intimacy settings, once believed to be safe havens (but probably never were), have been exposed as highly victimogenic settings, where children are subjected to incest, battering, sexual assault, sexual harassment, physical deprivation, and various humiliations (Pleck 1987; James and Prout 1990). Sexual trafficking in children is a global problem (Campagna and Poffenberger 1988). The results can be terrible and destructive. A kind of "cognitive cloudiness" pervades the thinking of persons who have been abused as children (Belenky et al. 1986). Neurosis, psychosis, psychosomatic disorders, learning problems, delinquency, and violent crime have been linked to abusive childhoods (A. Miller 1986; 1990; 1993; Zingraff et al. 1993).

Educational systems are often irrelevant, especially for inner-city and working class children, as they provide only a distorted view of society while masking their severely circumscribed roles within it (Kozol 1992). In fact, says Macedo (1994), the "mechanistic pedagogy" contributes to the "literacy of stupidification" for the entire youth population. Lack of economic opportunity, once confined to minorities and lower working class groups, is a generic problem among young people (Bessant 1993). Most young persons are expected to be, and are, profoundly apolitical. The political process remains a vague set of television images wholly disconnected from their lives. Modern existence is most likely to engender rage, rather than a dispassionate examination of political issues.

Child separation from adults and placement into bureaucratic institutions begins at younger and younger ages. The day-care movement has succeeded in institutionalizing children from infancy, exposing preschool children to the tyranny of experts before they have developed adequate language or self-consciousness to articulate their needs (Suransky 1982). Age segregated systems offer few opportunities to form meaningful relationships with nurturing (versus supervising) adults. This may contribute to a general decline in psychosocial competence among adolescents, as developmental tasks have been shortchanged or developmental conflicts left unresolved because of lack of environmental support (see White 1989, 29–30).

At the same time, young persons are subjected to extended social, legal, and economic dependency. The assumption is that youth should remain a "protected" category subject to adult supervision and control. Permissive trends since the 1960s granted limited adult status to those aged eighteen to twenty years, including drinking alcohol in some jurisdictions, leaving school, moving into either a full-time job or returning for tertiary education to achieve a higher-status position, the right to vote, and being legally responsible for criminal acts. But without genuine participation in mainstream society, youth privileges are often divorced from personal responsibility. "Playtime" is translated into a "license to deviate," a set of practices that establishes the tone for the entire teenage years, as children move into adult drinking, drug, and sexual roles in their early teens or younger (Inciardi, Horowitz, and Pottieger 1993).

Changes in the nature and distribution of work is a major culprit in extending dependency and restricting adult status. As a scarce resource, meaningful work—or work that is at the appropriate level of a person's background experience and job skills—is increasingly unavailable. For millions of young people, the declining "job" market implies that most jobs carry little prestige or benefits and may be merely part-time, occasional, or seasonal.

Surveys of job characteristics held by high school seniors show that 72.6 percent of males and 78.5 percent of females indicated that their jobs were unrelated to the type of work they expect to do after high school. Forty-four percent reported that the work was to a "considerable" or "great" extent only for money (U.S. Department of Labor 1994). Young people are also more likely to have disadvantageous work schedules, compared with adults—evening shifts, night work, and irregular schedules (U.S. Department of Labor 1994).

Jobs are unpredictable. They are not intended to sustain life, much less a decent standard of living. Young people moving into job markets today plunge headlong into a work world where they are a surplus product, one of hundreds or even thousands applying for the same position. Living off the older generation, even returning to their childhood bedroom, becomes a way of life for many young people in their twenties who are legally adults but socially children (Bessant 1993). Poor and minority children may never hold a job, or relate to the world of work. In New York City, four of five teenagers are out of work. Nine of ten black youths are jobless. And almost fifteen thousand jobs disappeared in one year alone (1992) (Fitch 1994). Young people have become part of the obsolescence built into technological society.

The so-called youth culture—as expressed in clothing, music, dance, drugs, and rebellious lifestyles—appears to be more a media artifact than an everyday reality for most young people. The commercialization of childhood and youth simply creates consumers at younger ages. Designer clothes, stereos, drugs, and a delinquent or hypersexual lifestyle does not necessarily create a collective consciousness geared around youth experiences and aspirations. Instead, young people *feel* they require consumer goods for both conforming and standing out. The consumer role plays an integral part of the construction of self identity in a risk society.

In "manufactured cultures" (Brake 1985, 184), young people develop unrealistic expectations promoted by advertisers that material possessions are equivalent to power and age-class cohesiveness. But such consumer wares are more likely to be divisive, separating youth in terms of class, race, gender, immigrant status, and access to resources (whether legal or illegal). Remnants of an identifiable working class youth culture may persist in ethnic gangs that are organized around masculine solidarity or economic gain, but these are usually little more than an interlude during the respite between school and settling down into marriage and parenthood (Brake

1985, 16). Such subcultures should not be confused with predatory urban gangs, which are products of severe economic dislocation and social alienation (see Chapter 10; Kratcoski and Kratcoski 1990; Hagedorn 1991).

These pessimistic assessments of the general state of childhood and adolescence are borne out in recent data on black homicide. Lethal violence is particularly pronounced among young African Americans. Among black males and females aged fifteen to twenty-four, homicide is the leading cause of death. African Americans constitute 13 percent of the U.S. population, but more than 45 percent of all homicide victims, and more than half of all perpetrators (Zimring and Hawkins 1991). In New York City, which has an overall high crime rate, the homicide rate is 27.5 per 100,000. Compare this to Harlem, where the homicide rate is nearly three times that figure at 71.3 per 100,000 persons (Garbarino et al. 1992). Inner-city educators and social workers express deep concern, as they observe that under conditions of chronic violence, the problems of children are reaching a new level of deviance and disturbance never before seen by educators (Curtis 1992).

SOCIAL CONTROL

Since 1760, with the Enclosure Acts and the rise of the industrial social order, the state has had a large involvement in the lives of children, and has assumed significant responsibility in the area of juvenile misconduct. Prior to this period, children were enmeshed in extended family and community networks, where their behavior was pervasively monitored (Davis and Anderson 1983). In colonial America, a juvenile classified as a "proper object" of reformation was covered by statutes that stemmed from three traditions: (1) American adaptation of Elizabethan poor laws that covered idleness, begging, vagrancy, and destitution; (2) Puritan-originated definitions of offenses peculiar to childhood and the apprentice status, that later became known as "status offenses"; and (3) State adaptations of common-law criminal offenses (Lerman 1990). Coercive power and punitive sanctions of the criminal law were used liberally to handle many problems that were clearly noncriminal. Paul Lerman (1990, 7) observes that "in the nineteenth century, the reformatory performed the social functions of a juvenile almshouse, a workhouse, and a house of correction" (see also Rothman 1971).

Competing and conflicting ideological perspectives regarding protection versus punishment, initiated in this early epoch, are with us still. A major source of confusion is the lack of a clear distinction between problems related to poverty, welfare, dependency, and those related to crime (Lerman 1970). The end result of a long history of child saving is that youth can easily lose their freedom for long periods of time for behaviors that are not criminal; or are less serious than charged. Reform movements have frequently yielded the incarceration of more children, not less (Lerman 1970; 1990). And because we do not have consistent policies, serious offenses can be treated much too lightly and trivial offenses much too seriously (Weisheit and Culbertson 1995).

Social control has invariably followed a zigzag course. Wholesale institutionalization of abandoned, neglected, and unemployed youth in the eighteenth and nineteenth centuries was followed by a recognition of the need for separate treatment in juvenile and family courts. By the 1960s, deinstitutionalization trends impacted on bureaucratic systems dealing with the young, and the modality shifted to "community-based" rehabilitation programs aimed to divert most youthful offenders out of the justice system. Rehabilitation models originally fixated on therapeutic modalities in locked institutions, but the lack of fit of traditional psychiatric diagnosis for adolescents together with institutional abuses undermined the mental health approach.

In the 1970s, short-term crisis intervention models pushed out long-term psychiatric care on the assumption that institutions were bad for everyone, but especially for kids. Public criticism attacked these institutions as offering neither correction nor cure, and in many instances as inherently destructive, or as creating additional problems; for example, juvenile suicides in adult jails, sexual exploitation in mental hospitals, reformatories as schools for crime and deviance, and arbitrary labeling as "violent offender" many juveniles who had committed lesser crimes (Weisheit and Culbertson 1995). A "get tough policy" in the 1980s reopened the debate on the use of incarceration for youthful offenders. States have changed their statutes to make it easier to transfer troublesome youth to the adult system (Bortner 1986). Imposing the death penalty on children has been one of the more egregious results of this policy (Streib 1995).

Decriminalization of status offenders and "overlooking" much juvenile offending by law enforcement has not lent clarity to bureaucratic systems of control. We are confronted with a thorny issue of a history of neglect, an absence of planning, and a general refusal to examine goals for the juvenile justice system, as well as other bureaucratic systems. Correctional and mental health systems continue to flounder without a clear mandate, while the problem of youth alienation deepens. The violent incorrigible adolescent who combines hostile, aggressive, acting-out behaviors with strong resistance to change challenges both systems. The need for long-term placement in a benign setting where disturbed children and youth would have structure, limits, and control simply does not exist. Such children usually end up in a correctional facility after committing many serious crimes, including murder (Agee 1990, 199).

Experts on crime warn of a "ticking time bomb" that will explode in the next few years as the number of teenagers soars (Butterfield 1996a). Between 1996 and the year 2005, the number of males fourteen to seventeen years old will increase by 23 percent. The coming jump in the youth population is predicted to be highly susceptible to criminal involvement. At the same time, the Council on Crime in America painted a bleak portrait of the criminal justice system as a "revolving door" that allows large numbers of violent felons to go free and commit more crime. The most serious criminals are males who begin committing crimes at a very early age, often before puberty. Prevention, not imprisonment, is the answer. Now, we recycle to those institutions that provide the possibility of preventing criminal careers among high-risk youth: family, school, and community. But, as we have argued, these institutions have been severely eroded by economic insecurity, corporate dominance, and lack of political will among elites. As a society, we appear to be preparing our own death shrouds.

GLOBAL CONSIDERATIONS

Cultural, economic, and political fragmentation has become a global condition bringing crime, disease, civil unrest, and war. The United Nations points out that despite a global decline in poverty in recent years, malnutrition plagues millions of the world's children and is a significant factor in over six million child deaths a year. The UN report linked child malnutrition and early death to discrimination against women and girls (girl babies are often given less food than boys in male-favored cultures) (*Vancouver Sun* (Canada), December 16, 1997, A3).

Youth crime commonly accompanies social disorder. A survey in Britain of thirteen thousand young teenagers revealed that more than half had committed at least one crime. On a national scale, crimes committed by youths under fifteen have increased by 54 percent since 1980, and they now account for 22 percent of all reported crime in that country. Even in Japan, where parental authority is held in high esteem, rapid industrial development has remarkably altered people's attitudes, values, and behavior resulting in increases in crime among juveniles and young people engaging in theft-type crimes. This is the result of the sudden shattering of the symbolic container by the post–World War II removal of the emperor as the embodiment of the mythopoetic Japanese self.

In Japan, the number of reported Penal Code offenders cleared in 1990, excluding traffic offenders, was 293,264 (about 42 percent). Of these, 182,308 (or 56 percent) were juveniles, many of whom were involved in serious crimes such as robbery, bodily injury, housebreaking, and rape (Voigt et al. 1994, 590). Such youthful criminality appears to be a worldwide trend (United Nations 1990).

In underdeveloped states, civil unrest and breakdown of law and order are common occurrences. Children are the more likely victims. A UNICEF report (1993) indicated that an undeclared war in Mozambique between a terrorist force and the government left an estimated 600,000 Mozambicans dead, among whom 494,000 were children. Psychological consequences may bear heavily on shaping the next generation because of protracted victimization and loss in that society. This condition, along with mass starvation, is duplicated in war-torn societies around the globe: Rwanda, Bosnia, Angola, Cambodia, the Sudan, and Somalia, among others (Kopperud 1994).

Ecological disasters have become routine problems in modern society and cast serious doubt about the future of our planet. Entire ecosystems are under attack from standard mining, forestry, fishing, and farming practices. Land, air, and water are regularly polluted from industrial effluvia, threatening livestock and food supplies. Across Asia, a pollution disaster hovers. In Gansu Province in Western China, one third of the peasants are mentally retarded or seriously ill. Most people die in middle age, the women report unending miscarriages, and many of the children never grow beyond the toddler size because of polluted water discharged by a local plant. Asia's "economic miracle" comes at a great price: Thirteen of the fifteen cities with the worst air pollution in the world are located in Asia (*New York Times*, November 28, 1997, A1).

Conditions are so bad in other parts of the world that extreme measures must be taken. In Poland, pregnant women, children, and elderly persons with respiratory difficulties have retreated to an underground salt mine to breathe clean air because of high smog levels. In Czechoslovakia, 50 percent of the drinking water does not reach minimum standards. In the former East Germany, cancer, lung and heart disease rates are up to 20 percent higher than in the former West Germany (Merchant 1992, 27). And population pressures threaten the livability, if not survivability, of vast portions of the globe (Ehrlich and Ehrlich, 1990). Corporate globalization processes are deeply involved, and have contributed to the degeneration of local environments that have condemned entire economies to poverty and underdevelopment (Laszlo 1994).

The entire industrial-era paradigm that has generated such prolific productivity, clearly has severe "steering problems" (Habermas 1975; Davis and Anderson 1983). The hierarchical, competitive, and mechanistic model that has governed human life since the mid-eighteenth century can no longer provide direction or scope for human societies. As the dominant paradigm for equitable distributions of resources, power, and justice, the model fails completely (Olsen, Lodwick, and Dunlap 1992, 35). (See Figure 2.1, which compares the techno-industrial model with an eco-sustainable model.)

1. It fails to promote one of the most fundamental functions of society, namely, to provide each individual with an opportunity to contribute to the society and to be affirmed by it in return.

2. It fails to foster more equitable distributions of power and justice.

3. It fails to create socially responsible management of the development and application of technology.

Figure 2.1
Components of the Old Technological-Industrial Worldview and the New Ecological Sustainable Worldview

Component	Techno-Industrial "control"	Eco-Sustainable "participation"
Definition of Nature	Static, inert; People control nature	Movement, flow, change; People live in harmony with nature
Dominant Metaphor	"Infinite," Unlimited resources; surplus product	"Finitude," limited resources; scarcity
Natural Laws	Humans not subject to laws of nature; special species status; exploitation of nature necessary and sufficient to maintain human control	Humans, like other species, subject to laws of nature; interconnectedness of living things; participatory evolution
Role of Natural Environment	Provide resources under technological control; reject conservationist "protectionist" programs as irrational interference	Biological context for all human activity; natural environment must be preserved for future human survival
Beliefs about Technology	Solves most human problems; continuous expansion and utilization of technology as means of control	Creates new problems even as it solves old ones; continuous monitoring of advantages and disadvantages of technology
Values	Secularization of the world; disenchantment & nihilism; materialism; economic efficiency; instrumental rationality; legalistic; cultural homogeneity; quantitative goals; present oriented; male gender dominant; ethic of competition	Sacralization of the earth; enchantment & awe; human development; social effectiveness; valuative rationality; "small planet" thesis; qualitative goals; cultural heterogeneity; future-oriented; male and female equality; ethic of cooperation
Perception of Children/Youth	Non-adult/non-worker lacks status; social and economic dependency; often burdensome; *tabula rasa* requires extensive, formal education; recognition of a few superior youth contrasted with larger population of nonachievers; Adult power-over mode	Child/youth have innate understanding and unlimited capacity for learning culture; recognized as developmentally immature necessitating protection & care; equality of unequals assures basic needs met

4. It fails to provide goods that will enlist the deepest loyalties and commitments of the nation's citizens.

5. It fails to develop and maintain the habitability of the planet.

The technocratic mode of thinking, which has growth as its central aim, has expanded the systematic and hegemonic application of technology to all levels of human activity. Technocratic control of all life has become the norm, reducing all phenomena to those features than can be quantified, controlled, and observed directly with the instruments produced by technology. By this means we *objectify* persons and nonhuman nature. Nature and humans are merely resources to be processed in a self-perpetuating and self-justifying system (Olsen, Lodwick, and Dunlap 1992).

Within this rubric, justice has been confined to procedural matters, treating as residual the social foundations of class, race, gender, age, and other socially defining characteristics and totally ignoring the eco-spiritual aspects of the criminal act. "Justice" refers to those phenomena of power that oppress, neglect, discipline, punish, and marginalize others. Conformity to these arrangements offers a closed set of principles for guiding action and constructing institutions. Hierarchy and adult dominance throughout all the control structures (e.g., family, law, economy, justice system, politics, social policy) have effectively denied the multiple realities of the young.

RISK MODEL: AN OVERVIEW

The youth crisis is an outcome of three components: (1) the high crisis condition of contemporary life both at the level of individual societies, as well as the global situation; (2) the high-risk society that often verges on the catastrophic event; and (3) the limited and arbitrary justice experienced by many young people. This model may be summarized as:

High Social Crisis + High Risk + Low Justice = Youth Crisis

The social crisis is essentially a deep break or cleavage in the routine social and moral order. Rapid and unassimilated social change may produce such a condition; so can failed normative orders, where an "anything goes" ethic prevails. Another is the loss of meanings and of community: the "who cares what happens to me" fatalism, or even more prevalent, "who cares about you; I've got my own problems." Critical thinkers frequently point to the dominance of a market society, which takes no responsibility for the collective well-being, as the essential cause of the current breakdown. A state of crisis invariably points to the judgment time: a requirement to recognize and repair the damaged social and political structures.

The high-risk society, to recapitulate, is one in which large masses of people are in a state of danger, or threatened with a state of danger, loss, life-threatening situations, or involvement with hazardous enterprises; conditions over which they may have little control. This societal state affects everyone, rich and poor, child and adult, alike, but it is especially pervasive among the poor and forgotten ones. Uncertainty characterizes our relationships with one another and defines the state of our institutions. Living in a high-crisis, high-risk society is often exciting, edgy, and adventurous. It is a society that successfully challenges the few, but undermines stability and security for the many. Subsequently, many people experience rootlessness, alienation, violence (as offender or victim), chronic stress-related illnesses, premature death, and social/economic failures for oneself and significant others.

Justice has been defined by philosophers as a state of balance, fairness, equity, and equality. But justice in the United States often has been identified with punishment; humiliation and degradation directed against the poor and weak. Social justice, a term with greater scope, entails the broadest spectrum of justice, including social, political, economic, educational, and moral considerations. Family justice, legal justice, restorative justice, medical justice, welfare justice, economic justice, political justice—these are significant and relevant aspects of social justice. In this larger sense of justice, we refer to the mutual obligation and responsibility we have for one another, inasmuch as we share a single planet, and in a spiritual sense, are one people.

As the book clarifies, it is possible to alter current conditions that undermine the life chances of youth. The model predicts that if you begin to reverse these factors—if you reduce social crisis (e.g., create new welfare programs, provide workers with a living wage), reduce social risks (e.g., practice risk management in children and adolescent lives, as in accessible health care, jobs, and low-income housing in inner cities), and create alternative justice models that aim to restore the excluded into society—you can get different results. In a word, we can begin at any point in the model to achieve a different outcome: a more habitable, loving world.

CONCLUSION

Chapter 2 reviewed characteristics of the risk society that generates high levels of crisis in the process of growing up. Global wars and conflicts; excessive capital accumulation without regard for human costs; race, class, and gender discrimination; corporate enterprises that ignore the safety and welfare needs of local citizens; punitive justice bureaucracies—these and other conditions all reflect the social upheaval that has its origins in the techno-industrial form of social order. We also showed how the postmodern epoch reveals a society that devours its own children, as youth problems continue to mount without effective intervention. If society is serious about reducing the risks associated with a severely disabled society, another social model must be devised. The chapter proposed an eco-sustainable worldview as a more balanced and life-enhancing approach to facilitate the global reality that dominates the new millennium.

The next chapter considers the history of childhood, where compassion was rationed by repressive ideologies. In the preindustrial world the largest proportion of children had a stable family and community, and even a predictable (if often limited) future. It was not without its dangers, though. Contagious diseases, highly authoritarian social structures, and death at an early age haunted the lives of children and adults alike. As industrialization proceeded, concern for children was confined to the affluent classes, with poor children destined to die at young ages from neglect and overwork. Modernism offered a conception of care as expressed in progressive social policies, but under legalistic shaping, care was translated into "rights," to be negotiated by formal structures of social control.

Genealogy of Childhood

3

The history of childhood is a nightmare from which we have only recently begun to awake.

Lloyd de Mause, *The History of Childhood*

The family is the first refuge in which the threatened individual takes shelter when the authority of the State weakens. But as soon as political institutions afford him adequate guarantees, he shakes off the constraint of the family and the ties of blood are loosened. The history of lineage is a succession of contractions and relaxations whose rhythm follows the modification of the political order.

G. Duby, *La Société aux XIe et XIIe siècle dans la region maconnaise*

WHY STUDY HISTORY?

History is a potential minefield that few sociologists care to tread (at least without some preliminary warnings). The peculiarities of evidence—diaries, journals, letters, literature, paintings, clothing, funeral effigies, tomb inscriptions, and other, sometimes arcane data typically assembled and interpreted by well-to-do classes—provide a very partial picture that requires historians to take giant leaps of faith to reconstruct an epoch. Nor do historians agree on major themes in the field. Take the concept of the "origins of childhood," as an example. The questions any historian of childhood must address are: What criteria should be used to determine whether a people had an idea that childhood is a separate condition from adulthood, and how many stages occur along the way? What kind of evidence can be brought to bear to make such an analytic cutting point? Why bother with historical materials at all, if historians cannot agree among themselves what constitutes childhood versus adolescence (or youth) and both categories from adulthood. And what difference does it make, anyway, given that children's voices have been muted throughout history? To paraphrase an old Arab proverb: Their voices are like the croaking of a frog at the bottom of a deep well (see J. Bernard 1981). In a word, young children do not bear witness for themselves; only adults can do that; and older children in past epochs, unlike the diarist, Anne Frank, in our own period, rarely left messages behind.

Keeping these issues in mind, let us construct a map for moving into this historical terrain. The coordinates for defining the point at which childhood or its various stages is said to have begun are as follows:

1. The historian recognizes that childhood is a construct, a human invention, that will be reflected in a number of institutional forms: law, language, art, artifacts, personal momentos, and so forth.

2. The historian acknowledges that available documentation is often biased in a variety of ways—most notably social class, ethnicity, religious affiliation, gender, age, and nationality—and preferably takes account of this in the historical narrative.

3. The historian is aware of contradictions, both in the evidence and in the arguments.

4. The historian provides a theoretical framework or model for organizing the material.

5. The historian offers alternative explanations to account for the historical "fact."

Such ideal history is not always available in the materials on childhood. In fact, the historical records appear to be quite sketchy or contradictory in places. Some accounts of childhood present fairly positive portrayals of an epoch, a kind of "upward and onward" social progress approach (e.g., Aries 1962). Another provides a psychoanalytical approach that is closer to a history of child abuse than a general history (de Mause 1974). A widespread reading of childhood is to lump the child/youth age cohort into the family history genre, and perceive childhood as primarily a set of beliefs, statuses, and practices that occur within the family context (Aries 1962; Shorter 1976; Demos 1986; Pollock 1983; Stone 1980).

Feminist work emphasizes that the condition of childhood remains contingent upon the status of women (Pleck 1987). Gender analysis also clarifies that family structures under patriarchy make women vulnerable by marriage. The family is by definition a structure of injustice (Okin 1989). The justice perspective has expanded into a growing literature of the history of childhood as the story of abuse and oppression (Pleck 1987; Gordon 1988; de Mause 1974; A. Miller 1984; Regoli and Hewitt 1991; Ch. 6).

Still another approach is to perceive childhood in developmental terms, and subsequently probe into early childhood practices (nursing, swaddling, weaning, presence or absence of mothers, and the like) (Pollock 1983) or stages of development (Erikson 1963). Research on the family structure as a dependent institution and inherently vulnerable social entity considers how children and youth have been both subjected to political interference and surveillance and protected against abusive parents by the state (Donzelot 1979; Lasch 1977).

The history of minority children for various societies remains largely unwritten (e.g., American Indian, African American, or Australian Aborigine), as does the history of children as gendered beings. In the latter case, witchcraft in the late middle ages primarily affected girls and young women, and female infanticide throughout European history from the ancient Greeks on was a well-established pattern (Shahar 1990). In sum, a single definitive history of childhood and adolescence does not exist.

Drawing on a differential stages model that emphasizes history as discontinuity, this chapter considers the *social context* of childhood/youth for two time periods—Preindustrial and Industrializing—by reference to three major concepts: *Culture, Social Relations,* and *Work.* The moral, social, and legal subordination of children to family and various authority systems without rights of appeal mark the historical record, and provide the social condition for the oppression of children and adolescents. We pursue these themes in various chapters when we consider the contemporary youth culture and its changing forms.

PREINDUSTRIAL PERIOD

Culture

To treat history as mere time capsules in which we deposit distinct events probably does a terrible injustice to the flow of actual happenings. But by the 1500s, it was very apparent that an entirely new reality, a distinctly different worldview, was emerging that would alter the face of Europe forever. As science began its breakaway from religious thought, it shifted from a cultural quest for God to a quest for new horizons. Discoveries were rampant. The cosmos was no longer centered around the earth, but rather around the sun, and the known universe was expanding into previously unknown continents. One historian observed that the change that occurred in the seventeenth century was thus not so much technological as mental. In many different spheres of life the period saw the emergence of a new faith in the potentialities of human initiative (Thomas 1971, 656).

Despite the Catholic Church's avowed concern for the "Holy Innocents," children continued to be viewed as incomplete, and if unbaptized, as inherently polluted. Once the Reformation was underway under the tutelage of Martin Luther and John Calvin, a surge of interest in children occurred. Part of this interest was related to the recognition that education must play a much more profound role in development of the moral person than had

earlier been realized, and that such education must begin with early childhood. The Protestant faith was not without its repressive elements, yet its
stance against medieval thought incorporated a strong measure of individualism. Capitalism was rearing its head as a new, dynamic economic order
that would sweep away fiefdoms, serfs, and rural ways of life that had
provided people with predictable, interconnected, and self-contained lifeways. These were supplanted with new modes of contractual production
lacking either social bonds or security.

Perhaps as the world becomes fiercer, childhood takes on more significance. By the seventeenth century, children were being idealized as loving
and brave—a figure of pathos because they were beings of nature, but
significant in this new order because of their contribution to the nation
state, and their role in perpetuating the family line. At the same time children were viewed as demanding and difficult—a pearl, but one that comes
at a great price. Whereas children remained gender neutral throughout
childhood, typically referred to as "it," (Shorter 1976), adolescents were
both sexual and angelic, a conflictual mix. Aries (1962) argues that the
concept of childhood as a special period of human life was first "invented"
during this epoch. Childhood was a "holy" thing, a unique status. Adults
were obliged to devote themselves to children through their love and protection, as well as to take into account the weakness and infirmity of the
young. Children, in turn, acted out their roles either as playful, loving creatures, entertaining adults; or meeting adult expectations as "precocious";
or among royalty, as "sensual," allowing the releasing of adult inhibitions.

Child iconography remained popular among the middle and upper classes. Artists portrayed young children as Eros, the cupid of love, and adolescents as both Eros and Angel. Representations demonstrated the
increasing differentiation of children and youth from adults. Adolescents
were featured in special costumes; normal child-like expressions and man-
ners were depicted in art form; and the birth of a commercial toy industry
began producing a wide variety of children's toys (e.g., miniature doll
houses, dolls, lead soldiers and weapons), and other child-centered games
and pastimes.

The sweetly sentimental attitude toward infants and small children may
have been for public consumption, because it apparently was intermixed
with a strong dose of parental rejection and fear of overindulging the child.
Scholars observe that lack of maternal affection even for young infants was
commonplace, a situation probably associated with infant separation from
mothers and the "boarding out" practice (de Mause 1974).

The culture continued to celebrate children's religious feast days, especially Circumcision for boys and the Presentation of the Virgin in the Temple for girls. First Communion was perceived as a great religious festival
of childhood in Catholic countries, timing the event when the child reached
the age of reason (seven years). The birthday, celebrated with such ebul-

lience in modern times, was not recognized among eighteenth-century Protestants. In colonial America, children were expected to prove the parent's worthiness in the world, as a way of attaining salvation, and neither birth nor subsequent birthdays were deemed to be significant.

Taboos that remained in force were infanticide, incest, rank disobedience by children, premarital sexuality, and excessive flagellation by parents, teachers, and masters against children. Horror stories of cannibalistic and sadistic mothers and stepmothers, that had reinforced the medieval witchhunts against women, were fading under the impact of increased education. At the same time, discipline became more rigorous under the new demands of the commercial order.

Social Relations

The hierarchical principle took new forms after the sixteenth century. Class structures based on wealth and achieved status moved into place, and state expansion began to edge out the Church as the dominant authoritative institution. From the sixteenth century on, the English family had become differentiated by clear class distinctions that endured until the 1920s. Abbott (1993) identifies five historical family types: landowner families, "plain folk"—families of farmers and craftsmen—middle class families, the families of the laboring poor, and the lower middle classes (the "blackcoated workers"). Courtship, marriage, relationships, socialization, education—indeed, all social relations—were defined within these identifiable categories.

In sevententh century England, the life expectancy of children (ages one to fourteen) increased, as the death rate dropped from 42.5 per 1,000 to 34 per 1,000, as a result of the "awakening of medicine" (Illick 1974, 312). At the same time the Enclosure Acts in England, and privatization of common land throughout large parts of Europe profoundly altered social relations. While this enhanced the professional and middle classes, who by now lived in a money economy, the life of peasants and urban working classes deteriorated (Laslett 1977).

Households were increasingly moving to small nuclear families, but unlike earlier European epochs, state power was beginning to usurp paternal control, especially among the dependent poor. A number of factors reduced parents' influence during this time. In addition to infant separation from mothers immediately after birth, fathers were older at marriage, and hence died before their sons entered adolescence. Extensive schooling and apprenticeships, beginning as young as age seven, implied that the traditional family assumed a lesser role than in the earlier period.

Once restricted to royal houses, the practice of hiring wet nurses spread to the middle classes, and eventually to any family that could afford it, almost all of whom boarded their infants out. One of the main reasons for hiring wet nurses was apparently the frequency of pregnancies. Couples did not abstain from marital relations during the nursing period, and most did not use contraception (Shahar 1990, 70–71). Wet nurses provided relief from the incessant demands of small infants, who were often compared with "parasites" who could drain the mother (Pollock 1983, 9.) Despite the gross number of boarded out infants who died from this practice, wealthy and middle class families went on putting their children out to nurse until the end of the nineteenth century, at which time hygiene and aseptic methods made it safe to use animal milk (Aries 1962, 375).

Socialization was discontinuous, and served to fragment the family. On the one hand, the evidence shows that throughout Europe and America extended separations between children and parents occurred from birth through early childhood, and in some instances until adolescence (Aries 1962). On the other hand, intimate relations between parents and children were either discouraged or nonexistent. Children were no sooner returned to their parents after the nursing period, when they were sent off again for school and apprenticeship training. Once philosophy entered its secular phase in the eighteenth century, the major critique of childrearing practices by thinkers such as Rousseau and Locke (see Okin 1989) focused on the deficiencies of the home and the hazards of childhood: infanticide, wet-nursing, swaddling, abandonment, and punishment. These attacks against the old order of childrearing provided the impetus for the ascendancy of new professional specialties, such as pediatrics and child guidance. As educational and state institutions began to assume more-direct roles in controlling the populace, the family unit was shrinking in numbers and functions (Popenoe 1988).

Education proved to be elaborate and intensive. The urban day school turned into a boarding school by the end of the period, and boys started school by age seven. Under the tutelage of the Beguines, a secular guild of women who set up schools in the late medieval to early modern period, some middle class urban girls were exposed to equally rigorous and comprehensive education as boys. But with the decline of the guilds, girls were generally kept out of the learning track and were expected to comply with their primary role of preserving traditional social values now threatened by rapid change. Girls' schools received their legitimacy by training in "marriageability," learning the domestic arts of music, needlework, and proper comportment. In Italy and France, the new "academics" offered a broad range of subjects, including humanities, business, and engineering, fields considered essential for the expanding commercialism of the period. The seventeenth-century Puritans had more at stake in education than secular careers. Because young children were "inclined to evil," education served to transform the child from a self-willed, destructive being to a Godly form (Illick 1974, 316).

Sex remained a taboo area for both men and women during this period, and both genders were required to remain virginal until marriage. Protestants recognized that the "natural constitution [being] exceedingly inclined to lust" recommended "mortifying duties to crucify the flesh" (Illick 1974, 322). To ensure that sexual attraction would take a sublimated form, the Puritan divines instituted a school program oriented around punctuality, restraint, self-discipline, and respect for the social code. This disciplinary regimen began at 6:00 A.M. and lasted until 5:30 P.M. for formal school and always included evening homework. It could be speculated that this "swaddling in Calvinism" served as a substitute, not only for sex, but for the physical controls that were gradually giving way to ideological precepts.

Reformation Europe depicted marriage as a shared responsibility between husband and wife, whose duties were clearly delineated. The operating principle, however, remained "father rule," with the stipulation that no wife could stand opposed to her husband (Ozment 1983, 50).

Shorter (1976) argues that another trend was revealing itself. A "surge of sentiment" has been identified with the making of the modern family in the eighteenth century, promoting courtship and romantic love, which superseded material considerations for marriage; fostering mother-infant relationships; and replacing love and affection for the former instrumental considerations in regulating the dealings of the family members with one another. The increased value of children *within the family*, though, came about as a direct result of economic growth rather than a shift of sentiments.

Sanctions gradually shifted during this period from physical to mental disciplines. Whereas extensive schooling became the norm for boys during the sixteenth and seventeenth centuries, it was not associated with a benign attitude toward the students. Aries (1962, 262) notes that there was an "insistence on humiliating childhood, to mark it out and improve it" by giving absolute power to the master. By the eighteenth century, corporal punishment had relinquished its hold, and new sanctions were applied. One was the appeal to affective individualism, holding out the prospects of opportunity and a "new morality" based on a rational approach.

Institutional sources of discipline were expanding under both state growth and private religious bodies. Foundling homes were in great demand as infant abandonment became the "poor man's" population control. For poor or illegitimate children, the orphanage provided an alternative to the street, but life inside was brutalizing, and often brief (Boswell 1988). Jails, prisons, workhouses, and poor houses became the landmarks of the European state, as the numbers of marginalized men, women, and children grew under capitalism (Rothman 1971). Despite the alleged newly discovered love for children—indeed, historians make much of this period as a "discovery" point for childhood—it was not merely any child that was desired and loved. Parents expressed an avowed desire for male offspring, perhaps as a response to the decline of the traditional family lineage. Some evidence suggests that the mother-child connection in those families that did not "put out" their children to wet nurses or early school or work commitments, weakened the husband-wife linkage. Girls, especially, remained close to mothers or female kin; whereas early and sustained separation of boys from their mothers was common (Ozment 1983).

Adult offenses against children took many of the same forms as in the medieval period, but the rationale that undergird the often draconian disciplines was more elaborated. Children experienced physical and emotional abandonment, infanticide (especially girls and illegitimate children), and various cruelties—sold to beggars, left at foundling homes, starvation, exposure to infection, neglect-induced accidents. At the same time, child abuse and incest were frequent events in families and any place where children were residing. Severe beatings as "normal" discipline continued well into the nineteenth century in Europe and remain today in many Asian countries.

Children's offenses against adults were the typical frictions between generations: disobedience, failure to learn, overt rebellion, leaving school, and refusing to work. Additionally, urban students in Europe, caged up in formal academies of learning under highly repressive authority and without parental nurturing, engaged in a variety of personal and collective violence against authority (Aries 1962; Davis and Anderson 1983).

Shame and guilt remained the punishments of choice for errant children and youth, but sanctions were hardly confined to these psychological approaches. Children were humiliated by public whippings—birching was every schoolboy's nemesis—fines; enforced separation from family, school, or caregivers; and other corporal means. Under the Puritans, Colonial America largely rejected the use of corporal punishment and incarceration for children or youth, but discovered another device: the stocks. Placing the culprit in public stocks for long hours at a time, or repeatedly dunking them into water were commonplace. Though such devices did not kill a person, it could seriously wound self-esteem, and dampen any efforts at autonomy. The militarization of ordinary schools was invented in the eighteenth century, creating a regimen of whistles, column marching, and solitary confinement. Children were never freed from punishment during this time, but rather had the threat of sanctions as a major form of psychological torture.

The historian John Boswell (1988) observes that the transition from late medieval to early modern Europe was "appallingly turbulent and violent" in many areas, and those at the bottom suffered deeply. Urban unrest was at its height, and in societies afflicted by plague, famine, revolution, civic disorder, poverty, religious conflict, and state oppression against religious minorities, mothers and children fared especially poorly. The plight of Jewish parents and children expelled from Spain in 1492 by the king depicts the tragedy of a premodern holocaust, in which

Many were consumed by hunger, especially nursing mothers and their babies. Half-dead mothers held dying children in their arms. . . . Many were drowned by the avarice of the sailors, and those who were unable to pay their passage sold their children (Senarega, quoted in Boswell 1988, 406).

Economic pressures on families to reduce the number of children contributed to an avalanche of child abandonment—estimated at one-third the number of births in the middle to late eighteenth century—and the eventual establishment of foundling homes. Rather than a solution to the social problem, the mortality rate of up to 91 percent for abandoned infants and 86.4 percent among all children admitted to these institutions reflects the total indifference of authorities to unwanted babies. The purpose of the foundling home or early orphanage system was not care of children, but disposing of the problem and eliminating parental responsibility. Even Rousseau, considered to be the founder of modern education, abandoned all five of his children to the orphanage. Boswell (1988) says of this widely accepted institution:

A major benefit of the foundling-home system was that the problem of unwanted children was removed from the streets and the view of ordinary citizens. The children disappeared behind institutional walls, where specialists were paid to deal with them, so that parents, relatives, neighbors, and society could forget. How would a parent know that the vast majority of such children died?

Among those few survivors of the foundling home, they entered the ranks of nonpersons: classless, familyless, unconnected adolescents with no claim on the support or care of any persons or groups in the community (Boswell 1988, 421). The emergence of a strong state did nothing to enhance the social condition of these young people; instead, it exacerbated the growth of a landless urban proletariat with little stake in the social system (Davis and Anderson 1983).

Work

Despite social turmoil and the decline of the patriarchal family, urban society began to take a definable shape with the expansion of occupations and guilds. Children from the laboring classes, whose families were no longer attached to the land, played a key role in the organization of work. Children were expected to do "hard service" in the homes of more-affluent families, beginning as young as age seven. The apprenticeship period was extended to fifteen and as much as eighteen years, during which the boy served under the master. Among peasants and lower classes, children worked as virtual family servants (de Mause 1974). Extended training for some more fortunate young men gave needed marketable skills and enhanced work stability, but did little to widen the horizons of ambitious youth who actually found their independence had been curtailed.

In an epoch in which children from pagan countries could be bought and sold as slaves, young children and adolescents worked as cheap indentured servants with no legal rights. On the one hand, children could be said to occupy the lowest social strata, in that they had social value only for their capacity to work, or for their future rights in lineage groups. On the other hand, children were socially invisible; they left no mark on history, or left impressions that were "too fragile to survive" (Boswell 1988, 5). Even older children and adolescents could as readily be disposed of in monasteries or convents, as put out for domestic service, prostitution, or begging or placed in a coercive marriage. For children, the lack of legal, social, or economic recognition, or of separate public and private spheres, confined them to a submerged state under parental or surrogate parental rule.

INDUSTRIALIZATION PERIOD

Culture

In an epoch where economic and state development were uppermost, social and political consciousness were shaped by mechanical images. A dominant view of the universe was the notion of an enormous machine with interlocking parts. The clock became the leading metaphor of the age, and people on clock-time felt the constant pressure to perform within an entirely new set of constraints: Time ruled by a machine. The rise of rationalism promoted contradictory ideas. On the one side, social and moral life were ruled by Calvinism with its doctrine of predetermined destinies. Because no one could be assured that he or she was saved, success became the operative principle. The Protestant ethic and the spirit of capitalism moved in tandem to produce the new cultural imperative of salvation through work (Weber 1977).

On the other side, revolutionary ideas of equality and liberty instilled deep distrust for authority among ordinary people, fueling revolution in Europe and America and promoting new political relationships of the citizen as a free agent under the banner of the social contract. But as the world's colonialized people, including women and children, soon realized, liberty was a discourse and practice restricted to males of European descent. Thus, the ethos remained divided, split between the demands of the industrial order that required a total disciplinary regime and the new individualism and independence promoted by the social contract. Under the constraints of industrial capitalism with its twin props of nationalism and militarism, individualism was increasingly restricted to affluent groups.

From the late eighteenth century onward, the separate-sphere doctrine prevailed. For children, this involved the concept of childhood as a separate time and place, largely confined to the family. For well-to-do classes, adolescence emerged as an extended period of education and emotional development. Contrast this official attention to the special needs of affluent youth with the indifference toward children of the poor and laboring classes, who were expected to perform as ordinary workers in the new industrial system. Working class children, once slotted into households of the rich or middle class, where they could perform minimally, now worked tortuously long hours in unregulated and unhealthy settings of mines, factories, and various urban work sites.

By the late nineteenth century, the horrors of industrialization—its utter disregard for women, children, and family life—had been amply documented (see Engels 1884/1985). At the same time, a distorted version of Darwin's idea of natural selection, captured in the class-antagonistic phrase "survival of the fittest," denigrated efforts to improve workers' lives (Davis 1980).

Perhaps the sheer misery of most children's lives contributed to the public myth of childhood as an "exalted state," symbolizing not only the lost innocence but also the center of a new domestic order. The home took on new significance as a "haven in a heartless world" (Lasch 1977), a hopeful shelter against the turbulent seas of social change. Still the images retained their oppositional quality: The "well contented" child was essentially the repressed child, or one who responded to the new disciplinary tutelage.

Children became individualized during this time, as depicted in individual portraits, or later, in photographs of children at all ages of life. Child-size furnishings and toys filled special rooms in larger homes, as children increasingly became separated from adults, especially the male parent, and in bourgeois homes more likely confined to nursery and kitchen. Instead of the medieval fairy tale with its child-devouring–adults theme, the period offered a sophisticated version of a children's literature and music that was primarily attended by educated adults.

Former childrearing practices died out, such as swaddling and the "putting-out" system (i.e., wet nurse), but new taboos arose. Masturbation was singled out as "self-abuse," the harbinger of insanity and various physical and moral infirmities (Esman 1990, 38). Premarital sex for girls was perceived as producing behavioral incorrigibility and moral corruption; and in an age where social appearances assumed moral reality, the incested child, the unwed mother, and the illegitimate child were central figures of depravity (along with the able-bodied unemployed man).

The sentiment structure during this time was remarkably dense. Childhood and domesticity enjoyed a highly valued status that often bore little resemblance to the callous and brutal behavior that characterized many families' relationships (Pleck 1987). Instead of industrialization producing a sense of psychological freedom, the hyper-disciplinary regimes of home, school, factory, and office generated highly negative emotions. As Freud's case studies show, fear, shame, and guilt governed the social consciousness, and what was evil or forbidden was repressed (Freud 1977 ed.). Sentimentality for children was one of the few allowable public emotions, and pity and sorrow over child victims flourished. The nineteenth-century melodrama captured audiences by its overdone pathos that from a contemporary perspective was absurd and even macabre in its effect, as in Charles Dicken's haunted children and the character of "Little Nell" in *Uncle Tom's Cabin.*

The sentimentalizing attitude was inconsistent with reality and appeared to cover up antisocial and nonempathetic feelings, as suggested by the profoundly widespread instances of infant abandonment, incest, "soul murder," child abuse, and juvenile prostitution (Boswell 1988; Pleck 1987).

Perhaps the child-centered rituals that were preserved acted to offset the essential indifference of most adults toward children not their own. Christmas became the premier child's feast day; birthday celebrations, now secularized events, followed in significance. The church occupied center stage for Christians, but the extension of school discipline into a Sunday school program dominated by adult-interpreted religious doctrine mirrored the parent-child separation and adult dominance found in other social arenas.

Social Relations

Industrialization introduced a class structure based on urban wealth and ownership of large enterprise, decentering the landed gentry based in rural areas. In the struggle between the demands of capitalism for a docile working class and the traditional morality, the work ethic prevailed and took precedence over family/religious/community commitments. The "new man" was born—a ruthlessly competitive, anomic, isolated entity. The revolutionary spirit that had fueled political liberty and personal independence was being co-opted by industrialists to conform to the new world order: dominance by captains of industry.

Households were increasingly woman-centered as the special-sphere doctrine—the mother is confined to the domestic sphere, and the father finds his primary location in the public arena—spread throughout the educated classes (J. Bernard 1981). The patriarchal nuclear family remained in form—the father retained his role as household despot—but protracted physical and emotional absence by fathers disallowed real authority. The Victorian family clearly was adapting to the contractual, individualistic society, but was doing so at the loss of a viable male role model and a decline of respect and deference to traditional authority (Mintz 1985).

Socialization of the young was rendered increasingly problematic, as critics noted how disruptive social change made it "infinitely more difficult to govern children than it used to be" (Mintz 1985, 29). Child guidance books provided new directives for mothers, and among new concepts, the notion of developmental stages that required differential treatment was especially appealing. Children and adolescents were to be distinguished by gradations of respect and privileges. Other conditions, though, intervened to erode the new science of childhood. The prevalence of the segregated nursery and the "nanny"—the ubiquitous child-care giver in affluent families—lumped all homebound offspring into a single category: dependent child. And because children continued to reflect family status and prestige (in affluent classes) or family wage earner (in laboring classes), children were unable to transcend their role of "other." Lack of family intimacy or of inherent respect for children, either at home or in the school, is a prevailing theme in Victorian society.

Under the impact of the social contract and Enlightenment philosophies extolling the "new man," education took on a new importance. Whereas the boarding school retained its importance for upper-class youth, middle- and working-class children stayed home and went to neighborhood schools. Mandatory education was consistent with the belief that work was equated with salvation and with reducing public alms and criminality.

Sex and marriage were invariably gender-structured. Although premarital sex was proscribed for both young men and women, males had ready sexual access to domestic servants, lower-class women, and prostitutes. In fact, prostitution flourished in Victorian society; in part, an outcome of economic deprivation, especially among orphans and runaways, but also a response to the growing problem of delinquent peer-groups in urban society and their overt social pressure on unsupervised girls (Gillis 1974, 63).

Victorian marriage was posited as a contract between two persons based on mutual consent; but without legal, economic, or social rights, women often had little choice. Delayed marriage was common—among middle-class groups, marriage might be delayed into the mid- or late-twenties for women, and a high rate of nonmarriage prevailed. While these practices restrained the population growth, they may have also reflected the down side of marriage as a contractual arrangement, not an intimate experience. Victorian marriages were organized on the basis of parallel lives. Nowhere was this more evident than in sexuality norms. Rose (1984, 12) observes:

Many cultural circumstances worked against the likelihood of sexual satisfaction. The inflexible taboo on pre-marital sex for middle-class women meant, among other things, that it was impossible to determine sexual compatibility before marriage. The law then made the wife absolute property of her husband and sexual performance was one of her duties. Imagine a young woman married to a man she finds physically repulsive. She is in the position of being raped nightly—and with the law's consent.

The absence of birth control made it impossible to separate sex from its reproductive function; women bore the heavier burden (Rose 1984). To be sexually active entailed the discomforts of pregnancy, the pain of childbirth, and the burden of children. For men, the middle-class taboo on premarital sex meant "sexual experience could be obtained only with prostitutes or working-class women . . . [which] breeds dangers in the erotic life" (p.13). Rather than unalloyed joys, marriage, sexuality, pregnancy, parenting, and childrearing were duties, simply another set of vehicles for imposing self-discipline and restraint on the population (see Mintz 1985, 133).

Sanctions against children represent a direct form of adult power. Intensive beatings and other harsh physical disciplines were commonly employed throughout history to coerce the young. The industrializing epoch imposed a disciplinary regime that was at once more subtle, even while it retained the fundamental purpose: humiliating and intimidating children and adolescents in the interests of reinforcing adult hierarchy. Whipping a child on his exposed buttocks or other sensitive body parts, cold water baths, emotional rejection, abandonment, forced labor, separation, and on a less physical level, telling psychologically terrifying stories, and forcing a child to repeatedly view corpses were all practices aimed to discipline the willful child (James and Prout 1990; Sommerville 1982).

More-serious child abuse, often masked as parental discipline, hid behind closed doors (A. Miller 1984). Pleck (1987) observes that the model of the "affectionate family" set apart from the public world sealed off domestic activities—including wife battering and child abuse—from community surveillance. A belief in family privacy made state intervention appear ever more "problematic, disruptive, and unnatural" (Pleck 1987, 48).

The family was clearly losing ground, however. Strong alliances between state and economy had been forged, and state officials increasingly had the power to oversee urban working-class behavior; including state intervention for managing poor families and out-of-control youth (Donzelot 1979). State-run foster homes and orphanages flourished. Schools, including boarding schools for affluent youth, were centers of discipline. At the same time, the "discovery" of delinquency in the mid-nineteenth century led to corrective institutions and eventually a distinct law enforcement machinery for juveniles (Lerman 1995).

State power prevailed over children through the doctrine of *en loco parentis*. This enabled the state to assume the parental role for neglectful and abusive parents, dispatching children to institutions with little public or parental interference. Incarcerated youth endured a mode of discipline that blended the factory regimen with military efficiency. Legal rights and appeals for miscreant youth were virtually absent (Lerman 1995, 10).

The separate-gender-sphere doctrine exerted an immense influence on all aspects of social life. Separate and unequal, girls and young women were excluded from prestige educational and occupational opportunities.

Whereas marriage offered financial security, the price was lifelong economic, social, and emotional servitude. The emotional distance between men and women and adults and children created various abnormalities: perceived isolation, mental disturbance, and sexual aberrations (Rose 1984).

Adult mistreatment of children and youth further contributed to a fear-based disciplinary regime. Physical and emotional abandonment, especially of illegitimate children, was common; so was exposure of immature and sickly children to workplace dangers that lead to premature death or chronic disability. Child abuse, sexual assault, and murder helped to create a society of small victims. Adult fear of masturbation as the ultimate degeneracy encouraged the use of physical restraints at night and the constant surveillance of the potentially degenerate child by the mother or nurse during the daytime (Mintz 1985).

Youth were not passive against the litany of adult abuses. They countered adult cruelties with sustained defiance (especially against fathers), refused to attend school, ran away from home, or engaged in a variety of deviant behaviors: passive withdrawal, rebellion, delinquency, illegal occupations, and violence. At one level youth problems were simply added to the plethora of urban social problems plaguing newly industrial societies that now included widespread family dislocation, destitution of women and children, civil unrest, parental alcoholism, welfare and crime costs, severe domestic violence, and widespread alienation (Davis 1980; Pleck 1987).

By the late nineteenth century, the industrial-capitalist order revealed itself at severe odds with both the revolutionary spirit and the rational educational mode. In the United States, intellectual and religious withdrawal from the brutalizing economic order left the mass of the laboring classes bereft of fundamental reforms. Patchwork remedies, such as the child-saving campaigns waged by charity ladies, attempted to tidy up problem families and their derelict children (Platt 1969). But private and public charity did little more than reinforce the denigrated status and virtual isolation of working-class families. Unemployed youth increasingly confronted a life of police surveillance and imprisonment that rendered them useless for work or family life (see Weisheit and Culbertson 1995).

Work

At first, the industrial machine was fueled by women and children, whose work was unrelieved by domestic or health considerations. Lacking any concept of child protection, industrialists were free to view such workers as mere cogs in the machine easily replaceable. For example, factory children worked the same fourteen-hour day as their parents, when work was available. Prior to 1850, overproduction and speculation in both England and America generated severe economic depressions, and the rates of welfare and vagrancy skyrocketed (Young 1953). Affluent classes sought to place their sons in the professions to avoid the irregular employment suffered by the mass of laborers. For working-class boys forced into the streets by unemployment and overcrowded domestic households, illegitimate employment such as thievery, prostitution, and robbery had a strong appeal.

The drastic shift in production that removed work from the home and scattered the family into different work sites wholly altered the timing and rhythms of family life. Accampo (1989) describes the more leisurely pace and mutually reinforcing activity of productive home labor in the preindustrial epoch:

When production took place within the home, work and family fused in a number of ways. Labor shared time and space with eating, sleeping, lovemaking, childbearing and childrearing, and socializing with friends and kin. Family and household concerns frequently and spontaneously broke up the sixteen-hour workday. Equally important, the bond between work and family had cultural significance. Men, women, and children often labored as a team. (p.3)

Compare this family-integrated productive organization with the newly emerging industrial model. With families splintered by economic necessity, child workers served as "independent contractors" in the sense that industry had no investment in their training or well-being, nor was the workplace responsible for health or safety. Characteristically, there was a total absence of child or worker protection under the factory piecework conditions, a situation that persisted until well into the late 1930s and the growth of trade unionism.

The old apprenticeship system, whereby the master took responsibility for the training and care of his charges, which was so entrenched in the preindustrial system, began its gradual demise. Because industrial work required little or no training—tasks were highly repetitive and required little specialization or competence—working people experienced a loss of skills with greatly reduced status for workers. While wealthy groups pushed their young men into extensive professional training that gave them greater autonomy and social privileges, the de-skilled worker had to be content with chronic underemployment or long bouts of unemployment (Young 1953).

Donzelot (1979) examines the effects of child poverty in newly industrial France, where children, forced to work to support their families, lived in subhuman conditions with lack of care, poor diet, scanty clothing, and other deprivations that "implied their death at an early age." Donzelot quotes from a French historian of the period that the dissolution of the family, civil revolts, and revolution could be explained by "those scrofulous, stunted, rickety children roaming about in bands . . . who grow up in wretched lodgings" (Donzelot 1979, 70–71).

Yet the impoverished, uneducated, and demoralized children were only a sign of the times. Industrial cities had begun to take on all the trappings of the contemporary city, where great wealth coexisted with profound poverty. In the nineteenth century, however, without modern hygiene or medicine, or a systematic family welfare policy to cushion the economic crisis, the premature and overly harsh work of women and children undermined any possibility of a meaningful family life. Additionally, the exploitative economy severely curtailed any benefits of the new order for a significant proportion of the urban population.

America offered a somewhat different profile, because the working class was essentially carved out of the mass migrations of manual laborers that fled Europe after 1830. Immigration offered a distinct set of issues, as Mintz and Kellogg (1988) note:

The heavy reliance on one's "own people" was a response to shared adversities. Immigrant families encountered a host of problems, including the language barrier, difficulties in obtaining jobs, inadequate income, frequent unemployment, and trouble finding housing. They faced the possibility of losing their own customs and values to American ways. The American stress on mobility and independence threatened Old World adherence to family solidarity and deference to parental authority. (p. 87)

In the New Land, under pressures of social mobility and the opening of the frontier, American families were to experience even greater degrees of nucleation and fragmentation than was the case in Europe.

Overall, boys and girls handled similar manufacturing work, except that girls were in greater demand in the burgeoning textile industry in England and America because of presumed greater finger dexterity. The more-prestigious professional and trade occupations strenuously resisted the admittance of women on grounds that intellectual development would lead to hysteria or an atrophied uterus (Belenky et al. 1986). Female occupations that emerged during this period included nursing, teaching, needlework, and clerical work. Despite rising expectations for self-fulfillment among most middle-class young women, the jobs were usually short-term, serving primarily as way stations to the female-destined career of wife and mother (see J. Bernard 1981; Mintz 1985; Popenoe 1988).

Although the Victorian family appears as a highly stable enterprise, the structure rested on weak moorings. Absentee husbands and fathers, whose word was law; unattached servants, whose influence was often deleterious; mothers without moral authority; lack of extended kin group; and rebellious children—all were among the influences that eventually weakened the nuclear family. As people pursued the value of individualism, the nuclear family became even more threatened. By the mid-twentieth century, child rearing was taken over by agencies outside the family, such as those controlled by the state (Popenoe 1988, 53).

CONCLUSION

A history of childhood reveals a fairly clear pattern of oppression that characterized growing up in Western societies in premodern times. At the same time, the historical record would be incomplete if we were to ignore the arenas of freedom allowed children and youth, and the surprising degree of attachment that in some instances occurred between the generations. What can we conclude about childhood from our brief historical overview?

First, from the Middle Ages on, a conception of childhood existed as a definite stage in human development. Parents were expected to respond to their children in terms that were appropriate to their age and experience.

Second, rather than being wholly indifferent to their children, preindustrial parents often expressed sentimental attachment to their young. High infant and child mortality undoubtedly contributed to a kind of parental pessimism regarding the likelihood of a child's survival. Religious belief in a spiritually enlightened hereafter helped to sustain those who lost beloved children.

Third, the structure of family life in preindustrial Europe, England, and America was entirely different to our own, adapted as it was to small communities or rural settings and the continuity of generations. Unlike the modern family, however, with its idea of domestic order as a private institution organized around the children, early families were likely to be father-centered and open institutions, often continuous with the extended kin group and local neighborhood or village. Boys might have been sent out to boarding schools or apprenticeship posts at very early ages, but this was to ensure for them a future niche in society.

Fourth, the tragic history of abandonment should be perceived in the context of societies that were utterly constrained by their limited resources. The Church's unswerving teaching on the sanctity of human life drastically reduced the infanticide rate, compared with earlier cultures. In no instance was infanticide condoned as it had been in ancient Greece or Rome. The Church pursued its doctrine by setting up a variety of institutions for destitute, illegitimate, and orphaned children. Lack of organizational skills and overburdened wet nurses and caregivers in the foundling homes and orphanages undermined the founders' good intentions.

Fifth, children in open-style families, who left home at early ages to pursue education, military, profession, or trade probably benefited overall from the flexibility of membership in multiple households. Parents that sent away a child to another household, a monastery, or a school could expect to receive others into their household for training. In theory, no household would be cut off from the world of growing children.

Sixth, there is a clear reminder in the historical record that children "let out" or "put out" at young ages also developed a spirit of independence and expressed this in both legitimate and illegitimate ways. Youthful workers might have pocket money, free time, and, for boys, opportunities for sex and other pleasures. Nor were these early youth silenced or intimidated by discipline and hardships. Adolescent rebellion and acting out is not confined to modern adolescence. Premodern youth left copious records of their misbehavior in boarding schools, manors, homes, and towns, as in mutiny, running away, delinquency, premarital sex, stealing, and other deviant behavior.

Seventh, not until industrialization emerged with its accompanying gyrations of the commercial markets and the loss of rural lifestyles organized around extended families and village life, did poor children really confront the horrors of societal rejection and abandonment. The work ethic, now extended to children barely out of infancy, symbolized the new salvation, and became the rationale for an entirely new series of disciplinary regimes. With industrialization, the cult of order emerged to dominate every relationship and institution, gradually strangling the spirit of freedom that had initiated the new social development.

Modernism promised an entirely new agenda for children and youth: full-time involvement in schooling, the absence of grueling labor, the reclamation of the family under trade unionism and state benefits, and the expansion of opportunities for skilled and educated labor. Despite a worldwide depression in the 1930s, Western societies flourished from the 1920s onward as the industrial machine expanded, first, for peacetime goods, then for war, and then during the post–World War II exuberance that led to the proliferation of production and consumption for all but the poorest families.

What happened to the promise of postwar freedom and opportunity? The 1960s demonstrated through a series of protests—women, African Americans, Native Americans, the elderly, poor, even prisoners—that much of the liberal promise was incomplete or distorted by legal, political, and media deceptions. Children offered the opportunity for schooling discovered that it was neither equal nor just. Class, race, and ethnicity determined one's future, and the right to life was *not* inherent in the Constitution, either before or after birth. Food, shelter, medical care, the basic necessities to carry on a physical existence—none have been guaranteed rights for children and young people.

In the empirically based chapters that follow, I assess the extent to which various aspects of contemporary young people's lives are throttled, damaged, and effectively denied. Individualistic and market-based theories of justice typically ignore our joint human enterprise proposed in the ecological model of a common web of life. In celebrating youth in all its diversities, I show alternatives to the narrowly defined age and gender isolated structures and life-constraining social scripts prevailing across most institutions of family, school, work, and leisure.

4

Schooling in an Unjust Society

Purgation through victimage is part of the ritual of school instruction and in a multicultural society there exists an abundance of victims to help cleanse the system of its foreign impurities. Not surprisingly, these victims are often the children of the poor, and usually from a minority background.

Peter McLaren, *Schooling as a Ritual Performance*

To address children first and foremost as human beings we must look beyond the models of education that serve the national economy or particular social agendas. As human beings, they can come to know, as inner experience, their unity with all other human beings, their kinship with all life on the earth. . . .

Jeffrey Kane, "Personal Reflections on
Sources of Illusion and Hope"

THE SCHOOL CRISIS

This chapter examines the crisis in public education as an issue of social inequality. The basic outlines of the U.S. educational system and the conflicts that periodically shake its foundations and shatter its development will be examined. Indeed they are best understood through an analysis of the contradictory forces operating on the system. The struggle between working people and the economy of class disparities has its counterpart in educational conflicts. Employers and social elites, on the one hand, have sought to use the schools for the reproduction of compliant workers, who are expected to adjust to working conditions set out by managers intent on extracting their labor for profit. On the other hand, parents, students, workers' organizations, blacks, ethnic minorities, women, and others have striven to use schools for their own needs: material well-being, culture, a just distribution of economic reward, and personal development, related to the possibility of having a fuller, more meaningful, and happier life. This class division is but one phase of the crisis of the public school.

What do critics mean when they announce that there is a "crisis in American education"? Observers could be referring to the dropout rate of one million students per year—11.3 percent nationally; that rises to 40 percent in some urban areas, and a 60 percent dropout rate in Newark, New Jersey. Or they may be pointing to unsafe schools: three million crimes on school property, the lack of safety inside schools, as well as outside them—streets, public parks, and student hangouts. Consider the drugs, gangs, and gun problem that terrorizes many students—4,200 teens between fifteen and seventeen were killed by guns in 1990. Add to this the growth of hate crimes against blacks, gays, lesbians, and other minorities, and increasingly, the physical assaults on teachers by out-of-control students.

Equality and equity issues invariably stand out as evidence that public schools are not what they appear to be: a democratic institution that provides increasingly diverse citizenry the opportunity to better their lives. Instead, schools mirror the more general social inequalities in society—income, race, gender, and age disparities. The gap between rich and poor families is wider in America than in all other European countries (except Ireland). Among inner-city schools, income differences translate into "savage inequalities" (Kozol 1992). As a result, poor children of all colors are consigned to a procession of overcrowded, underheated, textbookless, indifferently taught classrooms.

Another crisis involves gender disparities that have been linked to the "hidden curriculum"—girls are shuffled into nonrigorous courses, requiring little creativity, while boys are channeled into more challenging college preparatory, career-oriented courses such as math and science. Watchdog groups, such as the American Association of University Women (1993), claim that boys harass, attack, and punish girls to keep them in line. In a recent national poll of 222,653 high school students, 82 percent of girls complained of "disturbing" sexual harassment mostly by male students, but also by teachers (in *USA Weekend,* September 6–8, 1996).

Still other criticism from elite groups entails test scores, purportedly the chief indicator of national achievement levels. American students are reported to be intellectually stunted by television, poor teaching, the tyranny of low expectations, and a watered-down curriculum (R. Riley 1994). The National Commission on Excellence in Education, which convened in 1983, declared in their report, *A Nation at Risk* that other countries' schools were doing better in both quality and equality of learning. U.S. students now rank forty-ninth in literacy when compared to students from 158 countries in the United Nations. The study also said that only 15 percent of the students who enter high school complete college. Our schools

---

Box 4-A
The Baby Boom Echo

By the fall of 1995, there were more young people in our nation's public and private schools than at any time in American history—fully 51.7 million students. This new record is the beginning of a ten-year growth trend, that demographers call the "baby boom echo." By the year 2006 an estimated 54.6 million young people will be attending school every day. Of this number 40 percent will be minority students. This very large increase is also coupled with the disturbing recognition that although the nation's crime rate is down, the juvenile crime rate continues to escalate. The coming increase in the number of young people and the continuing rise in juvenile crime explain the accelerated efforts now underway to encourage schools, parents, and communities to find new ways to keep young people in school and to avoid drugs and violence.

Source: U.S. Department of Justice. 1996. "Estimating the National Scope of Gang Crime from Law Enforcement Data" (August). Washington, D.C.: National Institute of Justice.

---

have lost ground on all counts: physical plant, school management, curriculum, learning, equality, equity, and social order.

The Commission accused the schools of "a rising tide of mediocrity" that violates the democratic promise that "all regardless of race or class or economic status are entitled to a fair chance and to the tools for developing their powers of mind and spirit to the utmost" (quoted in Gagnon 1995, 66). With increasing numbers of students flooding the school system, the pressure is on to rectify the growing problems (see Box 4-A).

Another major crisis involves the substitution of computers for music, art, and physical education, as well as more-substantive disciplines. Oppenheimer (1997) sharply criticizes the overenthusiasm of educators for computer activities over more-traditional modes of learning. He cites a recent poll in which U.S. teachers ranked computer skills and media technology as more "essential" than European history, biology, chemistry, and physics; more essential than dealing with social problems—such as drugs and family breakdown or learning practical job skills; and far more essential than reading modern American writers (e.g., Hemingway) or the classics (e.g., Shakespeare).

Public school advocates—especially the National Education Association (NEA)—have launched a strong counterattack. NEA leaders claim that the crisis is "manufactured," mere rhetoric to debunk public education and to justify tearing down the public education system in favor of a more race-class system, in which rich children attend private institutions, middle-class children attend charter or parochial schools, and the poor are left with the dregs of the system, forced to attend dilapidated, demoralized public schools (Berliner and Biddle 1995). Though there is much truth to the NEA argument that conservative groups have opted for school vouchers and other government-financed schemes to avoid sending their children to the standard public school, the crisis is genuine. Both the overwhelming evidence of decline, especially in urban schools, and public perception that schools are not working reinforce a picture of a troubled institution (Bowers 1993).

These contradictory forces will be further clarified by taking up the following topics: (1) Origins of public schooling; (2) School and economy; (3) What do schools do?; (4) Social reproduction of inequality; (5) Schools as ritual performance; (6) Student resistance; (7) Sexual harassment; (8) Truancy; (9) Dropping out of school; and (10) Violence. A final section presents attempts to construct alternative models of schooling.

Origins of Public Schooling

The rise of industrialism and technology in the nineteenth century shifted the concern from Rousseau's ideal of "natural man" and the articulation of liberties to a far more somber purpose: adjusting the man to the machine by producing the "docile bodies" the new factory system needed (Foucault 1979). The asylum, the prison, and the school all took on the trappings of the factory system: a regimented, hierarchical, rule-ordained structure that denied those under their control both freedom of choice and self-expression.

In America from the colonial period to the mid-1800s, education bore little resemblance to European elite or factory models. Here the school was intimately linked with family and community, as was the apprenticeship system. In the colonies, young states, and territories alike, statutes mandated that children be instructed (Richardson 1994). The colonial Acts of 1642 and 1647 stipulated parental responsibility for the instruction of children. The states of Massachusetts and Connecticut instituted common schooling in 1647, grounded in the Puritan belief that all children should have the opportunity for "learning and labor" (Bailyn 1960).

The earliest elementary schools in the United States were, unsurprisingly, extensions of the home with little structure or discipline. Termed "Dame Schools," they were conducted by a literate woman in her own home, which provided the basic formal education available at the time. "Writing Schools," offering literacy and computational skills, coexisted with the dame schools, but they operated outside of the home. But as industrialization and the movement from country to city proceeded, a dual tracking system emerged. Among the well-to-do classes, schooling was highly informal; casual to the extreme. For the working classes and poor, military discipline and drill prevailed (Cremin 1961).

In the first half of the nineteenth century, political and educational leaders presumed that different races and classes must attend quite different types of institutions. In the South race-and-class divided schools prevailed, with most slaves remaining illiterate. But a minority opinion arose that challenged this undemocratic process and questioned whether it was not wiser to integrate the working classes into the same system to maintain more effective control, and to forestall such youth problems as habitual truancy and, among city youth, the rising specter of urban crime. To this end, different but equivalent educational structures emerged.

Richardson (1994) argues that American education developed as "a multidimensional institution," historically constituted by three worlds: the common school, the reform school, and the special school. He argues that the founding of the Illinois Juvenile Court Act of 1899 to "regulate the treatment and control of dependent, neglected and delinquent children" clearly represented a turning away from the penal principle of confinement to the "parens patriae" principle, the state as parent. This involves the interests of the state to intervene authoritatively on behalf of children to protect their welfare. This "legalized paternalism" with the family and school serving as models reflected the shift toward rehabilitation and prevention. The reach of state powers into the welfare of children had a double edge: one side promoted child welfare and education; whereas the other side extended the reach of state powers over families and communities (Donzelot 1979).

Mandatory education was slow in evolving. School formalization lagged because attendance was already high—as high as 70 percent in the North (Richardson 1994). Building programs were slower to evolve. By 1870 there were still only 160 public high schools in the country. By 1900 the figure had reached 6,000. Although public sentiment and state funding remained favorably geared toward the local school system (rather than a national program as in some European countries), the schools developed from a similar mold. Michael Katz (1971), an educational historian, claims that by the last quarter of the nineteenth century

American education had acquired its fundamental characteristics that have not altered since. Public education was universal, tax-supported, free, compulsory, bureaucratically arranged, class biased, and racist. (p.8)

School and Economy

Schools increasingly were formed in the image of the emerging economic system. According to Bowles and Gintis (1977), who focus on the large Northeastern seaboard cities, the expansion and continuing transformation of capital production led to unprecedented shifts in the occupational distribution of the labor force, necessitating drastic changes in job skills. The old apprenticeship system of training—which by custom committed masters for a period of up to seven years to supply their charges with room and board and minimal training in return for labor services—was no longer economically feasible. Periodic depressions and high costs of training and upgrading workers wiped out this system. Among large capitalist firms profits came to dictate the allocation of labor, not individual masters and their ill-trained labor.

As labor costs soared with scarcity of workers, plant owners turned to foreigners. By mid-century, immigrants became part of the growing urban proletariat. The failure of industry and commercial enterprises to absorb transient and foreign workers, as well as to raise living standards of American workers, began to pose unresolved problems of integration and control. Under pressure from the newly emerging workers' unions, public education was born. But it remained a far cry from the visions of Thomas Jefferson—who asserted the need for a "natural aristocracy" that can emerge from the common people—and Horace Mann, the educational reformer, who called for a more open school system. Mann argued as early as 1842 that one's stake in life should not be determined by name, birth, or family connections, but by one's own abilities and willingness to work. Theoretically, all Americans were to enjoy "an open and fair field of competition" (in Ballantine 1997, 56).

Horace Mann had correctly gauged the tensions generated by the "domination of capital and the servility of labor," which rendered workers as "servile dependents." The society and economy were out of balance, Mann reasoned, and only education could create a "new social edifice [that would be created by] sober, wise, good men" (in Ballantine 1997, 57). This nineteenth-century reformer strongly opposed the old teaching methods of authority, fear, force, and pain. Instead, he exhorted educators to create a relationship with students, focusing on affection, loyalty, and their higher motives. But reformers had little success in shaping the newer urban model of the public school systems, which increasingly resembled the factory, the railroad, and the asylum—strictly regimented structures aimed to produce a docile working class.

Public school expansion was not embraced by everyone. Ethnics, such as the Irish, fought to have their own schools. And professional and business elites were far more concerned with targeting the potentially explosive urban proletariat as school attendees than with the nuances of parochial schools, educational curriculum, and organization. In time, the relationship of industrial development to education took a now-familiar pattern. In the nineteenth century, Northeastern cities, such as New York and Boston, where wage capital thrived, attendance at public schools was more likely to be related to the percentage of the labor force employed in manufacturing (Bowles and Gentis 1977, 176). In other regions, especially the West, but also states such as Maine and Vermont, school attendance in rural and small-town America remained high, focused as it was on vocational education, which took place without the need for compulsory education laws or the factory-model common school (Richardson 1994).

What Do Schools Do?

If public education fails to produce the well-informed, disciplined citizen, as envisioned by Mann and other nineteenth-century school innovators, what does it do? The answer itself contains curious contradictions, because the public school in the United States, unlike Europe and Japan, has tried to be "all things to all people"— without ever succeeding. The more typical question has been: What *should* the school do? The Puritans answer was *discipline*. But this lacks a modern framework and fails to account for the abysmal failure of public education to instill discipline. How do educational philosophers regard this issue of school purpose?

One school of sociological thought, articulated by Emile Durkheim (1956, 1973) in the nineteenth century, stipulated that we cannot separate the educational system from the society for they reflect each other. Moral values, Durkheim said, are the foundation of the social order, and society is perpetuated through its education. Classrooms are "small societies," agents of socialization. Thus value transmission, not technical training per se, maintains the stability of society. Education works in a two-fold manner: It preserves the moral order, and it produces a disciplined labor force.

The functionalist perspective, as this approach came to be known, emphasized the fit between different parts of the social system, but typically from the "have's" perspective—those who own the means of production. It takes for granted the social order, and largely ignores the tensions, struggles, and disparities between "haves" and "have-nots." For example, a functionalist would be unlikely to perceive an equity problem arising from a largely female or minority teaching staff (who are paid at relatively low wages) and a mainly white male administration (who typically receive substantially higher salaries). Such gender disparities "preserve" the social order but are inherently unfair.

The conflict perspective posits an entirely different set of assumptions: Inequality and low-quality education accompany the institutionalization of mass education. This translates into the following (see Noddings 1995; Kozol 1992; Morrow and Torres 1995):

1. The American school as a mass institution functions to reinforce existing status discrepancies of class, race, ethnicity, gender, and age.
2. The social class relations that prevail outside the school are reproduced inside it, but not necessarily in a one-to-one correspondence (as will be shown later). For example, not all working-class boys grow up to be working-class men. Some may graduate into the professional class—doctors, lawyers, or professors—or

become business owners or managers. The class "stigma" may remain, however, as expressed in lifestyle choices.

3. Inequalities of power, control, and access to social and economic opportunities are legitimated in the day-to-day interactions and symbolic exchanges of students, teachers, and administrators. Rules of deference between ranks implies that students obey teachers, women defer to male commands, minorities honor the lifeways of dominant groups, even at the risk of violating their own cultural prescriptions.

Postmodern theory posits further modifications of both these positions and suggests that social status may be more fluid than is usually conceived (Morrow and Torres 1995). Some essential tenets include that social change is often drastic, dissolving old status barriers and erecting new ones. High school status evaluations rarely reward the "disciplined" student over the athlete or beauty queen. The transmission of values may go awry; the lower-class youth links up with mainstream opportunities and institutions, not necessarily on academic merit but on social and athletic skills. Similarly, in a status reversal, the affluent teenager gets hooked on drugs and drops out of school.

Families, schools, and communities are not necessarily linked in single pathways with "unhealthy" schools—those that are overly bureaucratized and regimented and contain mainly dysfunctional families and students— or those "healthy" schools, which are caring and supportive of students and incorporate a high proportion of achievers. Matters are far more complex.

Social mobility for lower working-class and minority youth, although not a manifest function of the school system, is possible but only under specific conditions. Success-oriented lower-class youth generally come from families that have supportive adult network structures, which promote mobility; restrictive family-community relations, which keep youth on task; and stringent parental monitoring strategies to prevent young people from identifying with peers over adults (Jarrett 1995).

Without school, the youth would remain immobilized, trapped in conditions not of his own making but that would define his existence for a lifetime. So, school remains a cultural imperative, not only to succeed in the world but to join fellow citizens in social and political action at any level of discourse. At the same time, school guarantees nothing; a high school diploma yields neither a good job nor a position in the larger community. A high school education says little about the individual and his or her achievements, because it has been severely devalued, its essential democratic meanings lost over time. In the present era, the functions of the public school remain amorphous: vague, indecipherable, multiple, and contradictory.

Social Reproduction of Inequality

How do schools transmit, or reproduce, class values from one generation to the next? Basil Bernstein (1977), a British sociologist, has argued in *Class, Codes and Control* that children from varying class backgrounds develop different "codes," or forms of speech during the early years of life, that affect their subsequent school experience. Bernstein's interest centered on *how* children use language and symbols that differentiate children from poor environments with children from more affluent backgrounds. Although the class structure of England is far more rigid than the one in the United States, Bernstein's ideas about class and differential communication codes are valid for all modern societies.

The speech of lower class children, Bernstein argues, represents a **restricted code**, a type of speech that is connected to the cultural setting of a lower-class community or culture. For example, lower-working-class people live in a familial or neighborhood culture in which certain values and norms are taken for granted and not put into explicit language. Parents in these settings socialize their children in concrete rather than in abstract ways—rewards and reprimands to correct behavior without reference to abstract ideas or relationships. When in school, these children display lack of curiosity, experience problems with abstract concepts, and use linguistic forms different than the teacher's. For example, the speech of some African Americans (black English vernacular) directly affects performance in mathematical school tests (Giddens, 1991, 522).

Children from higher-class backgrounds acquire a style of speaking that Bernstein calls **elaborated code**. Although children use restricted codes with one another on the playground, they can "switch over" from one to the other. These children are more able to generalize and express abstract ideas that are less bound to particular contexts. Children are socialized to understand why they should behave in certain ways. For example, if a child darts into the street, the parent from a higher educational background is more apt to explain the dangers of moving vehicles, rather than simply punish the child for disobedience. The elaborated code is also used by teachers and administrators, and thus, the child who can master this more complex language structure is more likely to be a successful student.

The concept of "cultural capital" developed by Bourdieu (1977) enables us to explore the interinstitutional linkages among schooling, family life, and individuals (Bourdieu and Passeron 1977). Moreover, the concept furnishes a theoretical lens to understand why social class influences family-school relations. Cultural capital, then, refers to the distinctly *different* resources that parents bring into the social situation, including education, income and material resources, occupational status, style of work, and social networks. Upper-class and professional families bring a large store of cultural capital and can effectively influence institutions, in this case, schools, on behalf of their children; middle-class families less so. Lower-class and working-class families with little cultural capital presumably have very limited ability to influence the school (Smrekar 1996).

The proposition that higher social class provides parents with more resources to intervene in schooling and to bind families into tighter connections with social institutions than are available to working-class families suggests the following:

1. More years of schooling provide parents with a greater capacity to understand the instructional language used by teachers and, thereby, be more responsible for helping their children with homework.

2. Higher social status allows parents to approach teachers as social equals or superiors and provides a greater sense of confidence in the educational setting.

3. Higher incomes make it easier for parents to purchase more educational resources—computers, language, travel—and to obtain child-care services and transportation to attend school events.

4. Upper-middle-class jobs more closely resemble the interconnection between work and home that teachers envision for students and their homework.

5. Upper-middle-class parents are more likely to be members of social networks with ready access to information on school processes and practices. (Lareau 1987).

Lareau's (1987) study of cultural capital left out two crucial elements: (1) The nature of the school—does it support or reject parental involvement and other parental commitments? (2) To what extent are parents free to pursue a school commitment, and how does that conflict with other family, work, and community commitments? Claire Smrekar (1996) pursued the cultural capital thesis to determine the degree of fit between class and parental participation in three distinct school systems: a neighborhood public school, a public-choice school (magnet school), and a Catholic school.

In the first place, schools differ remarkably in their capacity to provide a supportive milieu for parental involvement. Magnet, or charter schools, are alternative schools that draw students from a relatively extensive area, emphasize academic excellence, and provide options for parents who resist sending their children to the neighborhood public school. In Smrekar's research, the charter school, although drawing from a diverse mix of families, provided a high measure of internal cohesion—teachers and parents shared educational values and concerns. The Catholic school shared religious values and ideologies that helped build a school community. Only in the public school—with its economic, social, and value disparities among parents and school staff—was cohesion low or absent. Smrekar (1996, 12) posits that the public school reflected a "critical absence of social cohesion and communication despite a multifaceted parent volunteer program." Organizational processes within that system undermined community among parents, as well as connections between parents and school staff. Apparently, parents and school staff lacked the "common ground" to build disparate families into a "school community."

Perception of parents' involvement was vastly different in the three schools. Interviews revealed that magnet school teachers perceived parents as "committed partners"; Catholic school teachers saw parents as "meddlesome intruders"; and the neighborhood public school teacher viewed parents as "distracted absentees," essentially distant from and uninvolved with the school program.

The "cultural capital" model of social class and parent-school linkages requires modification. Parent involvement is not a simple resource issue. Other social facts intrude, like work and family commitments, that may undercut parents' efforts to participate in PTA, fund raisers, or home room visits. Smrekar (1996) concludes:

Across social class and school setting, parents referred to an accompanying state of general weariness and a lack of discretionary time as elements which structure their involvement in schooling. . . . For these [overwhelmed] parents, evenings are just a blurry and brief respite before another workday. Any expendable energy is spent preparing meals, organizing bath times, and helping with homework. (p.143)

Critics may blame the schools for their incapacity to involve parents—thereby contributing to students' alienation and lack of school connection—but the exigencies of parental work routines (outside factors over which the school has little control) and lack of cohesion in the school point to the greatly reduced capacity for the public school system to effect the necessary citizen-school based reforms to alter larger structural inequalities of class, race, and gender.

The social reproduction of inequality is far more complicated than it first appears. James Coleman's (1990) work on quality and equality in American education emphasizes the type and organization of school as crucial to student retention and achievement. Public schools overall are poorly organized, Coleman asserts, because there is a "crisis of authority" (p. 247). The problem revolves around the lack of consensus in a community defined by residence about what kind and amount of discipline should be exercised. Differences—based on race, class, family organization, beliefs, values—not similarities characterize the American community. The result is a paralysis of action, and the student suffers.

If a school system should emerge that offers "disciplined" learning, Coleman ponders, how would this impact on student achievement? His comparison of Catholic schools with public schools clarifies his hunch: Children learn in disciplined settings.

In our study of high school sophomores and seniors in both public and private schools, we found not only higher achievement in the Catholic and other private schools for students from comparable backgrounds than in the public schools, but also major differences between the functioning of the public schools and the schools of the private sector. The principal differences were in the greater academic demands made and the greater disciplinary standards maintained in private schools, even when schools with students from comparable backgrounds were compared. (Coleman 1990, 247)

From this Coleman concludes that *stronger academic demands and disciplinary standards produce better achievement.* From Coleman's analysis, we seem to have come full circle from the Puritans to a postmodern solution to the learning crisis.

But Coleman also recognizes that public schools are in a poor position to establish and maintain these demands—loss of authority of the local school board, superintendent, and principal to federal policy and court rulings; the rise of student rights (which help shape a student-defined curriculum); and perhaps, most fundamental to the breakdown of school authority, the lack of consensus among parents about high schools' authority over and responsibility for their children. Such conditions severely compromise an alliance of school/parents/community toward revamping public schools to upgrade student achievement.

Both overt and covert measures conspire to reproduce inequality in public schools. Take curriculum, for instance. We normally consider high school curriculum a straightforward matter of college preparatory versus technical or vocational training. But curriculum has two faces. The "visible pedagogy" entails courses and classrooms that meet state requirements for substantive content, methods, and period of study. In the case of tracking, the competitive grading system, and gender-related courses and activities (domestic arts for girls; carpentry and body-contact sports for boys), these highly visible structures remain entrenched in American education, and few dispute the normality of such arrangements (Smrekar 1996).

"Invisible pedagogy" is another matter, for this entails a manipulative strategy to achieve a more effective form of control. Educational assumptions are crucial to this model. Thus, lower-class children are presumed to have an intellectual or linguistic deficit; girls are expected to do poorly in math and science; and blacks and Hispanics are expected to be poor learners and eventually drop out of school. The school does little to examine these assumptions or change teaching practices to produce different results (Smrekar 1996).

Both curricula practice status placements, but in different ways. The visible pedagogy prepares students for future job placement by specific courses and relationship techniques (how to defer to people in authority) in terms of the student's preexisting family and community experiences (middle-class athletic "jocks" are given leadership opportunities). The invisible pedagogy structures classroom experiences to eliminate the "losers" and those that fail to fit the competitive norms (aggressive minorities, especially those lacking standard English usage). From these dual curricula derive a predictable array of outcomes—from high levels of success among those with strong cultural capital, to modest levels of success among those with minimal cultural capital, to exclusion among those whose families have few or no resources for launching the young person's future.

Schools as Ritual Performance

Jeffrey Kane (1995) defines adolescence as a "time without place"—a time for building lasting, definitive, and meaningful relationships; a time for learning to approach the world with reverence, wonder, and a sense of stewardship; a time for nourishing the inner self to develop a heightened sense of unity and purpose. And school should be the place where such lessons are learned.

What students really learn in school is an entirely different matter. They learn to interpret and address the world through academic subjects that are fragmented and routinized. They plod through the academic drill: English, social studies, science, and math, but without perceiving any intellectual connection between subjects or between school subjects and their own lives. Learning is a technical achievement that demands detachment, a separation of the self from others and one's own life. What school teaches is that knowledge is power, not loving embrace; that learning enhances external control over others, not self-control; and that lessons are ritualistic practices without reference to their own experiences, not a rich source of insight and understanding. School knowledge thus becomes an empty gesture, the educational process part of the "culture of pain" (McLaren 1993).

Kane (1995) attributes the lost opportunities of adolescence both to the organization of the school and drastic social changes.

The past decades have witnessed an increasing irrelevance of traditional rites of passage, a profound decline of parental authority, a near complete erosion of community, and a basic dislocation of the adolescent as a responsible, productive member of a family. Paradoxically, the contemporary adolescent is left to develop his or her new capacities in an environment where he or she is not needed and where his or her actions are viewed as less than substantial. . . . The central problem is that the contemporary adolescent dwells in a socially constructed vacuum [with] virtually no meaningful context for relation—for a sense of connection, inclusion, or identification. . . . The "I am" is left alone, without mooring, as a stranger in a strange land. (p. 3)

The adolescent thus cast adrift must flounder with other equally disoriented adolescents in desolate environments of school, street, or low-wage work. Early sex and motherhood, gang involvement, drinking, drugs, fighting, and dropping out of school offer momentary releases for their newly found intellectual abilities, passions, and physical powers. A dialectical process is inevitable, though. This means that the greater the external pressures for adolescent conformity in meaningless environments, the more likely the resistance. In short, school as an environment fails to address the diverse and growing physical, intellectual, and social capacities of this transitional age group, and this institutional deficiency generates student (and often teacher) alienation and resistance.

Schooling is not only tied to the economy, but it is inescapably political. Peter McLaren (1993) insists that power in the educational process works through the use of performative and regulatory rituals that are imposed over students' resistance. School, he argues, is above all a cultural production with enormous significance in the social construction and maintenance of power and domination. Ritual plays a crucial role in articulating these mechanisms of social control, such as the social distance between teachers and students (teachers can humiliate students; but if students act out or do likewise, it constitutes grounds for punishment).

McLaren's close ethnographic observations on the macro and micro rituals of power and privilege in a Catholic school, comprised of working-class Portuguese students, focuses on the somatic and usually unconscious modes of control that assert adult, Catholic, and middle-class power over these youngsters. Rituals embody a regular, repetitive, and prescribed format. The subjection of bodies in uncomfortable pupil seats for hours a day; the spacing of furniture to separate teacher from students; the authoritative bodily gestures of administrators; the rituals of instruction that feature conformity and "getting by"; the rush from one subject and classroom to another—all are modes of control that reinforce the power of the system.

Because school is such a ritual exercise, it means that all activities are institutionalized: circumscribed, nonspontaneous events that allow for little or no personal feeling or experience. Students are pushed through their paces, often without sufficient time to eat their lunch or go to the bathroom in a "tedious succession of unrelated episodes and the wearisome wait for instruction to end." School culture, McLaren says, is uniformly oppressive.

Students 'wore' the hegemonic culture of the school in their very beings; in their wrinkled brows; in their tense musculature; in the impulsive way they reacted to their peers; and in the stoic way they responded to punishment. (p. 167)

Students, like workers, are chained to their environments, and learn that debilitating feelings are normal. Like "spectral shadows," students endured the school day like a "factory worker, assembly line worker or laboratory technician" (McLaren 1993).

Coleman hearkens to "discipline" as the path to achievement. But what kind of achievement, for whose benefit, and at what cost? The radical separation of self into situational selves or distinct modes of consciousness, often with little connection between them, may be a direct outcome of such discipline. Students learn to divide themselves into segments. McLaren's research found four distinct "states," each calling for different forms of self and interaction, that extend over the course of the school day: student state, streetcorner state, home state (e.g., with parents and siblings), and sanctity state (e.g. prayerful, quiet). Rarely are these states perceived by students as self-conscious behavior. These states are created primarily by conditions imposed from outside—parents, teachers, shopkeepers, law enforcement, neighborhood adults—and, as such, provoke anger and engender resistance. Only the streetcorner state engenders a spontaneous expression of personal values and authentic interaction, but it also reflects a distancing between students and others. The streetcorner state is, by definition, a state of resistance.

The two states that most converge during school hours are the student and streetcorner states (see Table 4.1). Over the course of the day, students interchange between the student state—a docile, resentful, fearful, frustrated, task-centered, and rational self—with the streetcorner state, an emotional, sensuous, physical, playful, and formless state of being. McLaren calculates that students spend approximately 66 minutes of the school day in the streetcorner state, 4 minutes in the sanctity state, and 298 minutes in the student state. Only in the streetcorner state is there a sense of "aliveness"; being in the student state involves "slow, institutional death." The students seek to expand the boundaries of the streetcorner state into the classroom, hallways, lunchroom, and homeroom. The teachers seek to restrict the boundaries of the expressive state within the narrowest confines, which is accomplished by excessive rules, and by frequently doling out punishment in various forms (public humiliation, extra homework, letters to parents, after-school stays, forcible withdrawals from sports, and expulsion). Except for brief moments, the teachers invariably win.

Student Resistance

The streetcorner state is not the only form of student resistance to external control. As McLaren's ethnographic observations clarify, students are not passive in the face of oppression and discrimination. In their struggle against marginalization—of being overlooked, of being labeled "different" and "underachiever," of failing to make the grade—adolescents struggle with identity. Schools serve as a host site for "identity politics" (self-definition). Henry Giroux (1992) and other radical scholars claim that schools serve as potential host sites for *deep democracy* in inner-city schools. But in acting out their protest, oppressed groups may actually

Table 4.1
Structures of Student Conformity and Resistance

Street Corner State	Student State
Tribal	Institutional
Emotional, not rational	Cognitive, rational
Random gestures; imprecise	Planned gestures; precise
Expressive; excitable	Serious; lacks emotional involvement
Play	Work ethic
Experimental, creative	Conformist
Whimsical moods	Task oriented
Mind & body in synchrony	Mind & body separated
Inner resources stressed	Imitation of teachers
Informal; interpersonal skills	Formal; technical skills
Sensuous	Mechanical
High intensity interaction	Low intensity interaction
Cathartic activity—releases tension	Tension-inducing activity—builds tension
Peer-determined status	Institutionally determined status
Peer community	Anomie
Energy flow; relaxation	Energy barriers; stress-producing
Flexible; improvisational	Conventional; stereotypical behavior
Egalitarian relations	Hierarchical relations

Source: Adapted from Peter McLaren, *Schooling as a Ritual Performance*. 2nd ed. (London and New York: Routledge, 1993), chapter 3.

reproduce the conditions of their own oppression. As Aronowitz and Giroux (1991) aptly note:

Oppositional behaviors are produced amidst contradictory discourses and values. The logic that informs a given act of resistance may, on the one hand, be linked to interests that are class-, gender-, or race-specific. On the other hand, it may express the repressive moments inscribed in such behavior by the dominant culture rather than a message of protest against their existence. (p. 101–2)

Racial or gender pride is a product of shared identity making. This identity becomes an important asset for negotiating with institutions and authority persons. But in expressing a racial, ethnic, or gender identity, social actors may find themselves inadvertently contributing to the reproduction of racist or sexist attitudes and practices (e.g., "he's too ethnic"; "she's overly pushy"). How is this paradox played out in the context of the public school?

Miron and Lauria (1995, 36) take up the issue of identity making in inner-city schools. They observe that the public schools in urban areas provide places where the struggle for identity can be forged. Inner-city schools are uniquely situated to achieve this as changing demographics and global and national migration continue to construct schools as "host sites of identity politics. . . . School culture both shapes and is shaped by . . . students' real task in school: identity work."

Learning is not "busy work" but rather a struggle to overcome the limitations of negative collective identities (e.g., race, poverty, ghetto youth, deviant, underachiever). One of the stronger student responses is the reaction to inert government bureaucracies that ignore the impact of crime in the inner-city community. Students recognize that most African American residents react angrily to crime by African Americans. Being poor and African American, they argue, is not synonymous with being a criminal. At the same time, African American students and their teachers in inner-city schools conspire in "silencing . . . racial conflict and school violence" in an effort to achieve a semblance of order, and for the fortunate few, quality education and secure occupational future.

The students' struggle is not limited to race or gender pride, but challenges the foundation of the system. As such, identity making among self-aware students is part of "identity politics" (Miron and Lauria 1995; Giroux 1992). Mouffe (1988) articulates identity politics as

resistance to the growing uniformity of social life, a uniformity that is the result of the kind of mass culture imposed by the media. This imposition of a homogenized way of life, a uniform cultural pattern, is being challenged by different groups that reaffirm their right to their difference, their specificity, be it through the exaltation of their regional identity or their specificity in the realm of fashion, music, or language. (p. 93)

Significantly, the contemporary student self is not experienced as a single completed identity; but rather, as multiple, incomplete, and partial identities (Smith 1992, 31). The social context of inner-city school, the multiethnic student population, and the interface of race, class, and gender all contribute to the development of new and changing identities. What this implies is that student resistance does not translate into revolution, an organized effort to throw off oppression. Instead, in keeping with multiple identities, resistance may entail a number of strategies: withdrawal, resignation, aggression, willingness to compromise, enhanced motivation for success, utilization of legal channels to redress grievances, or participation in crime and violence.

Inner-city boys confront and resist territorial and political segregation by creating alternative social, cultural, and economic arrangements: gangs, violence, crime, and other urban disturbances. Ferrell (1995a) argues that urban graffiti demonstrates resistance to their increasing exclusion in the world of politics and work, as well as a protest over their lack of control of the urban environment. Participants in the graffiti underground undermine the efforts of legal and political authorities to control them. For female adolescents, who are often the victims of male violence, the repression often goes underground.

Female resistance is far more problematic than for boys. At the edge of adolescence (ten to thirteen years of age), girls begin to show signs of "losing voice," a newfound reluctance to speak about their feelings, thoughts, and relationships (Dorney, 1995, 58). Sometimes, the young women go "underground," their voices and knowledge hidden from the public arena, temporarily; or for some, silence may last a lifetime. Loss of self-esteem, voice, and authority is the outcome of educational and cultural messages that silence the voices and negate the knowledge of girls and women (Brown and Gilligan 1992; Dorney 1995).

Sexual Harassment

The AAUW's *Hostile Hallways: Survey on Sexual Harassment in America's Schools* (1993) reveals some of the reasons why girls lose voice. This report, based on the experiences of 1,632 students in grades 8 through 11, found that 85 percent of the girls and 76 percent of the boys experience sexual harassment at alarming rates. In the hostile hallways of America's schools, sexual harassment takes a far greater toll on girls than on boys. Girls who have been harassed in school feel less confident about themselves than boys similarly treated. Sexual harassment in school begins early; girls, African Americans, and gay/lesbian youth are the most likely candidates for sexual harassment. Along with increasing rates of sexual harassment of girls, many standardized tests contain elements of gender bias, and informal norms benefit boys at the cost of girls' silence.

Violence against girls remains an unacknowledged but deeply-rooted problem. Schools support violence against females and some males, based on deeply ingrained gender-role stereotypes and expectations. In addition to sexual harassment, girls experience date rape, battering, homophobic violence, and street violence (Women's Educational Equity Act [WEEA] 1995). These forms of gendered bias and violence undermine girls' self-esteem and discourage them from pursuing nontraditional forms of study, such as math, science, or business or of moving into leadership roles (AAUW 1995).

Parents, teachers, and administrators have been urged to foster girls' growth by encouraging them to experiment with the full range of strategies, bearing in mind that new options may generate opposition. The most-effective strategies often find girls balancing precariously between success and failure (AAUW 1996) (see Box 4-B).

Feminists are more likely than educators to perceive the paradox of conformity, in which the wish to be liked and approved of by peers and authority figures can incapacitate the young woman from developing her authentic self. Resistance is urgent, say feminists, who stress the importance

---

Box 4-B
Fostering Girls' Growth for Resistance

Speaking Out. When girls speak out, they tend to make their opinions heard at home, school, or community. They can be highly visible and publicly acknowledged as leaders in the school setting. In some circumstances, though, girls who speak out risk being labeled as troublemakers, and rejected by peers and teachers.

Doing School. When girls "do school," they usually carry out institutional expectations: complete their work on time, listen in class, respect teachers, and meet adult demands for conformity. On the other hand, doing school may result in suppressed potential for achievement. Conformity may not be the path to success for girls, after all.

Crossing Borders. When girls cross borders, they tend to move easily between different sets of norms and expectations and distinct cultures, bridging the gap between peers and adults or between racial or ethnic groups. This skill qualifies them as good communicators and mediators. Being a go-between can also be burdensome; a heavy responsibility that most young girls may not feel qualified to bear. Nor should they be expected to shoulder this new responsibility without school support. The AAUW report connects girls' success to school reforms, such as team teaching and cooperative learning with caring adults. Such norms benefit boys as well as girls.

Source: American Association of University Women (AAUW). 1995. *The AAUW Report: How Schools Shortchange Girls.* Washington, D.C.: AAUW Educational Foundation Research.

---

of women educators fostering healthy resistance as a form of political intervention. Most essential in this resistance process is teaching "self-authorization"—the "I am" as an essential form of opposition (L. M. Brown 1991). For many girls, though, it appears simpler to get pregnant, take care of younger siblings, drop out of school for a minimum hourly pay job, or withdraw entirely from the success track. Coping with violence or the threat of violence may be the most harmful situation of all. Under the best of conditions, the student state is problematical, if not wholly irrelevant, for many young lives.

Truancy, Dropping Out, and Violence

It should not be surprising that students react to an oppressive and irrelevant education by various withdrawal and acting-out strategies. As Aronowitz and Giroux (1991) emphasize, though, certain forms of race- and gender-identities that lend themselves to resistance against domination may also play into reactionary racial and gender views and practices. In these instances, the control system tightens its repressive grip, including labeling, exclusion, and punishment. Such is the case with three oppositional strategies students employ that we now consider: truancy, dropping out, and violence.

Truancy

Truancy, a status crime under current law, entails periodic, unexplained absences. Authorities view it as the first step to a lifetime of problems, including dropping out, unemployment, and criminality. Truancy is rampant in many cities and is directly related to juvenile crime. In 1994, state courts formally processed approximately 364,000 truancy cases, a 35 percent increase since 1990, and a 67 percent increase since 1985 (Ingersoll and LeBoeuf 1997). Truancy may be the first stage of more-serious offending. During a recent government survey in Miami, more than 71 percent of thirteen- to sixteen-year-olds prosecuted for criminal violations had been truant. In Minneapolis, daytime crime dropped 68 percent after police began citing truant students. In San Diego, 44 percent of violent juvenile crimes occurred between 8:30 A.M. and 1:30 P.M., prime school hours.

Whereas no figures exist for national truancy rates, selected cities show very high rates of truancy. For example, in Pittsburgh, each day approximately 3,500 students or 12 percent of the pupil population are absent without an excuse. Daily absentee rates in larger cities (e.g., Los Angeles) run over 30 percent.

Some of the truancy certainly is explained by the increased violence in schools (see also Chapter 10). One in five African American and Hispanic teens indicates that the threat of crime has kept them from attending school—staying home or cutting class (Butts 1996). To determine how extensive students' behavior has changed as a result of school violence and victimization, a USA Weekend Survey included 65,193 mail-in respondents from grades 6 to 12. Responses to school disorder ran the gamut from feelings of being unsafe to avoidance behavior (Ansley 1997):

- 37 percent did not feel safe in school
- 50 percent knew someone who changed schools to feel safer
- 43 percent avoided school restrooms
- 20 percent avoided school hallways
- 45 percent avoided school grounds

Dropping Out of School

A second strategy—dropping out—reflects students' response to both powerlessness as well as perceived opportunities. Coping with frustration and problems specific to their gender, social class, and other life circumstances, students who leave school—on their own volition or because of

Table 4.2
Differential Dropout Rates by Ethnicity (1993–1994)

Ethnicity	Percent
White	8.6%
African American	12.1
Hispanic (born in U.S.)	17.9
Hispanic Immigrants	46.2
Asian*	4.3
Native American*	8.9

*Data from St. Louis, MO. Tanna Klein. 1996. "Dropping Out of School." *Office of Social and Economic Data Analysis* 7(1). University of Missouri System, Lincoln University.

Source: National Center for Educational Statistics, quoted in M. B. Marklein, *USA Today*, August 11, 1997.

expulsion—have often given up on the institution (Fine 1991). Because school is associated with modernism, urbanism, and the need for a disciplined labor force, rural societies typically have high dropout rates (McMillen, Kaufman, and Whitener 1994).

The high school dropout rate in 1900 was 90 percent. In the 1930s only one-third of the youth population completed high school. By 1950 the number who graduated had increased to 59 percent. The dropout rate resumed its decline in the 1970s, but it was still nearly 28 percent nationwide. In 1996 the figure nationwide was 9.3 percent for students between sixteen and nineteen years of age, but in states with large numbers of minorities (e.g., California), the dropout rate was over 15 percent. By the year 2000, 42 percent of all public school students will come from minority groups. And because minority students are more vulnerable for leaving school early, it is predicted that dropout rates among poor, minority students will rise (Schwartz 1994) (see Table 4.2).

Reported dropout rates can be difficult to compare over time for at least two reasons: (1) dropout status changes over time—many students who initially drop out of school re-enter the system at some point and complete the requirements for either a high school diploma or a General Educational Development (GED) certificate; (2) school districts, state agencies, and researchers use different operational definitions of "dropping out." Students who have unexplained absences; who join the military; who sign up for the GED; or who drop out over the summer break may or may not be

---

Box 4-C
Why Do Young People Drop Out of School?

According to the Justice Department four in ten dropouts indicated that they left school because of failing grades or because they did not like school. An equal number of boys and girls left school because of personality conflicts with teachers. More males than females dropped out because of school suspension or expulsion. The dropout rate among sixteen to twenty-four-year-olds who had repeated more than one grade was 41 percent. This compares with 17 percent of those who had repeated only one grade, and 9 percent of those who had not repeated any grades. Dropout rates were highest among those who had repeated grades 7, 8, or 9.

Although school-related reasons were reported by most students, girls were more likely than boys to report family-related reasons. Twenty-one percent of females and 8 percent of males dropped out because they became parents. Another 26 percent of white female dropouts reported pregnancy as a motive for dropping out, compared with 31 percent of Hispanics and 34 percent of African Americans. More than 25 percent of those dropping out of grades 10 through 12 reported job-related reasons for withdrawing. Male dropouts (36 percent) were more likely than female dropouts (22 percent) to report finding a job as the reason for leaving school.

Source: Sarah Ingersoll and Donni LeBoeuf. 1997. "Reaching Out to Youth out of the Education Mainstream." *Juvenile Justice Bulletin* (February). Washington, D.C.: Office of Juvenile Justice and Delinquency Prevention.

---

considered dropouts, depending upon the school district (Jordon, Lara, and McPartland 1996).

In 1992 the National Center for Education Statistics reported that in 1992 approximately 381,000 students (4.5 percent of all high school students) dropped out of grades 10 through 12. In addition, approximately 3.4 million persons in the United States ages sixteen to twenty-four had not completed high school and were not currently enrolled in school, a figure that represents about 11 percent of all persons in this age group (McMillen, Kaufman, and Whitener 1994). Almost one in four students left school in St. Louis, Missouri. Ingersoll and LeBoeuf (1997) examined the reasons why young people drop out of school. Their research concluded that keeping young people in school was a national priority, because the consequences of dropping out are more momentous (see Box 4-C).

What has been referred to as "the new morbidities"—unprotected sex, drugs, violence, and depression—often bring with them the additional tragic result of school failure, which is a major contributor to dropping out (Carnegie Council 1995). The consequences are dismal. Dropouts are three and one-half times as likely as high school graduates to be arrested, and six times more likely to be unmarried parents. They are also less able to find steady jobs and contribute to the labor force; and when they work, their salaries are about one-third less than high school graduates.

Economic forces often intrude to raise the dropout rate. Counties with high dropout rates reveal two interrelated conditions that contribute to students dropping out: job growth and poverty. When employment opportunities rise, students readily leave school. Unfortunately, most of these jobs are service jobs requiring few skills and offering dismal future career prospects (M. Klein 1995).

Under- and unemployment plague the lives of school dropouts. Employment status of sixteen- to twenty-four-year-olds who dropped out of school between October 1991 and October 1992 indicates that 63 percent were unemployed: 40 percent were jobless and not seeking work; another 23 percent were unemployed but were looking for work (U.S. Department of Labor 1994). And while the real income (adjusted for inflation) of college graduates has increased during the past twenty years, the real income of dropouts has declined dramatically (Snyder and Sickmund 1995).

The federal government's interest in school dropouts is understandable, because a strong relationship exists between truancy, crime, unemployment, and premature school leaving. Urban schools have become the site of increasing lawlessness and danger. In 1991, approximately 56 percent of juvenile victimization happened in school or on school property; 72 percent of personal thefts from juvenile victims occurred in school; and 23 percent of violent juvenile victimization occurred in school or on school property (Snyder and Sickmund 1995).

Violence

Not only is school the site of a high volume of juvenile crime, but guns and violence have changed the way that schools manage and discipline students. A walk to the principal's office and a stern rebuke by an authority figure have been abandoned in favor of expulsion and arrest of troublesome students. Metal detectors, lock downs, security guards, and other security devices are more reminiscent of a prison than a school. Yet, such precautions are deemed to be required in inner-city areas, where one in seven male students in grades 9 through 12 reported having carried a gun to school more than occasionally (B. Brown 1996).

Experts point out that with each passing year, the occurrence of violence and assault in our country's schools becomes more dangerous and more frequent than in previous years (Walker 1995). Although violence in schools is not a new phenomenon, it is the recent growth and seriousness in violence that are new. As many as three million crimes are committed each year on school property—numbers that work out to sixteen thousand incidents per school day or one crime every six seconds. One in five high school students admits to carrying a weapon at least once during the school

Table 4.3
Factors Contributing to Increase in School Violence

Factors	Percent
Students lack conflict-resolution skills	57.7%
One-parent families	52.6
Student-to-student assault	45.7
Poverty	39.8
Gang-initiated	32.7
Racial/ethnic tensions	29.7
Access to guns	25.4
Student possession of guns	23.5
Students intimidated and fail to report weapons	19.2
Limited curriculum activities	15.2

Source: National Association of Secondary School Principals in TASB *Education Reporter Newsletter*, February 1995. For more information concerning NASSP services and/or programs, please call (703) 860–0200.

year; one in every six teenagers knows someone who has died in a violent incident; and 23 percent of students and 11 percent of public school teachers have been victims of violence in or around their school. With the anticipated growth of the teenage population, criminologists are anticipating a 114 percent increase in the rise in juvenile crime; and if nothing is done to prevent it, we can expect a jump to six million violent crimes in schools every year in the next decade (Jordon, Lara, and McPartland 1996) (see Table 4.3).

Blaming school violence rates on factors like poverty, single-parent households, racial discrimination, and other individual or family factors may not tell the whole story. A recent study on the causes of crime and delinquency has found that there are lower rates of violence in those urban neighborhoods—and by extension neighborhood schools—with a strong sense of community and values, where most adults discipline children for missing school or scrawling graffiti (Butterfield 1997a). The common ingredient in neighborhoods with low violence was "collective efficacy," a term the study group used to mean a sense of trust, common values, and social cohesion. This implies a "willingness to intervene in the lives of children" (quoted in Butterfield 1997a, A11) and an inclination to stop acts like truancy, graffiti painting, and streetcorner "hanging out" by teenage gangs. At the same time, the study acknowledged that poverty and joblessness "make it harder to maintain" cohesion in a neighborhood.

Violence is neither inevitable nor unstoppable, even in neighborhoods with relatively low cohesion. Delinquency and violence are symptoms of a juvenile's inability to handle conflict constructively. Conflict-resolution education reduces juvenile violence in schools, communities, and juvenile facilities. Conflict-resolution programs, such as peer mediation, have been very effective—peer mediators successfully resolved 86 percent of the conflicts they mediated in the Las Vegas school district (LeBoeuf and Delany-Shabazz 1997). Conflict resolution and peer mediation, as peacemaking programs, have been implemented in nearly ten thousand of our nation's elementary, middle, and high schools.

SALVAGING SCHOOLS

Is the public school worth saving? The dilemmas raised in this chapter point to deep internal cleavages and contradictions in public education. To pursue more of the same—alienated students, unequal education, class-, race-, and gender-biased systems (including the new push for private education), and massive dislocations, and disorder—severely undercuts the viability of the civil order. In the context of a global economy where capital and jobs have been uncoupled from local production, the marginalized school system can be simply ignored, abandoned to the poor inner-city minorities and their bureaucratic gatekeepers. As a culture, we cannot depend upon unrestrained capitalism and its social engineering techniques to salvage the schools.

New proposals have been advanced that point to the possibilities of creating a postmodern, ecologically sustainable culture—one that rejects the nineteenth-century platitudes about progress, prosperity, and personal discipline (Orr 1992; R. Miller 1993; Apple 1993). Bowers (1993) emphasizes that we begin with the natural world—the global ecosystem—as the vital matrix of human existence. A postmodern culture must be rooted in what he calls a "moral ecology," an ecologically sensitive and sustainable worldview. This requires a radical revision of the objectivist, individualistic, and technocratic assumptions that permeate modern culture. Postmodern education must be life-centered (Orr 1992) and focus on adopting ecological and community-nourishing values.

Postmodern educational scholars believe that schools are worth saving. Michael Apple (1993) acknowledges that the conservative agenda, although powerful, can be challenged and forced to compromise, if progressive educators organize and make themselves heard. Because schools are an essential component of both democracy and social justice, they remain one of the most important systems for acculturating children and youth to society. As other systems and institutions disintegrate, the public school has increasingly become the arena for a range of services formerly assigned to family, church, or neighborhood. Schools are also grounded in social movements that have been responsive to the events and conditions of society. The historical role of education as a vehicle for social justice, as well as current legal mandates to restore equity and eliminate violence, all argue for the restoration of public schools.

It bears repetition: The issues of schooling must be reframed in ecological and humanistic terms, not solely in terms of jobs and control systems. Under the traditional system, teachers act as gatekeepers who control rather than invite entry into their domains. A revitalized education begins with a "critical pedagogy" that embraces the knowledge and voices of adolescents, and operates within the context of a revitalized public sphere.

To address the social and racial inequalities that contribute to the slow leak of adolescents out of comprehensive public high schools and into the streets cannot be achieved by educational reforms alone. Michelle Fine (1991, 208) suggests that grass-roots efforts involving community-based collaboration may be most effective for school reform. She cites the efforts of the research branch of the National Education Association, which proposes a "rich image" of schools, trade unions, corporations, hospitals, churches, community-based groups, educators, parents, and students acting together to combine resources and experiences for generating locally tailored intervention to engage existing students, and to retrieve those who have left school.

Fine also points to a group of African American activist parents and community leaders in Milwaukee, Wisconsin, who, tired of promises from white parents to embrace educational integration, acted on their own. Enraged at high dropout rates (54% among African Americans and 75% among Hispanics), this community group opted for a shared commitment to an extensive and enriched context of parent and community involvement, eventually creating a bilingual, site-based managed, neighborhood speciality school.

Schools can reform from within, especially under positive community conditions. The Wheatley School of 600 students, on New York's Long Island, a wealthy suburb, has been cited as an innovative alternative school that challenges what we think we know about teenagers and schools. Tenth- to twelfth-grade youth were invited to be the devisers and implementors of educational policy in what eventually became a democratic community governed by student members. Their constitution commits students to a strong learning environment and "mastery of academic skills," while

promoting a nonauthoritarian and egalitarian education and community by promoting responsibility for one's own personal and academic growth, maximizing the opprtunities for citizens to learn from one another, developing leadership, [and] providing a unified and close-knit community environment.

Strong academics, a focus on human relations, and a vibrant student-led government make Wheatley School a continuing success according to close observers (see The Wheatley School Home Page 1997).

Whatever direction school restructuring takes, Americans of all walks of life can be involved as part of the regeneration of our civil society. Social change organizations should invite and listen to the multiple voices in the community. In low-income schools, issues such as tenant organizing, welfare reform, health care, newsletter for single parents, teen parenting programs, problems of homelessness, decentralized school governance, neighborhood crime—can feature prominently as topics for public conversation, using the school as the center for social transformation. Students and dropouts can be invited to witness and participate in social change. Fine (1991) says:

The point would be to enable young people to experience social problems as mutable, to position themselves as protagonists and makers of social history, to strengthen the sense of community and citizenship that schools intend to nurture, and to create among adolescents their own expertise and knowledge base which would migrate from community to school and back again. (p. 217)

CONCLUSION

That schools are in a crisis situation is beyond question. On the one hand, problems generated within late modernism—including poverty, deteriorating families and communities, blocked aspirations, economic marginalization, racism, violence and crime, unemployment, and other structural dislocations—impinge on the schools. On the other hand, schools demonstrate a weak structure, one that lacks the moral capacity and legitimate authority, at least as presently constituted, to change the direction or scope of the educational institution. Middle and high schools are particularly failing systems. They lack both unity of purpose and system commitment to teach all young people—rich and poor; black, brown, and white; boys and girls, abled and disabled—the elements of living together in a democratic society. Conflict and dissension provide the grist that drives the public school deeper and deeper into the backwaters of American life.

Reformers that propose to change schools too often work in isolation from one another on piecemeal projects that lack connection between institutional sectors. For example, troubled youth who engage in violence on school grounds may be placed in "special education" units that disconnect them from peers, or expelled and arrested. Social workers see the youth only *after* the child has failed (e.g., joined a gang, involved in crime, dropped out of school). Current alliances between education and juvenile justice are unlikely to generate the type of change that will turn around the school system. Education is overly bureaucratized; it lacks care and compassion. Juvenile justice is a punishment regime that launches far too many of its clients into criminal careers. Private education is not the answer, because it is inherently class- and race-biased.

Reinvigorating the public sphere may be a genuine hope, as has occurred in a number of communities. Coalitions of educators, advocates, union representatives, community representatives, parents, students, dropouts, academics, journalists, and formal school district representatives, can do more than foster educational dissent. Such coalitions can lead to creative efforts to retain students and to transform communities. Giving a "voice" to adolescents also promotes social responsibility and problem solving at both the school and community level. The next chapter, "Endangered Youth," demonstrates the extent of the challenges we have waiting for us.

5

Endangered Youth

It is not necessarily emotional deprivation that leads to psychic disturbance but above all narcissistic wounds—including sexual abuse. These
wounds occur at the time in life when the child is most helpless and
are concealed by subsequent repression. While this repression ensures
parents that their secret will be safe, the child's lack of conscious
knowledge blocks access to his or her feelings and vitality. Not being
able to talk about or even know about these wounds is what later leads
to pathological developments.

Alice Miller, *Thou Shalt Not Be Aware:
Society's Betrayal of the Child*

FAMILY MATTERS

In the unsafe and even "catastrophic" society the state of perpetual emergency threatens to become the normal state (Beck 1992). Nowhere is this
state of emergency more apparent than in the modern family. For never
has the family been more significant in the lives of young people, and at
the same time, never in the history of its nuclear form has it been weaker.
The family has been in decline for some centuries, of course. But more
recently, it has been becoming increasingly feeble, even as it relinquishes
social functions and power to other institutions, such as church, government, and school (Popenoe, 1991). And despite the vast array of models
of family life—corporate model, convenience model, team model, military
model, ethnic family, boarding school model, single-parent model, and the-
atrical model ("family life as an act") (Pogrebin 1983, 213–15)—most family models do not address the postmodern dilemmas of state/market control
and individual vulnerability, and the growing problem of what Popenoe
(1991) refers to as a "national parent deficit."

We should recognize that few families are able to escape the normal

Table 5.1
Increases in Child Abuse and Neglect from 1986 to 1993, from the Third National Incidence Study of Child Abuse and Neglect (Based on the Harm Standard)

Type of Offense	1986	1993	Percent Increase
Physical Abuse	311,500	614,100	97%
Sexual Abuse	133,600	300,200	125%
Emotional Abuse	188,100	532,200	183%
Neglect	507,700	1,335,100	163%

Source: U.S. Department of Health and Human Services, 1996, and National Center on Child Abuse and Neglect, Executive Summary, September 1996.

hazards of contemporary life, such as chronic underemployment, single-parent families, broken homes, family relocation, teen pregnancy, "latch-key" children, overstressed parents, mental or emotional illness, inadequate schools, racism, sexism, and substance abuse (National Council for Children's Rights 1996; Hauser 1991). The theme of endangered children and adolescents points to social conditions of the contemporary family that demonstrates its incapacity to prevent injuries to and destruction of children and youth, either by family members or by non-family persons (see Tables 5.1 and 5.2).

The oppression of children is a "normal" mode of socialization and is related to both traditional and postmodern elements in family organization. In the late twentieth century, the family—both the product of and foundation of industrial society—has demonstrated half industrial and half feudal social forms. The feudal component stressed family morality, hierarchical authority, division of labor by gender, strong sexual taboos regarding marriage and adult relations to children, and intergenerational "deep" connections. As industrial society triumphs, however, it promotes the dissolution of family morality; realigns the gender order; shakes off taboos relative to marriage, parenthood and sexuality; throws into disarray the maintenance of domesticity by women; and evacuates traditional roles that bind the generations (Beck 1992). These combined structural elements act to undermine family authority, exacerbate intergenerational feuding, and throw members into limbo regarding interactional codes and conduct. Violence and acting out are normal responses to this confusion.

Victimization of children shows parents as chief culprits in negligence and wilful harm. But this only presents the tip of the iceberg. Whereas birth families have a high likelihood of victimizing their own children, it is, per-

Table 5.2
Percent of Children Maltreated by Birth Parents,
Non-Birth Parents (Surrogates, Guardians, Caregivers) and Others

Type of Offense	Perpetrator	Percent++
Physical Abuse	Birth Parents	62%
	Mother	60%
	Father	40%
	Non-Birth Parents	38%
	Fathers	90%
	Mothers	10%
Sexual Abuse	Birth Parents	25%
	Fathers	58%
	Mothers	50%
	Non-Birth Parents	25%
	Fathers	90%
	Mothers	19%
	Other	50%
Emotional Abuse	Birth Parents	81%
	Non-Birth Parents	19%
Neglect	Birth Parents	91%

++Percents do not total 100 since both mother and father may be involved in any single incident.

Source: U.S. Department of Health and Human Services, 1996, and National Center on Child Abuse and Neglect, *Executive Summary,* September 1996.

haps, the failure of the various "new" forms of the nuclear family (e.g., step-parents, blended families, high-turnover partnered families) and caregivers (teachers, babysitters, neighbors, day-care attendants, youth workers)—as well as various predatory others—who can do serious harm to children that is the mark of our epoch.

An examination of the normative sexual exploitation of children and youth reinforces the powerlessness of the family, not simply in terms of predatory persons but also to make changes in the cultural messages that present distorted versions of children's sexuality and their alleged capacity for seductiveness. Developmental needs have been flagrantly abandoned in media shaping of child beauty pageants, exploitative advertising of children's bodies, and the promotion of the beauty myth among adolescent girls that contributes so profoundly to their sense of personal incompetence and self-denigration.

In this way, the lives of adolescents are pulled back and forth by the contradiction between dependency on the family as the primary source for human connection and protection, but which too often fails to deliver on its promises, and the culturally-promoted pursuit of individualization. In the latter case, unknown insecurities and risks await the dependent child, with especially profound impacts on the poorly-guided and often uncomprehending adolescent.

DIFFERENTIAL OPPRESSION

Oppression is the "unjust use of authority" and is both process and structure (Regoli and Hewitt 1991, 152). As process, oppressions consist of acts committed by adults that relegate children and youth to a subordinate (humbling and degraded) position. As structure, these denigrating processes collectively create and maintain a category of persons defined as inferior, not deserving of the same rights and privileges as adults.

The theory of differential oppression takes into account three distinct forms: (a) individual oppression; (b) institutional oppression; and (c) collective oppression. Parents, guardians, and caregivers may *isolate* and *control* the development of children by:

1. *Manipulating* their experiences to fit the caregivers version of reality.
2. *Projecting* their own weaknesses, failed dreams, and inadequacies onto their children.
3. *Pushing* children to grow up too soon, creating unnecessary stresses and strains.
4. *Demanding* that they play out roles that reflect parents/caregivers dissociated (denied) parts of selves (Regoli and Hewitt 1991).

Such oppressive practices are made possible because of cultural dependence on the nuclear family, essentially an isolated and fragmented structure in postmodern life, and also because of the lack of legal rights for children/youth. In addition, mandatory school attendance, lack of job opportunities, and virtually total economic dependence, as well as the entire series of arbitrary and class-/race-biased law enforcement practices all constitute the modern child as part victim and part survivor. We might also consider the modern child as part hero in his or her capacity for learning how to negotiate the often convoluted and incomprehensible adult culture. Regoli and Hewitt (1991) emphasize that oppression is neither uniform nor static. Instead, it is a continuum that shifts over the different stages of development from infancy to preschooler to school-aged child, adolescent, and young adult.

What are these different developmental needs? The infant needs total care, a sense of security, and responsive parents. The preschooler needs help with managing aggression and developing a gender identity, and a healthy acceptance of his/her body. The school-aged child moves out of the physical dependence into a different mode, that of needing help with developing moral reasoning, acquiring intellectual skills, and self-esteem; whereas the adolescent needs help with handling sexual drive, forming personal values, achieving independence, and successfully acquiring education and career goals. Finally, the young adult may need help with furthering a sense of responsibility and developing viable role models, and moving from a dependent status on parents to an equal one. Only too frequently, though, circumstances may intervene to undermine, prevent, or distort this adult help for young persons (Regoli and Hewitt 1991).

Parents or parent surrogates may respond negatively to inherent characteristics of the child—biological deficiencies, disabilities, appearance, or temperament. Or, parents may simply be overwhelmed with their own "stories" or miseries to provide the help needed at any particular developmental stage. Environmental factors within the neighborhood, play group, and family also may expose the child to dangers that are out of parents' control.

Social inequality, discrimination, and oppressions that originate from the culture and larger society (e.g., racism, sexism, classism) produce varying degrees of stress for children, especially those located at more-vulnerable points in the social structure. Poor children, children of color, disabled children, and homeless children must all endure disproportionate amounts of strain.

Individual oppression by parents, parent substitutes, caregivers, and family members is the most common and direct form of oppression. Forms other than individual oppression exist as well. Individuals oppress children—homicide has become one of the leading causes of death in children—but so does the culture. Its collectivities and institutions play a significant role in the mistreatment of children and youth.

Collective oppression, more subtle and pervasive than individual oppression because it potentially impacts all children (albeit at different levels of harm), entails the negative attitudes, beliefs, and practices of adult caregivers and entire communities who construct their lifeworlds to exclude or deny the young. At the same time strong (i.e., healthy) communities that organize young people in positive ways have the reverse effect—that is, the healthy community can help even the most vulnerable as well as average and high-asset youth. Thus, communities may foster collective oppression as well as positive experiences for young people (see Box 5-A).

Institutional oppression is also commonplace. Laws that promote adult interests, needs, and rights, while banishing young people's concerns to the margins or obliterating them altogether, reflect institutional oppression. Because institutions inevitably are structured around adult concerns, most

---

Box 5-A
Communities Make a Difference

An investigation by Blyth and Leffert into the effects of community context for adolescent development revealed that problem behaviors in twelve different communities varied significantly by the health of the community (as defined by such measures as structured activities for youth, youth connections to adults and attendance at religious services). Youths in the least healthy communities (characterized by negative environments, limited opportunities, low church attendance) generally had more problem behaviors which began at lower grade levels. These differences decreased in the higher grade levels. This trend was particularly strong for the problem behaviors, such as alcohol use and sexual activity that become normative as young people enter late adolescence and young adulthood. The research showed that the least healthy communities had youths whose "normative" problem behaviors generally started at early ages and the serious problem behaviors (e.g. antisocial behavior) remained higher longer than for youths in the healthiest communities. One of the more interesting findings was that even highly vulnerable youth benefited from living in a healthy community. This result indicates that "there may be need to worry less about the impact of one youth at risk on other youths (the proverbial apple spoiling the bushel) and more about the balance of behavior and strengths of the youth in the given community."

Source: Dale A. Blyth and Nancy Leffert. 1995. "Communities as Contexts for Adolescent Development: An Empirical Analysis." *Journal of Adolescent Research,* 10 (1): p. 85.

---

institutions remain oppressive, some more than others. In health, military, school, religion, even child advocacy, abuses of children are standard events because children's sensitivities and fears are typically disregarded.

All adult oppression denigrates and denies young persons' sense of security, self-esteem, and reality. Severe punishments, physical and sexual abuse, and parental homicide are obviously among the more damaging and lethal forms of individual oppression. But child victimization is far more extensive than standard repertoires of child abuse/neglect data would lead us to believe. Victimizations also include criminal victimization, child abuse and neglect, sexual abuse and molestation, and child abduction. According to David Finklehor and Jennifer Dziuba-Leatherman (1995) of the Family Research Laboratory, children are actually more prone to victimization than adults. For example, rates of assault, rape, and robbery against those aged twelve to nineteen are two to three times higher than for the adult population as a whole (Bureau of Justice Statistics 1996). The "hidden figure" of childhood victimization may be teased out by recognizing different categories of victimization, such as the very high rates of sibling violence.

TYPOLOGY OF CHILD VICTIMIZATION

Three broad categories of child victimization, according to their order of magnitude, have been proposed by Finklehor and Dziuba-Leatherman (1995) (see also Finklehor 1988; Finklehor and Baron 1990; and Finklehor et al. 1990). *Pandemic* victimizations occur among a majority of children (ages birth to seventeen). In the course of growing up, children are subjected to a variety of casualties, including assault by siblings; physical punishment by parents; theft; and, only infrequently recorded, peer assault, vandalism, and robbery. The next category, *acute* victimizations, are less frequent, but happen to a sizable minority of children, and are more likely to be of a generally greater severity. Among these are physical abuse, neglect, and family abduction. *Extraordinary* victimizations occur to only a few children but receive the lion's share of media and police attention. These include homicide, child abuse homicide, and non-family abduction.

Gathering reports from agencies across the country (which are admittedly very incomplete), Finklehor and Dziuba-Leatherman (1995, 42) found the following:

- 800 of every 1,000 children experienced assault by a sibling
- 311 of every 1,000 children reported assault by a nonsibling
- 499 of every 1,000 children have been subjected to forms of physical punishment, usually by parents
- 497 of every 1,000 have been robbed
- 258 of every 1,000 have been vandalized
- 118 of every 1,000 have been raped
- 23 of every 1,000 have suffered physical assault
- 6 of every 1,000 have been sexually abused
- 6 have been abducted by a member of their own family
- 3 have been psychologically mistreated

Although little public concern has been directed at pandemic victimizations, this merely shows how we neglect the concerns of children themselves. In a recent survey of 2,000 children age ten to sixteen, three times as many children were concerned about being beaten up by peers as were worried about being sexually abused (Finklehor and Dziuba-Leatherman 1995). Moreover, sibling violence, the most frequent victimization, has been largely ignored by researchers.

A key concept here is *dependency continuum*. The higher the dependency needs (young children, physically or developmentally disabled, and the like), the greater likelihood that the child will be victimized by family members or acquaintances. Neglect, family abduction, and psychological maltreatment are clustered on the high dependency end of the continuum. Sexual abuse and physical abuse are likely to fall midway on the dependency continuum, whereas homicide and stranger abduction are at the low or nondependency end of the continuum, and are more likely to occur among older children and adolescents.

Why are children at such high risk for victimization? The answer lies in their inherent vulnerability; their essential involuntary contact with high-risk offenders; and most importantly, say Finklehor and Dziuba-Leatherman (1995) "children have comparatively little choice over whom they associate with, less choice perhaps than any segment of the population besides prisoners" (p. 8). Thus, children and younger adolescents are not free or able to leave families that mistreat them; they cannot move when they live in dangerous neighborhoods; they cannot change or quit school when they confront a high proportion of hostile or delinquent peers; and they are not free to pursue other ways of life as adults do.

FAMILY VIOLENCE

Corporal punishment by parents is the use of physical force with the intention of causing pain, but not injury, for purposes of correction or control of the child's behavior (Straus and Yodanis 1993). The Bible exhorted parents to hit their children with a rod to enforce compliance. Hitting children in various forms is common in this country, as well as in many others. The current debate—what is "normal" bodily punishment and what is abuse—has not been resolved by experts (see Mason and Gambrill 1994, 222), because (1) the specific culture determines what is abusive and (2) there is only meager data on the effects of mild to moderate spanking. Nevertheless, enough evidence exists that much parental "discipline," including verbal aggression and emotional distancing ("I don't love you because you're naughty") to exact parental compliance, is excessive, cruel, and injurious. Undue punishment, especially when associated with parental rage, can threaten the mental and physical health of children (Straus 1993).

Straus (1991) has investigated the larger picture of family violence and argues that violence occurs in millions of "normal" families and is not the exclusive property of cruel or mentally ill parents or spouses. Because the family resides behind the closed doors of households, where norms of privacy from outside intrusion prevail, it is not usually perceived as the commonplace site of violence that it actually is. Measuring abuse acts versus injuries, emergency room attendants and child protection workers typically assess only injuries but frequently ignore the larger pattern of abuse. For example, official records show that only about 5 percent of physically abused children, compared with 37 percent of physically abused women, are injured severely enough to require medical care. These rates neglect to account for 95 percent of the acts of violence against children. Rates for

---

Box 5-B
Corporal Punishment in American Families

Cultural support for hitting children is integrated into our laws and childrearing practices. Corporal punishment is widely believed to be an effective and recommended form of discipline of children. In a national sample, 84 percent of respondents agreed that a "good hard spanking is sometimes necessary." Scholarly books on child abuse tend to ignore the role of corporal punishment in causing physical abuse. Code words for parental hitting include "spanking," "discipline," "being physical," and other neutral terms. Indeed, the virtual silence in the United States on hitting children provides a "license to hit," which can easily get out of hand if the parent is enraged, drunk, or severely stressed. The idea that "violence is permissible when other things don't work" is linked to the ingrained American idea that violence can and should be used to secure good results: the moral rightness of violence is rarely questioned. Compare this notion with Sweden and five other countries that have declared corporal punishment by parents illegal.

Source: Murray A. Straus and Carrie L. Yodanis. 1993. "Corporal Punishment, Normative Approval of Violence, and Assaults on Spouses." Paper presented at the American Society of Criminology Meeting (October).

---

family violence show that millions of persons and families are implicated in assault with one of every ten children *severely* assaulted by a parent, or a total of 6.1 million children who are known victims of family assault, which may be masked under the rubric of "discipline" (see Box 5-B).

Family and personal characteristics may engender a high level of conflict—stresses from work; relationships; poor health; limited coping skills; and for more and more Americans, the pressure of ordinary daily living. Add to these, built-in features of married life and childrearing—such as lack of privacy, required sharing, around-the-clock vigilance; isolated family life without a strong moral net and weak community connections; and sexist attitudes that place women and girls in constant jeopardy—and you have a volatile mix of components that may spark family violence. As stresses and conflicts build up, many families lack alternative means to express frustration and rage and may lash out against one another. In this way, sibling abuse, the most common child victimization, may not only imitate the rage and acting out behavior of parents; but it also reflects the larger culture's failure to teach people simple tools of conflict resolution and anger management.

Social risk factors have been identified by Ania Wilczynski (1995) for parental child homicide. She concludes that rather than a single inventory of parental risks, men and women in families confront a distinctly gender

Table 5.3
Social Risk Factors for Parental Child Homicide

Risk Factor	Female (%)	Male (%)	Total (%)
Performed sole/ primary child-care role*	94.7	15.0	53.9
Living with a partner	51.8	80.0	63.8
Biological parents not married at victim's birth	51.9	40.0	46.8
No or unsupportive partner	71.4	25.0	52.1
Dependency on welfare	33.3	45.0	38.3
Financial problems	35.7	60.0	45.8
Accommodation problems	60.7	75.0	66.7
Youthful parenthood**	46.4	45.0	45.8
Poor social support	68.0	63.2	65.9
Low education	71.4	94.4	82.1
Previous criminal convictions	17.9	70.0	39.6

* Non-neonaticidal offenders only
** Became parent when aged 21 years or less

*Non-neonaticidal offenders only.
**Became parent when aged 21 years or less.

Source: Ania Wilczynski. 1995. "Risk Factors for Parental Child Homicide: Results of an English Study." *Criminal Justice* 7(2): 193–222.

risk structure when it pertains to severely abusing their children (see Table 5.3).

For women, it is performing a sole primary child-care role—that is, being a lone parent, and without a partner, or having an unsupportive partner, as well as having poor social supports. For male parents or parent surrogates, it is cohabitating with a partner, financial problems and dependency, generally weak social supports, low education, and previous criminal convictions that distinguished men who killed children.

Filicide offenders—parents who kill their children—also tend to have become parents at a young age. Almost half the offenders first became parents or substitutes when aged twenty-one or under. Parental youthfulness and lack of training for parenting among parents or substitutes involved both female and male cases. It appeared that the offender had little conception of how to care for a child; thus the offender did not realize how "exhausting and self sacrificing parenthood would be, or had unrealistic expectations of parenthood or the child" (Wilczynski 1995, 201). Such parents often perceived the child as older, more competent or wilfully disobedient, although ignorance about child care and behavior seemed particularly apparent among the men.

CHILD SEXUAL ABUSE

Sexual abuse of children is a grim fact of life in our society, and far more common than most people realize. Some surveys say that at least one out of five women and one out of ten men recall sexual abuse in childhood (Sedlak and Broadhurst 1996). Child sexual abuse is any sexual act with a child that is performed by an adult or an older child. Such acts include fondling the child's genitals, getting the child to fondle an adult's genitals, mouth to genital contact, rubbing an adult's genitals on the child, or actually penetrating the child's vagina or anus (Wyatt and Powell 1988).

Physicians have been trained to identify various signs of child abuse that may entail physical and emotional signs, and in older children a range of psychiatric symptoms (Emans and Heger, 1992).

Physical Signs of Abuse

- Bruises or bleeding of the genitalia or anal area
- Lacerations, irritation, pain, or injury to the genital area
- Difficulty in walking or sitting
- Gonococcal infection of the pharynx, urethra, rectum, or vagina
- Pregnancy
- Recurrent urinary tract infections, difficulty with urination
- Vaginal discharge
- Frequent genital infections

Emotional Signs of Abuse

Younger children

- Nightmares or disturbed sleeping patterns
- Bed wetting
- Fecal soiling

- Clinging/whining
- Regression to a more infantile behavior
- Loss of appetite
- Unexplained gagging, reactions to certain colors or consistencies of food

Older children/Adolescents

- Depression and withdrawal
- Poor self-image
- Chemical abuse
- Change in school performance
- Running away or aversion toward going home
- Overtly seductive behavior/promiscuity/prostitution
- Eating disorders, sudden weight gain or loss
- Self-mutilation
- Suicide attempts

Psychological and emotional fallout for abused males has also been studied. Researchers find that abused male children show some symptoms that are particular to boys or appear to be more pervasive for this class of victim (Finklehor and Browne 1985; Gonsiorek, Bera, and LeTourneau 1994).

- Boys suffer confusion over sexual identity and fear of homosexuality.
- They display increased aggressive behavior after the abuse.
- They express strong denial or minimization of the impact of the abuse.
- Emergency room records indicate that half of the admissions of sexual assault involving boys are violent, and that boys are more likely to be physically injured as a result of sexual assault than girls.
- Boys have a tendency to re-enact their abuse by abusing other children.

Studies on high-risk children show that females, preadolescents (age ten to twelve), as well as those who experience social isolation, parental absence or unavailability, or those who have a poor relationship with parents, and those who report poor relationships between their parents are all at higher risk (Finklehor and Baron 1990). Finally, stepfather families—the presence of a nonbiologically related father—has been discussed as a risk factor for sexual abuse. Both class and race appear to have only weak associations with sexual abuse, although possible differences emerge for some ethnic groups. For example, in a Texas study based on a mail survey of driver's license holders, Kercher and McShane (1984) found that incestuous victimization rates for Hispanic women are considerably higher (21 percent) than among both white (9.8 percent) and African American rates (10.4 percent).

What features of the risk society propel adults into sexual contact with their own or other people's children? The answer lies in irrevocable changes in the traditional sex taboo that made sex with children both ideologically repulsive and practically very difficult (especially with large, extended families) (see Davis and Stasz 1990).

Permissive sexuality is the hallmark of modernism. But no society allows complete freedom of sexual expression. Yehudi Cohen says:

No society allows random and promiscuous expressions of culturally patterned emotions to anyone at all. . . . There are no societies in which sexuality is regarded as an ordinary biological necessity without the encumbrances of symbolizing and restrictions; there are none about which it can be said that sexual activity is free of profound conflicts and apprehensions. (Quoted in Davis and Stasz 1990, 250)

As the need for manual workers is replaced by white-collar, educated employees, state control has loosed its strictest control in establishing authority in the area of sexual behavior. Along with this easement—the state no longer controls family planning or contraceptive access, nor does it lock cohabitating couples in jail for fornication or adultery—certain trends suggest that sexuality is not as free and clear as advocates of free love would have it. Our modern sexuality has become increasingly depersonalized, violent, objectified, and commoditized (Davis and Stasz 1990, 250–53; Foucault 1978).

Child sexual abuse, which reflects the loosening of controls over sexuality, is perceived as a major social problem. It includes not only incest and sexual assault within the family and illicit sex contacts by acquaintances but also the sex trafficking, child molestation, and rape of teen girls under the guise of consenting sex. Once moral boundaries have collapsed or thinned out, eroticization enters the adult-child domain, evacuating more-protective feelings and practices from adult repertoires. Now, all manner of persons can be sexualized and exploited as part of the normal order of things.

Steele (1986) observes that the category of incest laws, once limited to sexual relations between individuals who are closely related by blood, marriage, or adoption, should be expanded to incorporate all adult sexual relations with a minor child. Incest constitutes abuse "when a child of any age is exploited by an older person for his own satisfaction, while disregarding the child's own developmental immaturity and inability to understand the sexual behavior" (p. 284). Scholars argue that children and young adolescents are unable to give informed consent due to the authority of the adult, her own dependent and less powerful status, and the age difference between them (Courtois 1988, 12; Knudsen and Miller 1991; Males 1996).

Subsequently, researchers have outlined a hierarchical continuum of sexual abusive behavior, including the idea that incest is invariably a "rape" situation (Brownmiller 1975).

CONSEQUENCES OF CHILD PHYSICAL AND SEXUAL ABUSE

Because incest is potentially an experience of "catastrophic proportion" (Courtois 1988, 20), victimization theory has focused on the traumatic stress reactions that follow the experience. Finklehor (1988) has identified four factors that are most related to its traumatic effects: traumatic sexualization, betrayal, powerlessness, and stigmatization.

Traumatic sexualization refers to a process in which a child's sexuality (including feelings and attitudes) is developmentally shaped in distorted and dysfunctional fashion as a consequence of the sexual abuse. *Betrayal* involves the child's recognition that someone they have intrinsically depended upon has caused them harm. In the case of father incest, the child may be doubly betrayed: by the father and the silence of the mother or stepmother. *Powerlessness* points to the process in which the child's will, desires, and sense of efficacy are continually contravened. For the child, it produces a pervading sense of hoplessness with no exit in sight. *Stigmatization* means the various negative labels—badness, sadness, shame, guilt, anger—that are communicated to the child around the experience and that then "become incorporated into the child's self image" (Courtois 1988, 532).

In intrafamilial abuse, the double bind of intimacy and humiliation creates a no-win situation, Speigel (1986) says:

Severe trauma inflicted by parents, as opposed to that inflicted by strangers, has elements of a macabre double bind. A beating or rape by a stranger, traumatic as it is, is in some ways easier to assimilate psychologically. It is a tragic event imposed from outside, seemingly for no reason. But rape by a father or physical abuse by a mother has the bizarre quality of combining intense and longed-for attention from the parent with pain and humiliation. . . . [Children] are made helpless to control both their own body and their own internal state. . . . Such patients become structurally or spatially fragmented, unable to incorporate their history of trauma and conflicting parental messages into a unified sense of self. The defense against trauma becomes itself a source of distress. (69–70)

Social functioning of sexual abuse survivors, though showing wide variability, ranges from isolation, rebellion, and antisocial behavior to overfunctioning and compulsive social interaction (van der Kolk 1984). Adults sexually traumatized as children suffer from a later "disorder of hope." Victimization has also been described as a "break in the human lifeline," which contributes to experiencing oneself and one's world as dead or constricted (Courtois 1988, 113). Long-term effects of sexual abuse typically

---

Box 5-C
The Emotional Effects of Testifying on Sexually Abused Children

Based on carefully controlled studies in North Carolina and Colorado by the National Institute of Justice, it cannot be stated conclusively that testifying is either harmful or beneficial to sexually abused children. Testifying may impede the improvement process for some children (the Denver study), or it may enhance the recovery of others (the North Carolina study). One of the major reasons for the different results may have been the different contexts for the children's testimony: criminal or child protection proceedings.

The studies drew the following conclusions:

• Before testifying, all children scored high on measures of stress and anxiety.

• Maternal support was associated with improvements in the children's mental health.

• Children who testified more than once tended not to improve as much as children who testified only once or not at all.

• Virtually all of the children improved with time, regardless of their experiences in the criminal justice system.

Source: Debra Whitcomb, Gail S. Goodman, Desmond K. Runyan, and Shirley Hoak. 1994. "The Emotional Effects of Testifying on Sexually Abused Children." National Institute of Justice, *Research in Brief*. U.S. Government Printing Office.

---

leave victims exhibiting various difficulties in both physical and psychological disorders that may persist over the life course.

Self-damaging behaviors also testify to the "revictimization" of self, whereby the individual has been so conditioned to the victim role and the stigmatized self concept that she continues the process, even after the original victimization has ceased (Courtois 1988). The issue of protracted emotional harm has been raised about children who testify in court. Although research to date has not revealed substantial long-term negative effects of testifying on most child victims, it has shown that some children need assistance in undergoing the criminal justice process to avoid suffering further harm (see Box 5-C).

The victimization experience often has a "ripple effect." The destructive impact of incest extends beyond the victim. Whereas the victim is directly affected, her intimates are secondarily impacted. Partners and other loved ones may suffer "contact traumatization," in which significant others develop their own set of symptoms (e.g., fearful, anxious, abusive, angry, resentful, depressed). From the therapeutic perspective, incest and child abuse represents an unmitigated horror that repeats itself indefinitely in the life of survivors.

Even with such a devastating experience, healing the sexual wounds is possible. Effective therapeutic intervention promises that a reconstituted self can emerge once the abused person is able to talk about or even know about these wounds. Alice Miller, a psychoanalyst who has written extensively about the incest wound, emphasizes the significance of acknowledging the trauma. "In a supportive environment the wound can become visible and finally heal completely" (A. Miller 1984, 182).

The issue of self-acknowledgement is not automatic. The unwillingness to self-confront or the use of denial acts as a major obstacle to healing. Widom and Morris (1995) found substantial underreporting of sexual abuse among known victims of childhood sexual abuse, despite such cases being substantiated in court. Given that victims of childhood sexual abuse are often asked to recall events that happened as long ago as twenty or thirty years earlier, gross underreporting is common. In fact, victim recall for a one-year time period has been reported to be as low as 30 percent (Widom and Morris 1995).

Sexual abuse survivors are not alone in their lack of recall or failure to report histories of childhood mistreatment. Nonreporting of crime victims in the context of victimization surveys has been known by researchers for years (Garofalo and Hindelang 1977). Apparently, "protective mechanisms" come into play, as in reluctance to report the incident because of embarassment; or memory decay and forgetting commonly occur.

ADOLESCENT HOMICIDE AGAINST PARENTS

Physical and sexual abuse, as well as protracted neglect by parents and caregivers, has been linked to juvenile and adult prostitution (Davis 1993a; Weisberg 1985); psychiatric breakdowns (Widom and Morris 1995); criminality (J. Gilligan 1996); and parricide (Heide 1992; 1993). In the extreme case of adolescent homicide against one or both parents, Heide's research shows

a. *"A pattern of family violence"* exists.

b. *"Adolescents' attempts to get help failed."*

c. *"Adolescents' efforts to escape the family situation" failed* (running away, suicidal thoughts, and suicidal attempts represented unsuccessful efforts to evacuate the scene).

d. The *"family situation became increasingly intolerable prior to the homicidal event."*

e. *"These adolescents as a group were isolated from others and had fewer outlets than other youths."*

f. *"Inability of these adolescents to cope with the familial situation typically led to a loss of control."*

g. Adolescent parricide offenders appeared to be *"criminally unsophisticated."*

h. There was *"easy availability of a gun."*

i. *"Alcoholism or heavy drinking in the homes"* was common among parents who were slain by adolescents.

j. *"The adolescent parricide may have been in a dissociative state during or after the homicide"* (e.g., amnesia, short-term memory loss, confusion).

k. The *"victim's death was perceived as a relief"* by the offender and other surviving family members. Few offenders expressed remorse (1992, 42–43; italics in original).

Professional intervention of sexual abuse victims opens up a complex set of conditions that should be considered in "risk assessment." The National Center on Child Abuse and Neglect provides a manual for intervention specialists that enhance the decision-making process (Faller 1993). Because families may be quite secretive, and because assessment may need to be made on an emergency basis without complete information, the manual advises paying attention to certain factors in assessing the degree of risk, such as

a. Type of sexual abuse (degree of intrusiveness)

b. Frequency, duration, and presence or absence of force

c. Age of the victim (the younger, the more vulnerable)

d. Relationship of offender to victim

e. Presence of other family problems, especially domestic violence

f. Number of offenders, particularly when multiple offenders are family members

Two models of intervention are especially persuasive: the family systems model and the feminist model. The family systems model assumes the fundamental cause of marital violence to be lack of interpersonal skills and a dysfunctional relationship. These shortcomings result in an escalating pattern of frustration and anger that eventually leads to violence. By contrast with the feminist model, which emphasizes power and equality for women, the family systems model proposes improving interpersonal skills among conflicting parties, especially negotiating skills, and correcting dysfunctional relationships. The model also emphasizes empowering the family to carry out its functions without resorting to violence (C. Dean 1994).

I would argue that the feminist model is more predictive of serious male violence against women and children, inasmuch as the patriarchal model of power-over represents a "deep culture" tradition that moves considerably beyond the dysfunctional family model. The primary criterion for a pattern of violence among men is their use of violence as a control weapon. Such men seek "to achieve, maintain, and demonstrate power over their partners to meet and further their own needs and desires" (Tifft 1993, 2). Empowerment of women is recommended as the primary method for preventing violence, and women-centered services and counseling, including mediation, the most effective for resolving conflict.

An adult male with a protracted history of violence against women and children requires more than a few lessons in interpersonal skills for remedying life habits. Whereas the family system model offers great possibility of changing poor communication patterns in conflict families that are nonviolent, violence intervention is more likely to be successful when intervention occurs early (as in adolescence) and separate support systems are in place for both victims—women and children—and offender (see Schuerman, Rzepnicki, and Littell 1994).

This does not preclude the fact that women, too, may be exceedingly violent, as in physical abuse and killing of their children or in spousal murder. Modern culture has strong undercurrents of violence, as expressed through racism, classism, ageism, and similar oppressions. Clearly, millions of men, women, and children each day are exposed to media conveying the value, acceptability, and even normalcy of violence, as well as specific themes of interpersonal aggression (Weiner, Zahn, and Sagi 1990). And direct confrontations with community violence is becoming a pervasive quality of everyday life for millions of Americans.

TEEN PREGNANCY AS INDIVIDUAL AND INSTITUTIONAL OPPRESSION

The popular myth, fostered by health agencies, sex experts, and especially the media, is that teenage girls are choosing early sexuality and pregnancy to satisfy unmet needs within the family. Reaching out to boys their own age for the love and affection denied them by parents, the younger adolescent girl shortly becomes pregnant, dropping out of school to have "his baby" and subsequently marrying the baby's father. Derogatory publicity surrounds this event, as headlines preach that "babies having babies" will undermine the strength—and pocketbook—of thrifty Americans who must carry this social problem on their backs (Thompson 1995). Adolescent males are blamed for their "raging testosterone," while their female counterparts are perceived as seductive and irresponsible, only too eager to become impregnated. These and other unexamined myths about women's sexuality demonstrate how the politics of youth sexuality distort both research and public information (see Tiefer 1995).

The reality is significantly different. Males (1996, 57) charges that officials have selectively exploited junior-high sex surveys that report girls as "being sexual," while disregarding serious questions of violence and exploitation by older males. The subsequent adult overreaction to discovery of voluntary peer sexual interactions totally ignores the issue of rape of young adolescents by older teens and adult males.

On closer investigation, it is clear that teenage pregnancy is a social prob-

Table 5.4
Sex and America's Teenagers

First Intercourse at Age	Rape Only	Rape & Voluntary	Voluntary
13 or younger	61%	13%	26%
14 or younger	43%	17%	40%
15 or younger	26%	14%	60%
16 or younger	10%	14%	76%
17 or younger	5%	13%	82%
18 or younger	3%	12%	85%

Source: Reproduced with the permission of The Alan Guttmacher Institute from The Alan Gutt-macher Institute, *Sex and America's Teenagers* (New York, 1994), p. 28.

lem that is not primarily caused by teenage girls. Instead, involuntary, adult male-adolescent female sex is the more common pattern. The National Women's Study of 4,000 women in 1992 found one in eight, a projected 12.1 million women, had been raped. Of the victims, 62 percent were raped prior to age eighteen, and 29 percent before age eleven. "The survey found that rape in America is a tragedy of youth, with the majority of rape cases occurring during childhood and adolescence" (National Victim Center 1992). The Alan Guttmacher Institute (1994) asked junior high girls what they meant by "having sex." The results strongly contradicted the equal peer sexual interaction story produced by officials. For 40 percent of the "sexually active" girls under age fifteen, rape had been their only sex (see Table 5.4).

Adult men have always fathered most of what we call "teen" births. In 1921, 98.6 percent of teen births to young adolescent mothers ten to four-teen years old were fathered by men aged 20 and older (U.S. Bureau of the Census, 1921, quoted in Males 1996, 49). By 1993, seven of every ten births among school-age mothers in California were attributed to an adult father. The Alan Guttmacher study (1994) found 74 percent of the births among eighteen- to nineteen-year-old women—some 220,000 per year—were fathered by men age twenty and older. Even more worrisome is that in these often coercive sexual interactions, teen girls are overexposed to sexually transmitted diseases compared to similarly aged boys. Whereas 54.8 percent of U.S. STD-infected youth are girls, age fifteen to nineteen, younger girls (up to fourteen years old) who experience coersive sex are at even higher risk, as their percent of STDs rises to 77 percent. And six of every seven heterosexual HIVs acquired by teens are in females.

Risks are greatest among children and younger teens, compared with boys: 91 percent of all heterosexual AIDS contracted by children twelve and under are female. Teen girls, thirteen to seventeen years old, contract

83 percent of heterosexual AIDS, and by age eighteen, older female adolescents acquire 67 percent of AIDS cases. Among those who are at greatest risk for AIDS, then, are young women and gay men, both groups of whom have been infected primarily by older men.

Not all teen women are at equal risk for premature pregnancies. Instead, among the 1.2 million illegitimate births, poor, minority, and sexually abused girls are more likely to become pregnant, and when they keep their baby, to be welfare-dependent and to have repeat pregnancies (Hughes and Sutton 1996; Alan Guttmacher Institute 1993; National Commission on Adolescent Sexual Health 1995).

- The illegitimate birth rate among low-income working-class white communities now exceeds 44 percent, and out-of-wedlock births are increasing more rapidly among whites than minorities. In inner cities the figure is typically in excess of 80 percent. In Arizona, 95 percent of pregnant teens, most of whom are Native American or Hispanic, are from poor backgrounds.

- Women with college degrees contribute only 4 percent of white illegitimate babies, whereas women with a high school education or less contribute 82 percent.

- Seventy-one percent of teen mothers were unmarried in 1992—more than doubling the rate in just one generation. In 1970 the figure was 30 percent; in 1950, 14 percent of births to teenagers were to unmarried mothers.

- Forty percent of all pregnant teens choose abortion. Hispanic and American Indian teens are least likely to make the abortion choice. In Arizona, these two groups comprise 57 percent of teen births in that state, but account for only 25 percent of abortions in 1994.

- Almost half of unwed teen mothers go on welfare within one year after the birth of a first child. By the time the baby is five years old, 72 percent of white teens and 84 percent of black teens have received AFDC.

- Nearly one of every five teens who has a premarital pregnancy will become pregnant again within one year. More than 31 percent experience a second pregnancy within two years.

- Growing evidence suggests that sexual abuse may be an important factor in early sexual activity. Several recent studies found that a significant proportion of teen women who become mothers also have a history of sexual abuse. Sexual abuse is also related to a higher frequency of sexual activity, as well as higher substance abuse, both factors that contribute to teen pregnancy.

Other dimensions of teen pregnancy include inconsistent and incorrect use of contraceptives. Among sexually active teens, the failure to use contraception or its misuse leads to unintended pregnancies. Approximately one-quarter of teens who do not use contraceptives become pregnant within six months of the initial sexual activity. About half will become pregnant within two years, but 20 percent will become pregnant in the first month following the initial sexual activity. Hughes and Sutton (1996) emphasize that increasing the use of contraceptives would be the most direct method of reducing both the rate of teen pregnancy and rates of sexually transmitted diseases. Making contraceptives readily available to young people both increases their use and markedly reduces teen pregnancy (Hughes and Sutton 1996). Because contraceptive knowledge and use are power tools for young women, they stand a greater likelihood of also avoiding entrapment by coercive and abusive men. In a recent twist, Lewin (1997) reports that teenagers are altering their sexual practices to avoid pregnancy, not by using effective contraception but by reliance on oral sex.

A final point: Motherhood, when achieved as a teenager and outside the bonds of matrimony, is regarded as problematic by outsiders, and stigmatized accordingly. Yet, motherhood for many young women is a reflection of their "authentic selves" and an approved status for women (Horowitz 1990). This discrepancy means that whereas sex and motherhood are culturally valued activities, they are only prohibited for certain categories of women (poor, disabled, underaged, unmarried, immigrant, and other politically suspect groups).

THE BEAUTY MYTH AS COLLECTIVE OPPRESSION

Unlike the visible and unremitting rupture from the individual oppressions of physical and sexual abuse and neglect, collective oppression plays a background role in children's lives. We turn now to the beauty myth. Although masked behind cultural screens of normalcy—after all, physical attractiveness in women has been a cultural imperative for centuries—the outcomes of this form of collective oppression can be as damaging as abuse in the long run for the well-being of individuals (Wolf 1991).

The dissemination of the American beauty myth, invariably a Caucasian model—slender, flowing hair, full lips and breasts, sculptured nose, long, slim legs, flat stomach, lean hips, and firm buttocks (Bordo 1993)—has penetrated the consciousness of American women, and may have global consequences. This idealized beauty standard, attainable by only a few, most of whom are professional models, has generated powerful industries: the $33-billion-a-year diet industry, the $20-billion-a-year cosmetics industry, and the $300-million-a-year cosmetic surgery industry (Wolf 1991).

More serious, the beauty ideal has produced a rash of food disorders. Anorexia nervosa and bulimia affect over seven million women, a figure that has doubled since 1970 (K. S. Schneider 1996). Although one million men also have been diagnosed with these serious food disorders, only women receive the cultural message that to find a husband and a job— "thin is in; thin is all there is"—the diet imperative must be pursued. Reality bears a close resemblence to the image. Hochschild (1989) argues that 75 percent of American women are employed in jobs that "stress physical attractiveness." Other research shows that men select youth and physical attractiveness as the two most important characteristics in their future wives (Buss 1994).

How do anorexia and bulemia, among the more damaging food disorders, impact on their victims? Anorexia nervosa entails refusal to maintain a minimally healthy body weight, intense fear of gaining weight, and a significant disturbance in perception of the shape or size of one's body. Bulimia nervosa involves binge eating—eating what the individual considers to be too much food in a way that feels out of control—followed by inappropriate compensatory behaviors (e.g., self-induced vomiting, excessive exercise, fasting) (National Association of Anorexia Nervosa and Associated Disorders [ANAD] 1996).

According to ANAD (1996), 86 percent of victims report that the onset of their illness occurred before age twenty. Usually considered to be the "adolescent girl" disease of the century, children as young as five have been reported to display symptoms of anorexia. Early onset and extended duration combine to yield relatively low cure rates (only 50 percent) and testify to the severity of the illness. Costs for inpatient treatment can be as high as $30,000 a month with many patients needing repeated hospitalization. Outpatient treatment, including therapy and medical monitoring, can extend to $100,000 or more without any guarantees of success.

It is not merely the pressure for weight loss that plagues teenagers; it is the *standard* of bodily perfection. Mary Pipher (1994), author of *Reviving Ophelia*, a best-selling book about the physical and psychological health of adolescent girls, says:

Research shows that virtually all women are ashamed of their bodies. It used to be adult women, teenage girls, who were ashamed, but now you see the shame down to very young girls—10, 11 years old. Society's standard of beauty is an image that is virtually just short of starvation for most women. (p.102)

In this context, the diet industry flourishes and contributes to the perpetuation of distorted body images and food disorders.

Is the beauty myth restricted to Anglo women? A 1995 University of Arizona survey suggests that this is the case. The survey found that 70 percent of teenage African American girls are satisfied with their bodies. But other research contradicts this, as in *Essence* magazine, directed at an African American readership, which claims that 54 percent of black women are at high risk for developing an eating disorder. "It's a generational and class issue," says Dr. Audrey Chapman, a Howard University psychology professor: "Many middle-class blacks who are assimilated into the white culture—and teenagers too—want to be thin, thinner, thinnest" (reported in *People* magazine, June 3, 1996, 68).

The next question probes into the key issue of food disorders. What is the source for the narcissistic fixation on body parts and sizes? At the immediate level, television bombards teens with unrealistic beauty images that, in the absence of more-substantive values and purposes, serve as a compelling focus for identity. More subtle in its psychological impact is that lacking power, self-esteem, and feelings of control over their lives, teenage girls control the one entity they can apparently (but actually never) master: their bodies. The task is accomplished by massive denial of their needs for self-nurturing and by savagely repudiating their physical needs for food.

A peculiar rendition of the beauty myth may be found in child pageants. The death of six-year old beauty queen, JonBenet Ramsey, who was found sexually assaulted and strangled in her Boulder, Colorado, home the day after Christmas 1996, galvanized critics who decry the sexualization of children. Televised footage of the small girl preening on runways in a feather boa, rhinestones, and makeup revealed a disturbing eroticism in pageants that could have opened the door to her sexual assault and slaying, social critics say (E. Bernstein 1997). Although baby-to-grade-school contests allegedly spotlight poise, grace, personality, and leadership, children essentially compete for recognition based on one definition of achievement: physical appearance. Critics also point out that the grownup pressures of pageants can steal a girl's childhood, not only in making the child appear and act much older than she is but also in the fixation on adult standards of beauty and behavior. Death may simply be the extreme end of adult exploitation of children. Boles (in E. Bernstein 1997) observes:

Making little children look sexual is a very dangerous thing to do because it arouses sexual interest. Because the child looks this way, the reasoning becomes that being sexual with her is not so bad.

Physical abuse and neglect, sexual abuse, food disorders, and child beauty pageants—all derive from a culture that faces outward, gazing on external standards of adult behavior that deny both inner and outer child. Girls, especially, have long been trained to be feminine at considerable cost to their humanity. Evaluated on the basis of appearance and caught in myriad double binds—"achieve, but not too much; be polite, but be yourself; be feminine and be adult; be aware of our cultural heritage, but don't comment on the sexism" are all examples of "false self training" (Pipher 1994, 44).

The beauty myth is also locked into the *child pornography* industry, where trafficking in children has become a major form of exploitation of ever younger children. Child pornography refers to the harmful use of children as sex objects in films, photographs, magazines, videos, and computer-generated images of children involved in sexually explicit acts, either with an adult or with other children (McCuen 1985). Over 260 different magazines in the United States portray children as young as three engaged in intercourse, masturbation, rape, and masochism (Hawkins and Zimring 1991). Although the medium and themes may vary, all child pornography carries a similar message: It caters to the adult consumer who associates sexual excitement with child nudity, victimization, torture, and even death. Child pornography is an even more lucrative business than adult porn, because it is relatively inexpensive to produce, using home video cameras, polaroid cameras, and computers. As a result, the child pornography industry is growing, and to a large extent, is a product of organized crime (Hawkins and Zimring 1991).

Seemingly unaffected by laws aimed to control it, the pornography industry had become a multimillion dollar industry by the mid-1970s, and flourishes today, largely unimpeded. As a result of the decriminalization and deregulation of the adult pornography industry in the United States, there is a virtual absence of law enforcement in bars, live sex shows, adult bookstores, and video rental stores. With the police largely removed as an agency concerned with regulating commercial sex, it has become markedly more difficult for law enforcement groups to keep child pornography and adult women pornography in separate worlds (Hawkins and Zimring 1991).

More recently, the Internet has surfaced as a source of sexual communication, as well as shared deviance. Pedophilia prospers in an environment in which child sexuality is publicly displayed as an everyday occurrence (e.g., child beauty pageants) and exploited by advertisers who promote child or child-like models in sexually suggestive poses. The fashion, media, and film industries all glorify the sexual image of young teenagers, gradually tearing down the traditional boundaries of child protection. Laws designed to protect children may be actually counterproductive, producing the social impulse that they seek to regulate. In response to this recognition, morality claims as the basis for controlling child pornography have been rejected as ineffective in the current hypersexualized milieu. The most recent approach to legal protection is the prohibition of the sexual use of children based on the *risk of child victimization* rather than on community morality (Hawkins and Zimring 1991).

Intervention for vulnerable individuals damaged by oppressive social practices does not erase the collective damage done to millions of young people, because of adult sexual and social perogatives (Okin 1989). For example, at a global level, female genital mutilation, slavery, and polygamy over vast parts of Africa and the Middle East—anachronistic customs from our Western perspective—represent entrenched traditions that systematically desecrate women and girls (French 1997).

MORAL PANICS AND TEEN ENDANGERMENT

A *moral panic* occurs when official reaction to a series of events builds a consensus about the presence and seriousness of a perceived threat (Davis and Stasz 1990). Once a public consensus occurs, the result can be the instigation of new control policies, and the emergence and growth of specialized industries to "handle" the problem. The *moral panic* concept draws attention to the official distortions, public denials, and governmental policy avoidance of the real issues that contribute to the problem. Thus, changes in policy have little or no impact on transforming the negative behavior.

Youth suicide and related behavior problems serve as catalysts for public reaction and the upsurge of psychiatric hospitals to deal with youth-specific problems. Such treatments may be more damaging than the initial problem. For example, among affluent groups with expanded medical coverage, youth with moderate behavior problems must submit to extended hospital stays, use of psychotropic drugs, and enforced contact with severely mentally ill and behaviorally disturbed young people. For young people with moderate behavior problems, the motto "Lock them up to cool them down" ignores the real needs of acting-out youth: parental attention and positive interaction with parents; social skills learning; smaller classrooms designed for flexible programming and maximum participation; receptive, strong community; and a range of job training/school options for promoting optimal choice.

Youth suicide certainly contributes to the endangerment of young people, but hardly in the numbers that suggest it as a major threat. The 1991 mortality statistics indicate that 1,899 teenagers committed suicide and the rates (18 per 100,000 for boys and 3.7 per 100,000 for girls) are substantially the same as in 1988, when rates for youth suicide peaked. For example, compare these rates with the number of children infected with AIDS, a killing disease. The U.S. Centers for Disease Control (1991; 1991–92) announced in September 1993 that 12,712 persons, who were diagnosed with AIDS between the ages of twenty to twenty-four, were actually infected between ten to seventeen; this number rises to 51,006 who were infected between the ages of fifteen to twenty-two, although not diagnosed until they were twenty-five to twenty-nine (Sweeney 1995). On a global level, estimates of the AIDS infection surpass all previous data (United Nations in Pear 1997) (see Box 5-D).

Whereas young adults who die of AIDS will die of opportunistic diseases (e.g., viral infections, pneumonia) that receive little public response, young people who take their own lives are most likely to kill themselves in a more dramatic fashion with firearms, which account for two-thirds of youth suicides. Add to this the 4,690 youths age 10 to 19 killed by firearms in accidents or by murder. According to Males (1996), the teenage firearms

---

Box 5-D
A Global Perspective: A New, Grimmer Portrayal of AIDS

The AIDS virus is growing at unprecedented rates, according to new estimates of the United Nations, and rates in some countries may have actually doubled over a one-year period (1996–1997). The U.N. study calculates that 2.3 million people around the world will die of AIDS this year, an increase of more than 50 percent from an estimate that 1.5 million people died of the disease in 1996. The United Nations data show that 1,600 children under 15 are infected with H.I.V. every day, up from last year's estimate of 1,000 children a day. Ten percent of all the new infections are in children 14 years and under, and more than half the remainder are in older adolescents and young adults (15- to 24-year-old). Most of these deaths are occurring in sub-Saharan Africa, Asia, and Latin America, countries which lack both money and medical resources for purchasing the new miracle drugs to abate the disease. Such drugs are readily available for affluent groups in wealthy nations.

Source: The United Nations in Robert Pear, "New Estimate Doubles Rate of H.I.V. Spread (*New York Times,* December 3, 1997).

---

accident rate is the highest for any age group, but the teen gun suicide rate is the lowest.

These data suggest the overavailability of firearms rather than the problem of youth per se. Death by firearms is more likely to be lethal, whether taking one's life, being involved in an accident, or murdered.

Firearm deaths among youth show the following patterns:

1. Male youth are overwhelmingly at risk for death by firearms, compared with female youth. Fifteen- to nineteen-year-old males are eight times more likely to die than females by suicide, accident, or murder.

2. Firearm-related death rates for both sexes reveal that the most vulnerable age group among young people is fifteen to nineteen, where their death rates from guns jump precipitously from younger teens.

3. Young adults, ages twenty to twenty-four, have the highest death rates from firearms among all ages. The greater accessibility of guns for young adults may account for these rates.

4. Combining teen death rates (ages ten to nineteen) suggests that teens generally are at high risk, with male adolescents at very high risk of dying from gun wounds. After age thirty, death rates from guns decline significantly (e.g., 14.3 per 100,000 for ages forty-five to forty-nine). The highest suicide rates are for persons over sixty-five, with white men over eighty having rates of 73.6 per 100,000.

Despite the lower suicide rate by females in all age groups, girls are four times more likely than boys to *attempt suicide.* The U.S. Centers for Disease

Control (1991–92) in their survey of seven thousand high school students throughout the United States found that close to 2 percent of older adolescents make suicide attempts, serious enough to warrant treatment by a medical practitioner each year. This translates into one-half million teen suicide attempts each year (Shaffer et al. 1996).

The psychiatric symptoms that especially flag suicidal youth are some form of depressive disorder, alcohol and/or drug abuse, physical and sexual abuse. Approximately 90 percent of teenagers who commit suicide have a psychiatric diagnosis (Pfeffer 1996). Their pathology reflects the additive effects of family discord, psychiatric disturbance among family members, violence, physical abuse, deaths/separations/divorce of caretakers, and other destabilizing domestic conditions (Pfeffer et al. 1993). Does psychiatric intervention help this domestically victimized population? The data strongly suggest that it does not. Adolescents over sixteen who had been admitted to a psychiatric hospital during childhood were nine times more likely to commit suicide than were adolescents in the general population (Pfeffer 1996).

Mental illness is not necessarily the driving force for most youthful suicides. Donna Gaines' (1992) study of cluster suicides among teens in a white ethnic suburb in northern New Jersey discovered that such youth suffer from "burnout," a sense of fatalism and despair. These young "burnouts" see themselves as a self-conscious group under seige by the larger society. Gaines says:

To outsiders, they look tough, scruffy, poor, wild. Uninvolved and unimpressed by convention, they create an alternative world, a retreat, a refuge. . . . They call themselves burnouts to flaunt their break with the existing order, as a form of resistance, a statement of refusal. (p. 9)

Gaines rejects the psychological and medical models of suicide that offer only atomized views of these vulnerable and severely disconnected youth. Instead, she emphasizes that we regard these "alienated kids" as historical actors, making reasonable decisions, even to death, in a society that has little place for them.

A New York study indicates that alcohol and drug abuse play a particularly important role among boys who commit suicide at age eighteen and over. Moreover, young males who had made a previous suicide attempt had an especially high risk for committing suicide later. Cluster or "copycat" suicides also appear to be a factor in suicide risk, especially among more-vulnerable youth (Shaffer et al. 1996). Intervention for both these precipitating factors tends to be too-little-and-too-late.

Physical and sexual abuse histories indicate a significant factor in suicide, regardless of social class. In a 1992 study of 276 low-income pregnant teenagers, a California pediatrics team found that physical and sexual abuse increased the risk of suicide fourfold (in National Commission on Adolescent Sexual Health 1995). Another study of five thousand entrants by *Who's Who Among American High School Students* found that one in seven girls who had been sexually assaulted were four times more likely to have attempted suicide, compared with students who had never been assaulted (17 percent versus 4 percent). The four thousand women identified in the study *Rape in America* (National Victim Center 1992) clarified that one-third of rape victims had contemplated suicide and that 13 percent had attempted it. By contrast, suicide attempts by females who had never been raped were negligible (about 1 percent) (see Males 1996; Bayatpour, Wells, and Holford 1992; U.S. Centers for Disease Control 1991).

Homosexuality is another strong indicator for suicide risk. In a study of 686 gay men, 337 heterosexual men, 293 lesbian women, and 140 heterosexual women, 35 percent of gay men and 38 percent of lesbian women considered suicide, compared to only 3 percent of heterosexual men and 14 percent of heterosexual women. The majority of the suicide attempts occurred before age twenty; nearly one-third were before age seventeen. More-vulnerable homosexual youth have even higher rates. In a study of homeless youth entering a shelter, 65 percent of the gay youth had attempted suicide, compared to 19 percent of the heterosexual youth. Lesbian and gay youth are two to six times more likely to attempt suicide than other youth, and account for up to 30 percent of all completed teen suicides (Gibson 1996) (see also Bell and Weinberg 1978; Larkin St. Youth Center 1984).

Prevention programs aimed at teen sucides have shown little effectiveness. The belief in the generic nature of teen suicide—as an "intrinsic risk" of adolescence or as residing in the personality or lack of coping skills of the victim—ignores underlying causes: lack of security for children and youth in families; social rejection of differences; poor supervision; inadequate treatment; and blaming the victim by adult labelers. It has even been suggested that prevention efforts may actually increase teen suicide. Males (1996) says:

The six-fold increase in teenage psychiatric hospitalizations since 1970 cannot be shown to have reduced teen suicide either on a societal level or among the individuals in question. The failure of current efforts can be tied directly to the attempt to single out teen suicide for special attention rather than recognizing the pivotal links between general and specific adolescent and adult suicide patterns. (p. 241)

Youth suicide is not a new phenomenon. Psychiatric claims that depression and substance abuse "cause" suicide miss the point. Suicide appears to be a complex response to hopelessness (based on an individual's reasoned response to life circumstances) rather than depression (a clinical state entailing feelings and brain chemistry). Intervention programs, classes, and forced treatments for youth that aim to alleviate depression may compound the sense that "something is wrong with me," rather than examine the social conditions giving rise to the hopelessness. The massive invasion of health and mental health professionals in youth affairs may require re-examination. Adverse environmental conditions cannot be solved by psychiatrists or mental health professionals, and much of what such health professionals do is to coerce labeled groups to comply to intolerable conditions (Males 1996).

CONCLUSION

In the high-risk society, youth are increasingly exposed to victimizing environments, where they may be physically, sexually, or emotionally injured by family members, caregivers, boyfriends, institutional agents, or life-denying features of the culture, such as beauty myths, widespread child pornography, and homophobia. Oppression is thus built into the social fabric of American life, whether the source of injury is from individuals, institutions, or the larger society. Treating teen suicide and other self-damaging behavior (e.g., pregnancy) as merely an "intrinsic risk" associated with adolescence also misses the mark. Children and teens who commit suicide, starve or purge themselves, have sex with older men, and engage in other life-denying behavior often have a history of victimization. Chaotic families, drugs and alcohol, exploitation by adults, and the intervention process itself are all implicated in creating a severely dangerous world for growing numbers of young people.

Chapter 6 next takes up the issue of youth homelessness. Taking into account psychological characteristics, while highlighting the major risk factors in the family, school, and society at large, the chapter defines the phenomenon of homelessness with reference to a Sydney (Australia) sample of homeless girls. A focus on factors that contribute to youth being cast out or prematurely leaving home reveals some of the same elements that feature in suicide and other teen endangerment: dysfunctional families, physical abuse, sexual exploitation and assault, rejection by family and conventional society, substance abuse, lack of effective prevention, and wholly inadequate, distorted, or absence of treatment programs.

6

The Descent into Homelessness

Among the estimated 100 million street children worldwide, the use of alcohol and other drugs is an immense problem. . . . Most street children describe major losses in their lives. Many have lost family members through AIDS, natural disasters, murder, and even death squads. Many have attempted or contemplated suicide. . . . Many children claim that physical and sexual abuse are the reasons for their leaving home.

World Health Organization, Geneva, 1993

YOUTH HOMELESSNESS

Why are so many children living on the streets of the world's cities? To answer this question is to raise issues about how policymakers devalue human beings, especially dependent young persons, and the role that violence and poverty plays in this process. Importantly, youth homelessness is not restricted to North America or Europe. Instead, it can be found in all societies, rich and poor alike. This chapter, focusing especially on homeless girls in Australia, reveals characteristic patterns of homelessness among young people in all developed societies. By examining homeless adolescent girls, the chapter emphasizes the special vulnerabilities of females for whom exposure to street life reinforces patterns of victimization and powerlessness experienced in early childhood.

Homelessness has become a generic condition in contemporary society. Almost one-quarter of homeless people in the United States are children (persons seventeen and under), the average age of which is nine. Few homeless children have escaped emotional, behavioral, and academic problems, and among those who have serious behavioral problems, few of the children receive any treatment. The homeless family population is one source for homeless children and youth. According to the National Center for Children in Poverty in less than a decade, New York City witnessed an astounding 500 percent increase in the number of homeless families, with close to 1,000 new families entering the New York City system each month (see National Coalition for the Homeless 1998; Burt 1997). Today, there are over 400,000 homeless families living in shelters in the United States (Homes for the Homeless, NYC 1998).

Homelessness among the poor is directly attributed to three main conditions: (1) reducing benefits and dropping people from assistance programs; (2) sharp rise in housing costs as construction of low-income housing fell, and thousands of existing single-room occupancy (SRO) units were taken off the market; and (3) economic displacement, people pushed out of their jobs through unemployment, underemployment, and the low-income housing pinch. According to Vanderstaay (1992), the supply of low-income housing shrank half a million units for every year of the Reagan administration.

Still, the largest proportion of homeless youth previously were attached to residential families, not homeless ones, and such youth have either been cast out, voluntarily left because of poverty, or have run away from oppressive home conditions, especially violence and abuse.

Parent-adolescent conflict is the major trigger that initiates the separation process. Black (1998) claims that running away, ostracism, separation, restrictive interaction, and other efforts to curtail, reduce, or end contact all represent expressions of "avoidance," a conflict-management strategy that arises to deal with perceived injustices and grievances. Avoidance is perhaps the most common way to deal with family conflicts, and may appear in various forms on a continuum from the voluntary and covert to the coercive and overt: exit (voluntary departure), exclusion (denial of access), expulsion (denial of membership), and exile (isolation). The coercive and overt strategy, if relentlessly pursued by either party, entails only limited risks for parents and caregivers, whose liability may be taken over by the state. But it invariably leads to drastic consequences for adolescents, for whom banishment, whether self- or other-imposed, rarely resolves the grievances but certainly may be fateful.

This chapter traces the steps into homelessness among adolescent girls by drawing on case materials from Australia (Davis 1993b; 1993c). In virtually every respect, Australia and the United States share the "culture of childhood," a pro-child ideology that constitutes juvenile homelessness as particularly reprehensible. Historically, Australia and the United States have a common ancestry, as well as embracing a legacy of democratic institutions and a welfare-oriented state. Unlike the United States, which has always been reluctant to expand the public sector, Australia has a far more developed system of state intervention. For example, low-income and homeless youth in Australia are frequently awarded a "Homeless Youth

Allowance," a subsistence income, which permits them to attend school or seek out-of-home shelter without resorting to crime.

The answer to the question of why children are on the world's streets without shelter or support lies in the sheer frequency and volume of violence directed at children by family members, and the mistaken belief by young people that escape brings salvation. As the chapter shows, the attempt to flee the domestic culture of violence—its very embeddedness in their young lives—is thwarted by the even greater dangers of street life. For homeless youth, especially females, whether living on the street or under "protective" or correctional orders, the search for a safe haven is futile.

DIMENSION AND SCOPE OF YOUTH HOMELESSNESS

Worldwide, there were approximately 100 million children in 1993 who live on city streets without care or shelter (World Health Organization 1993), a figure that doubled in a three-year period (200 million in 1996). The United States has over 2 million homeless and runaway (at risk of becoming homeless) youth; 16 percent of whom have run away more than five times (Terrell 1997; Regoli and Hewitt 1991). Los Angeles County alone has over 10,000 street youths. Canadian cities have 150,000 homeless youth, many of whom are at high risk for AIDS (Davis 1993b). Some have estimated that as many as 70 percent of homeless adolescents run away because of physical and/or sexual abuse and family conflict (Jenks 1994). Others flee for adventure or freedom, but often confront unanticipated risks, some of which are life-threatening. The "hard core" homeless youth may number as high as 500,000 in the United States, but services meet only a fraction of those in need (Baggett and Donough 1988).

Additionally, 500,000 juvenile prostitutes roam America's streets, many of whom are among the covert homeless and thus not included in statistical reports, because they ostensibly have shelter (Sereny 1985). In reality, they live a precarious existence with pimps or a series of boyfriends, or with other prostitutes (see also King 1991). On a global level, sexual exploitation is an enduring condition for girls (see Box 6-A).

Because we focus on homeless girls in Australia in a later section, it is useful to include some essential facts about youth homelessness in that country. In Australia, a country of under eighteen million people, the Human Rights and Equal Opportunity Commission (Burdekin 1989; O'Connor 1989) estimated that between fifty thousand and seventy thousand youth were homeless or in danger of becoming homeless. The same report stressed that homelessness was not merely a condition of being on the streets or the threat of homelessness, but in addition having a highly mobile life or otherwise lacking security without dependable caregivers.

The Youth Accommodation Association in 1991 estimated that in the

Box 6-A
A Global Perspective: Sexual Exploitation of Girls and Young Women

Child prostitution varies from individual cases to mass victims of organized crime. This may encompass a selection of children; some run away from home or from situations, some are sold by their parents, some forced or tricked into prostitution, some street children, some working part-time and some full-time, some amateurs, and some professionals. The effects of tourism on child prostitution has led to dangerous developments. Children of both sexes are involved in satisfying the sexual appetites of organized bodies of tourists, with pedophile tourists able to obtain profusely illustrated guides containing extensive information, including local agent, legal practices, and the "legal limits" of contact with children in each country.

Prostitution of very young children is known to occur in Asia, Latin America, Europe, and North America. In Bangkok, 30,000 children under 16 years of age and some as young as 6 years old are estimated to work as prostitutes. Anti-Slavery International reports approximately 200,000 child prostitutes in Thailand, where a relationship exists between tourism, drugs, prostitution, and the German Mafia. A legal investigation by the Thai Government found that 13 of every 19 children involved in prostitution had been deceived by promises of work or education, but were forced into prostitution. Another investigation uncovered that brothel owners had beaten up or drugged children who refused to work.

Countries of the Middle East tend to deny that the problem exists in the region. Yet, reports indicate that citizens of these countries travel to other countries, especially in Southeast Asia, in search of sexual services. In Brazil, they often support their entire family on their wages. Young prostitutes in Bogotá, Colombia earn 3,000 pesos from each client ($21), whose money may help support cocaine addictions and marijuana purchases. In Europe and North America, economic deprivation, domestic violence and abuse, family disintegration, and drug addiction are all significant factors leading to the increase in runaways, homelessness, and child prostitution.

The usual account of how a child gets into prostitution in North America is that he or she usually is a runaway newly arrived in a big city, and is picked up by a "sweet-talking" pimp, who treats the child well for a short time, and then demands favors in return. A recent study estimated that 5,000 boys and 3,000 girls below the age of 18 are involved in prostitution in Paris. In 1990, the legal age of consent in The Netherlands was reduced to 12 years old. Child sexuality has existed for two millennia or more, but the current industry of child prostitution may represent a more highly exploitative and destructive version, especially in light of the international AIDS epidemic.

Source: Encyclopedia of World Problems and Human Potential; See also Davis 1993c.

State of New South Wales alone there were between twenty thousand and twenty-five thousand young people, aged twelve to eighteen seeking accommodation because of homelessness (Coffey and Wadelton 1991). And this number does not include the discouraged homeless or those living in squats (abandoned buildings), sleeping outdoors, living in temporary housing arrangements, and other makeshift situations. Covert homelessness is similarly patterned in Australia as in the United States, where the practice of short-term live-in relationships with boyfriends or "sugar daddies" may account for the gross under-representation of girls in official counts (King 1991).

The Australian Institute of Family Studies research on youth applying for the Young Homeless Allowance found a number of recurring themes often associated with "extreme domestic disharmony" (Cass 1991, 48): (1) The repartnering of parents precipitating conflict; (2) Strong cultural and value differences between generations affecting young persons from different ethnic backgrounds wishing to adopt the values and practices of their Anglo-Australian peers; (3) Violence and sexual abuse affecting young women in particular; (4) Unemployment by parents or by youth; or lack of employment for rural or outer suburban youth who then seek jobs in the city, and inadvertently become homeless in the urban center as limited work, inadequate support and life skills lead to youth joblessness; and (5) Young women, especially, are more likely to be unemployed and remain so for longer periods, less likely to be in education and training, more likely to be found in marginal part-time or casual work, and more prone to seek employment in a narrow range of occupations.

A survey of two hundred homeless youth in Victoria State (Australia) found that the most significant factors contributing to loss of accommodations after leaving the family home were primarily relationship breakdown, including conflict with co-tenants, and eviction for rent arrears (Hirst 1989). The survey found that young women gained access to private rental through a male partner. When the relationship breaks up, the young woman's transition to independence is severely threatened, as she moves into a period of unsupported living (lack of job, no accommodation, inadequate income, and so on). The same report indicated that most had never experienced a stable home environment upon which to base their own living skills. Such trends are typical of the United States, as well as other post-industrial societies.

HOMELESS STREET YOUTH: VIOLENCE, PROSTITUTION, DRUGS, AND CRIME

According to the Burdekin Report, published in Australia in 1989, "homelessness" describes a lifestyle that includes insecurity and the transience of shelter not merely the absence of shelter. A number of American and British

---

Box 6-B
The Lives of Homeless Youth

Most street children describe major losses in their lives and the daily stresses of day-to-day living. Many have lost family members through disease, such as AIDS, natural disasters, murder, and even death squads. Many have attempted or contemplated suicide. In Rio de Janeiro, 55 percent of those interviewed claimed that they had attempted suicide. Every day, they search for food, shelter, and care, often fearful for their lives. Although poverty and rapid urbanization are major contributing factors to the problem of street children, many children claim that physical and sexual abuse were the reasons for their leaving home. The use of drugs is often quoted as a means of coping with this stress, pain, and suffering.

Source: World Health Organization. 1993; 1996 (updated). "A One-Way Street?" *A Report on Phase I of the Street Children Project. Program on Substance Abuse, WHO.* Geneva: Regional Office of the Western Pacific, p. 3.

---

researchers has argued that not only is the shelter temporary, but the homeless condition itself is only occasional or episodic (see Chamberlain and MacKenzie 1993). The "high turnover thesis" (Chamberlain and MacKenzie 1993) leads to official dismissal of the youth homeless problem on the basis that homelessness for young people is normal and transitory, even expected. This contributes to systematic neglect of the exploitation and misery that young people experience, as well as their increased likelihood of entering criminal careers.

The World Health Organization's report on street youth in ten cities wholly rejects the short-term thesis (1993). Instead, WHO argues not only that the street lifestyle exposes street children and adolescents to multiple forms of victimization, but that street survival entailing drug addiction, dependency on prostitution, or other street crimes may jeopardize the youth's return to mainstream society. In many instances, street activities simply kill the youth outright (e.g., drug overdoses, murder, suicide). In addition to the street lifestyle that precludes movement back to home and school, the equation of sexual abuse and homelessness implies a "forced exit" (Hirst 1989) and acts as an additional barrier to young people's returning to their abusive families (Robson 1992). Moreover, after months or years on the street, there may be a severing of all familial ties, physical retribution, and in some cases, going into hiding for some time with possible change of name and state. Homeless young people experience chronic loss and suffering (see Box 6-B).

Street life teaches harsh lessons. It promotes learning how to be abusive, dishonest, evasive, selfish, and irresponsible in order to "play the system" and uses violence, drug addiction, and criminal behavior as essential parts of the street survival kit (Robson 1992).

Violence is part of the routine order of street youth and involves peers, acquaintances, police, and strangers (Alder 1991a; Davis 1993b; Terrell 1997). Young people escape violent homes only to encounter further violence on the streets (Burdekin 1989). Among homeless youth, extensive histories of violence exposure—including witnessing violence, victimization, fear, and perpetrator roles—regularly occur. Kipke and associates (1997) report that among a Hollywood, California, homeless youth sample, 70 percent reported having been punched, hit, burned, or beaten; 33 percent indicated having been seriously hurt during a violent attack; and 44 percent reported having been sexually assaulted, molested, or raped. The Hollywood sample emphasizes that the increase in risk for violent victimization associated with life on the streets is particularly strong for females (Kipke et al. 1997).

Alder's (1991a; 1991b) intensive interviews with fifty-one homeless Australian youth under the age of eighteen reveal that almost two-thirds had been physically assaulted and half had been sexually assaulted in the previous twelve months. Distinct gender differences in victimization prevail, as "violence for males predominantly involves fights, while for females, it involves sexual assaults" (Alder 1991a, 10). Perpetrators of this violence were overwhelmingly male, including police attacks reported by 47 percent of females and 58 percent of males (Alder, 1991a). One of the most disturbing findings of Alder's research is the extent to which these young people suffer their violent victimization without seeking assistance or reporting the episodes to authorities.

In the United States, running away from home is a serious offense for young people punishable by arrest and jailing (Janus et al. 1987). Girls make up 63 percent of young people appearing in juvenile court charged with running away from home (Chesney-Lind and Shelden 1993). Because runaways are virtually without police protection, they are the most vulnerable group for violence and sexual exploitation (White, Underwood, and Omelczuk 1991). Once forced out, the movement into prostitution may follow shortly thereafter. A Miami study of one hundred seriously delinquent, drug-addicted girls shows the age at first time for prostitution was 12.6 years old (Inciardi and Pottieger 1991).

Street prostitution is undoubtedly the most violent-prone experience among all street activities, and follows a childhood of sexual assault, rape, and physical assault (Boyer et al. 1988; Davis 1993a; 1993c). Teenage prostitutes are drawn from the chronic homeless who often live in squats or "crash pads" in abandoned buildings without utilities or bathrooms (Beyette 1988). Several factors may be involved in a girl's taking up prostitution. She may be coerced, tricked, seduced, or blackmailed by a pimp, or learned in her abusive family to communicate primarily through sex

(Campagna and Poffenberger 1988, 65–66). Lack of shelters is a major factor in the girl's movement into prostitution (Davis 1993b; 1993c). But the most common form of teenage prostitution is a noncommercial transaction, "survival sex," by which the girl trades sex for "warm shelter for a night, drugs or perhaps a few 'Big Macs' " (Beyette 1988; see also Chesney-Lind and Shelden 1993, 38).

American data on drug use among young people show a strong association between substance abuse and delinquency, a trend that is increasingly occurring among younger ages (National Institute of Justice 1997). Today, age thirteen is becoming the average for early criminal participation (burglary, robbery, and serious theft) or early use of drugs other than alcohol and marijuana (Carpenter et al. 1988, 11). This drug-crime link may be especially pronounced among street youth because of the high availability of drugs as well as their intricate involvement with the street scene, such that widespread use of drugs by virtually all young street people has become the norm (Davis 1993c; Costello 1991; Inciardi, Horowitz, and Pottieger 1993; WHO 1993; King 1991). For example, crack cocaine has been estimated to be eight times as prevalent among runaway and homeless youth as in the general adolescent population (Kral et al. 1997).

Homelessness contributes to high criminality among youth. Results from previous research with homeless youth suggest that "hunger causes theft of food, problems of hunger and shelter lead to serious theft, and problems of unemployment and shelter are associated with prostitution" (Kipke et al. 1997).

McCarthy and Hagan's (1991) self-report study of 390 homeless youth in Toronto, Canada, found that although a sizable proportion of those surveyed participated in a number of illegal activities (most of them minor delinquencies) before leaving home, a significantly higher proportion of adolescents were involved in more-serious criminal activities *after* leaving home. Levels of crime show fairly profound increases for older street youth (sixteen years and up) and for those whose homelessness lasts more than a year. They propose that street life is inherently "criminogenic" in that it provides both opportunities for criminal offending as well as the necessity to sustain existence. The fact that the youth's participation in crime escalates after a certain period of time on the street points to the probability that crime may be adopted as a "conditional survival strategy" for coping with the economic and social strains that characterize homelessness (McCarthy and Hagan 1991).

HOMELESS YOUNG WOMEN: A SHELTER STUDY

To appreciate the larger processes that force girls out of the home and into the street, we present a case study of 105 young women interviewed in Sydney, Australia (1992), 50 percent of whom were living in a shelter at the time of the interview.[1] Another 14 (13 percent) were located in a girls' detention center. Among this group, the average number of shelters stayed at was eleven (see Table 6.1). Subjects' ages ranged from thirteen years to twenty-one years and all were currently or formerly homeless. Additional interviews were taken from 4 chronically homeless women between the ages of twenty-two and thirty-two. Most were white Australians from metropolitan centers (Sydney or Melbourne). Twenty-two girls were born overseas, and migrated with their parents as children to Australia. Nine were Aboriginal young women. Subjects tended to be unemployed, not attending school, and dependent on Homeless Youth Allowance (60 percent) or other community resources (20 percent). Almost 19 percent lived off their earnings or supplemented their income from prostitution, pornography, selling drugs, or other crimes.

Family History

Family histories reveal several significant themes. First, family breakdown through death, divorce or separation is common (see Table 6.1). Less than one-third grew up with an intact family, almost 20 percent because of a parent's death; and 50 percent because of divorce. Additionally, another 14 percent had lost siblings through death. Chronic disease also affected about 25 percent of the girls' parents or siblings, with many of the illnesses occurring when they were in infancy or throughout their childhood.

Second, parental employment patterns show that mothers or stepmothers (55 percent were usually employed) were much more likely to have professional or white-collar jobs, compared to fathers or stepfathers (48 percent versus 32 percent). Given the resistance to stereotypical gender roles, this status discrepancy may have been a contributing factor in the high rates of parental conflict and abusive drinking patterns.

These girls have experienced sustained abuse, some from infancy or young childhood onward, as shown by their self-reported statements on types of maltreatment (see Table 6.2). Physical abuse was experienced by almost 65 percent; emotional abuse was reported by 82 percent; and sexual abuse was a factor in the lives of nearly half the sample. Perpetrators were overwhelmingly fathers or stepfathers, although mothers counted among a significant proportion of those who were defined as emotional abusers (27 percent). Although fathers and stepfathers accounted for only 39 percent of the sexual abuse cases, other male predators, including older siblings, uncles, friends and neighbors, family acquaintances, or strangers had been involved in the abuse. When questioned about their experience with family counseling, given the pattern of family violence and substance abuse, 52 percent indicated that they had at least one or more sessions with a ther-

Table 6.1

Childhood Family Disruption and Victimization;
Including Psychological Assessment

Childhood: Family Disruption and Victimization

	Percent (Rounded)
Parent Death, Divorce, Separation	70
Parent Chronic Illness	25
Parent Alcoholism/Drug Abuse	
Mother	29
Father	41
Family Violence	64
Mother Hospitalized	22
Father Arrested	17
Court Hearing	14
State Intervention	
Foster Care	39
Custody/Detention	42
Physical Abuse	65
Starting at Age 1–5	39
Perpetrator	
Father/Stepfather	70
Mother/Stepmother	15
Other	15
(Sibling, Friend, Neighbor, Teacher, Minister, Priest)	
Emotional Abuse	82
Starting at Age 1–5	36
Perpetrator	
Father/Stepfather	57
Mother/Stepmother	27

Other	16
(Sibling, Friend, Neighbor, Teacher, Minister, Priest)	
Sexual Abuse	
Starting at Age 1–5	50
Perpetrator	35
Father/Stepfather	39
Mother/Stepmother	0
Other	61
(Sibling, Friend, Neighbor, Teacher, Minister, Priest)	

System Intervention

Statutory Order		22
Foster Home		39
Total Number of Foster Homes	(N = 41)	
Custody/Detention		42
Expelled from School		48
Living in a Youth Refuge (percent of sample)		77
Total Number of Different Refuge Stays	(N = 924)	
11 Stays Per Person	(N = 82)	

Psychological Assessment (Current)

Prolonged Physical Complaints	49
Expressed Fear of Caregivers/Family Members	66
Sharp Drop in School Grades	71
Frequently Sad or Depressed	90
Food Disorder	84
Sleep Disorder	76
Self-Injury	75

apist; only 11 percent found such intervention useful. Most of the young women complained that one or both parents refused to follow up either on the appointments or the recommendations of the therapist.

Psychological Well-Being

Despite the evidence that family life has been highly conflictual, if not impossible in some instances, many young women (60 percent) report that they had been under intense pressure to succeed, beginning as young as age four, but essentially throughout their childhood. Expectations of superior school performance by parents without adequate emotional support undoubtedly contributed to a variety of reactive behaviors and physical maladies among the girls. These include: prolonged physical complaints (49 percent); skipping school frequently (83 percent); fearfulness about certain people (66 percent); dramatic grade drops at one time or another due to family crisis (71 percent); persistent sadness or depression (85 percent); perfectionist tendencies (22 percent); abrupt changes in eating habits, including serious food disorders (anorexia, bulimia, gastritis, and so on) (84 percent); sleep disorders (76 percent); regression to childish behaviors (e.g., thumb-sucking, bed-wetting) (20 percent); self-inflicted pain (75 percent); suicide attempts (71 percent); injuring others (56 percent); injuring animals (11 percent); and destroying property (52 percent).

Because many young women in this sample remain in social limbo and have not recovered from their family trauma, or from experiencing the hazards of living/sleeping/working on the street, psychological adjustment may be said overall to be poor or very poor. Post Traumatic Stress Disorder (PTSD) is common: Eating disorders (84 percent), sleep disorders (more than 76 percent have difficulty sleeping; some with ongoing nightmares); jumpiness, generalized anxiety, and other psychological disorders are frequent occurrences. Feeling confused, being jumpy, having flashbacks of their early or current abuse, being nervous, anxious or forgetful are chronic conditions among a fairly large group of these girls. Even more serious is the feeling of "doom" and being out of control, an emotional state that then leads to a sense of hopelessness about changing the situation. It is significant that more than 90 percent of these girls admitted to being depressed "sometimes" or "often," a situation that can contribute to avoidance, denial, and hopelessness about their life circumstances.

It is all the more surprising to observe the number of girls who believe that they are personally responsible for their problems (38 percent), despite the overall powerlessness among most of these youngsters to personally alter their life patterns. Certainly, it is more realistic to "blame" their family, as in the abusive parent or sibling or other exploitative person, than to assume self blame.

Alcohol and Drug Use

Among these girls, heavy alcohol and drug use was common with 30 percent beginning drug use at age twelve or under. Almost 87 percent have used substances that were either illegal for minors or contraband for all persons. Alcohol and marijuana remained the drugs of choice (nearly 50 percent were currently using alcohol, and 51 percent admitted to current use of marijuana), but their drug experience extended to heroin, cocaine/crack, amphetamines, prescription drugs, methadone, inhalants, and barbiturates. Most youth workers I spoke with suspect that many young women are using contraband drugs in greater frequency than they reported, because we asked them to indicate whether a drug had been "previously used" or if they were "currently using." In either case, homelessness and street life are strongly associated with sustained and abusive alcohol and drug patterns. Clearly, this level of substance abuse for young women and girls has various severe consequences for health and safety, especially for an exposed population who are likely, while on the streets, to be totally in public spaces. Girls report being raped, mugged, beaten up, thrown out of shelters or apartments, losing friends, having accidents, experiencing blackouts, and other severe mishaps while drunk or drugged (although these incidents may happen when they are sober, as well). Many girls boasted about their high level of alcohol or drug intake, and apparently perceived little connection between their health and safety problems and their alcohol and drug use.

Health Issues

Life on the streets or even in institutions, such as refuges or detention centers, away from family, caring adults, and normal routines, has been shown to be hazardous to health. Fully 75 percent of this group have sought medical care since becoming homeless. The high medical risk of homelessness is apparent in the list of medical problems reported by this group that range from what medical informants emphasize are common ailments experienced by homeless persons, such as scabies, head lice, foot problems, and frequent colds. But in addition, this is a population of young women and girls who are exposed to high rates of violence; sexual coercion and unprotected sex that contributes to sexually transmitted diseases; pelvic inflammatory disease; and in three cases, a diagnosis of HIV-positive for AIDS. Almost 45 percent have been pregnant, itself a serious health risk, considering the age of some of these young women. Some reported illnesses have been complications from pregnancy or abortion. In addition, cuts and burns happen frequently, sometimes self-induced; sprains are common; and even broken bones have occurred among more than one of every four girls.

Stress appears to exacerbate asthma, a persistent condition for almost 40 percent of respondents.

Medical drop-in centers for street people, such as are available in the Sydney metro area and other large Australian cities, are a system response to the high-risk situations attendant on street life. These teenagers apparently sought out such services on a regular basis. Official or self-help efforts to prevent these accidents and illnesses appear to be negated by the general feeling of despair that pervades this group ("there's nothing I can do about it").

Contact with Law Enforcement

Although many of these young women have been more likely to be victimized than to be offenders, contact with police, court, and detention are fairly common occurrences. For example, 78 percent have been involved with the police, for a variety of reasons: arrests for status offenses or criminal acts, and others for welfare/protection causes. A significant number of girls (34 percent) experienced police violence (bashings), a few on repeated occasions, especially if they were Aboriginal or other minorities or failed to behave in conventional female ways (e.g., polite, deferential, soft spoken, and so on); and 42 percent had been held in custody or detention. What is surprising, in light of the literature on police oppression of vulnerable populations, is the relatively high incidence of intervention on *behalf* of these female youth. For instance, police have interrupted family quarrels and taken the affected children out of the home; they have come to young persons' aid when they have reported sexual harassment by other street persons, clients, businesspeople, or locals; or they have connected them to available services. Still, most girls reported that they avoided contact with police because police response could be unpredictable. They were as likely to be arrested (37 percent) as helped, especially because many of the young persons had been involved in episodes of street crime and violence themselves.

Institutional Engagement

These young women have a history of disruptions: family breakups, school interruptions or dismissals, and shifting foster or shelter care placements. Most had left school at one time or other, especially during longer-running episodes, and somewhat less than half had actually been required to leave school for extended periods of time, or had been expelled. Over two-thirds of the girls no longer attend school, most having left between fourteen and sixteen years of age. Nor do they plan to return to school. As described in these interviews most girls have had serious troubles at school, often unconnected to their actual school performances. Fighting, failure to relate to teachers or peers, lack of interest in the subject matter, and lack of social and economic support at home for school activities or inability to pay the costs of extracurricular projects are some factors that mitigate against girls' involvement in school.

Most girls have stayed in at least one refuge (77 percent), and a high proportion have moved from one placement to another, often without their consent but rather for the convenience of youth workers or the bureaucracy (especially in foster care placement). Even in refuge situations, girls may move weekly or more often. Separations, divorces, and remarriages often occur after the girl has left the family, and reconciliation is no longer possible because parental rules remain non-negotiable, or parents and siblings have restructured family relationships through virtual exclusion of the missing one. It is not uncommon to have girls grieving their loss of connection to a beloved mother because of the resistance of the mother's new boyfriend or husband, who perceives the girl as a threat to the new relationship or as too troublesome to take on.

THE DESCENT INTO HOMELESSNESS

Flight from Home

Social contexts vary for these girls. Some may be fleeing traditional family settings, where victimization is hidden and cripples the young person's efforts to grow up. Others are escaping crisis families, where single mothers may be contending with poverty, alcohol or drug abuse, and a series of unstable relationships. Such girls have a higher likelihood of being involved in serious delinquency, because of their delinquent patterns prior to their leaving home. The pathway to homelessness appears to be accelerated by institutional living. Girls placed in foster care, detention centers, or temporary shelters under bureaucratic control may be forced out by age, time served, or disciplinary action. And once homeless, the street culture becomes their "home," a survival setting, where adult authority is absent and where deviant peer networks dominate.

Leaving home is not a single act, but a process that occurs over time and space. For many young women, "running away" is distinguished from "leaving home" in that running is viewed as a temporary expedient to a singular crisis; whereas leaving home implies a decision to withdraw attachments and effort from a family situation, or literally being "kicked out" by parents. Hence, these young people may have already left home physically before leaving home emotionally. Few girls leave home for the streets. Instead, they seek shelter with grandparents or friends or try living in a shelter, and when these fail, they move into squats with other homeless youth. Some are forced to return to their own home or foster care situation or even to an institution after initially running away and wandering aimlessly in the city.

Girls leave home for a variety of reasons: adventure or freedom in the context of an authoritarian or disorganized family life, or because adults care so little. Emotional survival is a prevailing theme, as these statements show: "I was being blamed for other's wrong doing"; "I couldn't get along with mom (or stepfather)"; "I needed safety"; "I left for my own survival"; "I was abandoned"; "No one cared one way or another for me."

For a number of youth living in neglectful, substance-abusing families, the flight from home occurred at a very young age. A fourteen-year old girl, whose mother had earned a Ph.D. on a university scholarship, said that she was primarily concerned about her own "survival."

Mom was too involved with her work, and my father was too forgetful; he was on drugs. Love wasn't ever shown, and it was nothing but conflicts.

Protracted family conflict acted as a strong motivation to leave home. A seventeen-year-old girl, who began a drug habit at age nine, complained that physical abuse from the age of six, because of "Mom's different boyfriends," finally forced her out the door.

Me and mom's boyfriend never got along, and she [mother] asked me if she should ask him [boyfriend] to leave. I left so he wouldn't have to. She really wanted it that way.

Alcoholism and drug abuse accompanied by family violence appear to be endemic problems for these homeless girls. One young woman recalls the violent scene that occurred just before her escape.

Mom was weird—always drinking and throwing things. They had a fight. There was broken glass and holes everywhere in the wall. They always yelled at each other, too, especially at night.

Physical, emotional, and sexual abuse were everyday events for these adolescent girls. In some cases, it was other children in the family who were being victimized; but the effects were equally devastating.

There was plenty of physical abuse, but not on me. That's why I couldn't live there. There was lots of tension—a really bad atmosphere. I didn't want to be there.

Or the girl may be the object of parental conflict, as this statement suggests:

The fight was over me. Dad would hit me and mom said, "If you hit her again, I'm getting a divorce."

The father's violence against the mother may leave enduring scars. One girl tells the story of her unconscious mother, whom she deeply cared for, being viciously attacked.

Dad knocked my mother out. He leaves her when she's having an epileptic fit—that's when he picks her up and throws her into walls.

In these crisis-ridden families, children may be forcibly pushed out and placed in foster care, detention, or institutional custody. A girl with eleven years of experience as a state ward, and who detested the foster care system, explained how it broke up the family.

My sister and I left together [after] we were taken away from our home. But I ended up in lock-up (detention) until a foster family was found. None of us (six sisters) ever got back to our parents.

The authoritarian structure—father knows best—that is the taken-for-granted family organization may be a trigger for setting off adolescent resistance to control. A seventeen-year-old girl from an intact but alcoholic family describes the ordinary events that eventually drove her out of the house.

My father dominates all conversation. My mother agrees just to keep the peace. He is always right; everyone else is wrong. He physically abused me, then told me how sorry he was. I used to do things wrong just to be beaten, and then hear how much he loves me.

In some homes, the only communication is violence. Three young women comment on their typical experiences growing up.

One said: "Mum attacked dad with a knife; he then leaves and gets drunk." Another girl reported: "My mother said she was going to murder me, because I told her I was going to steal 50 cents from someone." Fighting was sometimes nonstop in these homes: "Mom and dad were always fighting—scary. Mom used to get drunk on weekends, before the divorce. Dad scratched a chunk out of mom's arms." The third said, "our family never talked. It was just BANG! Physical hitting and beating, mom always hit me; she never showed love."

When the embattled young people told their parents that they were running away, the response was surprising. Parents either insisted they stay, or they promised to work out their differences; often a repeated pattern of promises and disappointments. Usually, the situation worsened. One young woman described how her parents "bribed, forced, and threatened me, but once I decided to leave, I left." But frequently, it is not concern for the child as much as parental shame that leads to their entreaties to stay home. Subjected to regular beatings by her "mum," a girl comments:

They put the guilt shit on you [when you try to leave], and say, "How could you drag our name through the mud. You're ruining our reputation."

Some parents go further, and seek legal assistance to enforce compliance. A fourteen-year-old girl with a history of multiple suicide attempts, and who now lives in a shelter, said:

My parents want to get lawyers and legal shit to bring me back home. Even if she [mother] quit beating me, I wouldn't go back home now.

More common is parental manipulation—promises of safety and kindness, but parental performance that fails to resolve the underlying conflict. Parental incompetence and rage rarely achieve their intent, as this now eighteen-year-old homeless woman said:

When I told her I was leaving, first, mum was quiet. Then she went off her brain and said, "Get your arse back inside," and I said no, and walked away. There was a lot of screaming and yelling, but I just left anyway.

Because of long-standing negative interactions with adults, most of these girls did not consult with anyone before running away from home. The majority left without a support group or a sense of direction—whether to go across town or to a different state. A fifteen-year-old who reported to have run away "at least twenty times" said that she was seven the first time she ran away; her destination was eventually to land in the entertainment and vice district, "where the action is."

I went about 100 kilometers, first to a western suburb; then I went straight to the Cross (King's Cross District, Sydney).

Episodic runs were commonplace. A thirteen-year-old girl, born in New Zealand of Tongalese ancestry, describes her leaving-home pattern.

I've left about fifty times. I would go home on Monday and get kicked out by Mom on Saturday. It's because I used to fight with mom all the time.

Another said, "I just go in and out, but never stay. . . . I used to get violent and bash me mother, and I didn't like that."

The flight from domestic conflict and violence into the unknown represents for these youth a positive step, a leap into a more hopeful, promising future. At this stage of the drift into homelessness, the young woman believes that by resisting unloving, arbitrary, and cruel parents, she is taking control of her life.

Because the average number of runs for this group is 8.5, it is clear that these young women have had a wide range of leaving-home experiences, most of which have been negative. Victimizations, institutionalized care, a revolving-door shelter experience, and detention are all part of the pattern of homelessness. This may explain why girls try to return home again and again (sometimes with one parent's zealous efforts), further contributing to their sense of being angry, powerless, and out of control.

Street Experiences

"Where did you sleep last night?" may be an impertinent question asked of a person with a fixed address. It is a life-and-death question for young women on the street. A typical pattern is staying with same-age friends, extended family members, or family friends for a few weeks or months. Rarely does she locate a shelter the first time out. In inner city Sydney, there are considerably more young persons living in squats (abandoned housing) than is reflected in our statistics. We learned that this population is both less physically accessible and also more psychologically resistant to being interviewed (weapons are a common method for defending self and property in these settings). The fact that five young women reported having slept on the street is not surprising, given the shortage of shelters and the overly complicated referral system, at least for beginners to grasp.

Shelters, or youth "refuges" (in the Australian vernacular) typically were short-term arrangements with residential stays limited from one to two weeks to three months. Long-term shelters were unavailable for most of this sample; hence, the characteristic pattern was frequent movement from one refuge to another; or refuge to street and back again. Refuges were depicted by the girls in various ways. For younger residents, the shelter was a "lifesaver," a "safe place" to regroup, "a secure home away from home." But for others, such temporary landing places were defined as "overly short term," "revolving door," "too many rules and regulations," "too boring," "confusing and upsetting," "impersonal," "overcrowded," "violent," and "just a place to stay for a night until I sort myself out." One girl asserted that refuges are "horrible; the authorities stink, and I'm sick of going from one to another." A sixteen-year-old gay woman indicated that although she was "dying a slow death living with my parents," refuges also discriminated against homosexuals.

I've been in two different refuges. The first one I was there for five months, but I wasn't getting any support. I need a lot of support (because of her sexuality). Another was a youth house, which was run by the church. But they kicked me out because of my sexuality. I have to say that it [refuge] really sucks. When I was kicked out of the refuge because I was lesbian, it just added to the pressure. You feel lower than anyone else. It's taken a year for me to get alright for myself.

Among these homeless adolescents, the average age for first living on the streets is between twelve and fifteen, but some have been homeless at much younger ages—for instance, one was six and the other nine when first homeless. This population appears to be a relatively sophisticated street group with about 62 percent having been on the street for six months or more. More than 40 percent reported that they have been on the streets for over one year, usually moving from one situation to another.

One young woman, now eighteen, who first started living on the streets at eleven years of age, spoke about her transient living arrangements.

My stepfather came to live with us (family); he didn't have anyplace to live. But it didn't work out. My stepdad punched my mom and stabbed her too, so I left for the foster home cause I wanted to be treated good; like their child. It was really strict, but very posh. It made me uncomfortable. I didn't really fit in; it just wasn't me. . . . So over the next seven years, I moved back and forth from home to the streets to the refuge. But I never lasted more than two weeks at home.

Having a job or going to school stabilizes some young women, enabling them to develop friends and a less dangerous lifestyle. Sources of financial support are crucial to a more settled life. Among 60 percent of the respondents, social security provided an opportunity for regularizing housing accommodations and relationships. But peer involvement with drugs, alcohol, and partying invariably uses up most of the funding, reducing the likelihood that they can pay for an apartment and other basic needs. In some instances, the refuge was the site for parties; scores of young drifters that moved into a poorly supervised setting, and played all night.

I had every person in _____(district) sleeping there. It was just a big party. We spent two hundred bucks a day on alcohol. It was party all the time.

Ten percent of the sample currently were working as prostitutes, and another 3 percent as "models" to support themselves while on the streets. Prostitution was invariably defined as a "short-term proposition." This contrasts sharply with any sample of street girls in America, where lack of government funding or availability of menial jobs makes prostitution and property crime nearly inevitable choices for homeless girls (Weisberg 1985). Among this Sydney and suburban area group of young people, many have put together a financial package, combining community resources, jobs, and perhaps some illegal activity, that contributes to a sense of independence and competence. Not all the young women have discretionary income, however. Many that we spoke with had no money, or had only small change doled out by refuge workers. Community resources for youth in Australia remains a fairly new concept, and is by no means a guaranteed source of support. In most instances, the dole pays for little more than food and rent with "no money to do anything else."

Life on the streets remains a difficult, incredibly risky, if not dreadful, situation from a number of vantage points (see Table 6.2), and refuges are in short supply. Some young women are unaware of the existence of shelters (Australians refer to these as "refuges"), and simply must cope with street conditions unaided.

When I was on the street, I didn't know about refuges. Then, when I found out about them, I couldn't use them. My mother put a run report on me; that's why I couldn't get help.

Living in abandoned houses can have hidden dangers, as one homeless girl explains:

When I lived in the squats, it was always dark. Once I fell through the floorboards [to the floor below]. There are gang fights all the time. Everyone has weapons; someone with a gun or a knife is always waiting for you.

Another, who works as a prostitute, said,

I live with my boyfriend Andrew (who has a job) in the squats. There's no way to close the door; it's broken; unhinged. So anybody can walk in. There are always junkies leaving their stuff around. Recently, a friend we invited in took all our things and cleared out.

Young homeless people are constantly exposed to and involved in violence. Only 23 percent of this sample had not witnessed violence; whereas over half have witnessed ten or more violent acts. One girl reported that she had been exposed to 600–800 violent episodes over a three-year period of homelessness, and had personally participated in "200" of these. She described shootings, knifings, fights, beatings, rapes, muggings, death by overdose, and "fifty killings." Two young women claim that in areas such as King's Cross, Sydney, at least one person is murdered every night; a few have even witnessed a friend's murder or death by overdose. It is perhaps gratifying to see that shelters were not a primary site for violence (although violence did occur there with some regularity). The most common site is predictably the street. Intensive youth agency outreach programs in high-risk areas attempt to physically remove and relocate younger girls to safe havens, because of high physical, psychological and social risks (see Table 6.2).

Among their own peer group, violence may be perpetrated by a boy-

Table 6.2
Street Risks among Homeless Girls

Physical	Psychological	Environmental
- Drug/alcohol abuse	- Drug/alcohol abuse	- Drug/alcohol abuse
- Drug overdose		
- Infertility	- Delinquency stigma	- Poor foster homes; inadvertently leads to extended stays in brothels or living with series of men
- Sexually transmitted diseases (STD's)	- Sleeping/eating disorders	
- HIV/AIDS		
- Pregnancy		
- Cervical Cancer	- Hysteria	- Adult criminal associates
- Murder	- Sexual harassment	- "Shelterization"
- Rape		
- Suicide	- Peer pressure	- Dependency cycle
	- Emotional abuse	- Misguided/ contradictory agency care
- Physical Assault		
- Genital/facial/limb disfigurement	- Value loss contributes to confused sexual identity	
		- Victimogenic/ criminogenic milieus
	- "Post-traumatic syndrome" reinforces patterns of instability in relationships/ life choices	

friend, and for some, their relationship with men repeats the parental pattern of domestic violence. Street persons, both male and female, and youth gangs, are among the most violent; in some cases, the young woman herself was part of the fighting/mugging/raping, either as a victim or offender. These respondents indicated that they had reported over two hundred violent episodes to the police, but that only a few were followed up by police action. Additionally, there is fear that police would arrest or relocate them, suspicions that contributed to a cynical attitude toward policing activities in high-crime areas.

Victimization is rampant among street women. Sexual coercion may be a daily experience for those who are younger or inexperienced, and over 11 percent admitted to being forced to prostitute or pose nude against their will. Being injured, with or without weapons, having personal property stolen, and being forced to be vigilant against threats from older street persons, especially predatory males, made life on the streets a daily horror, according to those who have subsequently left. Many young women recognize that being female can be dangerous; rape, assault, and police bashings were frequently mentioned. One fourteen-year-old girl reported that police harassment was a regular street occurrence.

I was arrested twice for running away. They [police] put my name in a book, and said that if I do it again, I'll be a state ward. One time they called me a slut. They're so dumb; they call you anything just to shut you up.

At the same time, some respondents believe that street girls are better able to get protection than street boys, because boyfriends will intervene on their behalf. Yet these young women realize that all homeless young people are subject to random acts of violence, usually from other street persons, occasionally from police or other authority persons. Whereas most girls appeared to rely on boyfriends or other street peers, a few developed the habit of carrying weapons. Six girls carried a gun (usually taken from home), and twenty-eight girls (26.7 percent) carried a knife when on the street. None of these girls indicated that she used the police for protection or intervention at any time.

Life on the streets has its positive side as well, according to some of our respondents. Freedom from adult constraints, autonomy to make their own decisions, fun and adventure with peers, and learning to "stick together like a family" made street life worthwhile. Whereas some relish their freedom, many indicate that being away from the family is not considered a "best thing in life." The worst thing in life now for 30 percent remains the unresolved conflict with their family. Many regretted leaving home at all, even when parents ordered them out.

I've always thought, there's no place like home. Think before you act up. Why did I do it [run]? My parents said 'go,' so I left.

Among these girls, missing "mum" was mentioned frequently, regardless of how mothers had treated the young person. For many, the worst thing was simply being in their current circumstances, cut off from family, familiar routines, and their usual school and friendship patterns. Despite their outer veneer of toughness and acceptance of their situation, many young women demonstrated a deep sadness at their inexplicable fate. Without

extensive counseling, it is difficult to imagine these defamilized and disconnected adolescents creating a stable life for themselves as adults.

Illegal/Deviant Activities on the Street

The movement to illegal and deviant activities appears to be an integral
part of running away and exposure to sophisticated street persons. Thus,
deviance and crime may be directly related to survival mechanisms learned
on the street. Alternatively, the young person may have a prior history of
conflict with the law, and the push-out from the family merely underscores
the family's effort to construct boundaries for itself by excluding a disturbing element. In a word, there are two possible issues: Is deviance and illegal
behavior an outcome of running and homelessness; or contrariwise, is the
homelessness an outcome of previous deviant and illegal involvement? Let
us examine the data for an understanding of these two alternatives (see
Table 6.3).

First, most of these female youth have had some deviant involvement
prior to their leaving home or living on the streets. For instance, before
their movement into street life, over half had engaged in shoplifting; 15
percent had sold drugs; 35 percent had stolen property worth $50 or more;
19 percent had a history of forgery; 65 percent had been involved in fighting, with 24 percent of these using weapons (usually a knife); 18 percent
had stolen a car; over 28 percent had been involved in burglary and around
10 percent claimed to make money through gambling; and under 2 percent
had a history of voluntarily posing for pornographic pictures or videos.
This criminalistic pattern is especially pronounced among the older homeless girls, and those confined in the detention center.

Second, after moving to the streets, the pattern of illegal behavior is
exacerbated with the rates rising precipitously. Sixty-eight percent admitted
to shoplifting; 37 percent to regularly selling drugs; 56 percent to being
involved in theft; almost 27 percent to having committed forgery; 70 percent had a history of fighting, and most notable, almost 40 percent used
weapons; 36 percent had stolen cars; 48 percent had been involved in
burglary; over 30 percent had gambled for money; and over 10 percent of
the sample had engaged in pornographic modeling. Deviance and crime are
a persistent and widespread pattern for these street youth (see Table 6.3).
Although most street youth try to avoid giving or receiving harm, some
girls were matter-of-fact about their criminal exploits.

When I use [alcohol and drugs], I do crime. I've been arrested six times for drunken
disorderly, rolling people, and doing other things. When I'm wasted, I don't even
remember what I did.

Third, whereas only a small group indicated that they were currently
prostituting, about one out of three girls has been involved in prostitution

Table 6.3
Illegal/Deviant Activities before and after Leaving Home
or Entering Streets

Illegal/Deviant Activity	Frequency	Percent
Shoplifting		
Before	57	54.3
After	71	67.6
Theft (over $50)		
Before	37	35.2
After	59	56.2
Forgery		
Before	20	19.0
After	28	26.7
Break and Enter		
Before	30	28.6
After	50	47.6
Fighting		
Before	68	64.8
After	74	70.5
Use of Weapons		
Before	25	23.8
After	41	39.0
Prostitution		
Before	7	6.7
After	31	29.5
Sold Sex (when on street) for		
Food	21	20.0
Shelter	22	21.0
Drugs	28	26.7

for money while on the streets, and nearly the same number sold sex for drugs. This pattern contrasts with less-street-sophisticated girls who sold sex for food, shelter, love, or loneliness. Regardless of the specific motivation for selling sex, young homeless girls involved in prostitution constitute a high-risk group for serious victimization, drug addiction, and health problems, especially HIV-positive and AIDS.

Fourth, there may be two distinct modes of street adaptation here. On the one hand there are girls who become involved in crime and deviance, but never or rarely with prostitution. Early on they sought protection from an older male, and became part of a crime-dependent street culture. On the other side, there are girls who have rarely been involved in serious crime (although most of the older girls reported they had tried shoplifting a few times), who instead use their sex as "capital" to negotiate street life. Although only 2 percent of the sample identified themselves as "sex workers," girls who prostitute on a regular basis are apt to (1) not draw on homeless youth allowance; (2) live primarily off their prostitution earnings; and (3) have fairly chronic drug abuse histories. Isabel King, a researcher and youth worker at King's Cross, Sydney, emphasizes that homeless girls who prostitute for a living are invariably drug addicted (King 1991).

Unpredictably, most girls who prostitute did not identify themselves as "sex workers" (under 2 percent). The idea of sex as work, promoted by politicized sectors of prostitutes, rather than sex for survival or to feed a drug habit appears not to be a well-established concept among adolescent prostitutes. *Opportunistic prostitution* may be a better description of this form of street survival.

LEAVING THE STREETS

Among the 81 percent of young women who have been on the streets for any period of time, 72 percent mentioned that they had made the decision to leave (see Table 6.4). How serious is this commitment to alter their lifestyle? At the time of the interview, 45 percent had left the street three or more times, and nearly 12 percent had tried leaving ten times or more. Almost 29 percent had never left the street, regardless of their implied intention to do so. What are the major impediments to change in this case? Street friendships (retained by over 66 percent) have strong claims on this group. Life on the streets is living on the edge in a perpetual state of crisis that takes away any motivation for change. As explained by a seventeen-year-old, who originally came from a family of ten:

It's just lack of motivation; no one has motivation to do anything. Other street people say "You'll never get out of that life (street)." When I lived on the street, I gave away everything; somebody stole all my clothing [before that] worth $700. So, what's the use?

A persistent belief is that only one's streetmates understand the street experience. Moreover, streetmates will always share whatever they have: food, clothes, shelter, all without censure or judgment in a world where "you make your own rules."

Most girls made repeated efforts to leave the street. Life was unsafe, insecure, and dangerous. Being a girl on the street is different than being a boy, especially for very young girls:

It's worse being a girl on the street because with guys, they think we can be taken advantage of. Last night a friend of mine was raped. In the area I'm in now, a girl

Table 6.4
Major Reasons for Leaving Streets and
Services Received While on Run

Reason	Frequency	Percent
Lack of resources	22	21.0
Couldn't cope	19	18.1
Fears/Threats	8	7.6
Help from Friends	5	4.8
Health Problems	5	4.8
Help from Refuge	3	2.9
Police Intervention	3	2.9
Other	3	2.9
Total	68	
No Response	37	33.1
#Received Any Kind of Services While On Run	83	79.0

#Services include: drop-in center visits, medical, contraceptive, pregnancy, abortion, counseling, accommodation, material resources (food, clothing), drug/alcohol intervention, social security (CES), HIV/AIDS, travel, and stress/anxiety.

gets raped once a month. One girl I live with was raped by one of Dad's friends (she was only thirteen). She needs the support of her [street] friends to make it.

For many of these young women, lack of coping skills and resources make existence nearly or wholly untenable. Making the effort to leave represents a step away from danger toward a possible future. Thus, the healthy response is to keep trying despite setbacks, but mainly, stay away from street friends. Two girls provided their perspectives on how homeless young people could escape the streets.

When you walk away from your family, don't look back. My job is to straighten out my own life. I want my own home, security, a good relationship with someone who loves me. I'm willing to work it out, and stay away from the street.

Don't trust anybody (on the street). You've got to look out after yourself. You've just got to do things for yourself. You have to keep an awareness of yourself and other people. Don't lose reality; always keep in touch with it. Always, always, keep your head about you. Keep whatever you've got left of your self esteem [because] without self worth, you can't do anything, no matter how many opportunities you have.

Surprisingly, only 3 percent indicated that they received help from a refuge when they were attempting to shift lifestyles. Because this was an open-ended question with respondents providing statements without linguistic cues, it seems likely that among street youth, shelters are perceived as part of the street scene, and not separate from it. Because we also know from the interviews that there is a steady movement between the street and the short-term shelter system, a decision to leave may require a more established accommodation system than presently exists. A policy of shifting girls from one shelter to another, based on short-term housing availability or staff convenience, may undermine the belief that the shelter is a "taking off" point toward a better future, rather than merely an extension of the street scene.

CHRONIC HOMELESSNESS

Chronic homelessness implies a full-time street involvement with reduced or no contacts with family and conventional friends. Now the girl has lost meaningful contact with reality and has serious drug or alcohol dependency that involves illegal activity and a lifestyle that centers around the urban street culture. Whereas a few girls will be supported by welfare (a youth worker at an earlier stage helped her to fill out the form), most activity focuses on illegal or deviant activities such as prostitution, drug sales, and theft; and for a few, assault and armed robbery become part of the lifestyle. For an unknown number of young women, streets become their home, street youth their family and significant others, and street life their culture and society (Costello 1991). Such persons create a specific street lifestyle, "the culture of chronicity." A severely abused girl, who left home at fifteen years old, justified her current life of hanging out with a "mob of eighty people."

The streets aren't as hard as people say they are. Street life is not a social status; it's a separate culture. . . . We have emotional, financial support for each other. They take you in if they have somewhere to stay, but you have to stick to your own territory; your own people.

The open-ended question "What's a typical day for you?" elicited a standard response from street people:

I get up, find money, buy alcohol, pot; get drunk, stoned, go to sleep. When I'm on the streets, I just hang out; take drugs, shoplift; nothing much. Staying out of trouble can be difficult, if not impossible.

After a brief career as a "street kid," a sixteen-year-old, who described herself as "being severely abused," but now goes by her street name, "Rebel," listed the health dangers she encountered while "on run": "broken collarbone, suicide attempts, operations (lump removed from my breast), sexual assaults, cervical cancer, getting into fights."

A temporal profile of the homeless youth population shows that 60 percent to 70 percent of the population are homeless from some months to several years. There is a significant minority (estimates as high as 25 percent) who comprise a new "skid row" of chronically homeless youth (Chamberlain and Mackenzie 1993). Certainly, an argument can be made that having a street identity is better than having no identity at all. As members of the new homeless, youth are obliged to create their own culture, social space, routines, and networks. As a culture, street youth have a sense of belonging; a hierarchy based on gender, age, and physical size; an argot (much of it borrowed); and a special mode of communication, such as graffiti, that marks them as a special group. Street youth occupy territory, a large proportion of which is either shared with traditional homeless (usually male) and the mentally ill, or which they have expropriated, often pushing out former occupants (Costello 1991). Some of this culture is positive—supporting streetmates; forbidding adults or other street youth to injure children; serving as police against outsiders who harass or exploit "streeties"; and sharing their food, drugs, and material possessions.

Certain features of this culture are highly destructive, given the backgrounds of these youth. Death is an ever-present concern, and suicide attempts are common. Among girls, self-mutilation as in wrist and forearm slashing is both an activity—something to do to reduce the boredom—and a strong signal of distress. In the words of one thirteen-year-old girl who came from a very abusive home, life is hurting or being hurt.

For street kids, it's kill or be killed. I've been arrested twenty-nine times for robberies, attempted robbery, stealing, selling stolen goods, malicious damage, assault, beatings, B & E (breaking and entering), having drugs on me, other stuff. The police usually just bash me, and let me go. They punish kids by putting a phone book on your head, and bashing you to keep you from bruising. I used to hate getting locked up, but it's not so bad. I'd rather not be here (detention), but it's OK; it feels safe.

In a culture that represses and denies suffering, violence becomes a legitimate form of self-expression, as well as a statement of power relations, a situation that places untrained youth workers at considerable risk (staff interviews, Sydney, 1992). For females caught in the street culture of chronicity, the lack of clear boundaries and secure location is reinforced by violations from others of their physical and social space. Sexual assault, theft of personal possessions, invasion of living areas by police or other authorities, sexual harassment by police, adult men and street youth, give most chronically homeless girls a sense of frustration and despair.

Devices they use to cope with their powerlessness are often interpersonal violence, increase in street crime, alienation, and suicide. In Lauren Costello's (1991) words, they have become "the children our parents warned us about." The streets, and youth homelessness generally, generate a highly criminogenic situation, where crime becomes a "survival strategy" (McCarthy and Hagan 1991).

CONCLUSION

In this chapter, I have described a contemporary process of victimization of girls and young women who have become involved in the "culture of violence"—at home and on the streets. Many of these mechanisms and processes of female control appear to be direct, as in rape, where male hegemony is clearly articulated, and where law enforcement and the courts reinforce dominance by selective enforcement and nonenforcement (e.g., one out of every eight women in the United States has been raped, 29 percent when they were under age eleven years). Some of the control practices exerted against homeless girls are also a conscious and coherent policy of controlling female deviants. Such control is coercively implemented by external, usually state agents, as well as by families with varying degrees of psychosocial problems.

For most homeless teens, the streets remain an option for only short time periods, because both beliefs and practices about the violent lifestyle contribute to fatalism: "kill or be killed" or "an eye for an eye." Aggression and vengeance take their toll among young women, as injuries, illness, and hospitalization reduce their numbers through death, voluntary departure, or by becoming chronically disabled in a context of highly sophisticated male criminals, multiple drug addictions, and random street fighting. Suicide is a final solution: death by drug overdoses, hanging, or wrist slashings. A Sydney (Australia) study of homeless youth shows that 82 percent of the sample had attempted suicide (Howard 1991). Among the girls I interviewed, a significant proportion had attempted to kill themselves on more than one occasion (Davis 1993b).

What can we in the United States learn from the Australian experience of homeless youth? First, the problems of homeless youth are global and appear to be related to irreversible changes in both economic and family structures. Second, adolescent girls are especially at risk, because the nature of street life itself offers chronic exposure to violence—as a witness, victim, or perpetrator—but especially to sexual victimization. Third, although youth shelters are no panacea for the multiple problems of homeless young people, they deserve much greater public support and tax dollars than either country offers. Australia is far more advanced in the fundamentals of shelter care for this vulnerable and often difficult population—although they have far to go to develop a humane and appropriate long-term youth care system.

The United States offers a sharp contrast with Australia in the matter of human rights. Whereas Australia, as well as most countries in the United Nations, subscribe to the basic human right to shelter, the United States does not recognize the international right to adequate housing. The National Law Center on Homelessness and Poverty (Washington, DC), which has lobbied for an end to homelessness, points out that homeless people apparently have the right in the United States to be educated, as well as to sleep in public. However, they have no right to indoor or adequate shelter, Food Stamps, Medicaid, or Supplemental Security Income—basic programs urgently needed by homeless persons: youth, adult, and families alike.

To meet the special needs of young people, shelters should be organized to offer flexible programming at various stages of homelessness; and preferably in age- and gender-segregated settings, especially for younger females. At the very least, intervention should provide immediate relief from the unbearable stresses that homeless and runaway adolescents experience while living on the streets. This necessitates a policy of immediate relief for adolescents who are raped, assaulted, suicidal, or at risk of contracting the AIDS virus. Additionally, street-level clinics, observed in Sydney, should offer multidimensional treatment plans for coping with adolescents with chronic posttraumatic stress disorder, drug problems, mental health problems, and other illnesses.

Whereas homelessness for young people may be the ultimate form of powerlessness, and a visible symbol of social abandonment, alcohol and drug involvement throws up a far more confused set of images. Not only do alcohol and drug abuse patterns lend themselves to competing definitions, as we show in the next chapter; but also, in the midst of a government-waged war on drugs, young people from all walks of life pursue chemical highs as normal adolescent behavior.

NOTE

1. This study was sponsored by the Fulbright Commission, 1992, and included interviewing 105 young women located in shelters/refuges, detention centers, squats, drop-in centers, medical centers, food banks, and on the street, and in urban, suburban, and rural settings in the Sydney metropolitan area. All subjects signed an informed consent form prior to being interviewed. The length of interviews ranged between 1½ hours to 3 hours for each study participant, and included 220 items, 50 of which were open-ended allowing for an opportunity to elicit the experiences of these girls in their own "voice." Among this sample, their state-defined status included: state wards, delinquents, PINS (persons in need of supervision), runaways, and chronically homeless youth (or former delinquents,

runaways, or homeless persons). Additionally, I interviewed 50 youth workers, shelter directors, administrators, researchers, and reformers; as well as examined a wide array of agency documents. (See also Davis 1993b; 1993c.) My appreciation goes to Dr. Debra Gay Anderson, Oregon Health Sciences University, for her participation in the homeless-girl interviewing process. I am also indebted to Professor Suzanne Hatty, Southern Cross University in Lismore, NSW, for arranging to have the numerical data processed.

7

Youth, Addiction, and Control

Cocaine may be the prototypical postmodern drug because in this culture it enhances a personal sense of self-esteem, power, and control. A culture's drug of choice reflects its ability to meet people's needs; in the United States some people across all classes use cocaine, a stimulant, to medicate for their low sense of personal efficacy and lack of self worth. The common denominator is the desire to feel powerful, and what happens on the street in the inner city often parallels what happens on The Street, or Wall Street . . . with the glamorous lifestyle of the Wall Street Masters of the Universe.

David Forbes, *False Fixes: The Cultural Politics of Drugs, Alcohol, and Addictive Relations*

Living far from one's nature is not unusual in our culture, which is why the drug conquest of America is virtually complete.

Alice Walker, *Anything We Love Can Be Saved*

MODERN AND POSTMODERN PERSPECTIVES

This chapter asks you to suspend your usual preconceptions about why youth drink and drug. Poverty, low parent-child attachment, poor learner, boredom, peer influence, delinquency, lack of productive roles, and others—all have a place in understanding the origin of drug use. They will be explored in further detail as we move through the chapter. Now, the reader is asked to consider youth drug use and abuse as a matter of perspective—different points of view about how to define psychoactive substances yield very different conceptions of how to manage and control use and distribution. Because drug and alcohol use, among all the youth crises that we examine in this book, is the most susceptible to clashing viewpoints, contradictory explanations and wholly different policy recommendations that surface repeatedly.

To begin, let us consider two dominant approaches we have considered earlier: modernism and postmodernism. We have met these terms before, so you should be aware that **modernism** mainly reflects prevailing views about youth held by social control institutions. These include laws that articulate social and moral standards about young people's proper status and roles, such as the notions that young people are better off when not participating in adult institutions; that intoxicants are for adults only; and that adolescents who break the law are bad people. Overall, these beliefs govern much of our drug policy affecting youth created by the state, schools, business interests, political parties, the military, the criminal justice system, and other institutions.

The modernist perspective also holds that youth substance use and abuse revolves around control and denial: Youth must be protected against the use of alcohol and drugs until they reach a "magical" legal age (as determined by the state), where they supposedly will have adequate judgment to practice restraint and self-control. Legal substances, such as alcohol and medically prescribed drugs, must be restricted or ingested only under parental or medical supervision. Illicit substances, especially street drugs, are believed to be a homogeneous group of dangerous and addictive materials that, once tried, destroy young people's consciousness and their capacity to act rationally.

The self is monolithic: Either it is drunk or sober, stoned or clean, good or evil. Illegal drug taking is synonymous with delinquency and degradation. Casual use does not figure in this calculus, nor does the use of drugs as normal experimentation following young people's natural inclination to relish the risky endeavor. Excluding, rejecting, and punishing the user is believed to alter the negative drug behavior.

The alternative cultural perspective, **postmodernism**, takes a wholly different tack. In this analysis, drug-taking occurs under a range of circumstances, and reflects the more fluid sense of self as pleasure seeker and social experimenter, and of society as inherently fragmented, lacking unitary knowledge or purpose. Instead of the modernist forms of control over youth—especially denial of their feelings and experiences—the postmodern perspective points to the ubiquity of addictions over the course of life (Forbes 1994). Addictions characterize our ordinary existence: drinking, overuse of medically prescribed drugs, using/abusing illegal drugs, pleasure seeking, sex, working, shopping, gambling, popular music, and a host of other pursuits that offer freedom from the burden of daily living and an escape from ordinary awareness.

The result, as David Forbes (1994) shows is that as the self becomes overidentified with or overdependent on one form of life, it loses its relational aspect and becomes a fixed, rigid entity. The alcoholic, drug addict, sexaholic, workaholic, foodaholic, shopaholic are all "junkies"—all are hooked in their own way, insofar as the behavior is beyond the addict's control.

In the postmodern calculus, drug usage can neither be controlled nor denied. No war can abolish the chronic demand, because young people are using drugs in pursuit of identity and as a mode of peer bonding, and in similar ways as adults: to create meanings, relieve boredom, provide satisfaction, ease stresses. And it is becoming increasingly difficult to deny that, faced with poverty, exclusion, false promises, lack of opportunity, powerlessness, and meaninglessness, many young people will be attracted to drugs in their search for fulfillment and wholeness, however illusionary and futile the endeavor.

As long as the drug debate focuses on control and denial, society is doomed to perpetuate the current drug policy, spending billions of tax dollars on interdiction, arrest, imprisonment, mandatory treatment (that often has temporary effects only), and after-the-fact prevention. The following sections examine the drug debate, including the use of alcohol and illicit drugs, as issues of (1) conflicting explanatory models, (2) adolescent patterns of alcohol and drug use, (3) government drug enforcement, and (4) the treatment and prevention discourse.

CONFLICTING MODELS

Various efforts to explain youth drug use and abuse run the gamut from biochemical models to the pleasure-principle thesis. This section examines five prevailing models, some of which are mutually compatible, others that strongly oppose institutionally accepted explanations. The models include 1) the biochemical (disease) model, 2) the structural-situational model, 3) the historical model, 4) the risk model, and 5) the normalization model. Taken together, these models help clarify the current moral dilemma that dominates the institutional drug discourse. The addiction concept assumes a crucial role in most models, as it implies not only alcohol/drug dependence—with its attendant psychological disturbances—but also withdrawal of the adolescent from participation in family, schools, and other institutions.

The Biochemical (Disease) Model

A biochemical approach to drug use presumes that psychoactive substances—chemicals that influence the workings of the mind—have a direct and predictable influence on emotion, thinking, perception, and feeling. Researchers identify physical properties that result in intoxication: "getting high"; becoming addicted; losing physical, mental, and emotional control; narrowing of the perceptual field; and becoming aggressive. In some versions, the intoxication-aggression link is presumed to be invariant, because the ingestion of a known quantity of psychoactive substances leads to cognitive breakdown and disinhibition, and thence to disordered thinking and behaving (Fagan et al. 1990). Other versions refer to "underlying pathological states" that may be triggered by the alcohol or drug, inducing states of anxiety, hostility, paranoia, and aggression (American Psychiatric Association 1987). At least one study claims that alcohol may stimulate the production of cortisol, an arousal or stress hormone linked to aggression, which is most pronounced in males (Ylikahri et al. 1978). Another view is that prolonged substance abuse, as opposed to casual or occasional use, can produce pathologies or emotional states that lead to aggression, cognitive impairment, and various personality disorders (Schuckit 1990).

The disease model of alcoholism has won favor with physicians, law enforcement, treatment experts, and the general public. Also, it is the dominant metaphor of Alcoholics Anonymous, the leading self-help treatment program (Denning 1997). This highly individualistic approach calls for a zero-tolerance policy. Once the individual recognizes the "insanity" of drinking or drug taking, identifies him/herself as an alcoholic/drug addict, and turns over his/her life to a "Higher Power" (God, the group, or other entity), the individual can be saved. Despite program rejection of all intoxicants, treatment experts observe that cycles of sobriety and relapse are a normal part of the disease; addicts often remain psychologically dependent on the substance; and substitution behavior (e.g., food, work, gambling) can mask the inherent compulsivity that continues to drive the recovering addict (McElrath 1995).

The Structural-Situational Model

The structural-situational model of addiction is opposed to the disease model on a wide array of assumptions. Rather than uniform outcomes resulting from chemical use, sociologists emphasize that alcohol and drugs are first of all social in nature—their reality depends on social definitions, learned expectations, a given social context, historical referents, a specific network of relations, and a shared discourse of understandings. For example, men and women of all ages may both drink or drug excessively, but young adult males are involved disproportionately in violent behavior resulting from problem drinking (Fagan et al. 1990).

Instead of a simple connection between substance abuse and problem behavior, Fagan et al. (1990) argue that the nexus between substance use and aggression is a complex relation mediated by the type of substance and its psychoactive effects, personality factors, the expected effect of substances, situational factors in the immediate settings where substances are used (bar, street, or workplace), and sociocultural factors that channel the arousal effects of substances into behaviors that may include aggression.

From a structural-situational perspective, being a young, unemployed male from a violent family may be far more predictive of aggression than the psychoactive properties of a specific drug.

Cultural norms are far more significant in behavior than a strict medical model takes into account. For instance, aggression has been reported among crack cocaine users following intoxication and withdrawal, but it appears to conform with an "economic-compulsive" model of drug-related violence, rather than with a pharmacological response (Goldstein 1995). This means that "set" and "setting" (or situation)—time, place, persons, interactional norms, learned expectations, social control—in Andrew Weil's (1995) analysis largely determines how a person behaves.

Cross-cultural variations demonstrate that chemically related aggressive behavior is first, learned and transmitted by social and cultural processes; and second, that different forms of aggression may result—verbal assaults, physical assaults, sexual assaults, homicide, suicide, warfare. Some cultures have no association between intoxication and aggression. Members of the Camba tribe of Bolivia, for example, have been reported to get drunk on 178 proof rum twice a month but experience no verbal, physical, or sexual aggression (Heath 1983). Drinking for the Camba may represent a convivial "time out" from the arduous routines of these subsistence farmers. Alternatively, excessive alcohol use may contribute to motor paralysis, which accounts for the Camba drinkers' lack of aggression (P. Nelson 1997, in correspondence). Contrast these gentle folk with the fierce Lapp people of Finland who drink in periodic binges. During drinking episodes, fighting is commonplace and homicide a frequent result of knife fights. When sober, the Lapps display little of this antisocial behavior (Heath 1983). Cultural differences are significant here; but so are style and use, as well as type of alcohol.

Interpersonal violence occurs in some social situations more than others, and even varies between venues. For example, there is more violence in bars in the "tenderloin" district than in stable working-class neighborhood bars; aggression among players and fans occurs in some sports stadiums, and more often with certain sporting events (hockey, soccer). The extent and type of social control—condoning or prohibiting violence—shape expectations toward either aggressive or nonaggressive behaviors. In a word, not all drug use results in aggressive or other socially negative outcomes.

Rather than assuming that the term "drug" has a universal referent— evokes shared images and meanings for social members—we should consider how "drug" is a cultural artifact, a social construct. Erich Goode (1984; 1990; 1993), who has written extensively on drugs, says that "a drug is something that has been arbitrarily defined by certain segments of society as a drug"—that is, by labeling (Goode 1993, 16). In the case of the United States, federal law enforcement authorities define what a drug is, and this social definition shapes our reality about its psychoactive properties and physical effects. In a word, "nothing is a drug, but naming makes it so" (Bernard Barber, quoted in Goode 1984, 127).

The Historical Model

An historical approach is useful to appreciate the arbitrary and changing nature of alcohol and drug labeling (Siegel and Inciardi 1995). Colonial America was the site of home-brew alcohol, and it was liberally enjoyed by young and old alike. Homemade wines and beer were consumed daily and viewed "as essential as bread," an indispensable part of the diet (Lender and Martin 1987, 3). After Independence, the country shifted direction, creating a centralized government for purposes of collecting taxes and conducting foreign business. Nation-building took priority over traditional practices, and the federal government demanded tax money for alcoholic beverages. In this process, home manufacturing of spirits lost out and was declared illegal. Rum became the drink of choice for many Americans, a commodity that had high alcohol content and provided the federal government a regular revenue source. By the early 1800s heavy alcohol consumption was utilitarian—a normal part of personal and community life.

Alcohol played a devastating role in extending the American frontier, as frontiersmen were even heavier drinkers than colonialists, prone to binges as a respite from working nonstop under difficult conditions (Parker and Rebhun 1995). Native Americans also developed a reputation as heavy, violent drinkers, aided and abetted by traders. These Western-bound Americans believed that Native Americans and enslaved Africans became violently aroused once they imbibed alcohol (Levine 1984). But frontiersmen remained almost wholly unconscious of their own behavior under the influence. Fist fights, pistol duels, lynchings, beatings, and genocidal war against Indians have been an integral part of creating the American frontier. Heavy drinking accompanied conflicts over ownership of territory, rights to produce and sell goods, and struggles between ethnic groups and gender relations (Parker and Rebhun 1995).

What happened to change this national pattern of tolerance of excessive and violence-related drinking? Three forces combined to alter the country's drinking habits. Society moved from small farms and communities to larger cities, and in a few decades to industrial development. Tolerance for drinking in these contexts declined sharply. Second, medical opinion shifted from indifference to censure of hard liquor. When Dr. Benjamin Rush, signer of the Declaration of Independence, published *An Inquiry into the Effects of Ardent Spirits on the Human Mind and Body,* he attacked the routine consumption of distilled spirits, claiming that hard liquor could destroy a person's health and even cause death. Rush was the first physician to label alcoholism a disease characterized by compulsion and progressively more severe physical and mental debilitation (Goode and Ben-Yehuda 1994, 14).

A third influence, the Temperance Movement, had been launched, and by 1830 had 1.5 million members who took a totalistic view: complete cessation of the manufacture, distribution, and consumption of all alcoholic beverages as a matter of public policy. Over the nineteenth century the Temperance Movement rose in power and influence as it allied itself with the antislavery and feminist movements. Drinking increasingly became identified with suspect populations: immigrants, Roman Catholics, urban, and working-class people. The struggle against drinking increasingly took on the symbolic politics of class, status, and power, aligning rural and small-town affluent and established classes against urban ethnics and their alcohol-oriented lifestyles played out in saloons (Gusfield 1963). The "moral classes" had little pity for the struggling working classes, and none for drinkers. Goode and Ben-Yehuda (1994, 15) observe that "drinkers were not seen as unfortunate wretches to be helped so much as enemies of society who should be punished."

Prohibition, enacted in 1919, was identified as a moral victory and a patriotic achievement. Failure to obey the law became an act of treason (Gusfield 1963, 123). Shades of today's "war on drugs," the Temperance Movement came to be motivated by hostility, hatred, and anger toward the enemy. On the passage of the eighteenth amendment (Volstead Act), Billy Sunday, a famous Christian preacher, spoke to an audience of ten thousand believers with a message that sin and corruption were over; a new enlightened era had begun:

The reign of tears is over. The slums will soon be a memory. We will turn our prisons into factories and our jails into storehouses and corn cribs. Men will walk upright now, women will smile, and children will laugh. Hell will be forever for rent. (Kobler 1973, 12)

Legislating drinking behavior was not a success for long. Not only did a vigorous black market—"bootlegging"—in alcohol products emerge, but also crime syndicates substituted for legal industries. By the early 1930s, a new coalition of professionals and educated middle-class groups, who used alcohol for recreation and relaxation, voted out the "drys" (antidrinking groups) and elected Franklin D. Roosevelt. Under his leadership, the Great Depression was tackled with new strategies of government intervention, and the country repealed the Volstead Act. By late 1933, alcohol was legalized for adults but denied to minors.

To this day, efforts to control access to alcohol continue to meet with strong resistance, and even anti-drunk driver laws, initiated by Mothers Against Drunk Driving (MADD), have made little impact on curbing the highway carnage caused from drinking drivers. One-half of the fifty-six thousand fatal crashes involve drinking (Siegel and Inciardi 1995). Alcohol abuse is linked not only with automobile crashes, especially among adolescents, but other serious problems result: accidents, drownings, burns, trauma, crime, domestic violence, and child abuse. In the United States, there are an estimated ten million alcohol-dependent or alcoholic people, and twice that number of "problem drinkers." Up to 38 percent of high school seniors report regular binge drinking (Koper and Reuter 1996). Each year alcohol abuse costs the nation well in excess of $100 billion for loss of life, health care, property damage, and decreased production. Siegel and Inciardi (1995, 48) conclude: "We do pay a large personal and societal price for this chemical comfort."

Once alcohol was legal, the state turned its punitive attention to other drugs: marijuana, hashish, cocaine, heroin, and others. "Marijuana, assassin of youth," cried Harry Anslinger, Commissioner of the Federal Bureau of Narcotics (Anslinger and Cooper 1937). Antimarijuana legislation in the 1930s reflected the moral panic created by official efforts to control intoxicant use and distribution. The passage of the Federal Marijuana Tax Act was the result of the efforts of "moral entrepreneurs," who utilized scare tactics initiated by the Federal Bureau of Narcotics (FBN). The press colluded in the official doctrine that marijuana was a "killer drug," "weed of madness," "a sex-crazing drug menace," "a gloomy monster of destructions," and other lurid labels that linked marijuana use of any quantity to sexual excess, madness, and violence (see Goode 1984 and 1993 for an overview of marijuana).

In an important sense, public images of marijuana have shaped the social reality of users. Whereas in the United States and Central America marijuana has strong linkages with crime and aggression, its recreational "laid back" reputation in countries with tolerant drug policies produces very different results.

Reported violence associated with cannabis use in the United States comes about not only because of setting but also because when cannabis and alcohol are taken together, a frequent occurrence, they are mutually potentiating. Cannabis use alone has rarely been associated with violent behavior among noncriminal groups. Thus, two conclusions are possible: (1) Cannabis is a placebo for potentiating what is already going on (e.g., a violent milieu, drug war, and the like); (2) the liberal use of alcohol by many cannabis smokers is the primary source of limbic-cortical disinhibition with resultant emotional overreaction and violence. "Cannabis may add a paranoid cast to the user's perceptions, but it may take alcohol's disinhibiting properties to allow violence to break out."[1]

The Risk Model

Perhaps the most widespread approach to understanding adolescent patterns and impact of alcohol and drug use is the risk model. I proposed some versions of this approach in Chapters 1 and 2, where I discussed general trends of adolescents engaging in problematic behaviors that carried a high likelihood of negative outcomes. Additionally, we considered the more cumulative negative social patterns that have created the risk society (Bell and Bell 1993; Beck 1992). Here, we examine specific alcohol- and drug-related behaviors that increase the chances that regular or prolonged exposure will be detrimental to the health, safety, and well-being of adolescents (Hawkins, Catalano, and Miller 1992; Hawkins and Fitzgibbon 1993).

Intoxicating substances for adolescent and young adults are in and of themselves dangerous, especially under conditions of their physical and social immaturity, and the criminalization of drugs. Overdoses, death, cognitive impairment, loss of motivation, accidents, exposure to deviant persons and lifestyles, disattachment from family and conventional associates, unwanted pregnancies, arrest, imprisonment, suicide, and higher likelihood of contracting the HIV virus and other sexually transmitted diseases—all are possible outcomes of protracted or heavy use of intoxicants (Hawkins et al. 1988; Forst 1991).

Let us take a look at one drug, cocaine, and its highly toxic results, as a telling example of a serious adolescent drug problem. Adolescent cocaine abuse, high in the 1980s, has been associated with a number of psychiatric and psychosocial dysfunctions. Self-report data among 479 drug-abusing adolescent patients in five geographic regions across the United States reveal increasing psychiatric and behavioral symptoms as cocaine use progressed. T. W. Estroff, R. H. Schwartz, and N. G. Hoffman (1989), physician researchers, observed:

They [patients] were nervous, suspicious, and aggressive. They exhibited vegetative signs, including increase in fatigue as cocaine addiction progressed, difficulty in falling asleep, decreased appetite, and dysphoria (anxiety) when they were not using cocaine. . . . There was a significant (25 percent) [and other] self-mutilatory behavior. (p. 553)

Variations in levels of drug use accounted for distinctive risk structures. As Table 7.1 shows, among heavy users there was a cumulative array of disorders, including fighting, stealing, losing a significant other, being forced out of the home, passing bad checks, drug dealing, trading sex for cocaine, and others.

As the study shows, though, not every youth is at equal risk for serious dysfunctions associated with drug abuse. For example, light cocaine users were far less likely to steal from parents or stores, and very unlikely to be arrested for possession, compared with heavy users (1 percent versus 17 percent). Still, the data suggest that most of these adolescent patients had to contend with some serious setbacks in their lives, because as addiction increases, clearly an obsession with obtaining and using cocaine develops.

Table 7.1
Psychosocial Dysfunction among 341 Adolescent Cocaine Abusers

	Light	Intermediate	Heavy	P*
Stealing				
Stealing	12	41	58	0.001
> $500	6	28	54	0.001
Parents	4	17	50	0.001
Stores	4	23	30	0.001
Steal Car	7	21	44	0.001
Passing Bad Checks	15	32	42	0.001
Arrest for Possession	1	4	17	0.001
Fighting	26	48	64	0.001
Losing Girlfriend	27	51	50	0.001
Losing Boyfriend	17	33	78	0.001
Leaving Home	33	37	54	NS**
Parent Requesting Adolescent to Leave Home	21	38	56	0.001
Trading Sex for Cocaine	6	26	60	0.001
Drug Dealing	5	36	64	0.001
Tattoo	7	25	21	0.001

*P = Statistically significant.
**NS = Not significant.

Source: T. W. Estroff, R. H. Schwartz, and N. G. Hoffmann. 1989. "Adolescent Cocaine Abuse." Clinical Pediatrics 28(12): 553.

Increased use requires larger purchases, and eventually the addict must steal money to get his/her supply. Moreover, there is a tendency to abuse other addicting substances such as sedative hypnotics (Estroff, Schwartz, and Hoffmann 1989).

The risk model, then, is useful for specifying conditions likely to be associated with varying levels of use. For example, in the systemic risk model, violence is intrinsic to involvement with an illicit substance, depending upon a) the different types of substance use (e.g., casual, occasional, heavy); b) the different motivations of violent perpetrators; c) the different types of victims; and d) the differential influence by social context (Goldstein 1995). We know that in the United States, systematic violence is an integral part of the social and economic networks of illicit drug users and sellers, and a normal part of the drug lifestyle. Goldstein (1995) says:

Individuals caught in this lifestyle value the experience of substance use, recognize the risks involved, and struggle for survival on a daily basis. That struggle is clearly a major contributor to the total volume of crime and violence in American society. (p. 226)

Risk involves any of the following aggressive interactions (Goldstein 1995; see also Tonry and Wilson 1990):

1. Disputes over territory between rival drug dealers

2. Assaults and homicides committed within drug dealing hierarchies as a means of enforcing rules

3. Robberies of drug dealers and the violent retaliation by the dealer of his/her bosses

4. Elimination of informers

5. Punishment for selling adulterated or phony drugs

6. Punishment for failing to pay one's debts

7. Disputes over drugs or drug paraphernalia

8. Robbery that results in violence

Younger adolescents are least likely to understand the risks involved, especially drug trafficking or sharing needles, compared with older adolescents and adults. Conversely, intravenous drug-taking is related to the high probability of encountering an HIV-contaminated needle or syringe. Although virtually all intravenous heroin and cocaine users are aware of risks, few alter their risk-taking behavior. "Shooting galleries"—private places to shoot up drugs, located in users' apartments, homes, or hotels, as well as in abandoned houses or even outdoor facilities (e.g., parks)—are high-risk sites, as the drug fraternity share needles and sex with little regard for personal danger (Murphy and Waldorf 1991).

In youth studies, risk analysis is especially useful for identifying social, psychological, or ecological conditions that contribute to alcohol and drug experimentation and various levels of use (casual, occasional, heavy, addiction). Research (Johnston, O'Malley, and Backman 1995; Forst and Rojek 1991; Parks 1995; Brooks, Whiteman, and Balka 1997) shows that the risk of addiction is high for youth who reported having

- Low family bonds
- Initiated use at early ages (e.g., fourteen or under)
- One or both parents who are alcoholic or drug addicted
- Adverse school environments
- Peers who regularly use intoxicants
- Victimization
- Run away from home or become homeless (rates are twice to three times greater for homeless adolescents compared to those who live with families or in managed care)
- Scored low on family religiosity
- Actively participated in gangs
- Engaged in high-risk sexual practices (e.g., prostitution, gay sex)

Minority status and being male are not related to higher risk of addiction. Instead, white students are more likely than black students to have had exposure to legal and illegal drugs (Poulin 1991). Gender differences exist both for use and for arrests related to intoxicant use. White and Hispanic females are more likely than blacks or boys to smoke and use alcohol, and Hispanic girls, especially, show progressive use of alcohol, cigarettes, marijuana, and other illicit drugs (Morgan 1995). Although boys and girls are nearly at parity for alcohol and drug use, boys are much more likely to be arrested for drugs or alcohol-/drug-related behavior than girls (Chesney-Lind and Shelden 1993) (see Table 7.2).

Among inner-city teens, the prevalence of violence and sexual activity was directly related to drug use (Vanderschmidt et al. 1993). This suggests that young people use drugs to reinforce and enhance their experience but ignore the possible consequences (e.g., violence gets out of hand, a problem pregnancy ensues, and casual sex leads to a sexually transmitted disease).

In developing countries, a high percentage of youth (up to 60 percent of the total population) experience extremely low levels of schooling and high rates of un-/underemployment. This undermines their capacity to participate in society. In large parts of Africa, Asia, and Latin America, entire communities are degraded by poverty, disillusion, drugs, and alcohol. For example, as a result of the international cocaine business, youth have been drawn into the deadly war of trafficking and violence. Homicides in Rio

Table 7.2

Alcohol-Related and Drug Arrests of Persons under 18 by Gender, 1995 (Number and Percent of Total Arrests)

Offenses	Male Number	Male Percent	Female Number	Female Percent
DUI	8,074	0.6	1,491	0.3
Liquor Laws	55,548	4.0	2,421	4.7
Drunkenness	12,009	0.9	2,243	0.5
*Disorderly Conduct	82,793	5.9	26,512	5.5
Drugs	116,627	8.3	16,696	3.5

*Disorderly Conduct includes a variety of public disorder offenses that typically involve participants in drinking and drug behavior.

Source: U.S. Department of Justice, FBI. *Crime in America, Uniform Crime Reports.* Washington, D.C.: Government Printing Office, 1995.

de Janeiro have tripled in the last decade, and poor men are disproportionately involved in violent deaths, including death from AIDS (Zaluar
and Ribeiro 1995).

In addition to a diagnostic tool, the risk model emphasizes complex linkages between risk factors. Thus, among a group of persistent young adult
offenders in Manchester, England, recognition of the role alcohol plays as
part of a "poly-drug" use pattern related to subsequent criminal behavior
enabled researchers to show the intricate relationship between acquisitive
crime and violence on the one hand, and alcohol and drug use on the other
(Parker 1996).

Prevention and intervention models draw on risk analysis to develop
models to prevent or treat alcohol or drug use/abuse among youth (a topic
we take up in the last section). Teaching skills that will strengthen resistance
to alcohol and other drugs has proven successful under certain conditions—
an egalitarian environment for learning, adaptability of the model to
different problems and situations, and enhancement of community responsibility for all children rather than an exclusive focus on selective troublemakers (Homonoff et al. 1994).

What the risk model often fails to take into account is the *normality* of
alcohol and drug use among youth. Theoretically, nearly every youth is at
risk for this potentially troublesome behavior. Such a global approach has
little utility for predicting more-serious social problems emanating from
more-intensive use/abuse. A more useful tactic for predicting outcomes is
to identify *levels of risk* (e.g., casual, occasional, heavy, abuse), type of
drug (alcohol, marijuana, or other drugs), *differential motivation for use*,
and *situations and settings that encourage or deter* drug involvement.

The Normalization Model

When a social product that was once considered deviant (bad, mad, or
sad) becomes "normalized," it undergoes a significant shift in social frameworks. Not only do behaviors shift, but attitudes, values, beliefs, and meanings about the product can reverse themselves. Christopher Wren (1997)
argues that important social factors have created a more positive view of
marijuana: Media images of sex, drugs, and violence could be a contributing factor in delinquency; and contradictory beliefs and behaviors in
adult society about legal and illegal drugs influence young people's attitudes
and behavior to see the drug in more-favorable terms. The Internet influence may have a profound impact as well (see Box 7-A).

Cross-cultural data demonstrate that sites and situations play a crucial
role in drug use. For example, a study of young people involved in the
"rave scene" (dance clubs) in Glasgow, Scotland, found that fifty-one discrete drugs were used by the respondents (Forsyth 1996). Alcohol and cannabis (marijuana) were the most frequently used drugs among this group,

Box 7-A
An Internet Drug Culture Appeals to Youthful Eavesdroppers

Web sites are now open channels for purveying drugs, and teenagers need only have access to a computer to download the latest information on drugs and drug paraphernalia. With nearly 5 million children from two to 17 years of age using on-line services in 1996, and more than nine million college students who use the Internet regularly, the youth market may be a rapidly growing source of new drug users. High Times, which advertises on-line drug products, claims that "we are averaging 200,000 home page visitors a month."

The images are ready-made for youthful interest. Cartoons deliver the young potential patron into a mail-order house in Los Angeles, which promises all you need to know about "legal highs," "growing hallucinogens," "cannabis alchemy," "cooking with cannabis," and other "trippy, phat groovy things." A Canadian Web page offers "everything marijuana-and-hemp-related: books to bongs, clothes to cosmetics . . . hemp and marijuana seeds."

The Internet drug culture has proliferated in a number of ways. First, the tolerance or outright endorsement of illegal drugs, especially marijuana in on-line forums and chat groups; second, availability of explicit instructions for growing, processing, and consuming drugs; third, the emerging grass-roots sentiment for modifying or abandoning existing drug laws; fourth, the positive drug messages from on-line testimonials promising nearly instant access to drugs. A cocaine user said:

> I always enjoy the first toot (snort). I can place a phone call and within an hour get it delivered. It's as routine as coffee in the morning. And just about as necessary.

Sophisticated graphics modeled on alcohol and tobacco products promote drugs as recreational. In one counterculture Web site called Paranoia, a cartoon had a pothead announce: "You know this stuff should be legal! It can make an ordinary day so much brighter." Another cartoon character Pot-Peye, who resembles the spinach-guzzling Popeye, smokes his spinach instead. On-line chat groups offer misinformation, such as a seasoned user who responded to an inquiry about mixing methamphetamine with alcohol (a deadly combination) with "Yeah, you can drink on speed, and drink and drink."

According to reformers, drug prevention efforts appear fruitless against a technology that not only appeals to younger tastes (and often parents are unaware of children's access), but also undermines efforts to prevent young people from experimenting with drugs. On the flip side, the Internet allows an "unfettered discussion" about the legalization of drugs, and may become a major source for an expanded public dialogue on drug reform.

Source: Christopher Wren. 1997b. "A Seductive Drug Culture Flourishes on the Internet." *New York Times* (February 20): A10.

followed by Ecstasy, tobacco, LSD, and amphetamines. Inside these dance settings, amphetamine, nitrates, and Ecstasy were most commonly used, but dance participants used a variety of other drugs in other arenas (home, work, non-dance recreational settings).

Alcohol in the United States is illegal for anyone under twenty-one in most states, yet it is used regularly among adolescents of all social classes and environments. A New Hampshire study on rural adolescents' drinking behavior shows that in a three-year cohort-based study of 1,106 rural public school children, deterrence programs had little impact for preventing drinking alcohol. Among the senior high school cohort, only 6.3 percent had not initiated drinking (Stevens, Mott, and Youells 1996). Use of alcohol was associated with regular drinking in junior high school years. Adult role models contributed to tolerance and encouragement of alcohol use. Serious problems were more likely to cluster under conditions of early onset of regular use, such as drunkenness in sixth, seventh and eighth grades; friends that regularly used; poor educational achievement; and a high tolerance for deviance (Stevens, Mott, and Youells 1996).

The normalization of alcohol in American society is so complete that the origins of the historical connection between alcohol, crime, and violence have for the most part vanished (Parker and Rebhun 1995). This collective amnesia, in the absence of preventive policies, helps to explain why social control over alcohol consumption for youth is so ineffectual. In the model of aggregate youth consumption proposed by Parker and Rebhun (1995), a host of factors raises the likelihood of easy access and use, and with regular and heavy use, concomitant social problems. Access entails economic factors, such as relatively low price and low taxation rates, wide availability, urban settings, percent of young people unemployed, lack of alternative social and recreational opportunities, and legal minimum age. When you alter only one component—raising the minimum age of drinking—the model predicts that homicide incidence, a clear-cut indicator of violence, will drop (Parker and Rebhun 1995).

This model suggests that normalization processes can be reversed. We are witnessing such reversals in the reduced tolerance of tobacco smoking in public places, as an outgrowth of the antismoking movement; the reduced consumption of high-alcohol-content distilled spirits (e.g. whisky, rum, gin), in favor of beer and wine; and the ebbing of the youth crack epidemic in inner-city America, as a result of a change in the standards of the street subculture (Butterfield 1997c).

To further reduce alcohol consumption among youth and other high-risk groups will be an uphill effort. Even when persons have an accurate perception of their risk, they often continue to drink. A case in point is fetal alcohol exposure, which continues to be an important public health concern. Women who drink during pregnancy increase their risk for miscarriage, low-birthweight babies, and babies with fetal alcohol syndrome (FAS) (Peterson and Lowe 1992). FAS is now the third largest cause of birth defects in the United States and the major cause of mental retardation (Warren and Bast 1988). Such children are also at increased risk for learning disabilities, speech and language problems, hyperactivity, and attention deficit in childhood.

Programs aimed to prevent fetal alcohol exposure have had only minimal impact. Information campaigns, such as warning labels on alcoholic beverages, public service announcements, educational efforts, or actual alcoholism treatment programs (of which few have been targeted toward high-risk women) have not had their desired results. Despite the increased public awareness, 70–75 percent of women drinkers continue to drink during pregnancy. In fact, the prevalence of alcohol consumption at levels that may be harmful to the fetus is relatively high from a public health perspective. Between 3 and 10 percent of pregnant women report daily or heavy consumption of alcohol, a pattern that has been associated with harming the unborn. The low percentage undoubtedly reflects underreporting of alcohol use (Peterson and Lowe et al. 1992). Adolescents learn drinking behavior during an impressionable period, and similar to these intoxicant-using pregnant women, carry their drinking patterns into adulthood, often regardless of the consequences.

Normalization policies can operate in paradoxical ways, as well, as when public policies encourage some toxic substances to head off more dangerous drug usage. A concerted effort by the Netherlands to keep youth off hard drugs, such as heroin and cocaine, involves *de facto* legalization of soft drugs. This has opened the way for a hidden world of a small countercultural association of individuals whose livelihood and day-to-day activities revolve around the cultivation and distribution of cannabis products to "coffeeshops" in Amsterdam. Cannabis supply networks have their base in household settings, and dealers are guided by normative codes through which these particular social networks define themselves and one another (Korf 1990).

In the final analysis, young people's drinking or drugging is patterned on that of adult society and general social expectations, with variations of use in type of intoxicants and behavior outcomes dependent upon availability, age of onset, predrug psychosocial vulnerabilities, treatment experience, and other conditions. As long as underage drug use and male drunkenness reflect the relationship between tradition, morality, and belonging, as it does in traditional societies—for example, among Colonialists, early West settlers, and today, young people in Western Scotland—it remains largely unproblematic to social members (A. Dean 1990).

ADOLESCENT PATTERNS OF ALCOHOL/DRUG USE

A 1995 Columbia University Center on Addiction and Substance Abuse survey on adolescents and drug use showed that American adolescents overwhelmingly perceive drugs as the greatest problem they confront, outweighing all other issues (e.g., crime, sex, social pressure, grades). Adults and adolescents inhabit different universes when it comes to understandings about drugs. Thirty percent of the adolescents surveyed believed it was easy to obtain heroin or cocaine; 82 percent of adults queried indicated that they thought such drugs were readily accessible to adolescents (in Binder, Geis, and Bruce 1997).

What are major patterns of alcohol and drug use among teenagers? Four distinct patterns will be explored: 1) alcohol and drug use from 1980 to 1992 among high school seniors; 2) use among adolescents after 1992; 3) use patterns of juvenile male arrestees to compare a heavy-drug using population of adolescents with a normal sample of high school students; and 4) other adolescent drug risk patterns.

Alcohol and Drug Use, 1980–1992

Self-reported alcohol and drug use for four senior high school class cohorts—1980, 1985, 1990, and 1992—reveals that over this period, almost all substance use had declined. Whereas almost 88 percent of seniors were using alcohol in 1980, this figure decreased to 76.8 in 1992. Likewise, marijuana/hashish show very sharp drops in use over the twelve-year period: 48.8 percent in 1980 and 21.9 percent in 1992. Cocaine use, somewhat pronounced in 1980 (12.3 percent), declined to negligible amounts (3.1 percent) by 1992, whereas alcohol and marijuana and its derivatives remained the psychoactive substances of choice among seniors.

Drug Use, after 1992

But a few years can make a difference in drug use, especially among teens. The 1996 Federal Drug Survey (in Goldberg 1996) found that overall drug use nationwide remained flat from 1992 to 1995, and was far below the peak levels of the late 1970s among adults. For teenagers, though, the survey found that use of marijuana among twelve- to seventeen-year-olds rose 141 percent compared with 1992; use of LSD and other hallucinogens rose 183 percent; and use of cocaine rose 166 percent in the same period (1992–1995). At the same time, emergency room cases connected to marijuana rose by 96 percent, and those connected to heroin rose 58 percent (Goldberg 1996). Citing reasons for the sharp increases, authorities indicated lack of prevention, parental tolerance, "generational forgetting" (this generation does not know about the dangers of drugs the way the last one did), the glamorization of drugs in the media, as well as news reports favoring decriminalizing marijuana (Goldberg 1996; Wren 1997).

The volatility of student alcohol/drug preferences should be kept in mind. These drug preferences are not written in stone, but instead, change fairly rapidly with shifts in tolerance, or changed public attitudes about specific drugs. In 1996, heroin and methamphetamine use rapidly supplanted crack cocaine as the drug of choice among addicts, whereas a variety of "boutique drugs," along with marijuana, are now gaining favor among young people. The number of heroin addicts in the United States has been estimated at close to one million, and teenagers are among the more likely group for heroin-related deaths (Flores 1996). According to a study by the White House office of National Drug Control Policy, teen use of heroin and "club drugs"—hallucinogenic drugs, such as LSD—dispensed during late-night parties, is common practice. Young middle-class white users, in particular, have come to disdain crack as a "ghetto drug" (*Bellingham Herald* [WA], June 25, 1997: A9).

It is a mistake to combine all drug users into a single category, and presume that use equals abuse. The epidemiological statistics strongly suggest that the occasional use of drugs by most adolescents is nonproblematic, a different phenomenon from drug abuse, which is linked to an antisocial personality—or what criminologists refer to as a "deviance syndrome" (Hawkins et al. 1988). Drug abuse, especially in early and mid-adolescence, appears to be part of a general pattern of rebellion and nonconforming behavior; or possibly, of self-medication for untreated mental illness.

Research shows four levels of use: (1) drug initiation, (2) occasional drug use, (3) regular drug use, and (4) drug abuse (Johnston, O'Malley, and Backman 1995). Drug initiation in middle adolescence is normative behavior, as long as use remains very occasional and recreational only. But early onset of drug use predicts subsequent "misuse," leading to a variety of negative outcomes, including poor health, low social functioning, learning disorders, poor school performance, disorderly conduct, arrest, and incarceration for young users.

Juvenile Male Arrestees

The engaged adolescent, exhibiting no or low marijuana use, contrasts sharply with the disengaged, who may be polydrug abusers and who markedly lack social integration into adult norms and activities. Juvenile arrestees may offer the classic example of the socially nonintegrated modality.

Take the Washington, DC, data on juvenile male arrestees/detainees, for instance (National Institute of Justice 1997). Here we find some of the nation's highest reported drug use (among test cities), as determined by urinalysis testing. Compare this cohort's drug use patterns with the type of offense committed (see Table 7.3).

Whereas cocaine use is relatively low among this group, marijuana and other drugs are involved in the greatest proportion of these arrestees' offenses. The data also suggest a link between race, nonintegration into school, work, community activities, and crime. Because 95 percent of the arrestees were black, we surmise that lack of legitimate opportunities to-

Table 7.3

Percent Positive for Drugs, by Offense Category (N's in Parentheses)

	Cocaine	Marijuana	Any Drug
Total Males (390)	**9**	**61**	**64**
Violent Offenses (110)	4	48	49
Robbery (29)	3	52	52
Assault (51)	6	35	37
Weapons (25)	0	68	68
All Others (5)	20	60	60
Property Offenses (90)	**3**	**61**	**64**
Stolen Vehicle (67)	3	64	67
Larceny/theft (8)	0	50	60
Burglary (5)	0	20	40
All others (10)	10	70	70
Drug Offenses (97)	**16**	**77**	**80**
Sales (77)	18	77	80
Possession (20)	10	80	80
Other (92)	**13**	**58**	**62**
Public Peace (14)	15	57	71
Probation/parole violation (0)	0	0	0
All others (78)	13	58	60

Source: Adapted from *1994 Annual Report on Adult and Juvenile Arrestees,* National Institute of Justice. Washington, D.C.: Department of Justice, p. 73.

gether with family breakdown, poor learning environment in school, few jobs, low self-esteem, and other expectations for success all play a part in drug-related crime (we take another look at the link between drugs and crime in a later section).

Other Drug Risk Patterns

Not only does the evidence support the connection between drugs and social disengagement, including crime, but it also points to negative health practices that accompany regular or abusive drug use. Interview data were used to examine lifetime and current sexual and substance abuse behavior among a predominantly Hispanic and black gay and bisexual sample of adolescent males in New York City (Rotheram-Borus et al. 1991). These youth reported high rates of lifetime use: alcohol (76 percent), marijuana (42 percent), and cocaine/crack (25 percent), although none reported intravenous drug use. Such drug practices are significantly related to sexual risk acts. For example, condoms were never or inconsistently used by 52 percent of the youth (although 80 percent of the population engaged in anal sex), and 22 percent bartered sex for money or drugs (Rotheram-Borus et al. 1991). This has serious implications for contracting the HIV virus and AIDS, because of high sexual promiscuity and the practice of "survival sex" (sex for food or shelter).

Sexual profiles of delinquent and homeless youth in San Francisco and overseas reveal similar health risks for young people involved in drugs and sex. But in addition to deteriorated health and high levels of sexually transmitted diseases because of abusive drug practices, these youth have high rates of suicides and accidents. Alienation, lack of financial resources, criminality, and future exclusion from the labor market are tied to abusive drug use (Forst 1991), a condition that holds for similarly situated youth in Sweden (Hammarstrom 1991).

The impact of drug abuse upon adolescent suicide has been linked to escalated use of drugs, as a way of coping with perceived overwhelming stresses of life. In fact, drug abuse among adolescents has been proposed as a form of "slow suicide" (Downey 1990–91), a pain-numbing process that eventually reduces the individual's capacity to recognize signs of acute risk.

The suicide and drug data point to one reason why young people may choose to engage in abusive drug practices. For most youth, though, reasons for using drugs are far less sinister. Among a teenage sample of 2,537 students in rural Oklahoma, findings show five typical explanations for drug use: belonging, coping, pleasure, creativity, and aggression (Novacek, Raskin, and Hogan 1991). Even drug dealing among ghetto youth can be a "survival strategy." Both in the Caribbean and inner-city America, economic underdevelopment and poor schools relate to persistent social inequalities, of which drug abuse and drug trafficking are symptoms, not causes, of youth problems (Quimby 1990).

Native American youth reveal very high rates of alcohol and drug use, compared with non-Native Americans, and they tend to use these in ways that increase their risk. Getting very drunk, drinking while driving, and using drugs and alcohol together are pervasive practices among reservation youth (Beauvais 1992a). Young people's participation in heavy drinking, gambling, violence, drug abuse, and other compulsive behaviors weaken relationship ties and contribute to the degradation of Native American families and communities. Higher substance abuse rates among Indian youth compared with non-Indian youth are correlated with a low belief among these youthful users that drugs are harmful (which has a deterrent effect). Non-Indian youth, by contrast, report higher rates of perceived harm, congruent with their lower rates of drug abuse and negative attitudes about drugs (Beauvais 1992b).

The modernist version of adolescent drug involvement tends to pathologize drugs and their users. For example, the reasoning goes that adolescents use drugs because they cannot deal with the gruesome facts of their existence. As they become disengaged from institutional settings—family, work, religion, and community—their risks for using artificial props to sustain themselves in hostile environments accelerates. Drugs provide temporary relief from the ills of poverty, lack of opportunity, social alienation, and simply the pain of being alive (Flores 1996).

Jeff Ferrell (1995a) opposes this single line of reasoning and argues that young people often seek situated pleasures, and the shared excitement and "adrenaline rushes" that define the experience and meaning of crime for many of those who participate in it. Rather than labeling this behavior as individual pathology, Ferrell says that it should be perceived as social decay. Criminal pleasure associated with being a consumer of illegal drugs, pornography, prostitution, and other potentially risky situation has a thrill quality: It qualifies as fun or entertainment—"edgework" in Lyng's (1993) study. The "outlaw," who is part of a deviant or insurgent subculture, does not gain wealth or power from the activity, but instead relishes the rush of pleasure, excitement, and escape from the mundane. Drug use, then, should be redefined to take into account its function as an alternative avenue to identity and meaning in the context of "dead time" inside a decaying political economy (Ferrell 1995b, 9).

THE UNENDING WAR

The so-called U.S. "war on drugs"—involving massive government enforcement efforts at the federal, state, and local levels to restrict supply and punish dealers/users—is not just about cocaine and heroin, the "hard street drugs"; nor has marijuana been *de facto* decriminalized (see Inciardi 1992 for an overview). The fight against drugs involving over fifty federal agencies has degenerated into a war against minorities, poor people, and the young. In fact, today when we have a scarcity of prison cells for murderers, rapists, robbers, and other violent criminals, there are more people in federal and state prisons for marijuana offenses than at any other time in U.S. history (Irwin and Austin 1997).

Schlosser (1994a; 1994b) takes up this paradox in a two-part article on marijuana and the law in *Atlantic Monthly*, arguing that rigorous enforcement of marijuana laws has resulted in four million arrests since the early 1980s without diminishing the use of the drug in the general population. Arrests for drug crimes now exceed one million per year, and the number of people imprisoned has doubled since 1986. Drug offenders comprise more than 60 percent of the federal prison population, and nearly 25 percent of state prisoners (Bureau of Justice Statistics 1996). In a follow-up article, Schlosser (1997b) asserts that despite the most rigorous sentences doled out to pot users and dealers (more people are now incarcerated for marijuana than for manslaughter or rape), marijuana use among teenagers has actually risen. He concludes that a society that punishes marijuana crimes more severely than violent crimes "is caught in the grip of a deep psychosis."

Owing to mandatory-minimum sentences, which prevents judges from assigning penalties that are based on individual histories, many of those convicted for "soft" drug use are receiving stiff prison sentences, often for simply using or street-level dealing. In Alabama, a young man was given a life sentence for possessing a single joint (Schlosser 1997b). To make space for these drug offenders, violent criminals are released because of court-ordered rules on prison overcrowding (Irwin and Austin 1997).

What is this war, and why is it waged at such high social and economic costs? The drug war is the leading growth industry in federal funding. The annual budget rose from $1 billion per annum when President Ronald Reagan declared his version of the war on drugs to more than $16 billion today. The overall federal, state, and local effort has cost nearly $290 billion, according to Drug Strategies, a nonpartisan policy group (Frankel 1997). Roughly two-thirds of the annual drug budget or $10.5 billion has been earmarked to reduce the supply through law enforcement programs to eliminate production, especially in Latin America. Treatment and prevention receive the smallest proportion after all law enforcement requirements have been met. Yet treating drug users is a more cost-effective way to reduce consumption, than are law enforcement efforts to curtail supply. Drug traders appear to be the most spectacular winners of this war. The U.S. drug trade produces $50–$60 billion per year in illegal profits (Frankel 1997).

Social costs of drugs are equally devastating: over fourteen thousand dead from crime, overdoses, and illnesses and $67 billion in social, health, and criminal costs. A little-discussed travesty of the drug war is the militarization of the U.S.-Mexican border, which has resulted in local community outrage, and at least one death of an American teenage goat herder by a Marine sentinel (Verhovek 1997).

Bear in mind that drug enforcement primarily revolves around marijuana. The so-called drug epidemic involves thirteen million users, a little more than two million of these are cocaine and heroin addicts. Government prosecution in this country primarily focuses on the millions of users, growers, and dealers in violation of marijuana laws (Pollan 1997).

The first broadly defined mandatory sentencing of narcotic offenders was contained in the Boggs Act, which was passed during the McCarthy era of the 1950s amid the tensions of the Korean War and domestic fear of Communist subversion. Antidrug mandatory sentences were imposed in 1956, leading James V. Bennett, director of the U.S. Bureau of Prisons, to attribute the passage of such laws to "hysteria" (Schlosser 1994a, 85; Musto 1987).

By the late 1960s both political parties conceded that the antidrug sentences were a failure. Authorities found them overly severe, unjust, and ineffective at preventing narcotic use. In 1970 Congress repealed almost all the mandatory penalties for drug offenders, an act applauded by, among others, Congressman (later President) George Bush, who predicted that these "penal reforms" would "result in better justice and more appropriate sentences" (Schlosser 1994b, 87). In 1977 President Carter endorsed decriminalization of marijuana, and even the Drug Enforcement Administration was entertaining the idea. Eleven states, containing over one-third of the nation's population, had already taken the step (Pollan 1997).

The American antidrug movement was not silenced by the weakening of marijuana laws, or the ebullient youth outcry of "pot, freedom, license" (Schlosser 1994a, 52). Conservative parents' groups, under the aegis of the National Federation of Parents For A Drug-Free Youth, and other parent-led organizations created an alliance with the Drug Enforcement Administration (DEA), and launched a broad-based effort against marijuana. The new antidrug coalition claimed that not only was marijuana use reaching epidemic proportions, but also it was threatening to destroy the moral fiber of the young because of the fixation on pleasure and rejection of responsibility to society. The election of Ronald Reagan to the presidency brought the war on drugs into the White House (Nancy Reagan's "just say no" campaign). The DEA reversed itself from declaring that decriminalization was a policy worth trying three years before, to calling marijuana the most urgent drug problem facing the United States (Schlosser 1994b).

By 1984, politicians reversed the drug policy, and Congress began its deliberate calibrations of drug sentencing by relying on the mandatory-minimum sentences—mandating that offenders be sentenced for specific time periods, depending upon the drug/offense. Today, U.S. attorneys have sole authority to decide on sentencing. The only way a defendant can be

---

Box 7-B
Putting Pressure on Drug Defendants

In Kansas City, Tara S. Brown, a 19-year-old first offender with an 8-month-old daughter, cooperated with the government on a drug case involving PCP. Her mother had been involved with her in the case, but because Brown refused to implicate her mother, the government decreed that she was not being "cooperative." Brown was given a ten-year prison sentence without the chance of parole.

Source: James A. Inciardi, Ruth Horowitz, and Anne E. Pottieger. 1993. *Street Kids, Street Drugs, Street Crime.* Belmont, MA: Heath.

---

certain of avoiding the mandatory-minimum sentencing is to plead guilty and give "substantial assistance" in the prosecution of someone else. Guilty pleas and "cooperating with" the prosecution avoid expensive trials and supply valuable evidence. But naming others implicated in drug distribution can lead to extremely negative results: retaliation by members of the drug network, or a relationship crisis if a person betrays a friend or loved one. The dilemma for the defendant can be overwhelming (see Box 7-B).

FUTILITY OF THE ANTIDRUG CAMPAIGN

Stamping out cocaine has proved as futile as the government attack on marijuana. Over the past twenty years, governments have sprayed herbicides on fields of coca leaf; raided laboratories that refine coca paste; seized and destroyed tons of cocaine powder; arrested or killed thousands of smugglers; confiscated personal assets; and locked up dealers and users throughout their countries. Why hasn't the eradication program worked?

The cocaine habit is firmly enmeshed in American culture, and has survived market declines before. In the nineteenth century, cocaine and other narcotics were common palliatives, prescribed by physicians and available over the counter or from mail-order catalogues. Cocaine had extensive avenues for ingestion: sniffing for sinusitis or hay fever, drinking in Coca-Cola, and smoking, inhaling, or injecting for pleasure. Citizen concern over addiction—together with decreased public tolerance and the association of cocaine with violence, paranoia, and occupational failures—led to federal moves to control use. The Pure Food and Drug Act of 1906 was the first step, and entailed correct labeling of any "patent medicine" (including morphine, cocaine, and cannabis). The Harrison Act of 1914 was far more comprehensive in outlawing all narcotics. Within a century, the definition of cocaine shifted from a belief in its curative powers ("wonder substance") to counteract melancholy (depression), and the 1980's version of cocaine as a "crisis sweeping our nation" (Musto 1987).

The cocaine trade now links South and North America in a complex web of corruption and violence, one that threatens entire governments (e.g., Mexico, Colombia). Cocaine is not just any large commercial enterprise that rides and falls on public and government favor. The resilience of the cocaine trade has to do with a number of elements: very large profits for traffickers—Mexican drug traffickers earn up to $10 billion a year—extensive and successful bribery of officials and police officers; the sweatshop level of the industry that taps a limitless supply of cheap labor; and a global market of addicted customers (Wren 1997, A1, A10).

When cocaine began to lose its appeal in the 1980s, distributors created a new market: rock cocaine, made by cooking the powder with baking soda and water to make "crack." Crack's attraction for users resides in its instant high and cheap price. Powdered cocaine sells for around $30 to $40 a gram in New York City; a pebble of crack costs $2 to $4. Low price and high access have special appeal for poor youngsters (Inciardi, Horowitz, and Pottieger 1993).

The crack-cocaine connection has been especially devastating for younger female crack users, often involving relations of dependency and domination by men who use access to drugs for control (Mahan 1996). The social pathology associated with the crack subculture degrades all users, but exerts special hardships on women who experience humiliation and assault, degrading sexual encounters, unsafe sex, robbery, rape, and torture from men who invariably control the drug supply (Mahan 1996). The life of the crack prostitute signifies the lowest rung of the drug ladder. It also repeats the cycle of victimization these women experienced growing up (Mahan 1996; see also McCoy, Miles, and Inciardi 1995).

Writing for the Eisenhower Foundation, Lynn Curtis (1992) critically takes stock of the antidrug policy. He claims that the federal government has withdrawn investments from young, poor, and minority populations. Instead, by a series of systematic moves, the government has decreased the effective tax rate on the rich; reduced domestic policy spending on many effective programs for families and youth; encouraged a massive, but cost-ineffective prison-building program that doubled the prison population over a decade; and made the United States the leading industrial country in incarceration rates, surpassing Russia and South Africa. Additionally, Curtis points out that these trends have resulted in increased racial tensions, exacerbated child poverty, led to doubling in reports of child abuse over a decade, and contributed to a steady increase in crime in the same period.

Importantly, from the critical ecology perspective the most destructive aspect of a war on drugs is that metaphors of war distract us from the realities of class, race, and power; of poverty and disadvantage; of third world poor communities in the midst of first world prosperity; and of social exclusion and isolation of young people, minorities, poor families, and other vulnerable populations.

KIDS, DRUGS, AND CRIME

Research on the links between drugs and crime among youth have been comprehensively explored (Tonry and Wilson 1990; U.S. Department of Justice 1994a; U.S. Department of Health and Human Services 1996; National Institute of Justice 1997; The Lindesmith Center 1997; Inciardi, Horowitz, and Pottieger 1993). The drug/crime connection is one that continues to resist coherent analysis, both because cause and effect are difficult to distinguish, and because the role of the drug-prohibition laws in causing and labeling drug-related crime is typically overlooked (Nadelmann 1989).

The research identifies four connections between drugs and crime, at least three of which would be greatly diminished if the drug-prohibition laws were repealed.

1. Producing, selling, buying and consuming controlled and banned substances is itself a crime that affects hundreds of thousands of users. Decriminalizing drugs removes all users from participating in crime.

2. Many illicit-drug users commit crimes such as robbery and burglary, as well as drug dealing, prostitution, and numbers running, to earn money to purchase the often high-priced illicit drugs. Unlike the millions of alcoholics who can financially support their habit with relatively low-cost substances, many cocaine and heroin addicts spend hundreds or even thousands of dollars per week.

3. A drug/crime connection occurs in the commission of crimes, especially violent crimes, by people under the influence of illicit drugs.

4. The drug/crime link also involves the violent, intimidating and corrupting behavior of the drug traffickers. Illegal markets tend to foster violence, not only because they attract criminally inclined persons, but also because participants in the market have no access to legal institutions to resolve their disputes. Most law-enforcement officials agree that the dramatic increase in urban murder rates during the past few years can be explained almost entirely by the rise of drug-dealer killings. The current policy has failed to stem the tide of inner-city users, but it has led to juveniles getting caught up in trafficking and contributed to the demoralization of entire neighborhoods (Lindesmith Center 1997, 1).

Crack has had a particularly pernicious influence on the young. Among teenage users/dealers, crack serves to reinforce a sense of invulnerability, of immortality. Avoidable dangers—street violence, arrest, overdose, and death—are treated as part of the intoxicating experience with such dangers viewed as challenges to be overcome. Inciardi, Horowitz, and Pottieger's (1993) research on 611 inner-city "serious delinquents" in Miami reveals sustained drug use among these youth. The study found that alcohol use acted as the first stage in the drug/crime career of these serious delinquents. Very early onset of alcohol and drug use, often with an adult present, were some of the findings. Here are some median ages of this sample for first trying alcohol, age at first getting high, age of use without an adult present, using with peers, and using it regularly—three or more times per week (Inciardi, Horowitz, and Pottieger 1993):

- 6.8 First tried alcohol (N=611)
- 8.8 First time drunk (N=608)
- 9.5 First alcohol without an adult present (N=608)
- 10.8 First time drinking with peers
- 11.0 Started regular drinking (N=328)

Drug histories for this group, similar to alcohol, reveal early initiation and regular use of a wide variety of drugs. For example, over half the group tried cocaine at under thirteen years of age. Polydrug use and abuse also characterizes this Miami sample. Table 7.4 summarizes age of initiation and age at regular use for a variety of street drugs.

In addition to heavy drug use, the criminal involvement of this group is substantial. Among the 611 youths who reported committing some 429,136 crimes during the twelve months prior to interview, there was an average of 702 offenses for each youth (Inciardi, Horowitz, and Pottieger 1993, 175). About 60 percent of these crimes are "drug business" offenses, entailing retail sales of small quantities, but also manufacture of crack, drug transportation, and lesser offenses, such as serving as lookout during a sale. Among the 429,136 offenses, 92.8 percent entail four crime types: drug business, vice, shoplifting, and dealing in stolen property. Only 4.3 percent of the total offenses involved major felonies (e.g., robberies, assaults, burglaries, motor vehicle thefts). The research also highlights the importance of drug use as a causal factor in the development of adolescent criminal involvement, including violent crime. In fact, Inciardi and associates (1993) show that crack-market participation is strongly associated with more serious acts of violence (robbery and assault), as well as a large number of violent offenses per offender.

The research also distinguished gender differences in types of crimes committed—being male was positively correlated with major felonies and drug offenses, whereas being female was positively associated with petty larcenies, prostitution, and procuring. The study took note of the marked contrast in numbers of crimes committed between crack *users* (without any involvement in the crack business) and crack *dealers* + (those, who in addition to sales, manufactured, smuggled, or wholesaled the product). Non-crack-business youth committed a median of 375.9 crimes, and these highly involved crack dealers committed a median number of 1,419.1 offenses.

Overall, the criminological research over the last decade or so has em-

Table 7.4
Age of Drug Initiation and Regular Use

Age	Type of Drug	Percent Using
• 10.4	First tried marijuana	100.0
• 11.4	Regular use of marijuana	100.0
• 12.3	First tried cocaine	99. 2
• 13.0	Regular use of cocaine	93.3
• 12.8	First tried heroin	56.5
• 12.7	First regular use of heroin	16.2
• 12.6	First tried prescription depressants	75.8
• 13.2	First regular use of prescription depressants	44.7
• 12.7	First tried speed	59.9
• 13.6	First regular use of speed	14.9
• 13.6	First tried crack	95.7
• 14.0	First regular use of crack	85.6

Source: Adapted from James A. Inciardi, R. Horowitz, and A. E. Pottieger. 1993. *Street Kids, Street Drugs, Street Crime.* Belmont, MA: Heath.

phasized that neighborhoods with high crime and delinquency rates also have the highest prevalence of narcotics use (Tonry and Wilson 1990; Inciardi, Horowitz, and Pottieger 1993). Serious delinquency does not occur in a social vacuum, but rather flourishes in those city areas with poverty, low education, low occupational skills, poor housing, overcrowding, high drop-out rates, single parent households, and transience (Inciardi, Horowitz, and Pottieger 1993; Inciardi and Pottieger 1991; Inciardi and McElrath 1995).

What this research on the link between drugs and crime makes clear is that the attractions of a conventional adult life in these disadvantaged con-

---

Box 7-C
Youth and Drugs: Victims or Offenders?

James A. Inciardi, the senior author of *Street Kids, Street Drugs, and Street Crime*, together with his colleagues, conducted extensive fieldwork interviews, when analyzing their sample of 611 serious delinquents. Here is an interview that expresses the deep sense of hopelessness that many youth experience, once caught in the addiction trap with no place to go.

> In many ways you can say that I'm pretty close to the end of the line, maybe even past the end of the line. I'm 16 years old and I'm strung out on a couple of different drugs. I've turned at least a thousand tricks (prostitution); I've been raped so many times I've lost count—starting off with my father when I was 7 and ending off with a priest when I was 15, with an assortment of other chickenshits, assholes, and scumbags in between; I've stolen everything there is to steal; I've cut up a lot of people, a few pretty badly; I've been arrested 19 times and been fucked over by the system. . . . I mean literally fucked by a cop, a correction officer, and fucked again by my lawyer. . . . And to add insult to injury I'm probably HIV-positive, which means I'm gonna fucking die. What are you gonna do with me? Hand me over to some social worker? Tell me to clean up my act? Put me in a convent? Put me back in jail so I can be fucked over, or just fucked by somebody else all over again. How about college? Can you send me to college? Or you can get me a job, maybe something really good like making fries at Burger King? Give me a break and just leave me a-fucking-alone.

Source: James A. Inciardi, Ruth Horowitz and Anne E. Pottieger. 1993. *Street Kids, Street Drugs, Street Crime.* Belmont, MA: Heath, pp. 189–90.

---

texts may be particularly difficult to promote. Life in the streets is not only fun (at least initially), but can be economically rewarding for enterprising youth. A twelve-year-old drug dealer, a child not old enough for a legal job, can easily earn $100 a week, plus a daily bonus of two or three crack rocks. A seventeen-year-old in the drug business may earn $500 a week, including free vacation trips, and a larger daily crack bonus. By the time a youth realizes that drugs have jeopardized his/her future, it may be too late (see Box 7-C).

PREVENTION, INTERVENTION, AND LEGALIZATION

Keep this young man (Box 7-C) in mind when we consider the various policy proposals that have been advanced to prevent or treat youthful drug addicts. Among youth who combine drugs and crime in a street lifestyle, the likelihood of de-escalating their level of drug use or of kicking the habit entirely are remote. Short of drastic reorganization of families, work, and inner-city economies—which is possibly the only genuine drug prevention— many of these drug-oriented youth are destined to be a *problem drug use* population (Botvin 1990). Young people who begin their drug careers early and have a daily polydrug abuse habit by middle to late adolescence will inevitably experience severe and repeated adverse consequences: social conflicts, behavioral failure, emotional or psychological difficulties, physical impairments, and victimizations.

Among drug-oriented delinquents, repeated arrests and incarceration are likely to be the case. Even marijuana, once considered a benign substance by 1960s "hippies" and some politicians, when used frequently by drug-oriented juveniles, indicates *commitment to a lifestyle* (Inciardi, Horowitz, and Pottieger 1993, 47). This lifestyle may revolve around non-school attendance, unemployment, and involvement in property crime. Intervention for this population promises to be retributive justice only: law-and-order solutions, including arrests and lengthy prison terms.

PROPOSED SOLUTION: PREVENTION

Consider the array of non-criminal-justice preventive approaches in Table 7.5, and determine who you think could benefit from the different approaches. What assumptions are being made by policymakers regarding the "target" population? How effective would any of these approaches be for altering the drug practices of the street youth group discussed by Inciardi and his associates (see above section)?

The major limitation for successfully intervening upon street youth in either preventing or treating drug addiction is that the approaches outlined in Table 7.5 require a highly supportive environment. Such an environment must be capable of creating moral appeals against the use of drugs, of arousing a sustaining fear of drugs as dangerous substances, and of using techniques—such as "psychological inoculation"—which teaches youth by forewarning them of the likelihood of pressure for refusing drugs and alcohol, and by providing them with the necessary skills for countering these pressures (Botvin 1990). For nondeviant youth who have never tried drugs, programs emphasizing "resistance-skill" training could focus on some of the following:

1. Increase participants' resistance to negative social influences to engage in substance use.

2. Focus on cognitive-behavior training, including anxiety reduction, effective communication, and assertiveness skills.

3. Use peer leaders as program providers, who are typically older students with good mentoring skills.

Table 7.5
Overview of Major Preventive Approaches

Approach	Focus	Methods
Information dissemination	Increase knowledge of drugs, their effects, and consequences of use; promote anti-drug use attitudes	Didactic instruction, discussion, audio/video presentations, displays of substances, posters, pamphlets, school assembly programs
Affective education	Increase self-esteem, responsible decision making, interpersonal growth; generally includes little or no information about drugs	Didactic instruction, discussion, experiential activities, group problem-solving exercises
Alternatives	Increase self-esteem, self-reliance; provide variable alternatives to drug use; reduce boredom and sense of alienation	Organization of youth centers, recreational activities; participation in community-service projects; vocational training
Resistance skills	Increase awareness of social influence to smoke, drink or use drugs; develop skills for resisting substance-use influences; increase knowledge of immediate negative consequences; establish non-substance use norms	Class discussion; resistance-skills training; behavioral rehearsal; extended practice via behavioral "homework"; use of same-age or older peer leaders
Personal and social skills training	Increase decision making; personal behavior change; anxiety reduction; communication, social and assertive skills; application of generic skills to resist substance-use influences	Class discussion; cognitive-behavioral skills training (instruction, demonstration, practice, feedback, reinforcement); extended practice via behavioral "homework"

Source: Gilbert J. Botvin. 1990. "Substance Abuse Prevention: Theory, Practice, and Effectiveness." Pp. 461–520 in *Drugs and Crime,* edited by Michael Tonry and James Q. Wilson. Chicago: University of Chicago Press.

4. Teach students awareness of the techniques used by advertisers to promote the sale of tobacco products or alcohol beverages.

Most of the preventive techniques may be learned through modeling and reinforcement, which are mediated by personal factors—cognition, attitudes, beliefs, and experiences. For example, what kind of information about specific drugs has been provided program participants? What are their general attitudes and beliefs about drugs—awareness of danger versus attraction to experimentation? Do their peers use alcohol or drugs, and how extensive is the alcohol/drug involvement? If parents use alcohol and drugs, the chances are that young people will use them as well—approximately six million or 9 percent of all children under eighteen years old have parents who report having used illicit drugs in the past month of the survey (National Institute of Drug Abuse, in Wolfe, Wekerle, and Scott 1997). Additionally, general problem-solving and decision-making skills will play a crucial part in creating an effective prevention approach. A mentor program that empowers young people to examine the evidence and make their own decisions will have far greater impact than a fear-based approach (Wolfe, Wekerle, and Scott 1997).

INTERVENTION: INSTITUTIONALIZATION

Because a growing number of chemically dependent young offenders are being institutionalized, we should inquire about the efficacy of residential treatment programs and community-based programs in reducing criminal recidivism and drug-use relapse. Has there been any long-term success with these programs? Sealock, Gottfredson, and Gallagher (1995) examined seven hundred youths adjudicated for a variety of drug and other offenses, and studied the results of two program segments: (1) the residential treatment phase, and (2) the aftercare community-based services.

Their findings are instructive. Youths who participated in the residential treatment that was set up while in detention or prison, reported significantly decreased drug use and delinquency, increased knowledge about the consequences of drug and alcohol use, and increased cognitive decision-making skills *during their residential stay*. Once the offenders served their time and returned to the community for aftercare treatment, gains made during the residential phase of the program were actually reversed. And youth assigned to aftercare services performed more poorly than those returned home with no additional services. The reason: family-oriented activities and services were weak and ineffectual. In a word, the second segment of the treatment program lacked a supportive environment. The authors conclude that "residential treatment has a short-lived effect on offending behavior, but that the surge of misbehavior after release negates this positive effect in the long run" (Sealock, Gottfredson, and Gallagher 1995, 46).

The Ninth Congress of the United Nations on the Prevention of Crime and the Treatment of Offenders (1995) corroborates these findings from the 138 participating governments:

Rehabilitation was minimal when juvenile offenders were imprisoned. Once released, young persons ran a higher risk of reoffending than those sentenced to non-custodial sanctions. Children, who are still in the process of developing their personality, will suffer sometimes irreparable damage if detained. Juveniles should always be seen primarily as children, and only secondarily in the light of the offense committed. (p. 19)

Thus, we see that a severe roadblock to sound prevention programs in the drug/crime connection is the program delivery itself, where "the rhetoric is powerful but the reality of prevention practices is weak and marginal" (Hughes 1996, 225). Certainly, in a context of punitive treatment of juvenile offenders, courts may ignore any attempt at treatment in favor of harsh penalties. But "treatment" for juveniles too often involves long prison sentences, exposure to sophisticated criminals, and abuse by inmates and guards in training institutes that makes a mockery of the system's effort to provide rehabilitation.

In a "findings letter" by the U.S. Justice Department, based on a one-year investigation of abuses in four Louisiana youth training institutes, the department said they had "uncovered systematic life-threatening abuse" by guards. Records show that among younger inmates, especially, 83 percent of whom were black, guards had routinely hit, kicked, slapped, stomped, choked, and scratched juveniles (*New York Times* 1997c, A1, A10).

Literally dozens of juveniles are being seriously injured on a monthly basis across the four facilities, and the incidence of fractures to jaws, noses, cheeks, and eye sockets, as well as serious lacerations requiring sutures (usually also to faces) is disturbing. The abuse ranges from officers physically hitting, pinching or kicking youth (sometimes when they are handcuffed), to officers negotiating "contracts" with juveniles to beat up other juveniles. As a result of such abuse, infirmary beds at all four locations were "filled with children with serious injuries, such as broken jaws and noses."

HARM-REDUCTION APPROACH

Policymakers aware of these gross injustices are casting about for alternative approaches. An intriguing idea for lessening the most-serious impacts of drug abuse and related crimes, and whose time may have come, is the "harm-reduction" strategy. This approach seeks to *reduce* harm, that is, undesirable outcomes—not through changing persons, their habits, motivations, and lifestyles, or punishing offenders, but rather through modifying environmental or situational factors. For example, to counteract the spread of AIDS, agencies in some American and European cities have provided needles for intravenous drug users, which has had the desired result: slowing the AIDS epidemic.

An innovative program in Switzerland, which evolved to reduce street crime among heroin addicts, involved setting up clinics that would provide heroin or methadone to serious addicts (those with habits of at least two years' standing) as part of a conventional treatment (Kilias and Uchtenhagen 1996). Despite vigorous political protests against such practices, the program has shown a significant drop in some drug-related crimes (burglary and robbery), although other crimes have remained at about preprogram levels (vehicle theft and muggings). The heroin distribution program also aimed to reduce victimizations to which drug addicts are regularly exposed—for example, robbery, rape, sexual assault, physical assault, burglary, and theft in connection with buying or selling drugs (Kilias and Uchtenhagen 1996).

LEGALIZATION

A drug legalization plan has also been proposed by a number of scholars, although support is mixed (Nadelmann 1989; Wilson 1990). *The Drug Policy Letter* (Treback 1994) invites readers to reassess the existing criminalization program—which as most criminologists and policymakers concede has been an unmitigated failure in terms of discouraging drug supplies—and deal with virtually all illegal drugs as we now deal with alcohol. This idea has been suggested by many observers (e.g., The Lindesmith Center for Research on Drugs), although derided by prohibitionists as being naive, because alcohol is allegedly less harmful and easier to control than the currently illegal drugs. The *Letter* takes strong exception to this assumption.

Dose by dose, alcohol is one of the most toxic and violence-producing drugs human beings regularly consume. For these very good reasons, the national government prohibited alcohol from 1920 to 1933. However, we came to see that as bad as alcohol is, prohibition was worse for the country and its people [and] was therefore repealed. (p. 11)

Citing the question of "political reality," Treback (1994, 12) argues that "we live in cataclysmic, revolutionary times where the unthinkable today may well become the norm tomorrow. Traditional ways of thinking and sacred icons are regularly and rapidly smashed." Advocates for legalization ask the leading question: Why not undertake drastic drug law reform? The social benefits may be profound. And their answer is: There are two legalization routes.

The first is the medical option (drugs available from a physician or medical context), and the second approach is the non-medical option (drugs available outside of medical supervision with the proviso that users must obtain a "user's license" after passing a series of knowledge tests about the substances). One distinct benefit would be that street addicts could be included. According to Treback (1994: 12), "under this new system, even the lowest street addicts would be treated as basically rational people who have to make choices about their options."

The new law would include warning labels on the bottle ("this drug is addictive" or "This drug may cause seizures"), minimum requirements (e.g., over twenty-one years of age, U.S. citizen or lawfully resident alien, no convictions of a felony), specific packaging and labeling of doses, and restricted hours of operation for legal drug stores. Legalization, advocates propose, operates as a countermeasure to the failed eighty-year experiment with drug prohibition.

Whereas, the likelihood of an across-the-board legalization of drugs in the near future is undoubtedly nil (and could possibly present more drug-related problems than the current policy), the 1996 California Proposition 215 that legalized medical marijuana opens the door to a larger citizen-initiated dialogue about the war on drugs. Since the California Compassionate Use Act passed, it has been legal under state law for any "seriously ill" Californian to obtain marijuana upon the recommendation of a physician. Marijuana has been prescribed by physicians in that state even before the law passed. Clinical experience shows that the drug successfully combats pain and nausea associated with cancer, AIDS, and a number of other chronic health problems "where nothing else worked" (Pollan 1997, 40). A 1991 study of two thousand oncologists (cancer specialists) revealed that 44 percent of these physicians had recommended marijuana to their patients for pain and other symptoms (Zimmerman in Pollan 1997).

In May 1997, an ABC News poll found that 69 percent of Americans supported the legalization of medical marijuana—although 80 percent of Americans rejected the legalization of drugs for nonmedical use (Pollan 1997). So far, the federal government refuses to back down on the war against *all* marijuana use, and has prosecuted California physicians who prescribed it for their patients. After all, the war on drugs is really a statement of federal power. Both advocates and opponents of legalized marijuana recognize that the country's acceptance of medical marijuana could be the catalyst for a public debate on the general legalization of drugs. And how that struggle might affect adolescents' attitudes about using drugs remains a major stumbling block to an open agenda for policymakers.

Will the modern drug war with its emphasis on "zero tolerance" and punitive intervention prevail? Or will the medical marijuana issue send the message that there are different kinds of drugs and different reasons for taking them, and that drug use and abuse are not necessarily the same thing. For legitimation purposes, it only makes sense for the federal government to open the door to a wider discussion of drug use among doctors, scientists, moralists, politicians, and citizens.

CONCLUSION

The emotional hunger that drives the addictive impulse is the unacknowledged "secret" that underlies much excessive drug use for adults and young people alike. If we wish to transform patterns of drug use among young people, try first changing the hierarchical relations of the alcoholic/drug addicted family, the social distance relations between teacher and student, the unbalanced boss-employee relationship, and the perpetuation of male violence and domination. Race, age, gender, and other inequalities must be addressed, as well as changes made in the redistribution of income; in providing for work opportunities that pay a living wage; in political commitments to clean up community deterioration (especially in inner cities); and in reversing the undemocratic drift of the culture. This is a tall order. But until these changes are made, drugs will remain the symptom of the hunger for an intact self in a viable community. Addiction represents the pseudo-solution to the need for wholeness. Until we, as a society, understand this, our antidrug rhetoric will fall on barren soil.

Just as alcohol and drugs have entered the adolescent mainstream, so has violence—the topic we turn to next. Violence did not erupt on the American scene in the last twenty years, nor is it restricted to poor, minority youth. As our history books clearly show, America was created out of violence; first, in a revolutionary war; then war against Native Americans for land, and slavery for African Americans for cheap labor; various wars for empire building, especially the Mexican War in the nineteenth century; a civil war that geographically and morally divided the country; and in the twentieth century, two major world wars, followed by two wars in Asia—Korea and Vietnam—and a "postwar" strategy of perpetual buildup of armaments against enemies seen and unseen. Add to this, since 1980, "police actions" in Grenada, Iraq, Somali, Haiti, and Bosnia, have resulted in significant numbers of civilian casualties. Can youth be blamed for imitating their elders?

NOTE

1. Dr. Peter Nelson, a friend and reviewer, was especially helpful in clarifying issues in this chapter, particularly in delineating the physical and psychological consequences of taking certain drugs.

8

Youth in the War Zone

The riots start after the basketball game, hallway, outside East Camden Middle School gym. Unknowns fighting two to eight youngsters. And unknown get up in the two to eight face and then it is knives, razor blades, black eyes, busted noses, blood all over the halls, girls screaming, crying, people stepping on each other to get outside, 50 to 100 people fighting. Crazy. War inside the school. And even fists and knives is not enough. Guns. Someone duck out to get the guns. Bullets spraying the crowd out in the parking lot. Three girls, two dudes get shot that night. I carry my gun everyday.

"Riot at East Camden Middle,"
poem by a sixteen-year-old observer[1]

The weight in our culture is being carried by the young people. They are carrying some of the darkness that belongs to the whole society, and the redistribution of that will be very painful for everybody.

Michael Meade, youth advocate[2]

THE CLIMATE OF VIOLENCE

As I write these words, a bomb has just exploded in Olympic Park, site of the 1996 International Olympics. A year earlier, the bombing of the Oklahoma City Federal Building by white dissidents, resulting in the death of 168 persons, including 19 children, in May 1995, demonstrated the intense vulnerability of our taken-for-granted assumptions about public safety. In early December 1997 a fourteen-year-old in Paducah, Kentucky, shot and killed three classmates, and seriously injured another five youths as they gathered for their weekly prayer circle. The boy apparently had no motive for the crime. Still, most Americans prefer to believe that these and other violent acts are exceptions to the rule; that we, as a peace-loving democracy, uphold the principles of a non-violent society. Or do we?

The overwhelming historical evidence shows that institutionalized violence is a routine occurrence in the United States, and has become a general feature of our culture and lifeways (Davis 1987; Davis and Stasz 1990; Prothrow-Stith 1995; Rosenberg 1995; Arendt 1963, 1990; Currie 1985). Violence is institutionalized in formal ways, such as the media, political conflict, and warfare and in informal ways, including the socialization of males, street crime, and interpersonal violent solutions to frustration. In the United States, state and reactionary groups have engaged in continuous conflict and violence against native Americans, racial minorities, union organizers, homosexuals, and political dissidents.

America pursues a pro-crime policy. The United States leads the way in being the most violent country in the advanced industrial world with fifty-six thousand murders each year, and the crime rate is growing. Firearms are a major cause of death and serious injury. Yet, Americans remain divided on handgun control, with many citizens fearful of government interference in private lives. The government itself organizes criminal activity for its own ends without having to admit its illegality; for example, covert intelligence operations against private citizens; supporting piracy, drug, and weapons smuggling, and totalitarian regimes. And domestic violence represents the routinization of evil as a normal part of many families' daily existence (Pagelow 1984; Straus 1993).

This chapter examines the reality of youth violence in detail. As commonplace as violence may be—in fact, it often appears to be an epidemic in terms of its rapid growth and concentrated presence in inner cities—the problem requires a consideration of both general and specific trends, as well as an understanding of the social and psychological sources that underpin this destructive behavior.

PATTERNS OF YOUTH VIOLENCE

When concerned adults and school authorities turn to the problems of youth violence, they often refer to the growing collection of statistical data that demonstrates the scope of the problem (see P. Riley 1995; National School Boards Association Report 1993; Office of Juvenile Justice and Delinquency Prevention [OJJDP] 1995; 1996a; 1996b).

- In 1994 law enforcement agencies made over 2.7 million arrests of persons under age eighteen. Six percent of all juvenile arrests in that year were for a Violent Crime Index offense (e.g., murder, rape, robbery, assault, arson). Half of these arrests involved juveniles below age sixteen, half involved whites, and one in seven involved females (see Tables 8.1 and 8.2) (OJJDP 1996a).
- Juvenile arrest rates for weapons violations nearly doubled between 1987 and

1994. At the same time, the twenty-year trend in the rate of juvenile arrests for weapons law violations closely parallels the juvenile arrest trend for murder (OJJDP 1996a).

- About three million crimes occur on or near school property each year. Nearly three-quarters of students were aware of incidents of physical attack, robbery, or bullying, more than half witnessed incidents, and one-quarter indicated that they worried about such incidents. Altogether, 12 percent of students sixth through twelfth grade reported that they were victims of physical attack, robbery, or bullying in school (OJJDP 1995; 1996a).

- Younger teenage victims of crime were more likely to be victimized on or around school. Thirty-seven percent of the violent crimes against youth between twelve and fifteen years old occurred at school, compared with 17 percent of those sixteen to nineteen years of age (National School Boards Association Report 1993; P. Riley 1995).

- About 960,000 youths between ages twelve and nineteen were the victims of 1.9 violent crimes (rape, robbery, and assault) each year between 1985 and 1988. Even with a decline in juvenile homicides by nearly 20 percent between 1980 and 1984—from an estimated 1,810 to 1,460—in 1993 the number of juveniles murdered in the United States had grown to 2,840—a 95 percent increase in a ten-year period (OJJDP 1995; 1996a). There were 2,555 juvenile homicides in 1990. It is estimated that in the year 2000 there will be 8,000 (OJJDP 1995).

- In 1991, three of every ten juvenile murder arrests involved a victim under the age of eighteen (OJJPD 1995; 1996a; 1996b).

- About sixty-seven out of every one thousand teenagers were victims of a violent crime each year, compared with twenty-six per thousand persons age twenty and older. The murder rate for ages fifteen to twenty-two increased sharply. It is estimated that for this age group, 18,600 murders were committed from 1986 to 1992. In one year alone (1991), this age group generated an excess of 5,330 murders, or 21.6 percent of the 24,703 murders reported in the Federal Bureau of Investigation's (FBI's) 1991 Uniform Crime Report (OJJDP 1996b).

- The increase in juvenile murders has been driven by large increases in the number of male teens killed. For example, in the five years from 1990 through 1994, more than 5,700 males ages fifteen to seventeen were murdered—131 percent more than were killed during 1980 to 1984. By contrast, the increase for females ages fifteen to seventeen was 11 percent (OJJDP 1996a).

- Firearms are the leading cause of death for African American males ages fifteen to twenty-four. They are the second leading cause of death for all American teens (OJJDP 1995).

- Almost half of high school students reported weapons in their schools in 1993; up to 48 percent reported the presence of gangs.

- Schools with gangs had higher crime violence rates. Twelve percent of the students who reported gangs at school were victims of crime, compared with 8 percent of those who reported no gangs (OJJDP 1996a).

States may vary in their rates of juvenile violence. For instance, in Washington State, the youth arrest rate for violent crimes increased 165 percent from 1983 and 1994. And by no means does Washington lead the nation in juvenile violence (Aos, Lieb, and Barnoski 1996). In 1994—for the first time—the juvenile murder arrest rate exceeded that of adults in that state. Arrest rates for juvenile violent offenses show significant disparities from one state to another (see Tables 8.1, 8.2, and 8.3).

Should we, then, be surprised to learn that increasing numbers of young people are deeply involved—usually not as a matter of choice—as participants in lifestyles organized around violence; as victims in the deadly game of force; and as witnesses to violent attacks made against friends, acquaintances, or family members. Life in the inner-city war zone, though, is not merely a routine occurrence with its own set of rules, roles, and practices. Like other war zones, such as Cambodia, Beirut, Liberia, Mozambique, and other areas ravaged by violence, children suffer disproportionately when they are repeatedly exposed to violence, compared with adults (Garbarino et al. 1992; Garbarino 1991). According to one young African American man, Ron Foxx, life in the inner city is unbelievably hazardous (in Minton 1996).

I live in a war zone in America. Where I live, you could be home, watching TV and be shot. They'll come to your window while you sleep and shoot your house up, like it's Vietnam. Or your mother and father fight, and one of them pulls a gun—and the kids are watching and see their parents blown away in cold blood. . . . A while ago they had a shooting near my cousin's house—this gang drove by and shot a kid's face off. The police put him in the trunk of the car so people wouldn't have to look at it. The coroner didn't come for three or four hours.

On physical, mental, and emotional grounds, a child's human development may be stunted and distorted by the resulting stress and trauma of violence. For example, many inner-city children experience a mental-emotional condition of Post-Traumatic Stress Syndrome. This entails symptoms that may include sleep disturbances, day dreaming, re-creating trauma in play, extreme startle reactions, diminished expectations for the future, and even biochemical changes in their brains (Wright 1995). This can produce significant psychological problems that interfere with learning and appropriate social behavior in school and can disrupt normal parent-child relationships (Garbarino et al. 1992). Above all, says James Garbarino, president of the Erikson Institute for Advanced Study in Child Development, "trauma distorts the values of kids . . . [because] traumatized kids are likely to be drawn to groups and ideologies that legitimatize and reward their rage, their fear, and their hateful cynicism" (Garbarino et al. 1992, 22).

In war zones, traditional assumptions that characterize offender, victim, and witness as different psychological and social types are off the mark. Instead, there is significant overlap between youths who witness, are victims

Table 8.1
Percent of Arrests Involving Juveniles

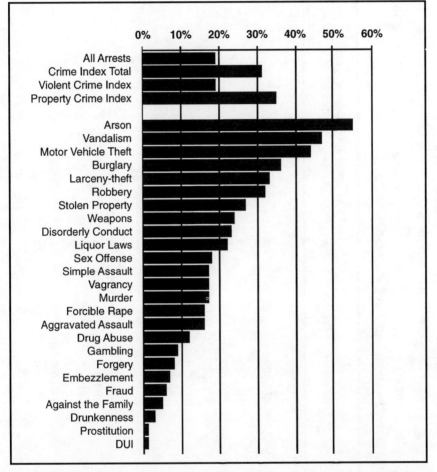

—Nearly one-third of all persons arrested in 1994 for robbery were below age 18, well above the juvenile proportion of arrests for murder (17%), aggravated assault (16%), and forcible rape (16%).

—Juveniles were involved in 1 percent of all arrests for driving under the influence and prostitution, but more than 40 percent of all arrests for arson, vandalism, and motor vehicle theft.

Source: FBI. *Crime in the United States, 1994.* Uniform Crime Reports. Washington, D.C.: Government Printing Office, 1995, p. 113.

Table 8.2
Age, Ethnicity, and Gender of Juveniles Arrested for Violent and Nonviolent Crime

Six percent of all juvenile arrests in 1994 were for a Violent Crime Index offense—half of these arrests involved juveniles below age 16, half involved whites, and 1 in 7 involved females.

Offense Charged	Arrests	Female	Ages 16-17	Percent of Total Juvenile Arrests			
				White	Black	Native American	Asian
Total	2,714,000	25%	45%	69%	29%	1%	2%
Crime Index Total	898,300	23	40	65	32	1	2
Violent Crime Index	150,200	14	49	48	50	1	1
Murder & Nonneg. Manslaughter	3,700	6	71	39	59	1	2
Forcible Rape	6,000	2	43	55	43	1	1
Robbery	55,200	9	50	36	62	<1	2
Aggravated Assault	85,300	19	48	55	43	1	1
Property Crime Index	748,100	25	38	69	28	1	2
Burglary	143,200	10	40	74	24	1	1
Larceny-Theft	505,100	32	36	70	27	1	2
Motor Vehicle Theft	88,200	14	46	56	41	1	2
Arson	11,600	12	19	80	18	1	1
Nonindex Offenses	1,815,700	26	48	70	27	1	2
Other Assaults	211,700	26	39	62	36	1	1
Forgery and Counterfeiting	8,700	36	73	80	18	1	1
Fraud	23,600	26	54	53	44	1	2

Offense	Number	%	%	%	%	%	%
Embezzlement	1,000	35	81	68	30	<1	1
Stolen Property; buy/recv/possess	44,200	11	50	59	39	1	2
Vandalism	152,100	10	33	80	17	1	2
Weapons; carry/possess	63,400	8	49	62	36	1	2
Prostitution & Commercial Vice	1,200	49	75	65	32	1	2
Sex Offense (non-rape/prostitution)	17,700	8	31	71	27	1	1
Drug Abuse Violations	158,600	12	65	60	39	1	1
Gambling	1,700	5	64	23	74	<1	2
Offense Against Family	5,400	36	46	70	27	1	3
Driving Under Influence	13,600	14	92	91	6	2	1
Liquor Law Violations	120,000	29	74	91	5	3	1
Drunkenness	18,400	16	70	87	11	2	<1
Disorderly Conduct	170,500	23	45	65	34	1	1
Vagrancy	4,300	19	54	71	27	<1	1
All other offenses (except traffic)	422,300	22	53	67	30	1	2
Curfew & Loitering	128,400	29	47	76	21	1	2
Runaways	248,800	57	30	77	19	1	3

—71% of juvenile arrests for murder involved 16- and 17-year-olds.

—91% of juvenile arrests for driving under the influence and for liquor law violations involved whites.

—The majority of juvenile arrests for running away from home (57%) involved females.

Note: UCR data do not distinguish the ethnic group Hispanic; Hispanics may be of any race. Detail may not add to totals because of rounding.

Source: Office of Juvenile Justice and Delinquency Prevention. Juvenile Offenders and Victims: 1996 Update on Violence. Washington, D.C.: National Institute of Justice, 1997, p. 10.

Table 8.3
Juvenile Violent Crime Arrests:
Arrest Rates in the United States, 1992

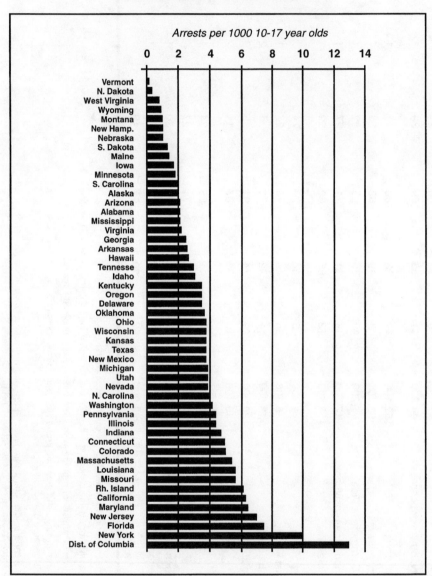

Source: U.S. Dept. of Justice. *Juvenile Offenders and Victims: A National Report.* Washington, D.C.: U.S. Government Printing Office, August 1995, p. 28.

of, and who participate in violent acts. A study of over one thousand African American students from four of Chicago's South Side public middle and high schools clarified that nearly 75 percent had witnessed a robbery, shooting, stabbing, and/or killing; another 46 percent had been victims of violent events (being robbed, having a gun pulled on them, being knifed, being raped, being the victim of attempted rape, being shot, being shot at, or being stabbed) (Uehara et al. 1996). Almost 27 percent of the sample admitted to committing at least one of the following types of violence: robbery, knife pulling, rape, shooting, stabbing, or killing.

The study identified consistent patterns of victimization (Uehara et al. 1996). For example, being male consistently is related to higher probabilities of perpetrating aggression (see also, NIJ 1996). Other conditions, such as age range, school, and weapons carrying are all significantly associated with victimization. Whereas carrying a weapon was singled out as most strongly associated with perpetration of violence, the study concluded that the clear overlap between youthful victims and participants, and the cumulative pattern that appears to characterize youth encounters with violence, suggests the presence of a strong environmental influence. The authors also emphasized that conditions in certain inner cities are hazardous to children's physical health, mental well-being, and social adjustment (Uehara et al. 1996).

THE DEADLY NEXUS

Alfred Blumstein (1995) argues that violence by young people expresses a "deadly nexus," whereby age, race, gender, fear, guns, and drugs combine to generate high rates of violent crimes. After a period of relative stability in the rates of juvenile crime, a major turning point occurred in 1985. As a result of the crack trade, which was concentrated within the inner cities, inside a period of seven years, the rate of homicides committed by young people, the number of homicides they committed with guns, and the arrest rate of non-white juveniles for drug offenses all doubled. Among sixteen-year-olds, the murder rate before 1985 was consistently about half that of young non-white persons ages 18-to-24. But by 1992, sixteen-year-olds convicted of homicide increased 138 percent over the seven-year period (from 1985). Blumstein also calculated the "excess" murder rate committed by young people, and concludes that the number of "excess" murders is estimated to be 18,600. This represents the number of murders that would **not** have been committed had the youth murder rate remained at its earlier, pre-1885 average. In all, juveniles are responsible for over 30 percent of the growth in violent crime between 1988 and 1994 (Snyder and Sickmund 1995) (see Table 8.4).

Age is a crucial variable in crime rates; in fact, its relationship to offending is usually designated as the "age-crime curve." This curve, which typ-

Table 8.4
Juvenile Contribution to the Crime Problem, 1994

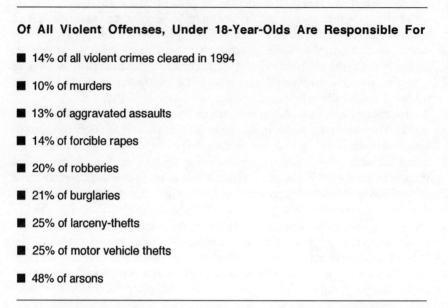

Of All Violent Offenses, Under 18-Year-Olds Are Responsible For

■ 14% of all violent crimes cleared in 1994

■ 10% of murders

■ 13% of aggravated assaults

■ 14% of forcible rapes

■ 20% of robberies

■ 21% of burglaries

■ 25% of larceny-thefts

■ 25% of motor vehicle thefts

■ 48% of arsons

Source: Office of Juvenile Justice and Delinquency Prevention. 1996. *Juvenile Offenders and Victims: A National Report,* p. 13.

ically peaks in late adolescence, emphasizes that crime is committed during an offender's younger years, and declines as the offender matures. Murder rates for young people have undergone dramatic change. Between 1965 to 1985, persons in the age group eighteen to twenty-four were the most likely to commit murder; after the mid-30s, the rate dropped to half the peak. After 1985, the new peak age for murder was eighteen, implying that ever-younger juveniles were involved in killing (Blumstein 1995, 3–4). In fact, over half of all violent offenders initiate their violence between ages four-teen and seventeen (Elliott 1994).

Race is a second variable that reveals a major trend shift. Prior to 1985, murder rates among African-American males ages fourteen to seventeen have been about four to five times higher than among white males of the same age group. After 1985, the rates for both white and black males rose, although the growth rate was much faster among blacks. For white males in this age group, their annual rate for murder was 8.1 per 100,000 in the years 1976 to 1987. Within four years, it had almost doubled (13.6 in 1991). In this same time period, the arrest rate for murder by black males ages fourteen to seventeen more than doubled (from 50.4 to 111.8 per 100,000) (Blumstein 1995). At the same time, most juvenile homicides involved victims and offenders of the same race. Ninety-two percent of the black juvenile victims were killed by blacks, and 93 percent of the white juvenile victims were killed by whites (Snyder and Sickmund 1995).

The next factor, gender, receives strong biological, psychological, and cultural support that shows that males are overwhelmingly involved in aggressive behavior, in this case, violent acts. Juvenile males account for approximately seven out of eight serious violent offenses. Nevertheless, males are not inherently criminal, nor do they suddenly become homicidal (except under unusual circumstances).

Antisocial behavior has many precursors, including biological, family, and school conditions, as well as emotional, cognitive, social, and cultural factors. A common, growing, and dangerous psychological syndrome, identified by Scott Sigmon (1994), is the "Youth Violence Syndrome." This condition is characterized by at least nine behaviors: (1) hopelessness; (2) a complete or great disregard for the laws followed by most Americans; (3) a short temper combined with a lack of empathy; (4) a desire for respect from others where such respect has not been earned; (5) an act or acts of violence against another person; (6) unemployment or employment in a minimum- or low-wage job; (7) an extremely high desire for expensive consumer goods; (8) acting-out to obtain expensive consumer goods illegally; and (9) a high school dropout or a high school graduate with deficient reading and math skills. Additional factors that play a critical role in the Youth Violence Syndrome should be included (D. F. Hawkins 1995): lack of opportunities; lack of skills; lack of recognition; and failure to bond with family members, teachers, and other adults. Undoubtedly, the reasons for the much greater incidence of male involvement in criminal violence are social expectations, including expressions of "machismo" or hypermasculinity and its use in the quest for personal power, when more-legitimate channels remain closed (a topic we examine in more detail in a later section).

Fear of strangers plays a vital role in defensive postures taken by youth caught up in a "culture of violence" (Mock 1996). First, young people tend to engage in random violence, primarily against people they do not know. Anxiety and fear generate the higher levels of recklessness associated with much youth violence. When victims are selected at random, anyone can be a target. Blumstein notes that the FBI's Supplementary Homicide Report for 1991 indicated that 28 percent of the homicides committed by people under age twenty-five were against strangers, whereas only 18 percent of those committed by offenders over age twenty-five were against unknown persons.

Guns may be a more causative factor in juvenile violence than the average citizen supporting permissive gun laws realizes. The FBI Supplementary Homicide Reports (1996) clarifies that among juvenile offenders, ages ten to seventeen, the likelihood that a juvenile homicide involved the use

---

Box 8-A
Teen Gun Deaths Hit New High

According to the Federal Centers for Disease Control in Atlanta, U.S. teens are killing each other with guns at the highest rate since the government began recording the deaths 30 years ago. Almost 4,200 youths, ages 15 to 19 were killed by guns in 1990, or about 11 every day. Lois Fingershut, an epidemiologist at the National Center for Health Statistics, emphasizes that "these are just the deaths. We're not talking about the kids who are shot and don't die."

The Centers for Disease Control also show that 25 percent of all deaths between ages 15 and 24 were the result of shootings. Of grave concern is that 39 percent more teens die from gunshots than from disease. And while the primary cause of death for black males ages 10 to 34 was guns, the death rate among white teens is increasing the most rapidly. This means that death and injury from gunshot wounds is not limited to drug trafficking and other criminal activities. Instead, according to one mother of a 17-year-old boy, who was shot and killed by an Eagle Scout, any youngster can become a victim:

> There is a misconception by the general population that murder happens to others, that the kind of violence that turns into murder is only by people doing drugs or one race against another. . . . The truth is . . . it can happen to your child as easily as it happened to mine.

Source: "Teen Gun Deaths Hit New High," *Daily Report Card News Service*, vol. 2, no. 195, March 25, 1993.

---

of firearms is over three times greater than when other weapons (i.e., knives, stones, and so on) are used (1992 data). Guns also intensify the fear of crime among youth in inner cities, and account for the self-reported increase of weapon carrying among young people as a means of "self protection and status seeking" (Blumstein 1995, 6). Because few juveniles are equipped with the training and restraint necessary to handle rapid-fire assault weapons, settling disputes often leads to excessively violent outcomes (see Box 8-A).

THE DIFFUSION HYPOTHESIS

A "diffusion" process appears to account for the widespread use of guns, not only among inner-city youth, but also among white youth as well. The evidence of the diffusion suggests that guns are diffused from drug markets to the larger community through juvenile recruits. According to Blumstein (1995, 6), the escalation can be related to an "arms race," a situation in which the presence of guns in a community incites others to arm themselves. "Thus begins the escalation: as more guns appear in the community, the incentive for any single individual to arm himself increases, and so a local 'arms race' develops." A working hypothesis about the growth in juvenile violence has been proposed (*The Criminologist*, Special Issue, 1995, 7).

- When crack cocaine hit the streets in 1985, it changed illegal-drug-buying habits and distribution patterns. The number of transactions increased markedly, as people bought one "hit" at a time, rather than large quantities that could be stored for later use.
- To accommodate the higher number of transactions, youth (primarily African Americans in the center-city areas) were recruited into the drug market.
- Because they could not easily ask the police for protection, the new recruits needed guns to protect themselves and their valuable wares.
- Their tight networking through schools and the streets led to a broader diffusion of guns into the larger youthful community, primarily for self-defense but also, additionally, for status.
- Because of the presence of guns, the fights that routinely occur among youths can rapidly turn from fist fights to shootings. Adult gun carriers, even those in the drug market, seem better able to exercise restraint.
- As more young people carried guns, they provided an incentive for other youths to arm themselves, resulting in an escalating process of gun-carrying (the familiar "arms race"), which, in turn, has led to a greater propensity in any dispute for either party to use his gun before the other person does.

Despite the apparent absence of white youth in the drug markets, the growth of their involvement in homicide (80 percent increase) strongly supports the diffusion hypothesis. This diffusion of guns into the larger community has had a profound impact on the nation's schools to the extent that nearly 10 percent of junior and senior high school students across the country avoided school and school locations because of fear of victimization (Lab and Clark 1994). In fact, in a violent, divided society, where impoverished, crime-ridden neighborhoods have the most rundown and poorly equipped schools in the metropolitan area, schools have become a major social problem in their own right. Plagued by massive dropout rates (greater than 50 percent in some districts), gangs, drugs, weapons, violence, chronic sexual harassment of females, and high rates of nonattendance, schools, as currently organized, contribute to the brutalization of poor children and the exceedingly poor performances that characterize many American schools generally (see Chapter 4).

JUVENILE VIOLENT CAREERS

The National Youth Survey is a projected longitudinal study of a national probability sample of 1,725 youths age eleven to seventeen in 1976.

Nine waves of data are available on this youth panel, which included persons age twenty-seven to thirty-three when last interviewed in 1993 (Elliott 1994). What these data show is that despite the impulsive, reckless, and random nature of much juvenile violence, it is possible to track the career trajectory that occurred among this group from onset, through the developmental course, to termination. Delbert S. Elliott (1994) proposes that by employing projected longitudinal designs and self-reported measures of violence, we may better understand the causes and developmental course of violent careers among all youthful violent offenders.

First, the onset of serious violent offending is in **younger** adolescence; the highest risk of onset is found at age fifteen for blacks and age sixteen for whites. By age eighteen, nearly 40 percent of black males have become involved in serious violent offending, compared with 30 percent of white males; at age twenty-seven these rates are 48 percent and 38 percent, respectively. Comparing lower-class blacks with whites, though, strongly argues against a racial explanation for violence. Approximately seven blacks to every six whites of low income are violence-involved.

Second, minor forms of delinquent behavior and alcohol use are added to the "behavioral repertoire" before serious crimes of criminal theft and violence occur. Additionally, minor delinquency precedes all forms of illicit drug use.

Third, a progression from least serious to more serious offenses tends to prevail. Elliott shows that aggravated assault precedes robbery in 85 percent of cases and rape in 92 percent. Similarly, robbery precedes rape in 72 percent of cases. Thus, the typical sequence is from aggravated assault to robbery to rape. Aggravated assault, reported by 88 percent of all serious violent offenders, remains the most frequent form of violent behavior.

Fourth, the variety of minor offenses tended to increase in the year before the onset of a serious violent offense (SVO). The addition of a SVO to the behavioral repertoire was accompanied by an increase in the offending rates for all types of offenses in the individual's repertoire. Elliott (1994) concludes:

Thus, the behavioral progression through the career for serious violent offenders is characterized by an add-on pattern, not a substitution pattern; the general trend is toward diversification in offending, not specialization, and toward adding more serious offenses to the behavorial repertoire. (p. 19)

How do we characterize the transition into the adult years in terms of continuity or discontinuity in serious violent offending? Continuity rates have been examined for race, gender, and social class. Among these three variables, only race operated as a clear demarcation with nearly twice as many blacks as whites continuing their violent careers into their twenties. Gender surprisingly revealed little difference between males and females, despite far fewer females involved in violent offending (22 percent of males versus 18 percent of females continued their offending into their twenties). Social class also showed little difference in the rates of continuity between the underclass and working-/middle-class youth. These data support the "maturational reform hypothesis." This stipulates that the transition into responsible adult roles leads to desistance from crime and violent behavior (Sampson and Laub 1993).

Elliott proposes that higher maturation processes among whites may be explained thus: 1. Whites are more likely than blacks to be living with their parents in conventional settings with more support, and 2. Blacks are more likely than whites to be involved in the illicit economy, particularly the drug trade. Both conditions contribute to the findings that blacks apparently have longer criminal careers than whites. The fact that fully 25 percent of all seventeen-year-old males failed to terminate their criminal careers in this early sample points to the alarming continuity of criminality from juvenile deviance to petty crime to serious violent offending. With the presence of handguns these young men represent a serious and protracted threat to organized society. By 1997, a comprehensive assessment of serious and violent juvenile offenders questions the maturation hypothesis (U.S. Department of Justice 1997):

1. SVJ offenders are a distinct group of offenders who tend to start early and continue late in their offending.

2. From childhood to adolscence, SVJ offenders develop behavior problems, including aggression, dishonesty, property offenses, and conflict with authority figures.

3. Many potential SVJ offenders below the age of twelve are not routinely processed in juvenile court, and community services for these very high-risk offenders are unnecessarily fragmented.

More significantly, if young people in a culture are in trouble, then the culture is in trouble. These violent youth are a symptom of a serious cultural disorder (Meade 1996).

JUVENILE VICTIMIZATION

What is the prevalence and incidence of youth victimization? Who are their offenders? How often are firearms involved? How many juveniles are murdered each year? These questions permit us to continue the discussion of child and adolescent victimization pursued in Chapter 5. Here, we specifically consider criminal victimization of teens, ages twelve through seventeen.

Much of criminal violent juvenile victimization is hidden from public view—crimes are not reported, offenders are not arrested, and data may not even be collected. For example, the National Crime Victimization Survey (NCVS) under the Bureau of Justice Statistics, does not capture information from, or about, victims younger than age twelve. Only older juveniles are covered. Despite limitations of the data, some unexpected patterns in criminal victimization of youth emerge from the NCVS statistics (Snyder and Sickmund 1995).

The risk of violent victimization in 1991 was greater for a twelve-year-old than for anyone age twenty-four or older, although the risk of violent crime varies substantially within the juvenile age groups. The risk of being a victim of a violent crime for a seventeen-year-old was 33 percent greater than the risk for a twelve-year-old. In 1991 juveniles ages twelve to seventeen were as likely to be the victims of rape, robbery, and simple assault as were adults ages eighteen to twenty-four. Aggravated assault was the only violent crime for which young adults had a statistically higher victimization rate.

Most offenders who victimize juveniles are family members, friends, or acquaintances. Only 22 percent of personal crimes against juveniles were committed by strangers. This compares with 42 percent of crimes against adults that are committed by strangers. If we consider only rape and robbery, however, the figures for juveniles and adults show less disparity. Strangers are involved in 33 percent of juvenile rape, and 39 percent of adult rape; and 44 percent of juvenile robbery and 51 percent of adult robbery.

As for choice of weapons, a gun was used in one of four serious violent offenses against juveniles in 1991. More suggestive of the high risk of street crime is that in 67 percent of serious violent crimes involving juvenile victims, the offender was armed.

Next, compared with other juveniles, black youth are more likely to be the victim of a violent crime. Black juveniles had a violent victimization rate 20 percent higher than that of white juveniles.

Personal crimes with juvenile victims occurred most often in school or on school property, including property and violent crime. Figures on violent crime on school grounds reveals that 23 percent occurred most often in school or on school property.

Whereas there are about 1.5 million violent victimizations against juveniles ages twelve to seventeen, the crimes are only rarely brought to the attention of police. In 1991 only 20 percent of these personal victimizations against youth were reported. By contrast, 37 percent of adult personal victimizations were reported to police.

The risk of violent victimization has increased for juveniles and young adults in recent years. Between 1987 and 1991 the risk that a person between the ages of twelve and seventeen would become a victim of a nonfatal violent crime increased 17 percent. Over this period the risk of violence increased from 61 to 71 violent victimizations per 1,000 juveniles. During the same period the risk of violence for those aged eighteen to twenty-four increased 24 percent from 66 to 81 per 1,000.

Additionally, the homicide rate for youth, ages fourteen to seventeen—the best indicator of serious criminal victimization—has nearly doubled since the mid-1980s, while the rates for younger juveniles have remained relatively constant. After age thirteen, the homicide victimization rate increases throughout adolescence, especially for boys. Firearms explain the higher death rates among juveniles. Older teens (ages fifteen to nineteen) were more likely than any other age group to be killed with a gun.

Finally, homicide victims ages ten to seventeen were more often killed by a friend or other acquaintance (61 percent), rather than by a family member (16 percent) More than 70 percent of these homicide victims were shot to death. The large majority of juvenile homicide victims in this age range were male (73 percent) (Snyder and Sickmund 1995).

DISCLAIMERS TO THE VIOLENT YOUTH THESIS

The fear over violence in general and violence committed by young people in particular has reached what Altschuler (1995) refers to as "epidemic proportions." As evidence of the scope and nature of violence committed by persons under the age of eighteen demonstrates, there certainly is a juvenile crime problem, and it is one that is increasing in seriousness. But this is not to say that youth violence is the same thing as an epidemic. Instead, it could be argued that it is the public fear that surrounds it, as well as the lack of political will to address the problem, that are at the root of the youth violence problem. Consider, too, the number of factors that show youth crime to be far less damaging than the outraged public reactions against it (see Acland 1995).

In the first place, most juvenile crime (i.e., crimes committed by persons under the age of eighteen) is substantially property crime, and less serious crimes against persons. For example, the single largest increase in youth violent offenses is for simple (not aggravated) assault (Whitehead and Lab 1996).

A second point: The largest proportion of all violent crime arrests involved persons eighteen or over (FBI 1996). The juvenile contribution to the crime problem in the United States for 1994 was 14 percent for all violent crimes cleared, and 25 percent of all property crime cleared. Based on 1992 clearance data, about one in eight (1:8) of all violent crimes cleared involved juveniles. Clearance rate, however, may underestimate the real participation of youth in crime, because youthful victims of peer violence often fail to report the crime to police.

A third consideration, Snyder (1994) calculates that 19 percent of the increase in violent crime overall was attributable to juveniles, meaning that in the last ten years adult violence was responsible for just over 80 percent of the **increase** in violent crime.

Next, it is largely property offenders, not violent offenders, who are most prone toward reoffending (Altschuler 1995). Altschuler and Armstrong's (1990) review of prediction research reported that risk factors associated with juvenile reoffending behavior include: (1) a combination of justice system contact factors (e.g., age of youth at first justice system contact, number of prior offenses and referrals); and (2) need-related factors (e.g., family dysfunction, school disciplinary problems, negative peer group influences, drug involvement).

A final observation: Despite the greater attention paid to youth violence, crimes of violence among juveniles has actually declined slightly. Preliminary data compiled by the FBI from local police reports show that the arrest rate for homicide for youths ages ten to seventeen had fallen 22.8 percent since reaching an all-time high in 1993. The overall rate of juvenile violent crime, which includes assault, robbery, and rape, as well as murder, declined 2.9 percent in 1995 (Butterfield 1996b). More-effective law enforcement strategies may account for some part of the decline. Another factor accounting for the decrease, according to James Alan Fox, is because the juvenile homicide rate almost tripled in the past decade. "It was inevitable that at some point it would go down" (in Butterfield 1996b, 1).

POLITICAL RESPONSE TO VIOLENT AND DEVIANT YOUTH

Prior to the creation of the juvenile justice system in 1899 by the Cook County, Illinois court, youthful offenders were adjudicated in adult court and received similar penalties as adults. The invention of the juvenile justice system was devised to divert youth away from the harshness of adult criminal justice with the state taking on the role of *parens patriae*, or the state as surrogate parent. Now, the state could act in a complex role set: fatherly overseer, administrator of discipline, and protection of juveniles. At the same time, due process rights and advisements, afforded as a matter of course to adults, were believed unnecessary in the juvenile court system. Not until 1967, when the abridgement of juvenile rights came before the U.S. Supreme Court, were due process rules changed to recognize the legal status of juveniles in the criminal process (see Whitehead and Lab 1996 for a history of juvenile justice).

The state's role as protector collided with its chief role as social control agent. As a result, many youthful miscreants have been removed from their homes and communities and placed in either adult jails or in juvenile facilities, where they are purportedly free from negative influences and the commission of further delinquent or criminal activity. Regardless of the nature of the wrongdoing—violence, property crimes, disorderly conduct, status offenses (e.g., truancy), and even neglected and abused youngsters—all were subject to uniform handling with high rates of detention and incarceration. Unofficial processing of very minor transgressions contributed to large numbers of young people entering the system. For example, making noise, sledding in the street, playing in the street, riding bicycles on the sidewalk, and throwing paper into the sewers became the subject of these unofficial cases (Whitehead and Lab 1996; Rothman 1990).

The failure of this policy soon became evident. Detention centers and training schools offered the recruit new and more-sophisticated opportunities for lawbreaking. Once inside these juvenile facilities, victimization is rampant. The "exploitation matrix" serves to reinforce a hierarchy of youthful inmates with the strong prevailing over the weak. The most vulnerable and fearful youths are subject to intimidation, and coerced by violence and threats of violence by older, larger, stronger, or more dangerous inmates into handing over their food, personal possessions, and sexual favors in exchange for protection and companionship. The quantity of goods and services surrendered without a fight keep the weak in a permanent "pecking order" of subordinate/superior relations (Braswell, Montgomery, and Lombardo 1994).

Juvenile detention remains a "hidden closet for the skeletons of the rest of the system," said Patricia Wald in 1975 (in Schwartz and Barton 1997), and little has changed over twenty years. But the number of youths admitted is rising dramatically with more than 880,000 youths admitted to juvenile facilities each year, and 77,000 incarcerated in adult jails and prisons every year. On any given day, 90,000 teenagers are locked up in juvenile facilities across the country. As for detention centers, these number 422 in the United States, more than twice the number of training schools, with admissions to these centers at over 500,000 annually (see OJJDP 1996c).

Juvenile detention centers are essentially jails for allegedly "dangerous" juveniles who have been arrested and are awaiting trial. Such facilities not only are overcrowded and in poor physical condition but also hold many youths who do not seem to require this type of secure confinement. Additionally, they are a very costly use of scarce juvenile justice resources—for example, Florida in 1988 allocated fully 40 percent of its delinquency programs budget to the operation of detention, with operating costs for new detention facilities estimated at $75,000 to $100,000 per bed. Their greatest handicap, of course, is that they essentially fail to provide either punishment or treatment, but perform a brutalizing role instead. As described by Schwartz and Barton (1997) young people in these "hidden closets"

sleep in tiny, barren cells, often wear "institutional green" uniforms, march single file to and from classes and meals, and sometimes remain locked up for several weeks, and even months, only to be sent home after they finally have their day in court. (p. 1)

And adult jails—the most severely underresourced and holding the vast range of adult criminals, both those awaiting trial and those doing time— have been active sites of individual juvenile corruption and self-destruction. For example, youth held in jails have higher suicide rates, compared to those placed in detention. Even more damaging is the reality that time spent in prison or jail **increases** the risk of reoffending among juvenile offenders once they are released to the community (Hagan 1991). Moreover, evidence supporting a deterrent effect of incarceration of juvenile offenders is alto- gether lacking (Altschuler 1995). Based on its review of research, the Panel on High Risk Youth concluded that

the U.S. justice system is overburdened, and that its emphasis on punishment is expensive, unproductive of the desired gains in reducing levels of crime, and prob- ably productive of increased hostility toward itself in ghetto communities. (Quoted in Altschuler 1995, 11).

Mental illness is another factor that complicates the juvenile incarcera- tion policy. According to the OJJDP (1995), mental illness is a strong con- tributing factor in juvenile crime. Although precise prevalence rates are unknown, experts in mental health and juvenile justice estimate that the rate of mental disorder among youth in the juvenile justice system is sub- stantially higher than among youth in the general population. Information on the specific types of conduct disorder are typically lacking, but OJJDP emphasizes that at least one-fifth, and perhaps as much as 60 percent, of the youth in the juvenile justice system can be diagnosed as having a con- duct disorder. Recently released figures from the State of Virginia revealed that more than 75 percent of all youth in the State's secure detention fa- cilities exhibited at least one diagnosable mental disorder. Among this group, 8 to 10 percent had mental health needs described in the study as "serious," and another 39 percent were assessed as having needs in the moderate range.

To offset these injustices, reformers sought to divert youth out of the administration of justice into community-based custody and service-type sentencing. These diversion trends emphasized treatment and rehabilitation, and the integration of adolescents into the communty rather than their removal from it. The reasoning has been that in a community setting, errant youth are allowed to make some degree of amends for their offenses. In- stead of being punished by being taken off the streets and being forced to give up all that is familiar to them, they can continue to attend school, live in their homes, go to work if they have part-time jobs, and otherwise be out in the community at large. Offending youth can also be held accountable for their behavior by paying restitution in the case of thefts, property damage, or minor medical bills, or by doing community service, especially if it related to the type of crime committed. The social integration strategy is obviously the more positive, hopeful approach to dealing with youthful offenders by offering them a "second chance" to become productive members of society, whereas social control options tend to negate or limit such possibilities (see Weisheit and Culbertson 1995).

But juvenile offending has remained a highly politicized event, subject to rapid shifts in policies and programs that alternate between demands for stricter social control from alarmed citizens and the media to calls for more-effective and sustained levels of treatment from reformers. Prosecuting today's teen criminals as adults appears to satisfy current political pressures. Politicians and angry citizens have urged that serious juvenile offenders no longer be provided with the luxury of the juvenile court and its more benign interventions.

Protection is off, control is on. Under the "three strikes—you're out" law, which stipulates that offenders who commit three felonies be imprisoned for 25 years to life, young offenders—who may be as young as thirteen or fourteen years old, and who have committed serious crimes—are frequently mandated (transferred) to adult court, where they are more likely than adults to be given long sentences in adult prisons.

Even first-time offenders fall under this repressive umbrella. For example, on a recent tour of a Washington State women's correctional institution I took with my students, we discovered that a sixteen-year-old girl, charged with a violent felony, had been sentenced to life without parole. No mitigating circumstances—first offense, age, gender—intruded to modify the harsh sentence.

As the research clarifies, adult treatment of juvenile offenders produces little incapacitative or deterrent value, and punishing a teenager for life strongly suggests a cruel and unusual punishment. A study conducted by researchers at the University of Florida and the University of Central Florida concluded that juveniles tried as adults actually committed new and sometimes more-serious crimes at a higher rate than those whose cases were handled in juvenile courts (*Law Enforcement News*, 1996).

The Florida study compared a group of 2,738 youths, whose cases were transferred to adult criminal courts with a matched sample of youths sentenced in the juvenile system during 1987. It found that 30 percent of the transferred youth were rearrested in the year after their release from custody, and only 19 percent of youth, whose cases remained in the juvenile justice system, committed new offenses.

What we found was that those that were transferred to adult court came back more often, more quickly and were slightly more likely to come back on felonies rather than misdemeanors. (*Law Enforcement News* 1996, 445).

Trying kids as adults apparently makes good politics, but its contribution to public policy remains counterproductive.

In a survey of police chiefs by Northeastern University's Center for Criminal Justice Policy on the effectiveness of four different approaches to reducing crime and violence, few chiefs opted for harsh punishment. Only 14 percent of the 540 police chiefs surveyed chose the policy of trying more juveniles as adults and sentencing more of them to adult prisons. Most police chiefs—one of every four big city chiefs and three out of five in the overall sample—said the best way to reduce crime and violence is to increase investment in programs that help all children and youth get off to a good start (in Broder 1996) (see also *Journal of Adolescent Research*, 1995).

At this juncture of history and youthful demographics, when we expect a population explosion of youngsters over the next decade—there are currently thirty-nine million children under age ten—now is the critical hour for implementing innovative, pro-social programs that can prevent the younger brothers (and sisters) of today's teenage violent offenders from following the same devious and self-destructive path.

THEORIES OF YOUTH VIOLENCE

Perhaps our national reaction to youth violence stems from our sheer misunderstanding of the underlying causes and conditions that trigger or fuel this antisocial behavior. Comprehending the reason *why* a person acts or behaves in a particular way is the first step toward compassion, an essential element in any effort to prevent violence and reintegrate marginal youth into the community. This approach takes strong exception to the conservative criminologist James Q. Wilson (1975), who is the leading advocate of a punishment-centered approach to the crime problem. Wilson asserts that there is no such thing as "underlying causes" of crime; and that we should abandon the attempt to discover and ameliorate or eradicate these so-called causes. Instead, he urges that as a society we continue to deal with crime in our customary fashion; namely imprisonment and punishment.

Rather than a single, comprehensive theory—which in any event does not exist at this stage of social science—this discussion will focus on some leading (and in some instances, interrelated) explanatory frameworks that contribute to our understanding of serious criminal behavior, especially violence among young men. I propose six approaches: (1) intergenerational cycle of violence; (2) mental health perspective; (3) theory of masculinities; (4) social-economic conditions; (5) psychoanalytical approach; (6) public health model.

Intergenerational Cycle of Violence

A series of ongoing studies (sponsored by the National Institute of Justice, the National Institute of Alcohol Abuse and Alcoholism, and the National Institute of Mental Health), has been examining the lives of 1,575 child victims identified in court cases of abuse and neglect dating from 1967 to 1971. By 1994 this sample would be in their late twenties and early thirties (National Institute of Justice 1996). These data show that almost half of the victims had been arrested for some type of nontraffic crime with 18 percent arrested for a violent crime. Rates of arrest were at least 25 percent higher among black victims. Another key finding is that neglected children's rates of arrest for violence were almost as high as physically abused children's. Compared with the control group, differences in arrest rates began to emerge around the ages of eight and nine.

Abuse and neglect appear to magnify preexisting disparities between the races. Black individuals who had been abused or neglected as children were being arrested at much higher rates than white individuals with the same background. In this sample group, 82 percent of black males and 50 percent of black females had been arrested for some type of offense. Fifty percent of black victims as children had an arrest for violence.

Whereas males seemed to be at increased risk for antisocial personality disorder or psychopathy, females appeared to be at increased risk for alcoholism and prostitution. Contrary to the researchers' expectations, no relationship existed between childhood abuse and teen pregnancy.

Abuse and neglect, then, act as the initial trigger for a spiral into violence. Bear in mind that not all abused and neglected children have their cases brought to court, and among those who come to the attention of the court, not all move into violent careers. But the very high rates of arrests among this sample testify to the strong relationship between childhood victimization and later criminal/violent conduct. The general lack of a proactive, preventive stance to stop the cycle of violence implies that the coercive intervention that typically characterizes the justice system's confrontation with problem youth may have further contributed to the cycle of violence.

Mental Health Perspective

Agee (1990) takes a mental health perspective to review the case histories of certain violent youth, whom she refers to as "aversive treatment evaders" (ATEs). The analysis highlights the complexity of programs that must take into account the circumstances of these violent children's lives. Not only do these youth, as a group, cause more problems than all other adolescents, but also, they cost more in terms of time, money, and effort to schools, law enforcement, and treatment providers than all other problem adolescents.

Agee observes that most of these aggressive, assaultive, and otherwise violent youth, who eventually come to be perceived as "untreatable," have been abused, abandoned, or rejected by parents, who frequently have alcohol, drug, mental, or emotional problems themselves. Such family backgrounds result in children who often have trouble trusting others and who have an inability to form and maintain relationships. Agee surmises that the violent behavior serves as an outlet for the rage and fear they endured as powerless small children, as a result of their abuse, deprivation, and neglect. Lack of motivation by parents to change their own behavior—much less participate in family counseling to correct their child's conduct—along with resistance by youth confounds the healing situation.

Other factors, Agee notes, that contribute to the failure of treatment include the dearth of specialized training among mental health professionals, who are unfamiliar with violent youth or with family/group therapy, as well as with unmotivated clients; inappropriate treatments, such as talk therapy that actually is counterproductive, because it requires a level of verbal and interpersonal skills these youth lack; and the reluctance by system managers to make a long-term commitment for these violent, troubled youth. Consequently, throughout childhood and adolescence, these children are bounced from one facility to another; from home to foster care to lockup placements in a seemingly endless cycle of institutional settings. The violent, criminal career is forged from these beginnings.

Theory of Masculinities

Men commit over 90 percent of violent crimes. According to Campbell and Muncer (1994), "violence and the male sex are virtually synonymous—the two are interwoven seamlessly in our minds as part of the natural order of things." Yet women also have a capacity for anger and aggression—as infants, they cry and tantrum as frequently as boys, and as adults experience anger as often and as intensely as men do. Why, then, are men more identified with aggressive and violent behavior? No matter how much the media promote the idea of violence as "senseless" or "mindless," masculinity as a role is inherently mired in aggressive behavior, although expressed differently, depending upon social class, age, race, and occupation.

Male violence manifests itself in acts as disparate as school bullying, sexual harassment, date rape, stranger rape, bar brawls, robbery, assault, homicide, serial murder, and a variety of other serious violent offenses (Polk 1994). All these violent behaviors, despite their seeming spontaneity and impulsiveness, serve a clear instrumental purpose and achieve interpersonal ends.

Gendered differences in social representations of aggression may be traced to contemporary structural factors, especially differential socialization of boys and girls. Boys learn in peer groups, which are large and hierarchically organized (Maccoby 1980), how to compete in hierarchical settings, and the significance of using aggression for asserting interpersonal control and achieving respect. This message is clearly reinforced in electronic presentations of the "superhero," who single-handedly defeats his opponent by violent means.

If men across cultures learn to control and manipulate their lifeworlds through violence and coercion, why, then, are not all men violent? History and personal experience certainly offer examples of gentle, loving men—Jesus, some Catholic male saints, Mahatma Gandhi, Martin Luther King, Jr., and even some members of our extended families. The key is in recognizing the diversity of masculinities. Above all, power differentials are relevant to the use of instrumental aggression among men. Hannah Arendt (1990, 56) observes: "Power and violence are opposites; where one rules absolutely the other is absent. Violence appears when power is in jeopardy." Men whose positions are under threat, or who lack social status and recognition, are most likely to engage in instrumental aggression. Whereas middle-aged, middle-class men are more likely to hold jobs with built-in power, working-class boys are more likely to be unemployed and to reside in areas where the demonstration of physical prowess and violence is accepted as a source of status (Campbell and Muncer 1994).

Traditional working-class patriarchy has been thrown into a prolonged material and ideological crisis, as increasingly large numbers of men are unable to reproduce what some theorists have called "hegemonic masculinity" (Connell 1987; Messerschmidt 1993). The restructuring of the global economy has most severely impacted on ethnic and immigrant groups.

Phillippe Bourgois (1996) conducted ethnographic fieldwork while residing next to a crack house in El Barrio, New York, for five years. The second- and third-generation Puerto Rican immigrant men he encountered have experienced profound social and economic marginalization, subsequently turning their rage and impotence against women and children in the family and against other men in the ghetto street. Unable to replicate the rural-based models of masculinity and family structure of their grandfathers' generation or to develop either an industrial working-class role (i.e., subordinate status) or a service-oriented ethic (i.e., high social skills) in this deindustrialized, high-tech inner city, these marginalized men have taken refuge in the drug economy. In this context, Bourgois says, they "celebrate a misogynist, predatory street culture that normalizes gang rape, sexual conquest, and paternal abandonment." In the absence of prosocial roles organized around traditional masculinity (to procreate, protect, and provide), a distorted identity arises based on "fear of disrespect." These data point to one conclusion: Until American society shifts from the de facto apartheid thinking that tolerates rising levels of misery among the working poor, interpersonal violence and community destruction will only get worse.

We should consider the diverse ways that men accomplish masculinity in the "risk society," especially when they are excluded from conventional routes to masculine identity. Among underclass youth, sex, drug dealing, drug taking, "normal" crime, and violence are central in creating a street style of "spectacular consumption, excessive drug use and edgework—the attempt to live a life at the edge of order and on the edge of chaos" (Jefferson 1996, 345).

Social-Economic Conditions

As an explanatory schema, social-economic conditions offer a structured analysis that often ignores the subjective mind-set of the social actor. Still, this approach points to systematic efforts to situate violence in relation to broader social relations, such as the notion of a "culture of violence" (Luckenbill and Doyle 1996; Mock 1996). Newer models of social structure are more likely to include the psychological impact of inequality and its capacity to generate shame, humiliation, rage, and other emotions (J. Gilligan 1996).

In his discussion of crime in America, Currie (1985, 146) comments that "there is an accumulated fund of sophisticated research linking serious crime with social and economic inequality." Whereas some studies have found a relationship between poverty and crime (for example, Taylor and Covington 1988), other scholars indicate that income inequality (the degree of relative poverty) is a better determinant of crime than absolute poverty. Braithwaite and Braithwaite (1980) conclude from their study of homicide rates in thirty-one nations that higher homicide rates are strongly related to economic inequalities. Their measures of economic inequality included the gap between the rich and the average wage earner, the disparities in income between workers in different sectors of industry, and the percentage of gross national product spent on social security.

In the United States, Blau and Blau (1982) found that high rates of criminal violence were strongly related to economic inequalities, particularly when these inequalities were based on race. Others have argued that the important factor for understanding criminal involvement is not whether a person is out of work, but rather the nature of that person's relationship to the work force. The increasing marginalization of some groups, particularly the young (Polk 1988), and the development of an "underclass" (Duster 1988) imply that some people are not simply out of work, but they are so far out that they have ceased looking for it (Currie 1985, 117).

We have already seen that violence and its control are men's work. Gender, then, is a defining structure in analysis of violence (Davis and Stasz

1990; Felson 1996). So, too, is race as we glimpsed earlier in our discussion of the greater risk for serious crime among African American children who experienced abuse as children, compared to whites (D. F. Hawkins 1995). Having considered in the case of the New York Puerto Rican barrio men how the postindustrial society has largely swept away the need for physical labor—inexorably creating a surplus population of men without traditional work or identities—this analysis requires that we attend to the deep social, cultural, and economic crises that afflict some postindustrial countries.

Joachim Kersten's (1996) work on sexual assault against women questions why reported rates and media visibility of rape are high in Australia, low in Japan, and in Germany somewhere in between. In Japan, it would appear an entire host of factors—cultural, organizational, and even architectural—combine to protect Japanese women and dissociate masculinity and assaultive behavior. Japan's streets are far safer for women than those in Western countries.

Australia, by contrast, is a society where the "national male character" of independence and physical prowess (i.e., frontier man) is being undermined by the continent's "deep social, cultural and economic crisis which has implications for gender relations." Large-scale farming in Australia, long associated with maleness and the physical strength of the individual farm worker, has been undermined by a shifting economy of high-tech electronics, a complex service industry, and tourism, all affecting youth (see Box 8-B). Neither Japan nor Germany has such large-scale agricultural productions; both countries have traditionally divested farming from masculinity; and their economies are more firmly established along the lines of postindustrial products and services (Kersten 1996).

Class and caste both play integral roles in the etiology of behavioral violence, once the emotional impact of social inequality is taken into account. Sennett and Cobb (1973) investigated the psychology of social class in America through a series of interviews with manual laborers and their families. They conclude that the terrible thing about class in our society is that it sets up a "contest for dignity," wherein those on the bottom rung of the social ladder by definition lose. The class structure operates impersonally at one level to create a set of social conditions that generates feelings of deep inadequacy and shame on those at the lowest end of the hierarchy. It should be emphasized that it is not poverty or deprivation in an absolute sense that causes shame—not the lack of material goods or services, as such—but rather the loss of dignity, self-respect, and pride. It is the disparity between rich and poor—between those at the top and those on the bottom—that allows the arrogance of elites to humiliate those members of lower-status groups. Marx referred to "shame" as the "emotion of revolution," so powerful that it can mobilize millions to cast off their oppressors by violence (see Fanon 1968).

Admittedly, most of this propensity for violence against the "haves" by

---

Box 8-B
Global Perspectives: The Australian Case

Changes in the labor market and in state policy have resulted in creating the "youth problem," according to recent research by Rob White and Associates in Western Australia. It is a problem of many dimensions, ranging from soaring levels of suicide, unemployment, and poverty through to an increasing problem of homelessness and violent victimization among young persons. Over the last few years a greater proportion of young people have been excluded from the wider society; they feel left out and marginalized. This is expressed both in terms of their reduced role in the social-economic relations of production and reproduction, and their minimal role in the consumption of the goods and services generally available.

Based upon a major survey of youth workers in Western Australia, the research emphasizes how social exclusion, homelessness, and violence work in a systematic process to negatively affect the emotional and physical disposition of large numbers of youth. Placed outside the mainstream of economic life, many young people have taken to the streets and youth shelters as a means to escape the conflicts in the parental home, and because of the inadequacies of social welfare policies. Among users of youth services, high levels of violent victimization regularly occur among the homeless group, resulting in 86 percent of the respondents reporting that they have been physically hurt by someone since leaving home (96 percent of males, 74 percent of females). A sizable proportion of the sample reported that police officers have threatened, bullied, or bashed them. Lack of legal redress for young people raises serious questions concerning the link between "legitimate violence" (against marginal and suspect populations) and "legitimate rights" (which are denied homeless and unemployed youth).

Source: R. White, R. Underwood, and S. Omelczuk. 1991. "Victims of Violence: The View from the Youth Services." *Australian-New Zealand Journal of Criminology* 24: 5–39.

---

the "have-nots" has taken distinctly different forms than those envisioned by Marx. Displaced violence against women and children is certainly more likely today than the mobilization of armies of the poor against the tyrannical elite. And terrorism, backed up by weaker governments against more powerful ones, is played out by individuals or small groups in rituals of violence that erode safety and security of dominant groups but that fail utterly to displace ruling classes (e.g., Israel and Palestine, Iraq and the United States) (see Davis and Stasz 1990).

Social caste—race and ethnic disparities in status, wealth, and honor—provides another condition that conduces to violence, a point we cannot overemphasize. Malcolm X (1966), a gifted African American leader, came to interpret the race situation in America as different from his original analysis of the individuality of racism. It was not a matter of the individual white man, he reasoned after his pilgrimage to Mecca, but rather, the American political, economic, and social atmosphere that automatically nourishes a racist psychology.

> The white man is not inherently evil, but America's racist society influences him to act evilly. The society has produced and nourishes a psychology which brings out the lowest, most base part of human beings. (p. 34)

Thus, it is not the race of a people, but their social circumstances that contribute to violence. This analysis is supported by anthropological studies of native African populations with intact cultures whose homicide rates are far below those among blacks in this country (Bohannan 1960). These data support the conclusion that the elevated, black homicide rate in America is not a function of race, biology or heredity, but of the conditions to which blacks have been subjected.

The racist ideology that has so overwhelmed many African Americans with extremities of shame, inferiority, humiliation, and soul mutilation has not had an equally deleterious effect on other minority groups. Whereas an intact culture can provide people with a powerful means to protect themselves and to bolster their self-esteem, this is not the case for weak cultures, whose traditions have been eradicated and whose new ones are often dysfunctional, because of historical exclusion (Fanon 1968; J. Gilligan 1996). Among minority groups, such as Jews and Asians, discrimination has not diminished their cultural integrity. Among these cultures, widely shared and collectively shared norms of education and achievement have reinforced effective mechanisms learned in the family for maintaining self-respect and diminishing individual and group vulnerability. The high level of professional successes among these groups further acts as positive feedback to support personal and group integrity.

Psychoanalytical Approach

The psychoanalytical, or depth psychology, approach that has so enhanced the social structural analysis, inasmuch as it takes account of the nonrational and feeling elements of individuals, works with four assumptions:

1. Social structure is mediated through personal experience, language, feelings, and rituals.
2. Human action involves the nonrational (or unconscious) as well as the rational component (minded behavior).
3. Meanings that are repressed (shut down) or suppressed (aware, but not expressed in everyday language or action) may take symbolic (and often devious)

forms. These include slips of the tongue, bodily symptoms, acting-out behaviors, and other nonlinguistic expressions, including violence against oneself or others.

4. Individuals acting out of unconscious drives or repressed behavior may be wholly unaware of their meanings. Instead, they may displace their "unthinkable" or "unspeakable" precognitions or feelings into symbolic behavior that takes compulsive or ritual forms (e.g., serial murder) (J. Gilligan 1996).

Projection is another defense mechanism that enables persons out of touch with their unconscious to blame or credit other persons with their own psychic "stew." In still other cases, persons may blame themselves for what clearly is out of their control. Thus, the trained psychoanalyst's task is to uncover the mystery that the symbolic behavior presents; in a word, to lay bare the essential meanings of the symbolic acts. For example, women survivors of rape, who blame themselves for the violence perpetrated against them, will often take frequent and extensive showers to "cleanse" themselves from what they feel is a polluted self. Not until they "get in touch" with their own lack of culpability—their essential guiltlessness—can the healing process begin (Courtois 1988).

How does this analysis pertain to violent youth? According to the depth psychology approach, personality traits—such as hypersensitivity to ridicule, self-pity, fear of shame, and sense of inadequacy, as well as the overbearing need to prevent others from laughing at oneself by making them weep instead—serve as the dominant motives for violence (J. Gilligan 1996). The criminologist Jack Katz (1988) described murderers' conception of what they were doing as performing an act of "righteous slaughter." As exaggerated as this may sound, murderers have "simply gone back to the behavioral origins of the ritual sacrifice of humans" to displace their overpowering feelings of shame (J. Gilligan 1996, 77). Thus, the violent youth can be said to be communicating symbolically through his body to the body of his victim, saying, in effect: "I am not a wimp, a punk, and a pussy—I am not shamed by others, I will shame them instead" (J. Gilligan 1996, 78). This implies that bodily actions serve as a mode of communication and symbolization that can function as an alternative to language.

Shame is the driving force behind different forms of violence, whether toward individuals, groups, or entire populations. James Gilligan (1996) a Harvard-trained psychiatrist, who has worked with violent men in prison for twenty-five years, clarifies the meaning of violence:

The purpose of violence is to diminish the intensity of shame and replace it as far as possible with its opposite, pride, thus preventing the individual from being overwhelmed by the feeling of shame. Violence toward others, such as homicide, is an attempt to replace shame with pride. (p. 77)

Not all men who feel ashamed will inflict lethal or life-threatening, mutilating, or disabling injuries on others. James Gilligan (1996) observes that

three preconditions must be met before shame can lead to the full patho-
genesis of violent behavior. The first precondition—and a carefully guarded
"secret"—is that violent men often feel "deeply ashamed, chronically
ashamed, acutely ashamed, over matters that are so trivial that their very
triviality makes it even more shameful to feel ashamed about" (p. 111).
Such a shame-based psychological state may gravitate around a sense of
inadequacy about appearance, ability to attract women, intellectual capacity, occupational skill level, or other self-defined deficiencies.

Additionally, for young men in prison, "the inmate . . . is figuratively
castrated by his involuntary celibacy," contributing to deep anxieties about
his own maleness (Sykes 1958). The inmate, shut off from the world of
women, may experience more damaging psychological outcomes than the
physiological ones associated with castration, as he is now "in danger of
becoming half complete, fractured. . . . His sense of himself as a man" is in
jeopardy (Sykes 1958, 70–72).

This implies that the greater the shame, the greater the need to conceal
the shame, because shame threatens their adult, masculine, heterosexual
identity, their very selfhood. Violent men often hide this "secret" behind
the mask of "machismo," arrogance, bravado, or studied indifference. Behind the mask of "cool" or self-assurance that many violent men reflect in
their faces to the world is a desperation over the fear of losing face.

A second precondition that leads up to the violence is when the men
come to have a definition of the situation as having no nonviolent means
of warding off or diminishing their feelings of shame and low self-esteem.
Violence then is a last resort for staving off their fear of becoming a non-
person.

A third precondition for engaging in violent behavior is that the person
lacks the emotional capacities or the feelings that normally inhibit the violent impulses that are stimulated by shame. Love and guilt toward others
and fear for the self—these capacities are required to stop violent expressions. At the time the men committed the violence, they were incapable of
feeling love, guilt, or fear. Because punishment alleviates the feeling of
wrongdoing, it exonerates the individual offender from guilt. This is why
the more we punish criminals or children, the more violent they become.
As punishment increases their feelings of shame and at the same time de-
creases their capacities for feelings of love for others, and of guilt toward
others, the person is free to strike back in the belief that not to do so would
erode or destroy his fragile self.

Public Health Model

An epidemic of violence—violence as a disease, as a contagious illness
that moves into and afflicts specific populations who may be "at risk"—
offers both an intruiging analysis, as well as a policy-based approach. In-

itially, "epidemic" was perceived as a metaphor, simply a way of talking about the soaring rates of violent crime; an image of violence as a cancer with endlessly reproducing cells that eventually destroys its host. Most recently, violence as "illness" and "disease" can be understood and conceptualized in medical terms as a "bio-psycho-social" problem, as a phenomenon that simultaneously causes and has effects on biological, psychological, and social systems. James Gilligan (1996) proposes a literal meaning of violence as "disease":

Violence, and also the social and psychological forces that cause violence, create biological pain, injury, mutilation, disability, and death just as literally as does any bacillus or malignancy. . . . Violence [is] a bio-medical problem, a problem in public health and preventive psychiatry. (p. 99)

Whereas James Gilligan's conceptualization of violence borrows heavily from psychiatric models of intervention, another approach by J. David Hawkins (1995) proposes a more classic public health model as appropriate for use as part of a criminal justice strategy. As applied to disease control, Hawkins draws on an example of the process used to prevent cardiovascular disease.

First, researchers in the field identified risk factors; that is the factors whose presence increased a person's chances of contracting the disease. Tobacco use, high-fat diet, sedentary lifestyle, high levels of stress, and family history of heart disease—all were identified as raising the possibility of the onset of heart disease.

Second, researchers determined what protective factors—for example, aerobic exercise, relaxation techniques, diet, nutrition, weight loss, and so forth—helped prevent the development of heart problems.

Third, the goal was to reduce or counter the identified risk factors for heart disease in the population at large. Their strategy involved launching a massive advocacy campaign that would impact the media, corporations, schools, government, and the general public, and that aimed to eliminate "at risk" behaviors (and the attitudes supporting them). The success of this campaign has paid off. There has been a 45 percent decrease in the incidence of cardiovascular disease, due in large measure to "risk-focused prevention" (J. D. Hawkins 1995, 11).

A similar process can work for violence, says Hawkins. Using the public health model to reduce violence in America's communities calls for a two-step process. First, identify the factors that put young people at risk for violence in order to reduce or eliminate these factors; and second, strengthen the protective factors that buffer the effects of exposure to risk. Here we are, back to structural conditions, as well as individual circumstances, that raise the likelihood that youths will turn to violence to resolve conflict.

In this model, four sets of risk factors may be identified: community factors, family factors, school-related factors, and individual factors (J. D. Hawkins 1995; Blumstein 1995). The specific risks may vary from individual to individual, just as they would for a medical disease. Furthermore, research and prevention may identify additional factors that play a significant role in the etiology of violence (Hawkins, Catalano, and Miller 1992) (see Table 8.5).

Community factors play a critical role, as well as generate risks for young persons. In many lower-income communities, laws and norms favorable to crime operate as a positive reinforcement for youth to "try out" criminal activities with few community barriers to prevent it. Neighborhoods characterized by extreme economic depression, especially in a society surrounded with images of affluence and high levels of transition and mobility, tend to foster crime as an alternative to poverty and neglect.

It is not merely the poor and financially depressed neighborhood that generates a risk structure for young people, but also the character of that neighborhood. Persons who reside in debilitated communities often have little or no attachment to place, particularly when the neighborhood is highly diverse, and in transition from one usage or population to another. Gentrification, a process whereby upper-middle, professional groups move into low-income neighborhoods because of relatively inexpensive housing, but displace the former residents, often triggers local crime waves (see W. J. Wilson 1987). The presence of gangs and firearms is invariably linked to high rates of violent crime (Greenfeld and Zawitz 1995). In such neighborhoods, young people may join gangs out of coercion and carry guns out of fear.

Family factors, too, make a significant contribution either to enhancing the risks of growing up to be a violent man or to reducing such possibilities from occurring. Certainly, poverty plays a crucial role, because being poor may not only reduce a family's capacity for providing a decent living standard, but it also limits where you live and who your friends are. Parental skills may not have been learned in their own childhood, and thus, low-resourced parents may be maladroit or even destructive in their management of children. Single parents, unemployed parents, overwhelmed parents generally may unwittingly set their children up for early home leaving and criminal behavior. Children who are not recognized for their positive behavior (e.g., bringing home good grades); who receive inconsistent or harsh punishment; who have few or no parental expectations for achievement; and whose parents fail to monitor their activities are all placed in high-risk circumstances (J. D. Hawkins, 1995). When you add to this the presence of intergenerational family violence and parental alcoholism or drug addiction, you have a toxic blend of ingredients that makes for very high-risk outcomes for vulnerable youth (Pagelow 1984).

School-related factors are often neglected in risk analysis. As critics have

Table 8.5
Risk Factors for Health and Behavior Problems

Communities That Care®

Risk Factors	Substance Abuse	Delinquency	Teen Pregnancy	School Drop-Out	Violence
Community					
Availability of Drugs	✔				✔
Availability of Firearms		✔			✔
Community Laws and Norms Favorable Toward Drug Use, Firearms, and Crime	✔	✔			✔
Media Portrayals of Violence					✔
Transitions and Mobility	✔	✔		✔	
Low Neighborhood Attachment and Community Disorganization	✔	✔			✔
Extreme Economic Deprivation	✔	✔	✔	✔	✔
Family					
Family History of the Problem Behavior	✔	✔	✔	✔	✔
Family Management Problems	✔	✔	✔	✔	✔
Family Conflict	✔	✔	✔	✔	✔
Favorable Parental Attitudes and Involvement in the Problem Behavior	✔	✔			✔
School					
Early and Persistent Antisocial Behavior	✔	✔	✔	✔	✔
Academic Failure Beginning in Late Elementary School	✔	✔	✔	✔	✔
Lack of Commitment to School	✔	✔	✔	✔	✔
Individual/Peer					
Alienation and Rebelliousness	✔	✔		✔	
Friends Who Engage in the Problem Behavior	✔	✔	✔	✔	✔
Favorable Attitudes Toward the Problem Behavior	✔	✔	✔	✔	
Early Initiation of the Problem Behavior	✔	✔	✔	✔	✔
Constitutional Factors	✔	✔			✔

Adolescent Problem Behaviors

© 1996-1998 Developmental Research and Programs

Source: © 1990–1998. Reprinted with permission from Developmental Research and Programs, Inc., Seattle, WA., developers of the Communities That Care® operating system for research-based prevention. For information call 800–736–2630.

emphasized, the school plays a fundamental role in shaping the next generation (Kozol 1992). In many urban school districts, inadequate resources—out-of-date books, lack of programs taken for granted in wealthy districts (such as music), unmotivated students who fail to see the relevance of school for their own constricted lives—all are factors in reproducing the poverty and crime that young people see around them. Many schools are facing earlier onsets of antisocial behavior, children who disrupt classes but are too young to expel. How do schools manage severe deficiencies in students' capacity for learning, such as Attention Deficit Disorder? Failure to intervene early in a child's life may lead to unredeemable outcomes, such as dropping out of school, teen pregnancy, gang involvement, drugs, and violence.

Individual factors must be examined to assess the larger risk picture that prevails for many young persons. Some risk features are linked to family of origin, such as failure to bond or only weak bonding with family members, teachers, and other adults. Family dynamics may also account for a nonresilient personality, one that is rigid and uncompromising, or development of negative social attitudes that preclude effective coping and learning. Low self-concept, when linked to shame, offers an especially precarious situation for young people; as does the early onset of substance abuse (Robins and Ratcliff 1979).

Cultural factors, it should be noted, are not included in Table 8.5. How do cultural factors affect violent behavior? Cultural conditions, such as racial, gender, ethnic, and class distinctions and ideologies, conduce to violent resolutions to intergroup conflict. For example, learned values of masculine dominance are highly associated with sexual violence (Messerschmidt 1993). Among the "have-nots," lack of legitimate opportunities for work and participation in the larger community may set the stage for violent attacks against the "haves," including primitive and reactionary group violence (e.g., looting) (Davis and Stasz, 1990). Media portrayals of violence are a society-wide problem, in the sense that the media present ready-made "solutions" to complex problems of living as manageable through violence. Marginal youth may be most affected by such violent scenarios.

Identifying risk factors provides only half of any public health model. The model must also take into account why some youth, although exposed to multiple risk factors, do not succumb to violent, antisocial behavior. J. D. Hawkins (1995, 13) indicates that three major protective factors reduce the impact of negative risk factors by "providing positive ways for an individual to respond to these risks."

- *Individual characteristics*: A resilient temperament and positive social orientation

- *Bonding*: Positive relationships with family members, teachers, or other adults

• *Healthy beliefs and clear standards*: Beliefs in children's competence to succeed in school and avoid drugs and crime coupled with establishing clear expectations and rules governing their behavior

CONCLUSION

Having delineated the scope of criminal violence and victimization among youth, and having offered some leading theoretical frameworks for understanding or preventing this serious problem, we arrive at an impasse. Until the society as a whole is willing to take responsibility for what is destroying our young people by changing the root sources of the problem, matters will only grow worse, despite the temporary and minor decline in youth violence. It is probably woefully true that not until the culture undergoes radical transformation can we begin to ameliorate the rage, shame, and impotence that we, as an entire society, heap on the most vulnerable of our young people. The society is ripe for such a shift. If we choose to collectively engage in a spiritual regeneration, a revaluation of values, and a human-centered children's policy based on care and compassion, we may yet salvage this fragmented society. To do otherwise is to continue to invite the forces of violence that imperil our world.

Next, Chapter 9 takes up the issue of gangs—their sources, organization, and consequences—and concludes that gangs are not so much parallel communities operating to meet the interests and needs of their members—a mythical view proposed by some observers—as much as an amorphous collection of marginal young men (and to a lesser extent, young women). These youth seek identity and a sense of community, but their activities, frequently illegal and sometimes violent, threaten the integrity of the larger community within which they operate.

NOTES

1. U.S. Senate Hearing on the Status of the Juvenile Justice System in America, November 26, 1991, Washington, DC.

2. *Eugene* (OR) *Weekly*, March 30, 1995.

9

The Gang as Pseudo Community

One lives in a community, one enjoys the advantages of a communality.
. . . One dwells protected, cared for, in peace and trustfulness, without
fear of certain injuries and hostile acts to which the *man outside*, the
"man without peace," is exposed . . . since one has bound and pledged
oneself to the community precisely with a view to injuries and hostile
acts. What will happen if this pledge is broken? The community . . .
will get what repayment it can, one may depend on that. . . . Quite
apart from this, the lawbreaker is above all a "breaker," a breaker of
his contract and his word with the whole in respect to all the benefits
and comforts of communal life of which he has hitherto had a share.
. . . The wrath of . . . the community, throws him back again into the
savage and outlaw state . . . it thrusts him away—and now every kind
of hostility may be vented upon him.

                                      Friedrich Nietzsche, *Ecce Homo*

THE GANG AND COMMUNITY

The "gang problem," and our society's attempts at controlling the more
violent aspects of youthful delinquency and crime, has preoccupied ordinary Americans, law enforcement officials, researchers, and youth specialists for generations. Philosophers, such as Nietzsche, and even the ancient
Greeks, most notably, Plato and Aristotle, were no exception to this concern, as they pondered the problems of youth and how to socialize and
inculcate in the young the values of the community. As early as 1555,
England struggled with control of the "ragged classes": the destitute, handicapped, orphaned and delinquent youth (Brake 1985). Today,
gangs, drugs, and guns severely complicate society's efforts at social control
of young people.

In the nineteenth century, Nietzsche (1969) asked the poignant question:

What happens when the social contract, the written and unwritten rules of society, no longer has meaning or promise for the young persons living in marginal circumstances? The social "instinct," the notion of striving to be an important and valued member of one's community, does not simply wither away. Those individuals who have been cast aside, aware that they are not respected, still have a "will to power" (Nietzsche's phrase) and will seek other channels to exercise their demands for empowerment and inclusion. "Everyone wants to have power over their world," rapper Ice-T (1995) argues in "The Killing Fields," even if it requires the total negation of the larger community.

Gangs were born out of this chaos—the inner city. When you grow up in South Central [Los Angeles], and you've never had anything in your life you control, you seek control. Gangs offer you ultimate control to do what you want. Just getting that for a minute is very intoxicating. Gang members are out there trying to control their own little world. It's only a little tiny block they live in for years, and in some cases their entire lives. It's theirs. That becomes their whole world. Everyone wants to have power over their world.

In this sense, gangs reflect the unraveling of community in favor of competitive relations between micro life worlds; a life strategy, we argue, that is calculated for self- and other destruction.

PSEUDO COMMUNITY

It is useful to retain the concept of community as we explore a parallel construct of the "pseudo community." Briefly, the community embraces the idea of a social group whose members live in a specific locality, share institutions and governance, have a common heritage, experience a sense of mutuality, and in viable communities, care for one another. In the sociological sense, the term *community* evokes images of security and familiarity (McNall and McNall 1992). A community is also characterized by diversity: variations in population, social and occupational groups, and interest groups, which combine to create a social organization of common character.

The gang as pseudo community has adapted some of the familiar institutions of society, such as work/business/money activities, extended family structures, social relationships, and fraternal organizations' rituals and membership rules. The gang, however, has restructured this apparatus into a quasi-tribal or premodern social organization that mimics a feudal economic order. For example, with some exceptions, much of the "feuding" between gangs is organized around "turf," or areas demarcated as one gang's territory or boundary. The gang's attempt to create parallel social, economic, educational, and political structures to replace those its individual members believe they have lost—or, more likely, never had—has failed.

A widely recognized gang characteristic includes alienation from the traditional foundations of community—home, school, work, as well as adult and elderly role models and associates—which serves to isolate the gang, rendering it apart from the fabric of society. This chapter examines the methods by which youth and street gangs seek to create a sense of community. Gangs are formed from the commonalities of ethnic identity, neighborhood residence, language, cultural background, financial pursuits, hobbies, economic deprivation, close associations built upon interests, affiliation, hierarchical relationships, gender, or age—considered together, these could conceivably fashion a community. But a community is also about caring for its members—providing a collective sense of security; offering opportunities to earn a livelihood on a sustained basis; and ensuring the durability of the community for future generations. At this point, the lack of fit with the community concept is pronounced.

There may be some exceptions, as a closer examination of the Chinese gangs demonstrates. However, our thesis that youth and street gangs only superficially resemble genuine community will be borne out by the data we examine here.

DEFINING GANGS

We first draw upon the widely cited definition of gangs by Malcolm Klein (1971, 13), a distinguished researcher of gang life. A gang is any identifiable group of youngsters who (a) are generally perceived as a distinct aggregation by others in their neighborhood, (b) recognize themselves as a distinct group (almost invariably with a group name), and (c) have been involved in a sufficient number of delinquent incidents to call forth a consistent negative response from neighborhood residents and/or law enforcement agencies. The second part of this definition has been expanded by Vigil (1990, 61) in his discussion of the marginalization of ethnic minority youth, who actively seek a "sense of belonging." Some of his gang informants drew almost exclusively upon the gang for their sense of self and place in the social order, although this identity varied with the individuals' commitment to the gang (p. 62).

Cohen (1990, 10) notes that when criminologists refer to gangs, "they usually are thinking of collectivities [that] emphasize size, organizational complexity, urban location, hierarchy, leadership, territory . . . plus some propensity to disruptive, 'antisocial' or criminal behavior." Esbensen and Huizinga (1993, 569) emphasize that "in order to be considered a gang, the groups must be involved in illegal activity." But Short (1990, 3) rejects the delinquent status as a defining characteristic; instead, he admonishes researchers to "understand gang identity and behavior, and the reactions of others to gangs . . . and the *significance* of names, for gangs, and for others" before assuming delinquent behavior to be the overarching characteristic.

Fleisher (1995, 147) has conducted extensive fieldwork among gangs and street hustlers in Seattle and offers a grounded perspective of the gang as a social group

composed of adolescents who form a weak social network with intergenerational longevity. . . . A gang has a coherent expressive culture, which denotes the network's outer boundary through various symbolic markers such as a distinctive name, origin tales, specialized vocabulary, and secular rituals and traditions.

The unique distinguishing feature of this expressive culture, Fleisher adds, is its fatalistic ritualism predicated on a "mythology of death." In fact, funerals are the only events at which all members of a gang gather together (Fleisher 1995, 143).

Teenage gang members in the Kansas City metropolitan area purchase their own coffins, decorate them with gang graffiti, and pose inside the coffin for "death photographs."

In addition to group rules, leadership structure, internal sanctions, initiation and exit rituals (e.g., especially death), Fleisher contends that the intergenerational nature of gangs—the gang lasts more than one generation, or put another way, gangs do survive beyond their membership—be recognized as the distinctive gang feature. This quality, above all, separates delinquent groups from neighborhood gangs (Fleisher 1995).

Rather than creating community, many gangs in the 1990s represent the antithesis: undermining community through alienation, random violence and law breaking, and their numbers are growing. Precise counts of gangs are difficult to determine, as police contact is the basis for obtaining statistical crime data. And who is a member of the gang may vary with the purposes and methods for defining "gangs" (Ball and Curry 1995). For example, W. B. Miller (1981) has identified twenty types of law-violating youth groups, including robbery bands, local criminal cliques, assaultive affiliation cliques, drug-dealing networks, and others. Only two types constitute the classic "gang" concept: turf gangs and fighting gangs; the others have only ganglike features.

Another perspective, subculture theory, lends credence to the pseudo community notion we have proposed. The subculture concept earlier dominated the study of gangs, and continues to offer insights into gang formation (Miller and Cohen 1996). Theorists stress that some environments are characterized by atypical, criminogenic values and normative systems, making deviant behavior more or less normal in that setting. These environments effectively prevent gang members from integrating into the dominant society, as well as causing open or covert conflicts.

Subculture theory offers a rich mine of studies on gangs. Short (1990) observes that youth criminal subcultures comprise boys from poor and ethnic backgrounds who perceive few or no legitimate opportunities and live in low-resourced families and communities. The gang serves as an alternative to rejection. The gang as subculture represents a "collective response to a shared problem" (Miller and Cohen 1996). Fleisher (1995, 149) sees few benefits in such subcultures. Instead, he notes that "gangs are a visual symbol of depraved families," the outcome of intracommunity poverty and society's political and economic neglect. Robert Bly (1996), a poet and mythologist, depicts troubled youth as expressing the "rage of the unparented." Hence, gangs serve merely to act as parent substitutes for emotionally abandoned youngsters.

Although it could be argued that no two gangs are alike, a number of characteristics appears consistently in a gang member's profile. Ethnicity strongly factors into gang membership, particularly if the individual is a member of an ethnic group that has experienced significant difficulty and discrimination in work, housing, residence, income and socioeconomic status, education, language, or other social indicator. Typically, the minority gang youth's family is poor or underemployed. If the family has recently immigrated to the United States, the parent or parents may be preoccupied with financial survival and may not have time or attention to devote to the youth. Particularly among Latino youth gang members, poor performance in school is closely associated with the propensity to join a gang, because success in school is a predictor of financial and occupational achievement. Conversely, achievement in school for Latino youth can be the bulwark against future gang involvement (Los Angeles Police Department 1990b).

For many minority youth, the ethnic community of which he or she is a part may not provide the strong ties of kinship and relatedness for the American-born or newcomer ethnic youth. The alienation experienced by these youth may not be understood by the family, and the young people may quickly assess the reluctance of their "mainstream" or "Anglo" peers to accept them into their social groups. The gang becomes the "substitute" or "surrogate" family, as well as the primary youth cohort group. Gang researchers have identified a number of discrete groups that comprise youth gangs: African-American, Mexican-American and Puerto-Rican, female, Chinese, Japanese, Cambodian, Vietnamese, Samoan, Filipino, and ideologically inclined Caucasian youth gangs, such as Skinheads.

Age is a critical variable in youth gang membership. Typically, gang members are between ten to twenty-two years of age, but children as young as five and adults (less frequently) up to age thirty-two have been reported to be involved in gangs (see Ball and Curry 1995, 235). The National Gang

Crime Research Center (1995) reports typical age-related events among a large sample of gang members (see Box 9-A, which includes Figure 9.1).

One of the earliest gang researchers, Frederick Thrasher (1927), used age as the most identifiable gang characteristic. Thrasher (1927, 46) observed that the gang is

an interstitial group originally formed spontaneously and then integrated through conflict. . . . The result of this collective behavior is the development of traditional, unreflective internal structure, *esprit de corps*, solidarity, morale, group awareness, and attachment to local territory.

The term "interstitial" is a sociobiological one, and refers to an entity that is in between one place and another. Adolescence is the stage of life to which Thrasher refers; he saw gang development as a transitional, age-related stage in the youth's life. Above all, Thrasher recognized that weak social controls are a major factor in gang development (Miller and Cohen 1996).

Contemporary theorists have added other dimensions. Bursik and Gras-mick (1993) perceptively argue that "interstitial" refers to a geographic locality in cities; "interstitial" neighborhoods are adjacent to the central business district and the more-upscale neighborhoods. Characterized by high residential mobility and marked urban decay, in recent years, urban "renewal" has resulted in high-rise housing primarily for low-income households and the construction of freeways. In this way the city has created virtual boundaries guaranteeing the institutionalization of poverty in urban neighborhoods and the effective isolation of their hapless residents. The young captured in these neighborhoods are among the most impoverished of all age groups. Nationally, one of every three children lives in poverty; in inner-city areas, one of every two children is condemned to poverty.

It is not surprising, given the high concentration of persons in poverty, neighborhoods in distress and decay, and a perception of the intractability of one's personal circumstances, that the impetus for adolescent crime is in place. Is delinquency the primary motive for gang membership? Sociologists disagree. Delinquency may be the by-product of intense peer relationships among adolescents, who typically are high-end risk-takers. Some of the payoffs for the typical youth gang member, according to the Gang Activities section of the Los Angeles County Sheriff's Department (1994) are the following.

First, gang membership confers status and identity for the young person, often with the added attraction of standing out from the crowd with gang insignia, colors, nomenclature, language, hand signals, and the like.

Second, gang membership can provide the youth with the feeling of being protected from harm, because he or she typically lives in a gang-prone

Box 9-A
Mean Ages for Major Life Events among a Large
Sample of Gang Members

Project GANGPINT, sponsored by the National Gang Crime Research Center, reported in its 1995 survey of 1,994 gang members that the age range was from 10 years to 56 years, with 88.8 percent of the respondents under the age of 18 years. Almost all of the gang respondents were male (91.3 percent). The average length of time spent in a gang for this group was about 4.5 years, and nearly half (46.7 percent) had tried to quit the gang at least once. The responses to age-related questions show that early onset of gang influences tend to prevail among large numbers of inner-city youth, as Figure 9.1 shows.

Figure 9.1
Mean Ages for Major Life Events among a Large
Sample of Gang Members

Major Life Event	Mean Age
First heard about gangs	8.9 years
First met someone in a gang	9.2
First fired a handgun	11.3
First saw someone killed or injured due to gang violence	11.3
First joined a gang	12.0
First time taken into police custody	12.3
First got permanent tattoo	13.0

The authors conclude that while the average age for information about, and initiation into gangs, was relatively young—about 65 percent first joined a gang when they were between the ages of 11 and 14 years—older gang members were a clear presence, and were clearly the leaders. Thus, "youth gangs" are often led by middle-aged adults.

Source: Edward Tromanhauser. 1995. "A Descriptive Survey of Selected Characteristics of Street Gang Members in the United States," from a preliminary data analysis conducted by the National Gang Crime Research Center. Paper presented at the Meeting of the American Society of Criminology, Boston, November 16.

neighborhood and will surely be at-risk from other rival gangs. Gang ideology is infused with *de facto* contractual obligations of the gang to support individual members if attacked, and to provide backup for retaliatory attacks if wrongdoing by other individuals or gangs is perpetrated against the member.

Third, the gang "promises" to be the substitute for the family, offering support and safety. The youthful gang member may never have experienced an interpersonal relationship offering affiliation and acceptance. Hence, even the meager version the youth experiences in a gang could be the most significant experience the youth has encountered.

Fourth, the specter of threats to the youth's physical safety often make the gang appear to be the only "safe haven" to which he can turn when repeated intimidation takes place via practices, such as stealing personal expense money or physical assault. LAPD Detective Suarez notes that this pressure may be so severe that "If a particularly violent gang war is in progress, recruitment tactics used by a gang can be extremely violent, even to the point of murdering the non-member to coerce others into joining the gang" (LAPD, 1990b, 2).

The current state of gang theory is best summarized by the concept of "urban underclass," considered to be an established social class beneath the traditional lower class. Underclass theorists recognize that a distinct subculture has emerged that disrupts family and community controls, and promotes utilitarian crime. Hagan (1993) proposes that the activities of gangs are a natural response to the harsh realities of social inequality.

[Gangs] are not intergenerationally transmitted expressions of cultural preferences, but rather cultural adaptations to restricted opportunities for the redistribution of wealth. Put another way, these youth have substituted investment in subcultures of youth crime and delinquency for involvement in a dominant culture that makes limited structural or cultural investment in their futures. (p. 328)

The causal relation between the underclass and gangs is widely accepted today in sociological criminology (Miller and Cohen 1996; Hagedorn 1988; 1991; Vigil 1990; Padilla 1995; Anderson 1990; see also W. J. Wilson 1996 for a critique of underclass theory). The theoretical limitation for social policy inherent in the theory is that it fails to account for the diversity of gang types, as well as their new formations in nonurban centers. For example, two distinct theories may be necessary to explain gang proliferation, depending upon the ethnic structure of the community. Underclass theory, especially when linked with institutional racism and pervasive alienation, primarily explains the emergence and spread of gangs among African Americans. Subculture theory, with its focus on identity and belonging needs, accounts more completely for the cultural gang traditions among Hispanics (M. Klein 1995).

NUMBER AND SCOPE OF GANGS

The search for gang numbers remains an inexact science. A Washington State journalist, writing about her home town of Chicago, estimates that it has at least 50,000 gang members (*The Olympian* [WA], March 14, 1995, A7). Malcolm Klein (1995) asserts that nearly 800 towns and cities in America have gangs. In California, street gangs thrive in 196 cities, with over 200 gangs in Los Angeles County alone. Orvis (1996) calculates that there are more than 100,000 youth gangs with a combined membership of over 1,000,000 juveniles and adults in the United States. The U.S. Department of Justice Survey (1994b) offers a statistical profile that reflects actual numbers reported by survey respondents. Bear in mind that the nation's gang crime problem is underestimated because many cities do not have the capacity to compile statistics and to report on gang-crime activity.

The Justice Department figures for 1993 yield a total of 8,625 gangs with 378,807 members and a total of 437,066 gang-related crimes (U.S. Department of Justice 1996). Malcolm Klein (1995) also emphasizes the precipitous increase in gang-involved cities from 54 cities in 1961 up to 766 cities in 1992 that reported gangs, a multiplier effect of 14 times the original number of gangs over a thirty-year period.

What has struck researchers of late is the rapidly increasing numbers of gangs in settings other than urban areas. Specifically, in suburban, small-town, and even remote rural areas, such as Indian reservations, gang activity has been found. Gangs have been initiated by youth who have never been exposed to urban environments. Instead, they draw upon other sources, such as "pop" music, movies, advertisements, or other media coverage of the gang phenomenon (M. Klein 1995).

GANGS AS CRIMINAL ORGANIZATIONS

The legal community has paid particular attention to a recent phenomenon of what may be described as sophisticated urban street gangs (U.S. Department of Justice 1995c; 1996; Orvis 1996; Miller and Rush 1996). Because of the effectiveness of the 1970 federal RICO antiracketeering statutes in breaking up the power of the Mafia, a vacuum was created in the importation and distribution of illegal narcotics. This void has been quickly filled by juvenile street organizations, which have evolved to resemble the hierarchical, traditional authoritarian social structure and rigid divisions of labor of the Mafia's *La Costa Nostra*. The aim: to produce and market a highly lucrative product—crack cocaine and heroin.

Originally, the Department of Justice applied the RICO law for prosecuting federal crimes associated with Mafia operations, such as usurious loan making, gambling, and narcotics distribution. The RICO law provided the government a means to prevent illegal profits from being used to finance legal business ventures. Urban drug gangs share with more-established criminal enterprises certain characteristics of organized crime. As such, many drug gangs no longer can be considered simply as adolescent delinquent groups, especially if they have numerous characteristics of criminal organizations (e.g., sustained criminal hierarchical structures) (Orvis 1996; Abadinsky 1990).

Urban street gangs in many localities have made the shift from unorganized juvenile groups to organized criminal enterprises, again largely through the foothold of the cocaine or heroin trade. Conflict and violence serve as the "glue" uniting members toward a common purpose. Procuring boundaries and creating a hierarchy facilitates efficiency in operations. Petty criminal activities, ostensibly for raising money, combines with turf protection to secure geographical exclusivity. Drugs, an easy venue for money, invites greater involvement by the working gang (Padilla 1995). This, in turn, often creates the need for more violence to protect the market cornered by the gang, to minimize competition, and to increase customers and profits. Reputation and power are enforced by violence. A highly lucrative and solid base of operations, founded upon a virtually inviolable territory, offers the opportunity to solidify the organizational structure, capped with an authoritarian leader to direct and manage every aspect of the gang's criminal activities (see Skolnick 1995; Maxson 1995).

Gangs can evolve into relatively large criminal enterprises that are primarily devoted to maintaining drug operations. Some gangs are considered by authorities to be major crime and terrorist organizations (U.S. Department of Justice, 1995c). The extent of illegal acts ranges from racketeering (apart from narcotics), robbery, extortion, bribery, kidnapping, multiple homicides, and obstruction of justice. The evolution of an anonymous juvenile street gang into a sophisticated and organized criminal operation, successfully prosecuted under federal criminal statutes, has become more common in the past ten years.

The spread and escalation of gang violence—sometimes reported to be synonymous with criminal gangs—actually reflect elements of collective behavior, rather than highly structured organizations (Decker 1994). Block and Block (1993) clarify the nature of gang violence as an intergang rivalry problem, exacerbated by the availability of high-caliber automatic or semiautomatic weapons. Their research indicates that

Gang-related, high crime neighborhoods can be classified into three types: turf hot spots, where gangs fight over territory control; drug hot spots, where gang-motivated drug offenses concentrate; and turf and drug hot spots, where gang-motivated crimes relate to both. . . . Gang involvement in violence and homicide is more turf-related than drug related. Only 8 of 288 gang-motivated homicides were related to drugs. (p. 1)

Drive-by shootings have emerged as a major conflict strategy and serve as a "protective" measure in gang-generated situations. Though highly risky in terms of counterstrikes by rival gangs and police apprehension, the drive-by can be conducted by anyone capable of riding in a car and shooting a gun. They remain the quintessential form of loosely organized gang violence (Sanders 1994).

Ethnicity seems to be a less salient variable than it is in more loosely-organized gangs. For example, the notorious "Westies" gang from the Hell's Kitchen section of the west side of Manhattan, originally American-born and naturalized Irish, was an extremely violent and fearsome organization. The federal government successfully prosecuted them using the RICO laws. Similarly, another challenge to RICO drug gang prosecutions was upheld in the case of the EL Rukns gang from Chicago (see Destro 1993 and Orvis 1996 on the applicability of RICO to gang situations).

A more ominous threat appears to be the trend of the street ruling the cellblock, in which inmates keep their gang loyalty inside the nation's prisons. The Florida Department of Corrections has identified members of 240 separate street gangs in the state's prisons. In addition, it has recognized a disturbing trend: The gangs are forming alliances. Greene (1996) reports that prisons are discovering that old population management strategies don't work when inmates behave like drug gang members. In Connecticut, state officials realized that up to 70 percent of the prison system's most severe violence, including homicides, stabbings, and riots, were gang related. Officials worry that the generation of inmates now entering America's prisons may not settle down during their long sentences and that unless corrective steps are taken, they will become more violent, not less, as time goes by (Greene 1996, 6).

As we pursue different types of gangs, bear in mind that street gangs and criminal drug gangs are very different entities. The bulk of drug trafficking continues to be operated by organized adult criminals (Lyman 1989). Malcolm Klein (1995, 132) provides some salient differences between street gangs and drug gangs (see Table 9.1).

ETHNIC GANGS

Street gangs, a far more familiar gang type in city and small-town streets across America, paint a wider brush, as it is far more likely that these youth are involved in lesser-organized gang activity. Bear in mind: Some criminal actions of gang members—as well as the consequences of these actions for undermining community—may be equally serious as those of more-established drug gangs. Here, we turn to the primarily affiliation-based juvenile street gang. Outlining some of the major ethnic youth gangs operating in urban neighborhoods allows us to contrast some of the salient

Table 9.1

Common Differences between Street Gangs and Drug Gangs

Street Gangs	Drug Gangs
Versatile ("cafeteria-style") crime	Crime focused on drug business
Larger structures	Smaller structures
Less cohesive	More cohesive
Looser leadership	More centralized leadership
Ill-defined roles	Market-defined roles
Code of loyalty	Requirement of loyalty
Residential territories	Sales market territories
Members may sell drugs	Members do sell drugs
Inter-gang rivalries	Competition controlled
Younger, on average, but wider age range	Older, on average, but narrower age range

Source: Adapted from p. 132 of *The American Street Gang: Its Nature, Prevalence, and Control* by Malcolm W. Klein. Copyright © 1995 by Oxford University Press, Inc. Used by permission of Oxford University Press, Inc.

Table 9.2
Race and Ethnicity of Gang Members for a National Sample

Race or Ethnicity	Percent
African-American	48.7%
White-Caucasian	14.8
Mexican	19.3
Puerto Rican	3.5
Asian	5.5
Native American	3.4
Other (e.g. Samoan, Filipino)	4.9

Source: National Gang Crime Research Center, as quoted in Edward Tromanhauser. 1995. "A Descriptive Survey of Selected Characteristics of Street Gang Members in the United States." Paper presented at the Meeting of the American Society of Criminology, Boston, November 16.

characteristics of each gang, and to clarify how the concept of the pseudo community can be understood in terms of how these youth see themselves within the protective confines of the gang. The urban ethnic gangs include Latinos, Asians, and African Americans. We also break down larger ethnic categories into smaller ones, such as Chinese and Vietnamese gangs within the larger category of Asian gangs, particularly because each group's immigration patterns present striking differences. Table 9.2 plots percentages for race and ethnicity from a national study of 1,994 gang members conducted by the National Gang Crime Research Center (Tromanhauser 1995).

Latino Gangs

Latino gangs have emerged in areas where large numbers of immigrant or migrant populations have settled, primarily in the large urban areas of the Northeast, Midwest, and West Coast. Particularly in California's larger coastal cities, Latino youth have been joining gangs for generations. According to Vigil and Long (1990), the conditions that gave birth to gangs have not changed substantially in over fifty years (see also Vigil 1990). Market forces in the United States have sought sources of cheap and willing laborers for agricultural and manufacturing jobs residents spurned. Each set of newcomers settling in Southern California sought housing and community near those previously established, creating new neighborhoods (*barrios*). Accordingly, the difficulty in providing the necessary support for those succeeding groups caused pressure both within and without the community for schools, social services, job placement, and socialization to their new surroundings.

Although most of these youth have not found their way into gangs, Vigil and Long assert that the marginalized—or what they term the *cholo*—subculture has involved adapting some of the Anglo youth cultural norms to distinctive Mexican cultural patterns. This hybrid culture provides both identity and a place for youth seeking another way to express their authentic cultural experience.

The *cholo* subculture of Southern California was born in marginal urban areas where small houses exacerbated the crowded living conditions for large families. Poverty and discrimination in employment generated continual stress within these households. Few parks and playgrounds existed in these areas. The youths who created the cholo subculture and those who have maintained it have been excluded by distance and discrimination from adult-supervised park programs. They have experienced failure in school because of language and cultural differences, and limited encouragement from school personnel who expect little of them. Add to this, parents who are preoccupied with day-to-day economic crises, and it is no wonder that the streets have held such attraction for these youths (Vigil and Long 1990, 60).

The values of these young people revolve around social relationships with their friends. As in Vietnamese youth gangs, they employ terminology creating familial relationships where none previously existed. The primary focus of attention is on having a good time, or "partying," and responsibilities to others not in one's family of origin or in one's social network evoke little interest. Positive performance in school is of little concern, and paid employment is viewed as a means to "taking it easy."

Vigil and Long (1990) note that the Mexican male value of *machismo* has been reinterpreted as an exaggerated capability of consuming heavy amounts of drugs and alcohol, having a way with women, and a willingness to fight anyone, anytime. The other part of the construct of Latino manliness is that of taking responsibility for one's family and protecting those needing care. Again, gang values have co-opted this value, and reinterpreted it as "defending one's honor and family and backing up friends in altercations" (Vigil 1990, 120). Most authority figures, including family members, law enforcement personnel, and school professionals, are outside the circle of trust for these youngsters.

Motivations for joining the gang are primarily to seek a place where they can feel "a part of" something larger than themselves. Their peers are effectively "pre-selected," with whom they can have instant camaraderie and family feelings, or *carnalismo* in Spanish. Mexican American youth adhere to both *macho*, exaggerated male values, and to crazy behavior; combining these extremes leads to many battles with rival gangs. The hypersensitivity to criticism and an artificially inflated sense of pride make these youth easy targets for casual insults, which quickly escalate into violent episodes and injury to themselves or other gang members.

Cloward and Ohlin (1960) earlier noted that the adolescent subculture of conflict creates opportunities for status enhancement by manipulating violent episodes. Risking injury to defend oneself or the gang reinforces who that person is: someone not to be "messed with." However, if the adolescent accepts gang norms that define violence as the key to maintaining self-identity, he will interpret situations as threatening and will employ violence to that end. Successfully negotiating the pitfalls of collective street conflicts bestows respect, an important Mexican social value. Failure to do so brings shame, criticism, expulsion, or death (see J. Moore 1992).

Latino gang socialization begins at an early age. According to the Los Angeles County Sheriff's Department (1994), junior members of the gang may be brought in by older family members from the age of ten. Between ten and thirteen, these children are labeled "pee wees" or "li'l winos" by older gang members. By age fourteen, adolescents are full-fledged gang members enforcing gang rules and perpetrating crimes committed by the gang. If members survive past the age of twenty-two, they are considered *veteranos*, or the gang's "elder statesmen," giving advice and counsel and occasionally a place to stay if a youth is a fugitive from the law. Other chores for the ex-officio street soldiers involve destroying weapons or other evidence from the commission of crimes, and establishing a residence for the gang's social activities and meetings (see also LAPD 1990b, 7).

Role differentiation takes place in Latino gangs, primarily in the commission of crimes. A division of labor may take place, with certain members selected for their expertise in property crimes, such as burglary, or who may be more adept at the psychological domination required for extortion. The "plunder" from illegal activities is strictly shared among all members equally.

One of the defining characteristics of Latino gangs is the preoccupation with territory, or turf. Gang members consider themselves to be "stewards" of the neighborhood or barrio and assume responsibility for protecting it from intrusion from nonresidents. Typically, these are members of rival gangs. The gang's status and prestige are dependent upon maintaining a dominant profile in the neighborhood, and losing face is considered an intolerable consequence of failing to prevail in a challenging situation. Membership in Latino gangs could be visualized in a series of concentric circles, each larger than the one in the center. The center circle would be the "hard core" gang members—those most involved in crime and violence, who know the streets and neighborhoods in their territory and beyond, and whose leaders are knowledgeable about gang business and affairs—

with associates, peripheral gang members, and cliques comprising the outer circles.

Latino gangs tend to maintain ethnic membership and have appropriated a strong sense of group solidarity that supersedes the significance of the individual member. This is drawn from Latino culture, which prescribes the same relationship between the family as a whole and individual members of the family. The Latino family is also the source for the ethic that all members must become equally involved with any violation or violator of the gang's rules or well-being. The potential loss of the member's life is considered part of the unwritten contract of belonging to the gang.

It is highly unlikely for a Latino adolescent, despite a marginal economic background, to be involved with gangs if experiencing academic success. In fact, the Latino youth's self-esteem is likely to be closely associated with a positive school experience. Thus, alienation from school is highly predictive of juvenile delinquency and subsequent gang involvement (Curry and Spergel 1992). Clearly, the gang offers an arena whereby disaffected and marginalized Latino youth can find excitement, attachment, and a sense of purpose, albeit in criminal and antisocial activities.

The pseudo community of the gang offers a seemingly benign environment for Latino young people having large amounts of unstructured time to be engaged in a wide variety of deviant behavior: petty and serious criminal activity; socializing with excessive amounts of drugs and alcohol; fighting for sport, for expression, and for the purpose of establishing or reinforcing power, boundaries, and, perhaps most significantly, for promoting a sense of identity that transcends family, neighborhood, nationality, or region.

An East Coast Gang, Los Solidos Nation, hailing from Hartford, Connecticut, had seventeen members arrested under violation of federal racketeering charges (*New York Times*, December 25, 1994, 13). The Los Solidos gang succeeded in generating a favorable environment for creating a sense of family, of belonging, and an ideology that can scarcely compete with the meager offerings that the neighborhood or barrio, or even the family can offer. For example, who would wish to take issue with an organization describing itself as an "empowerment organization" in its charter, and which offers an "Achievement Plan" for members to be integrated into society's mainstream? These are heady promises!

The pseudo community created by the gang may not be legitimate, but it aspires to be an authentic community. A later section turns to the largest presence in the urban gang scene, the African-American youth gang, where we note significant similarities between these two ethnic groups. Now, we turn to Chinese and Vietnamese gangs to explore the extent to which their activities are motivated by community or family norms.

Asian Gangs: Chinese

Prior to 1965, rates of crime among Chinese communities were extremely low. Most Chinese were immigrants, and they were characterized as law-abiding, industrious, and peace-loving. Violations of the law consisted primarily in abuse of drugs or alcohol, prostitution, and inappropriate public behavior. Part of the explanation for this low crime and delinquency profile was the absence of teenagers, due to federal laws that excluded Chinese from entering the country, including the Chinese Exclusion Act of 1882 and the National Origins Act of 1924. Greater permissiveness in federal immigration policy after 1965 enabled more Chinese to come into the country as families and groups rather than as individuals (Joe 1994, 405).

Traditional Chinese support systems, such as families and neighborhood associations, were overwhelmed with the influx of immigrants. The newcomers had to find their own way to obtain housing, jobs, education, and to negotiate the system for help with other problems. Amid this large demographic upheaval, organized Chinese gangs emerged to capitalize upon the lack of social control traditionally exerted in community relations. Instead, immigrant Chinese in their large urban communities lacked unity or cohesion. Although it has been estimated that fewer than two thousand Chinese belong to gangs, the 1980s witnessed dramatic increases in gang-related violence. Some of these activities included narcotics trafficking, smuggling aliens, laundering money, and other large-scale organized illegal operations (Chin 1990, 129).

A brief demographic profile of Chinese gangs in New York City shows the membership as predominantly male with an extended age range: from 13 to 37 years with a mean age of 22.7 (Chin 1990; 1995, 47). Overall, most are in their late teens or early twenties. Gang members are primarily from Hong Kong or Taiwan, and speak Cantonese. The average size of the gangs is between 20 to 50 intensely involved members. New York law enforcement officials estimated that perhaps 200 to 400 individuals are actively participating in gangs, although only 192 are registered gang members (Chin 1995).

The gangs are hierarchically organized, with larger gangs having four to five leaders, *tai lou*, or "big brothers." Smaller gangs will have single or dual leadership. The underbosses, or lieutenants, supervise street operations. "Privates," or soldiers, at the lower end of the hierarchy, are sent out into the streets and are involved with the bulk of criminal activity, such as street fights, robbery, and extortion. The term to describe their role is *ma jai*, or "little horses." The gang leaders work closely within the traditional social structure of the tong, or "gathering place." These associations are sometimes, but not always, led by visible and well-thought-of male leaders of their communities (Chin 1990, 130).

Recruitment patterns are grounded in fear of reprisal from hostile gangs that developed after 1970. Formerly, associations were based upon friendship. Within the current nexus of narcotics and gang activity, new members have been coerced, or "persuaded" by being taken out for an expensive meal, shown gang members' flashy cars, and offered female companionship. If the prospective member fails to appreciate the advantages of gang membership, the ante is upped by employing the "privates." These underlings serve the gang by working the streets to assault those refusing to join.

More often than not, it works. The candidate for membership is likely to be an academic underachiever or a youth who has given up on school altogether. Limited English ability makes it more difficult for the boy to negotiate among the mainstream culture and to obtain employment. Those with a great deal of time on their hands who "hang out" in public places are likely recruits. Once a youth has been selected, an initiation ceremony modeled after Chinese secret societies mandates the youth to

take his oaths, burn yellow paper, and drink wine mixed with blood in front of the gang leaders and the altar of General Kwan, a heroic figure of the secret societies. The oaths taken by the new recruits are, in essence, similar to the 36 oaths of the secret societies. (Chin 1990, 133)

Chinese gangs possess distinct characteristics, to the extent that some scholars hesitate to group them in the youth gang category. One reason is the maintenance of close ties with the traditional Chinese community power structure, and the unlikelihood of eclipsing them in power. Another feature is the goal of taking illegal profits and laundering them in legitimate businesses into which the gang leaders are fully involved. A third distinction is the national and international spectrum of gang networks.

Fourth, few other ethnic gangs have the strong cultural roots and heavy involvement with traditional structures, such as the secret societies and historical and philosophical links to centuries-old practices adapted for the New World. Fifth, there is an absence of socialization to increasing levels of individuals' participation in violence. Recruits may be just as likely to implement serious or deadly assignations as the more seasoned members. A sixth difference is the primary focus upon profit and of procuring power and financial control of Chinese community businesses (Chin 1995, 145).

Sociologists have noticed another remarkable distinction among Chinese youth gangs that appears to be lacking in other ethnic gangs, and even in other Asian gangs. This is socialization into an adult criminal organization based upon intense personal relationships between the more mature criminal actors and their youthful protégés. Adult criminal groups will cultivate gang youths, offering them employment and a future in complex criminal enterprises. Because of the close affiliation with adult organizations, such as the tongs, or meeting halls, and associations offering assistance to fellow newcomers, many criminal operations have been institutionalized in the Chinese community. The violence associated with street gangs in a traditional city, such as New York, tends to be played out in newer ethnic enclaves, including Flushing, Queens, and Brooklyn, where other ethnic gangs have not penetrated. Rivalry between gangs often stems from group appeals for "turf," which offers more than simply gang boundaries. Such conflicts are directly linked with income from protection rackets. The Chinese gangs also fight over slights to members' "respect," and will instigate battles to seek revenge for injuries or killings perpetrated by rival gangs (Chin 1990; 1995, 10).

Conflict between members of the same gang tends to be focused around money, particularly around gambling debts. Fights can break out if money from criminal operations is perceived to be unfairly distributed by the gang leader. Gang members can also be at odds over women. Factional disputes grounded in power struggles can result in serious bloodshed; factions may operate territories independently from the "upper management" of the gang leader.

The pseudo-community concept may not be as salient an explanation for the cohesion among Chinese gangs and their connection to the Chinese community as a whole, because of the close relationship with traditional cultural institutions, such as the "Triad" secret societies—linking humans, the earth, and the sky in the form of a triangle—and based on political and historical experiences in China in previous centuries (Chin 1990). Chinese gangs have co-opted important vestiges of the Chinese experience into the milieu of crime and delinquency. On the one hand, there is an unusual mix of mentoring by members of the organized adult criminal enterprises, blended with participation in a variety of serious crimes, including racketeering and extortion, robbery, physical assaults, and murder. On the other hand, Chinese gangs also participate in the more mundane and delinquent offenses learned in the American urban milieu, such as fist fights and intergang fights, petty theft, and turf battles.

Although the gangs are arguably antisocial in their preoccupations and activities, the goal of money and profit remains foremost in motivating both youth gangs and the organized criminal enterprises found in Chinatown sections of large North American cities (Vancouver, British Columbia; Seattle; Los Angeles; New York; San Francisco; and Toronto, Ontario). The ultimate aim of their criminality is not power, deviant ethnic identity, or turf, as such, but rather to generate income with which to underwrite legitimate business activity. It could be argued that such criminal activity serves to support the mainstream ethnic community, in that it offers legitimate employment opportunities and social standing for an otherwise marginalized immigrant population. The Chinese community is the oldest and most established Asian ethnic group, and it has—albeit illegitimately at times—generated a new social structure into which newcomers could be channeled and given a sense of place and of belonging (Fessler 1983).

As we explain next, this luxury has not been afforded one of the newer immigrant Asian groups, the Vietnamese. The resulting cultural dislocation has placed a heavy burden on these young immigrants, who have responded by creating their own negative version of community.

Asian Gangs: Vietnamese

Vigil (1990) has employed the term "multiple marginality" to describe the legacy of racism, institutional neglect, ghettoization of neighborhoods and communities, and the pervasive negative economic forces serving to prevent Chicanos in Southern California's urban areas from achieving the dream of a better life after immigration from Mexico. Paralleling this experience, Vigil and Yun (1990, 148) assert, is that of the recent immigrants from Vietnam, who fled Southeast Asia following the fall of Saigon in 1975. Despite the efforts of the federal government to disperse the emigres nationwide amid a generally high level of hostility among the American people, they flocked to Southern California. There were two waves of immigrants: the first were middle class, economically stable, well-educated, and were primarily young people with their families.

The second wave were the "boat people"—those who remained after the Americans left and who were subject to starvation, abusive political indoctrination, and random searches and seizures by the newly installed authoritarian regime. After arduous sea travel in which many died, they settled in refugee camps and were subjected to privation and discrimination in addition to serious handicaps for adapting to their new country: lower educational levels, lower socioeconomic status, and unfamiliarity with urban life and the demands of a market society.

With 40 percent of Vietnamese settling in two counties in Southern California—Orange and Los Angeles—the social service net was stretched to a breaking point, as was the patience of Californians in the wake of being held responsible for the resettlement of this newer wave of war-torn Vietnamese (Vigil and Yun 1990, 150). Lacking the stable foundation of the previously settled and well-established Vietnamese community, the welfare system was the support of last resort, providing the most marginal means for individuals lacking an economic foundation. Their first task was to learn the English language, enabling them to cope with the bewildering demands of modern American society in the context of a political climate holding them responsible for their unfortunate social conditions.

Poverty has been the legacy for many of these families, and their children have struggled to adjust to the unrelenting demands of suburban life. School has been a particularly painful arena for some of these youth, many of whom lacked basic language proficiency and were enrolled in classes with young children. Failure in school has been an important predictor of alienation for Vietnamese youth, and a precursor to gang development. Vietnamese families have traditionally supported middle-class educational values, but family support and the stability undergirding the family structure have been undermined by influences of popular culture, consumerism, instant gratification of material wants, and the bombardment of media information loudly taunting youth that it is "all there for the taking."

According to Vigil and Yun (1990, 153), "Not only do the youths reject their parents' values, they learn to reject the traditional role of parenthood itself." Vietnamese parents are often absent from the home to work long hours for low pay, and the youth express ambivalence about seeking financial support from their parents. The conventional avenues of educational striving and hard work do not generate opportunity, but rather frustration, anger, and shame.

Vietnamese youth gangs are drawn from young people who have not measured up to the American Dream; those who have not been able to overcome the multiple barriers of low income, limited English proficiency, racism, failure to achieve in school, and lack of fit between the traditional Vietnamese values and those of modern American society. All form obstacles to economic achievement and serve as incentives for the Vietnamese young person to join a gang. The gang provides tangible needs for these youths: financial support, independence, affiliation, and something to do (Vigil and Yun 1990, 156).

Similar to Chinese gangs, money is a primary motivator, and illegal activities—stealing cars, burglary, robbery, and brutality associated with small groups of gang members robbing other Vietnamese in their homes—is the *modus operandi*. What is particularly striking is that some of these youth were similarly brutalized by communist soldiers in Vietnam. The victimization of other Vietnamese is made even easier by the fact that suspicion of the government led them to spurn using banks or otherwise investing their money. The victims, timid about asserting their rights, seldom report these crimes to the police. The luxurious lifestyle such criminal activity supports is made evident in spending sprees of buying automobiles, eating in Vietnamese restaurants, and partying and socializing with women in bars. Some youth aspire to join organized Vietnamese crime enterprises, which seek steady income from extorting protection money from businesses, but this usually requires sophistication and knowledge of the community these youth lack.

Although the primary focus is money, Vietnamese gangs do not display the obsession with acquiring turf and the fights accompanying such struggles. Vietnamese gang members strictly avoid being recognized by the police, and thus eschew obvious gang indicators, such as distinctive clothing styles, tattoos, or hand signals. Los Angeles police Gang Activities Section report that these ethnic gangs are more likely to operate in business suits (LAPD 1990a, 2). Drug dealing, a major occupation of other urban gangs, is typically considered a poor business risk. At the same time, gang members may have no compunction about "recreational" drug use, such as cocaine and marijuana.

Relationships among the youth in these gangs is close and intense. They bestow familial titles to one another, such as the males calling one another *ahn*, or brother, or giving each another nicknames (Vigil and Yun 1990, 167). They describe their relationships in the gang as those of kinship. They vow to protect and defend other members and express this to the extent of risking their lives for one another. These relationships have clearly superseded those they left behind in their families of origin.

The pseudo community of the gang offers a contradictory blend of features: a haven in a rejecting world, thrillseeking, "easy" money, and freedom from the ties of neighborhood, job, community, or of traditional obligations to duty and family. The dichotomy between the old values and the new ones is too great to be bridged via institutions of school, work, civic and community affairs, or non-gang relationships. Long-term gang members, fragmented and alienated as perhaps no other ethnic group examined in this chapter, are highly likely to advance into long-term criminal careers. It is a skewed and twisted path to the American dream.

Other Asian ethnic groups with documented gangs are the Filipino and Samoan communities in Honolulu, Hawaii (Curry, Ullom, and Foster 1993), and Japanese, Filipino, and Korean gangs in Los Angeles (Los Angeles County Sheriff's Department 1994). The Filipino gang members identify themselves as Pacific Islanders, yet have many similarities with Hispanic gangs, such as graffiti and nicknames (*placas*). However, they do not display the same interest in maintaining and defending territory.

African-American Gangs

Surveying gangs in Chicago, early gang researchers noted the paucity of "Negro" gangs—fewer than one in ten (Thrasher 1927). In those days, the youth joining gangs reflected ethnicity from immigrant groups arriving in the first two decades of this century: Irish, Jewish, Polish, Scandinavians, Eastern Europeans, and Germans (Skolnick 1995). African Americans were only a couple of generations removed from slavery, and the vast majority were living in strictly segregated Jim Crow southern cities or in rural hamlets, cut off from the most commonplace public conveniences. The youth were also detached from institutions of higher education, detached from all but the most menial work, as well as forbidden entry into the professions, and were harassed and excluded from exercising their constitutional rights of voting, sitting on juries, or other citizen rights. If former slaves or their children dared to challenge the status quo, they were victimized and terrorized by domestic hate groups, such as the Ku Klux Klan.

The federal government did not specifically renounce segregation in the armed forces until an executive order was signed by President Truman in 1948. This was because the power in the United States Congress was held by Southerners, who refused to move forward. Even a unanimous Supreme Court decision in *Brown v Board of Education* (1954) had little effect in integrating public schools until the nation experienced the shameful attacks upon protesters and marchers exercising their First Amendment rights in the summers of 1963 and 1964. Only then were public accommodations and institutions finally opened to minorities. Even the most fundamental right—that of choosing to live where one wishes—was not protected until the Open Housing legislation passed by Congress in 1968.

In the intervening time, race riots, beginning with Watts (a section of Los Angeles) in 1965, rapidly followed by other cities, exploded the myth that integration was only a matter of time. Americans were eyewitnesses via their television sets of the foreclosure of a peaceful, legal resolution of racism. For some African Americans, the dream of a new and free America died with the assassination of the Reverend Martin Luther King, Jr., in April 1968, followed by the violent death of Robert Kennedy in June 1968 who represented for many oppressed citizens the hope of renewing the vision set in motion by his brother, the late President John F. Kennedy. This turbulent political period gave way to great economic dislocations, whereby large urban manufacturing concerns, often sources of stable employment for African Americans, began moving out of central cities and "outsourcing" the work to foreign countries, or simply moving to suburban areas that were inaccessible by public transportation for most urban minorities.

Joining a gang is often the last step in a process that begins in the earliest stages of life. The common thread of violence between persons and aggressive behavior that undergirds so many daily interactions in underclass urban neighborhoods reflects the conditions of large numbers of impoverished young people and their families: the extremely limited job opportunities, racism, the havoc wrecked by the dominance of the drug culture and of the addicts who patronize it; and the disconnection all this produces in individuals who have lost hope for a better life (Anderson 1994, 81). These sentiments have been incorporated in the "code of the streets," to which all, regardless of level of participation in street activities, must adhere. Respect is not understood or perceived as an internalized value, but rather, it is something exogenous to the individual, something granted or obtained from another. Anderson (1994) reports that respect involves an elaborate set of interpersonal rules. Respect

must constantly be guarded. The rules of the code in fact provide a framework for negotiating respect. The person whose very appearance—including his clothing, demeanor, and way of moving—deters transgressions feels that he possesses, and may be considered by others to possess, a measure of respect. With the right amount of respect, for instance, he can avoid "being bothered" in public. If he is bothered, not only may he be in physical danger but he has been disgraced or "dissed" (disrespected). Many of the forms that dissing can take might seem petty to middle-class people (maintaining eye contact for too long, for example), but to those invested in the street code, these actions become serious indications of the other person's intentions. Consequently, such people become very sensitive to advances and slights, which could well serve as warnings of imminent physical confrontation. (p. 82)

All of this, Anderson suggests, is a direct result of the alienation inner-city African Americans feel about the institutions of law enforcement and the judicial system. Generally, nonresident white officers have failed in their duty to "preserve, protect, and defend" minority neighborhoods. Now many of these inner-city communities have devolved into a Hobbesian life that pits neighbor against neighbor and is "nasty, brutish, and short." The ease with which guns can be obtained and the ubiquitousness of drug operations make negotiating the shoals of urban streets highly uncertain and dangerous, especially for persons who cannot muster an adequate support system to maintain a reasonable quality of life.

Enter the gang. Some of the these African-American gangs have become household words through their quick proliferation from, for example, inner-city Los Angeles to points north and east. Extensive discussion among sociologists has focused on whether such notorious gangs have evolved in different regional locations independently, or whether there has been a concerted effort by gang principals to "plant" gangs as a type of collective strategy (Maxson, Woods, and Klein 1996). Preliminary data show that African American gangs tend to be less focused upon a neighborhood identity and turf, as opposed to Latino gangs, and thus are more mobile and available to change gang loyalties and identities over time. The issue of gang migration is often associated with a particular product or activity in which the gang is involved; for many, it is the production and distribution of drugs.

Violence is employed to initiate members into the African American gang, particularly in Los Angeles gangs. The appellation "homeboy" can only be bestowed to those who have been properly and officially installed. "Getting jumped," or assaulted by several gang members simultaneously, is usually the method, but it can also include high-risk behavior, such as going into the street to sell drugs or killing a member of another gang.

Gangs offer many positive benefits. In addition to having a ready-made community with prearranged social and economic activities, gang members receive instant recognition from fellow members by wearing distinctive colors, by employing gang terminology descriptive of their gang, and in particular, by joining an in-group for waging war against rival gangs.

Visible symbols are crucial for establishing the gang member's identity.

Box 9-B
Everyday Risks of Gang Members

As the story goes, Lamar Lewis, a seasoned 21-year-old member of the Los Angeles Grape Street Watts gang, had been shot and paralyzed by a rival gang for trespassing into a street not secured by his gang. Despite being confined to a wheelchair, the gang's dictates forced him to continue the relentless pursuit of dominance and control of the street by participating in drive-by shootings. Other gang members and their victims are not as fortunate. Some 700 persons are murdered annually in gang-related incidents in Los Angeles County alone.

   Although such statistics may seem at the least, daunting, and at the most, horrifying, gang members, such as Lamar Lewis, have been inculcated with street gang values by parents. His father helped to found the Kitchen Crips gang and was incarcerated. Having joined a gang by the age of 13, and placed in juvenile lock-up for almost half of his life, Lamar was intimately familiar with adult jails, where he had served time for assault, possessing weapons, and attempted murder. Four years after his disabling assault, he was determined to fight on. Lamar spoke with a *New York Times* reporter about the urgency of violence against a rival gang:

   We've got to slow them down . . . We've got to go over there and shoot everyone up, shoot up their children, shoot up their women, just jump in a car, roll down the window, and let the guns fly.

Source: New York Times. (March 19, 1995: A7).

Because it is an identity that is essentially established outside of the self, the acquisition and display of objects communicates one's social status and imputed value in the eyes of others. Much gang activity revolves around the ability to violate another person's sense of security or well-being, or to steal his or her belongings. The taking of something from another—the acquisition of status based on transgressing upon the boundaries of another person—enhances the sense that there is indeed something to which one must take up arms and defend. Ownership of material things—clothing, jewelry, automobiles—or of intangibles—respect, or "juice," fearlessness, manhood, or "nerve"—are constantly in a state of flux, dependent upon reevaluation by one's peers.

The gang battle seemingly never ends, even if gang members are injured or disabled, as Box 9-B details. (African American youth are discussed further in the next chapter).

Curry and Spergel (1992) propose that African-American gang involvement is predicated upon social or interpersonal variables, especially extensive exposure to gang members in school and at home.

Another type of gang exists, both a hybrid of those examined thus far, yet having qualities separate from the essentially male gangs. We turn now to female gangs.

FEMALE GANGS

A number of scholars has examined the complex relationships of young women involved with delinquency and gangs (Chesney-Lind 1993; Campbell 1991; 1995; Fishman 1995; Swart 1995). Until the last ten to fifteen years, the subject has been largely dismissed by male scholars in sociology and criminology, and has been generally treated with prurience and sensationalism in the media. The 1992 NIJ National Gang Survey reported ninety-nine independent female gangs spread over thirty-five law enforcement jurisdictions (Curry and Decker 1998). Estimates of female gang membership in New York City range between eight thousand and forty-thousand members, 10 percent of whom are female (Campbell 1991, 5). Like male members, they become active in their early teens, and may maintain gang membership into their thirties. Many have children, and although marriage is not commonplace, neither is it rare.

Campbell (1991; 1995) asserts that traditional scholarship in female gangs has mythologized the roles taken by such girls. A primary myth is that girls join gangs for upward mobility. Despite their lower-working-class status, these young women are basically choice makers, determined to improve upon their family's circumstances. Middle-class values and lifestyles include postponing the fulfillment of immediate wants in favor of future goals and making an effort to improve oneself. Girls envision marrying for love, having a supportive husband for bearing the burden of raising the children, and living well. These girls have been viewed as "dabbling" in gangs, as part of an adolescent phase, but eventually left behind as the virtuous role of "good girl" takes over.

The other prong of the gang girl myth is that she is "bad." She holds no illusions about her socioeconomic status and the lack of opportunities it affords. She is likely to have performed poorly in school, particularly if English was not the language spoken in the home. The struggle for money is relentless, and she is taunted by television stories of the wealthy and prominent, but knows this will never materialize for her unless she "wins the lotto." Being "bad" provides an outlet, a diversion from the monotony of her life and that of her friends. Possessions and partying are major preoccupations. Authority figures provide opportunities to prove toughness and control in challenging situations.

With both female stereotypes, males figure prominently. With the "good" girls, they compete as peers, fighting with the boys, backing them up. Gang girls are stereotyped as "tomboys," even taking up criminal activity, such as robbery. The major difference between the two—and they are both engaged in promiscuous sexual liaisons—is that the former maintains her affiliative relationships with other females, whereas the "bad" girl, now denigrated into a "sex object," focuses exclusively upon male relationships. This restrictive role portrayal does justice to no one, for, according to Campbell (1995),

These types of roles tend to suggest a no-win situation for gang girls. As Sex Objects, they are cheap women rejected by other girls, parents, social workers, and ironically often by the boys themselves. As Tomboys, they are resented by boys and ridiculed by family and friends who wait patiently for them to "grow out of it." (p. 70)

Among lower-class women, the "independent woman," as often as not, raises her children in an all-female household. In so doing, she becomes the target of government, academic, and media concern by those who accuse her of rearing a new cycle of delinquents or, if she works, of ousting the male from the labor force by taking low wages.

Clearly, female participants in gangs share some of the characteristics of male gang actors. However, there are some factors that may offer additional explanations for why young women are attracted to gangs and gang violence. First, there has been a significant increase in gang activity, particularly in areas outside the major population centers. As gangs grow, more young people are drawn into gang activity: siblings, friends, and sweethearts. Girls are urged to consider themselves equal to boys, and a significant amount of their male points of reference are comprised of relationships that are grounded in abuse and violence. It is not merely physical abuse; it is overwhelmingly sexual abuse. In Seattle's King County juvenile lock-up, a recent survey found that 98 percent of incarcerated girls, compared to 65 percent of boys so detained, were victimized sexually (Mendez 1996, A7).

James Washington, a gang intervention specialist with King County in Washington State perceptively observed: "Girls are continuing the pecking order. They've been abused by men, their families, and society, so they're busting out" (Seattle Post-Intelligencer, October 27, 1995, C1). This is reflected in sharp increases in crime among girls. However, the U.S. Department of Justice (1993) documents that just 13 percent of felonies, such as assault, weapons charges or robbery, were committed by young women. In King County in 1993, females were 17 percent of all youth incarcerated in juvenile detention. These numbers, however, have been stable over the last ten years.

A more typical pattern for gang participation among females is to join a male gang, rather than to join or found an exclusively female one. Rites of initiation can include the "jumping in" ritual described in African American or Latino male gangs, which involves multiple beatings. A deviation sometimes practiced upon females wishing to join a gang requires submitting to gang rape by the male members. Seattle gang informants reported that this practice was limited to girls requesting such an initiation (Mendez 1996).

Girls who engage in high-risk sexual behavior experience a gender-specific exploitation not encountered by male gang members. For example, girls can be invited to join a gang to be primarily sexual outlets for the males, or in more extreme cases, to work as prostitutes to generate income for the gang. In a few cases, girls refusing to be so degraded were violated sexually with objects by other female gang members.

The female gang members interviewed in Seattle took a traditional view of females in gangs: Those who could fight and "hold their own" were accorded more respect (a male gang construct). Those who used more conventional means to gain acceptance, sexual willingness and availability, were accorded less respect, or no respect whatever. The lines are stark. One girl, aged 21, revealed the following:

There are two ways girls get into gangs. She comes in as a slut, or she comes in as a homegirl. If she wants to jump from homeboy to homeboy, then she's going to be seen as a slut. But no one's forcing her. Her sister added, "Don't these girls think about what they're doing?" (*Seattle Post-Intelligencer*, October 27, 1995, C2)

The appellation "homegirl" captures a complex set of meanings immediately connected with the gang context. Girls who allow themselves to be abused physically or sexually are not accorded this honor. It is only those who "act like boys" and can conduct themselves with respect and defend themselves as well as the men who are duly recognized. As one girl explained: "Homegirl is more solid than friend. I think of a friend as just someone you work with. But if I say, 'What's up, homegirl?' that means I trust you. And these are my homegirls" (*The Seattle Post-Intelligencer*, October 27, 1995, C2).

Fighting thus protects the female gang member from sexual victimization. Indeed, membership in a gang provides a number of discrete functions that provide a bulwark against a very hostile environment. Often coming from families where they are extremely isolated, female gang members tend to be "loners" and may find a sense of belonging never before experienced. The promise of familylike relationships inside the gang, intensified by conflict coming from without, draws gang members together. Expressions of "sisterhood" are commonly exchanged, and the ideology of gang togetherness often covers up intragang conflicts, many of which are focused upon competition over male attention. The young women are extremely male-referenced, and gang membership, even as auxiliaries, provides a continuous connection with men in dominant roles. Many have not experienced a significant relationship with a father-figure, except in the role of victim.

Joan Moore's (1992) research emphasized the social harm, not liberation, associated with female gang involvement.

In lives filled with boredom, the gang interjects excitement and "something happening." Literally, no arena in their lives exists where they can be considered successful. School is a road that leads to nowhere; and emancipation and independence are out of reach, given their limited family and community networks.

As Campbell (1995) points out, avenues of opportunity for urban underclass girls are blocked by several sobering realities. Most lack any possibility of access to a career, which normally requires not only obtaining a college education, but also knowing persons who work in a professional capacity—parents, relatives, friends, or associates from places other than the neighborhood. Their role models typically are their mothers and grandmothers, who, if they are native-born, may be second- and third-generation welfare recipients.

The pseudo community of the gang provides a haven for sexually abused and battered girls who, having no genuine sense of safety, of being significant, or of the promise for a better life away from their neighborhood or community, join in the hope of finding something they have never experienced. But the various evils—poverty, racism, ignorance, sexism, violence—none is escaped, even in the gang. The irony of gang membership is that the more heavily involved the young person is, the more at-risk she is for injury or violent death. The protection and security sought is illusory. The appeal of the gang is in an idealized, romanticized life that confers prestige and honor in the commitment of often base and horrific acts (Campbell 1991). John Irwin (1970) observes that this collective delusion is not only a youthful activity, but generic to criminals who engage in distortions of reality by which they "fool" themselves.

The gangs born out of the disarray of the urban underclass are not the least of the new gangs on the scene today. For some observers, it is the gangs emerging out of the last generation's racial, class, and economic cleavages who appear to be the biggest threat to civil society. They are a chilling revisiting of the scourge of fascism of some fifty-plus years ago. These are the hate gangs: groups holding rigid ideologies of white racial supremacy and of the elimination of all "enemies" of racial purity. A resurgence of such groups has occurred; first in Germany and throughout Europe, and now in the United States. We turn to them next.

IDEOLOGICAL "HATE" GANGS

Ideological hate gangs come from a strain of American culture that emphasizes nativism, fear of foreigners, and what historian Richard Hofstadter (1955) has termed "the paranoid style of American politics." Schlesinger's (1963) description of Americans drawn into fascistic movements during the Depression years resonates with the resurgence of militaristic-style youthful skinhead activity today. He noted:

New forces had been released in American politics; . . . These forces drew their strength from stirrings in the nonpolitical, xenophobic lower middle classes. The new activists had little experience of party politics and little understanding of democracy. Moved by envy and suspicion, they would follow any leader who promised to advance their status and foster their self-respect. (p. 51)

By definition, skinheads are explicitly not street gangs; the latter organized around oppressive social and economic conditions, especially racism and poverty, which often does not involve violence (Hamm 1993; Hagedorn 1988; J. Moore 1978). Instead the skinhead "movement" expresses strident racism, and the dedication to violence against racial, religious, gender, and sexual minorities (e.g., blacks, Jews, feminists, gays). Today, the movement has come a long way from the crude messages broadcast over radio or newspaper editorials by communist-fearing publishers attracted to the rhetoric and discipline promised by Hitler and Mussolini.

The Anti-Defamation League (ADL) has been monitoring the skinhead movement, and has found that skinhead activity spans thirty-one countries, and includes homicides, assaults, fire-bombings, incidents of racial harassment, and other activities by small groups of lawless individuals bearing shaven heads and other military regalia. Although small in number, they are far from isolated. Their medium of exchange is heavy-metal music and racist publications, supplemented by computer linkages, affording instant access to global marketing and technologies. The *New York Times* (July 2, 1995, 7) reported that the ADL tracked only those skinheads affiliating with anti-Semitic Nazi ideology. Its adherents range in age from thirteen to twenty-five, and worldwide may number as high as seventy thousand.

A consistent pattern is selecting an "other" whom, skinheads believe, the world would be better without. The ethnic group targeted is typically a minority having little political and economic power, but is nonetheless perceived as "taking away" the liberties of Caucasian residents of the community or country. There is also a global perspective (see also Box 9-C). The report on this international phenomenon notes that

In Germany, they have mobilized against the Turks; in Hungary, Slovakia the Czech Republic, the Gypsies; in Britain, the Asians; in France, the North Africans; in Brazil, the Northeasterners; in the United States, racial minorities and immigrants; and in all countries, homosexuals and those perennial 'others,' the Jews. In many places the targets include the homeless, drug addicts and others who are the down-and-out of society. . . . The countries skinheads are found in the greatest numbers are Germany (5,000), Hungary and the Czech Republic (more than 4,000 each), the United States (3,500), Poland (2,000), the United Kingdom and Brazil (1,500

Box 9-C
The Global Perspective

The German skinhead scene is particularly instructive, as it has employed the power of heavy metal music to capitalize upon excessively nationalistic feelings that have historically spawned racist movements based upon hatred of other nationalities. The German government has only recently banned explicit racist music and propaganda; one particular action in 1993 involved a raid of Rock-O-Rama, a recording company, which has subsequently limited its connection with skinhead music after having some 30,000 recordings confiscated. Because racist groups may openly purvey their philosophies under the protection of the First Amendment to the Constitution of the United States, they are easily distributed to international audiences. German skinhead groups have been strongly influenced by American skinhead groups and the literature of the militia movement. This is evidenced by references to the American hate movement, exemplified by expressions such as White Power, the White Aryan Resistence (WAR) commonly employed by German skinheads. This international movement is organized around the ideology of neo-Nazism, supported and sustained by a specific style (shaved heads, Nazi regalia, Doc Martens, racial/ethnic violence, and white power rock). Mark Hamm also describes this movement as a *terrorist youth subculture*.

Source: Mark S. Hamm. 1993. *American Skinheads.* Westport, CT: Praeger.

---

each), Italy (1,000 to 1,500), and Sweden (over 1,000). (*New York Times*, July 2, 1995, 1)

The Midwest has been the first region of the country witnessing the development of the skinhead movement. In 1985, skinheads from Chicago made their first major appearance at a rally located on the farm of a retired Michigan Ku Klux Klan leader. Loose alliances exist with older hate groups, such as the Aryan Nation, Church of the Creator, and the White Aryan Resistance. Skinheads are considered to be in the vanguard of white racist activities, and are referred to as "front-line warriors" (*New York Times*, April 4, 1995, 7).

Skinheads are easily recognized: shaven heads, earrings, tattoos, heavy military style black boots, and leather jackets. The young people interviewed in Allentown, a city two hours' distance from metropolitan New York, expressed disgust at the influx of minorities to the formerly white enclave. Each may have a specific resentment, covertly expressed by an item of clothing, such as shoelaces. Clothing thus communicates fury over what is perceived as the cause of current unrest or crisis.

Consistent with gang mythology, skinhead gangs profess family bonds with prospective members. According to Anne Van Dyke (National Public

Radio, April 4, 1995) of the Pennsylvania Human Relations Commission, "Hate groups will say to young people, 'We want you to be part of our family. We will be family with you,' and this is at a time where many of these young people don't feel like they have family or are estranged from their natural families." To bestow an additional sense of being esteemed, skinhead gangs will offer incentives for youth to attain a positive reputation and command of the gang organization. In the vacuum of these young people's lives, this is nearly irresistible.

In the event that the Nazi ideology—supported by gang myth-making—fails to draw the young person into skinhead society, fundamentalist Christianity provides an additional incentive, enabling the righteous to embrace the idea of a racial holy war in which they will be the victors. In a perverse marriage of religion and politics, the gang advocates moral superiority combined with a swaggering, bullying racist ideology. This blends seamlessly into the adolescent desire to be feared, to be strong, and to be admired. Skinhead regalia is physically imposing, intimidating, and often repulsive to nonadherents.

In some areas, skinheads are not a homogeneous group. Instead, they comprise two distinct youth gangs: white supremacists and integrationists. For example, in Antelope Valley, located in Northern Los Angeles County, street wars between the Nazi Low Riders and a rival gang of antiracist skinheads, who call themselves Sharps, have resulted in serious injuries and death. Both gang types, as well as the two hundred or more other youth gangs in the Valley, have evolved from similar social conditions: rapid population growth; sudden economic disaster as defense plants closed down; overcrowded, chaotic schools; high dropout rates (45 percent); alarmingly high juvenile crime rates; and up to one-half of children who remain unsupervised from dawn until late evening, because of parents' "epic commutes" to jobs, only available outside the Valley (Finnegan 1997).

GANG PROLIFERATION

Gangs do not grow in a vacuum. They emerge and flourish in the social context of the larger community. As Malcolm Klein (1995, 53), the leading authority on delinquent gangs, emphasizes, "Street gangs are byproducts of partially incapacitated communities." Klein identifies three structural variables in the making and proliferation of gangs: underclass, onset, and maintenance (see Figure 9.2).

Underclass variables play an especially crucial role in gang development. Malcolm Klein's model enables us to draw some conclusions about the relationship between underclass variables and gang emergence.

1. A dynamic worsening of the underclass is associated with a large increase in new gangs. A static underclass is associated with only few new gangs.

Figure 9.2
The Structural Variables Model for the Emergence of Gang Cities

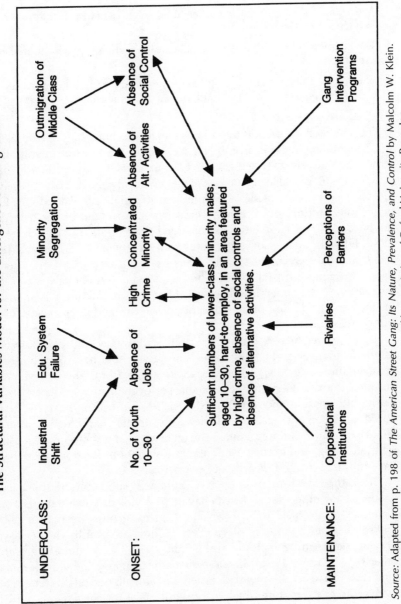

Source: Adapted from p. 198 of *The American Street Gang: Its Nature, Prevalence, and Control* by Malcolm W. Klein. Copyright © 1995 by Oxford University Press, Inc. Used by permission of Oxford University Press, Inc.

2. Lack of job opportunities and a high proportion of youth populations (ages fifteen to twenty-four) leads to increased gang presence.

3. Racial segregation significantly predicts gang emergence.

4. A low proportion of people in the neighborhood/area in the labor force is related to higher gang emergence.

5. The interaction between loss of manufacturing and unemployment predicts the rise of gangs.

6. The recent proliferation of gangs has disproportionately taken place in cities with a preponderance of black, rather than Hispanic gangs.

The so-called "diffusion hypothesis" suggests that gangs spread as a result of members moving from place to place; a kind of out-migration pattern. The idea is that gangs move from city to city primarily as an outgrowth of illegal drug involvement, especially crack cocaine (see Lee 1993). This thesis provides the dominant rationale for federal and urban police intervention. But this hypothesis is not borne out by the data. First, the bulk of newer gang cities has emerged since 1980; and especially since 1984. Fifty-six percent of larger cities with street gangs have emerged since 1984, and 76 percent of smaller cities have surfaced into view after this date. This gang-diffusion process has occurred coterminously with the deterioration of the underclass, because of loss of manufacturing jobs, massive unemployment, failure of the educational system, and intensification of racial segregation.

Second, other factors intrude to create gangs as a kind of cultural icon of youth. Inadvertently, gang experts and the media have played a role in augmentation of gangs, as knowledge of gang patterns and behavior styles becomes known. Certainly, the media performs a major role in disseminating information about gangs (Klein 1995, 206). Gangs are both dramatized and romanticized in movies, TV dramas, and news programs. Suburban school children imitate the inner-city gang symbols, such as gang signs, clothing, and graffiti. Gang life as a symbol of freedom and rebellion has infiltrated into the heartland of America.

Third, the transformation from a delinquent subculture that engages in vandalism or other nonviolent behavior to a violent street gang is a more common occurrence than law enforcement groups recognize (Ferrell 1995b). Consider the case of "taggers." These are youth who seek walls, bridges, signs, and vehicles to spray-paint their "tag"—initials, graffiti, or other signs (Krauss 1996). In California cities, tagging individuals and tagging crews have come up with a variety of colorful, personalized tags, using merely three letters, but which have significance for their users: NFR (No Fucking Respect), EWF (Every Woman's Fantasy), DTS (Destroy To Survive), YGW (Youth Gone Wild), and many others. But tagging crews have surfaced that bear a strong resemblance to gangs: gang loyalty, intergang rivalry, fighting, territoriality, and a variety of criminal offenses. When police confuse the nongang taggers with gangtaggers, as is often the case, the situation swiftly accelerates into full-scale hostile relations between the youthful vandals and the authorities, resulting in the creation of the now-familiar gang pattern and behavior style.

Fourth, institutional suppression frequently has had counterproductive results in actually promoting gang affiliation and cohesion, which contributes to higher crime rates. How is this possible? When groups are deprived of self-expression and normative outlets for their rage, other means will be found to make a public statement. Sociologists have also long observed the process of "deviance amplification" (Davis and Stasz 1990). The reaction to deviance by expanding social control can produce the unanticipated consequences of an escalation in deviance. When police counter gangs with "zero tolerance" and antigang street sweeps, picking up everyone available on already-existing warrants, and arresting them for gang-related behaviors (e.g., flashing signs, wearing "colors") and minor offenses (e.g., violating curfew), they set up a process of neighborhood resistance and gang member cohesion. Another case: When schools dismiss students for wearing gang clothing (e.g., baggy pants) and displaying gang insignia or "hanging out" in close proximity, the students are more likely to drop out rather than comply with what appears to be arbitrary control.

Malcolm Klein (1995, 170) counters the tendency for draconian suppression of gangs by emphasizing how social control groups have systematically created an "institutionalized distortion of street gang realities." Klein emphasizes that terrorism does not apply to most street gangs or members; the terminology confuses the nature of street gangs. Most street gangs are not criminal in nature; gang membership is related to identity, status, companionship, and protection against perceived threats. The gang does not have "purposes"—only members do. Similarly, until external suppression (along with intergang rivalries) force gang members together in a cohesive mass, the gang may have been merely a disparate and fragmented youth group. Membership is a judgment call rather than a clear identity. Many youth claim membership that they really do not have. Finally, Klein points out that a vast array of "crack-down" tactics under the guise of "deterrence" can backfire and produce the now-cohesive, nothing-to-lose violent crime gang.

"War" declared against gangs and violence tends to be implemented by highly confrontational units of law enforcement: heavily-armed paramilitary police forces and SWAT teams, employing still more violence to achieve dubious, if nonquantifiable, ends. Threatening young criminals with even the death penalty for violating the social contract provides virtually no disincentive, inasmuch as many youth living in the underclass have little hope of living into adulthood. Zimring and Hawkins (1973, 317) confirm the relationship between punishment and gang proliferation as one of providing "incentives" to embattled members to function as a gang and the likelihood that they will convert stigmata into status symbols. Moreover, prosecuting gangs has been a major problem for law enforcement, because victims and witnesses fear subsequent gang intimidation.

COMMUNITY ALTERNATIVE TO GANG PROBLEMS

As long as law enforcement groups monopolize intervention through the suppression policy (arrest, detain, and punish), the prospects of gang proliferation appears assured. As the infrastructure of American cities continues its downward slide, gangs reflect one adaptation by youth to garner some measure of resources not available by legitimate means. As a society, do we have a choice? Should we simply sit back and let the inevitable happen?

This is not a rhetorical question. Community-based research and development points to alternative strategies that can be employed in any city or town in which youth gang-related problems exist. A research study by Irving Spergel and David Curry (1995) offers a National Youth Gang Survey of 254 criminal justice and community-based agencies and grass-roots organizations in 45 cities and at six special program sites. The survey was intended to encompass every agency in the country that was currently or recently engaged in organized responses to gang crime problems. Chronic gang cities were characterized by large populations, by a long history of serious gang problems, and by gangs that were better organized and had greater involvement in serious crime and drug trafficking activity. Emerging gang problem cities tended to be lower in population and only recently had recognized an acute gang problem (since 1980).

Researchers surveyed the agencies about the five most- and least-effective types of intervention strategies to reduce gang presence (Spergel and Curry 1995). These include: community organization, social intervention, opportunities provision, suppression, and organizational change and development.

The findings strongly recommend a community, rather than law enforcement, approach to curbing the gang problem. Two factors were especially relevant among this agency group: Opportunities provision (better schools, jobs, resources) and community organization (mobilizing the community, building community trust, educating and changing the community and in general creating an enhanced social context for growing youth) receive strong support. Organizational change and development also play a significant role in creating a more positive community, approaches that were especially positive when an independent advisory board was present to deal with the agency's problems. The research clarifies that the suppression policy, entailing police, prosecution, and court, was not an effective preventive strategy. The social intervention approach, which superimposes professional values and lifestyles on oppressed communities, proved to be the least effective.

This research strongly recommends generating a public policy that replaces suppression and intervention with collective responsibility to all young people. The social commitment to the most vulnerable among us has been lost and must be renewed to counter the marked deterioration of families, neighborhoods, and communities during the past forty years. The Children's Defense Fund emphasizes not only public policy but also advocacy and direct action to raise public awareness and to encourage citizens to proactively address the needs of children nationwide. Gangs and gang violence are a symptom of our social ills, and clearly solutions must be community-based.

CONCLUSION

This chapter explored contemporary gangs from a number of perspectives. Gangs are not only age, class, ethnic, gender, and race structures, but they can also function as organized businesses, especially in the drug trade. Gang problems arise in American communities because of entrenched poverty and few or no legitimate opportunities. They flourish in areas of high residential mobility and striking urban decay. "Underclass" youth, those who are most economically and socially disadvantaged, are most likely to be attracted into gangs at early ages—for example, poor African American, Latino, and Vietnamese boys. Gangs are no longer confined to inner-city spaces, but are located in rural, small, and medium-sized cities and suburban communities, as well as on Native American reservations.

The gang phenomenon reflects weak community, neighborhood, and family structures, wherein young people seek identity and social connections among street peers that may involve full-time criminal lifestyles. Although gangs present a community-like facade, their amorphous organizations generally lack essential qualities—security, legitimate opportunities, and durability—that comprise a genuine community. As a quasi-tribal social unit organized around turf and intergroup conflict, gangs are especially successful in indoctrinating alienated neighborhood youth.

Above all, we should remember that the youth gang is an historical structure, not a social inevitability. Paying attention to community building, creating greater opportunities for youth and their families, and providing humane intervention with local leaders may not produce dramatic results, but they can be most effective for reaching a gang truce.

We turn now to the crisis of survival among African American male youth, where the social crisis manifests most devastatingly. The next chapter considers how racism, as a preeminent cultural attribute, generates additional risks, because it contributes to despair and instability among an entire age cohort of young people, especially those trapped in inner-city communities.

10

Race Matters: The Case of African American Youth[1]

We black folk, our history and our present being, are a mirror of all the manifold experiences of America. What we want, what we represent, what we endure is what America *is*. If we black folk perish, America will perish. If America has forgotten her past, then let her look into the mirror of our consciousness and she will see the *living* past living in the present, for our memories go back, through our black folk of today, through the recollections of our black parents, and through the tales of slavery told by our black grandparents, to the time when none of us, black or white, lived in this fertile land. The differences between black folk and white folk are not blood or color, and the ties that bind us are deeper than those that separate us. The common road of hope which we all traveled has brought us into a stronger kinship than any words, laws, or legal claims.

Richard Wright, *12 Million Black Voices*

A CRISIS OF SURVIVAL

Although the distinguished African American writer, Richard Wright, pointed to a post–World War II vision of a "common road of hope" which binds us all—people of color, whites, young and old and middle aged, women and men, and of varied cultures in kinship and community—this dream was not to be. A generation later, America confronts the legacy of slavery, poverty, institutional racism, and segregation in the nihilism of young, poor African American men who see neither promise nor possibility in the seriously flawed American society. They are not alone, of course. The Los Angeles riot of 1992 was neither a race riot nor class insurrection. As Cornel West (1993a) emphasizes, this "monumental upheaval"

was a multiracial, trans-class, and largely male display of justified social rage. For all its ugly, xenophobic resentment, its air of adolescent carnival, and its downright barbaric behavior, it signified the sense of powerlessness in American society. (p. 1)

It is tempting to blame the riot exclusively on the oppression of the black masses, the growing criminal underclass or the political revolt of the racially disenfranchised, because these are grounds enough for a mass uprising. Among those arrested, though, only 36 percent were African American, more than a third of whom had full-time jobs, and most were indifferent to politics. Instead, as West (1993b, 1) asserts, the 1992 riot was the "consequence of a lethal linkage of economic decline, cultural decay, and political lethargy in American life." Race was only the "visible catalyst" rather than the primary cause. Yet race matters in the question of power and morality, and in its devastating impact on African American families. Among youth, especially males, it is also a matter of life and death.

YOUNG BLACK MALES: A POPULATION IN SEVERE CRISIS

Ronald B. Mincy (1994) examines the social conditions of black youth today and raises the question: Which black males are in crisis? Mincy demonstrates that by the end of the 1980s, black men had nearly reached parity with whites in terms of the proportion who finish high school and go on to work. Trends reveal that 80 percent of black men between twenty-five and thirty-four years old completed four years of high school or more in 1989, compared with 86 percent for white males; and 75 percent of those black high school graduates went on to work, compared to 90 percent of white high school graduates. But growing racial gaps in employment and earnings place these new young workers in jeopardy. Black high school graduates, rather than moving into family-wage jobs, have become stuck in low-wage jobs that go no where. Some supplement their earnings with income through drug sales and, therefore, expose themselves to the violence and incarceration associated with drug selling. Thus, black males between ten and fifteen years old who are likely to graduate from high school in the next three to eight years can be counted among the population in crisis.

For young black men who have not completed high school, the picture is much more bleak, Mincy continues. Only 56 percent of black male high school dropouts between twenty-five and thirty-four years old worked in 1989 and less than a third of those who were between eighteen and twenty-four years old worked. Only about half of the older cohort and just over a quarter of the younger cohort worked full-time and full-year (Mincy 1994, 12) (see Tables 10.1 and 10.2).

This provides some idea of the population in crisis, and suggests that young black males who are at risk of becoming high school dropouts should be the major focus of crisis intervention. Recent declines in school achievement, however—over 50 percent of blacks between ten and fifteen

Table 10.1

Black/White Mean Earnings Ratio, 1989

Age/Employment Status	Total	4 Years High School or Less	High School Graduate	Some College	College Graduate or Higher
18–24 Year Olds					
All Earners	0.79	0.64	0.79	0.84	N/A
Full-Time/Full-Year	0.87	N/A	0.96	0.76	N/A
25–34 Year Olds					
All Earners	0.73	0.68	0.77	0.85	0.79
Full-Time/Full-Year	0.80	0.86	0.81	0.95	0.80

Source: U.S. Bureau of the Census (1991), Table 6, as quoted in Ronald B. Mincy, ed. 1994. *Nurturing Young Black Males.* Washington, D.C.: The Urban Institute Press, p. 11.

Table 10.2

Percentage of Earners Working Full-Time, Full-Year, 1989

Age/Employment Status	Total	4 Years High School or Less	High School Graduate	Some College	College Graduate or Higher
White Males					
18–24	39	33	48	29	43
25–34	76	65	75	77	83
Black Males					
18–24	36	26	40	36	45
25–34	64	50	68	61	77

Source: U.S. Bureau of the Census (1991), Table 9, as quoted in Ronald B. Mincy, ed. 1994. *Nurturing Young Black Males.* Washington, D.C.: The Urban Institute Press, p. 12.

years old were two or more years behind their grade level—have both dampened retention, as well as reduced post-school employment. Thus, the pool of low achievers expands as the percentage of high school dropouts grows. At the same time, the college entry rates of black males have fallen compared with whites since the late 1970s. By 1988, the college enrollment rates of black males were about 20 percentage points lower than those of white males (Mincy 1994).

Now as in the past, poor labor market prospects for less-skilled workers are correlated with increases in criminal activity, a situation that affects both white and black youth. Among black youth, though, drug-related crimes greatly exceed white criminal involvement, and the rise in homicide and aggravated assault over a ten-year period depicts the destructive outcomes of the crack-cocaine and other illegal drug trade among inner-city youth (see Table 10.3).

Changes in criminal justice policy also impact on young black men, where a shockingly high number of these youth has been arrested and incarcerated. Freeman (1992) estimates that in 1988, more than 75 percent of black male high school dropouts were in prison, on parole, or on probation. Studies from major metropolitan areas, such as Baltimore, Washington, D.C., and San Francisco, also reveal that 30–60 percent of young adult black men (seventeen to twenty-four) are involved in the criminal justice system (Mincy 1994). Low achievement, poor wages, few jobs, drug involvement, and a ruthless punishment policy are what is meant when we say that a high proportion of young African American males are in a severe crisis.

FROM SLAVERY TO THE MILLION MAN MARCH AND BEYOND

Chattel slavery as a systematic institution in North America emerged in 1619, when the first shipload of slaves arrived in Virginia (B. Davidson 1980). As early as the sixteenth century, Spanish-influenced sectors of the New World had attempted to enslave Native American populations, but with only limited success. Two factors account for the failure. Indians proved to be disease-prone because of lack of antibodies to European diseases, and they died in large numbers. Another reason for the inability of the Spanish to enslave Indians was because of their protection by Spanish missionaries. African blacks proved to be a hardier and more productive labor force.

At first, slavery developed extremely slowly, such that in Virginia there were still only two thousand black slaves versus six thousand indentured laborers of European origin by 1681 (Mannix 1962). By the American Revolution, slavery actually appeared to be declining, only later to be revived. Three conditions contributed to the proliferation of the slave trade

Table 10.3

Percent Change between 1980 and 1990 in Juvenile Arrest Rates for Crimes Related to Violence (Arrest Rate per 100,000 for the Age Group 10–17)

Offense	Whites	Blacks	Black/White Ratio
Violent Crime Total	43.8	19.2	0.44
Murder	47.4	145.0	3.06
Forcible Rape	85.9	8.5	0.10
Robbery	12.3	- 15.6	- 1.27
Aggravated Assault	59.2	88.9	1.50
Weapons Violations	57.6	102.9	1.79
Drug Abuse Total	- 47.6	158.6	- 3.33
Heroin/Cocaine	251.1	2,372.9	9.45
Marijuana	- 66.7	- 47.5	0.71
Synthetic	- 34.1	144.7	- 4.24
Non-Narcotic	-34.6	223.3	-6.45

Source: Federal Bureau of Investigation (1991), Table 5.1 as quoted in Ronald B. Mincy, ed. 1994. *Nurturing Young Black Males.* Washington, D.C.: The Urban Institute Press, p. 16.

in the late eighteenth and nineteenth centuries: the intensive cultivation of tobacco, and later sugar and cotton; the growth of the plantation economy, demanding heavy utilization of a pacified labor force; and the invention of the cotton gin in 1793 (Buxton 1968; B. Davidson 1980). In fact, the slave trade between the west coast of Africa and the Americas reached enormous proportions, becoming the most lucrative trade of the time and constituting a considerable proportion of traffic as a whole, eventually totaling fifteen million blacks that were transported to the New World (Buxton 1968). By 1808, the slave trade was officially banned, but normal procreation of slaves constituted a steady internal traffic for slave traders.

Africans in America, as described by W. E. B. Du Bois, were hauled off their auction blocks in Charleston, Baltimore, or Alexandria, Virginia, bereft of family and clan, having been thrust chained and disoriented into a social situation that debased black women, corrupted black men, denied any vestiges of family life, disallowed personal possessions, and silenced any vestige of a political voice. Du Bois (in Lewis 1993) says:

Home had deteriorated; political authority and economic initiative was in the hands of the masters, property as a social institution [for the slaves] did not exist on the plantation. (p. 222)

Despite the masters' ruthless efforts to squelch any sign of indigenous movement among the mainly illiterate slaves, slave rebellions were a common feature of Southern plantation life, culminating in John Brown's singularly destructive raid against the military arsenal at Harper's Ferry (1859). Together with the white abolitionists, who were morally opposed to slavery, and the resistance by Northerners against the spread of slavery into new territories on economic grounds, the situation was ripe for a national conflagration.

The victory of the North in the Civil War and the subsequent passage of the Thirteenth Amendment in 1865 may have emancipated the slaves, but the bitter heritage of poverty and racism had taken firm hold in America (Mandle 1978). The sequence of anti-Negro legislation, Jim Crow laws, job and housing segregation, and racially discriminatory practices in health care, education, and justice lay bare the white supremacist ideology: Race hatred and institutional racism has prevailed over the more moderate voices of integration, albeit taking different social forms over time (Marable 1981).

For example, the Jim Crow "laws" (actually informal rulings) were devised by the Southern states to retain the racial separation first created by slavery. A variety of edicts declared that all public facilities, including education, transportation, restrooms, drinking fountains, hotels, bars, even cemetery lots, must have separate facilities for black and white. It was an apartheid model that permeated all race relations throughout the Southern states.

A reign of terror settled into black communities throughout the Southland that lingered until its overthrow with the Civil Rights Movement in the 1960s. Initially promulgated by custom and informal edicts (however unconstitutional), the strict racial hierarchy was upheld by threats and unprovoked killings. Thousands of innocent black men were lynched under the guise of attacking white women. The rise of secret, chiefly antiblack, societies, notably the Ku Klux Klan, denounced tolerance, and professing Americanism, maintained terrorist organizations in the Southern United States. These groups, together with the economic advantages of white supremacy, served as strong incentives to state legislatures and local politicos to keep the racial barriers intact: America for white Americans; penury, marginalization, and subordination for blacks (Tolnay 1994; Tolnay and Beck 1994; NAACP 1919/1969).

Southern black migration into Northern cities in the 1900s to 1920s that offered blacks jobs and physical proximity with whites in urban centers, a favorable Supreme Court ruling in 1932—namely, the Scottsboro case that upheld the right of blacks to a fair trial—and World War II were historical events that began the gradual transformation of the black community from slave society to democratic participation.

The Civil Rights Movement of the 1960s heralded for blacks and whites alike a new era of human rights. The roots of black activism can be traced to the influence of World War II, which had an enormous impact on U.S. society and politics. During the conflict, more than a million African Americans served in the Armed Forces, and countless other black workers were offered economic opportunities never before available. Yet the racial divide persisted, both in the military and in employment. President Roosevelt had enunciated that the purpose of the war was "to uphold the doctrine that all men are equal in the sight of God." Civil Rights leaders took exception, not only to the segregated military, but also to the extensive employment discrimination throughout industry and the professions.

New York was first to pass the Anti-Discrimination Act (1945) that prohibited the use of racial criteria in employment. Two years later, President Truman desegregated the Armed Forces, and by 1961, twenty-one Northern states had adopted statutes similar to New York's. President Johnson followed Kennedy's lead in pushing for a nondiscrimination policy to build the Great Society. But it was Martin Luther King, Jr., and the Southern Christian Leadership Conference in the Selma, Alabama, march of freedom, not the presidents or legislative groups, that made possible the enactment of the 1965 Voting Rights Act. King's charismatic message in "I Have a Dream" spoke to the entire nation. The 1964 Civil Rights Act, more than any other single piece of legislation, reinforced for African Americans and other struggling groups that ordinary people could build a peaceful revolution, an ideological banner that helped women, Hispanics, Native Americans, the elderly, and the handicapped with their own campaigns against discrimination (See J. Q. Wilson 1992, Ch. 19, for an overview of civil rights).

The new equality assumed two forms. One expression was a heightened consciousness among historic minorities about their subordinate status leading to challenges to domination. The second push for equality was more cultural in nature, contributing to changed attitudes toward political rights and social behavior. The consequences of these changed attitudes and collective willingness to confront discrimination by whatever means contributed to greater opportunity and participation for African Americans throughout the 1970s, although less so in the 1980s because of conservative policies.

The Vietnam War revealed the darker version of opportunity. Black men were proportionately far more likely than their white counterparts to serve as foot soldiers with subsequent higher likelihood of dying in battle. Embittered and frustrated with the apparent slowdown in racially-integrated progress, many leaders ignored the signs of civil chaos. Yet, until the Million Man March in October 1995, and the Million Women's March in October 1997, the Civil Rights Movement—with its emphasis on economic and political equality—has been effectively dormant in America over the last decade.

Today, with the attack on affirmative action programs and a revitalized conservative agenda, a highly vulnerable African American community confronts the significant shifts in social structure and social policies that directly contribute to young African American male nihilism and rage in the 1990s (see Taylor 1995; Banner-Haley 1995).

First, as delineated in Chapter 1, capitalist society is in process of radical restructuring in a world economy where profit, not people, count. Massive destructuring of American industry has both severely weakened the economic foundation for working-class communities and families who have depended upon full-time, good paying jobs with benefits in the primary labor market. In their place the market has substituted part-time, often temporary, low-wage service jobs in the secondary labor market. And because capital is highly mobile, it can shift to Asian and Latin American labor markets, where workers are paid a pittance and rarely demand benefits, much less a raise (see Thurow 1995).

Second, capital and industrial development has moved out of many older industrial inner-city areas, where investors' risks are perceived as too high for easy profits. Functional illiteracy, systematic "deskilling," crime, poverty, and despair are not features that attract international capital. At the same time, the educational system that serves African Americans offers a largely irrelevant array of white biased scholarship or dead-end technology classes that have little or nothing to do with these adolescents' lives (Kozol

1992). Meanwhile, whites fled to the suburbs, where today 86 percent of white suburban Americans live in neighborhoods that are less than 1 percent black (West 1993a, 4).

Third, the economic rationale behind recent welfare "reform" requires poor women and children to carry the heaviest burden—resulting in the poor growing poorer—thus further limiting young people's future. This approach conveniently ignores the structural dislocations that have had their most profound impact on African American families and youth (Lipsitz 1995). Instead of cushioning the blows of capital restructuring and the injustices of racism, conservatives are hastening to further deprive the most-destitute citizens with diminished support. Virtual decimation of affirmative action programs, deep cuts in welfare for poor women and children, elimination of medical programs for uninsured citizens, and punitive approaches to force mothers with young children to work are all part of the master plan to cut the deficit, regardless of the human costs (see Verhovek 1995, A1 and A10).

Fourth, the issue of black male rage and angst is not a new phenomenon. In 1963, A. Philip Randolph, a Civil Rights leader, told President Kennedy how seriously institutional racism was affecting the young. Randolph said

They have no faith in anybody white. They have no faith in the Negro leadership. They have no faith in God. They have no faith in the government. In other words, they believe the hand of the society is against them. (Herbert 1995b, A11)

Thirty years later, the cultural buffers of black religious and social institutions that sustained family and communal networks of support during and after the slavery period are threatened by the market-driven forces that are shattering all civil society, but especially black communities (West 1993b). Market calculations and cost-benefit analyses that now shape the larger culture exacerbate the undermining of the moral community and make any future prognosis for African Americans even more dire now than in 1963. West (1993b) says:

Black people have always been in America's wilderness in search of a promised land. Yet many black folk now reside in a jungle ruled by a cutthroat market morality devoid of any faith in deliverance or hope for freedom. Contrary to the superficial claims of conservative behaviorists, these jungles are not primarily the result of pathological behavior. Rather, this behavior is the tragic response of a people bereft of resources in confronting the workings of U.S. capitalist society. . . . The nihilistic threat contributes to criminal behavior. It is a threat that feeds on poverty and shattered cultural institutions and grows more powerful as the armors to ward against it are weakened. (p. 16)

Whereas most of the anger, rage, and despair of young black men are directed against fellow black citizens, especially toward black women, the nihilistic threat has recently surfaced in the larger American society, attesting to the general cultural decay, as unemployment, suicide, delinquency, crime, and alcohol and drug addiction rates continue to spiral upward among the young of all ages, regardless of race or nationality, but with particular ferocity among African American youth (West 1993b, 18; Vaz 1995; Taylor 1995). Inner-city blacks now have unemployment rates as high as 50 percent or more. In these settings, the legacy of racism conspires with industrial restructuring to eliminate entire populations from legitimate work.

The Million Man March, led by Louis Farrakhan, attempted to address these issues of the African American community, primarily as they affected males, but the March failed to incorporate Black women and girls. Although Farrakhan's recurrent calls for individual accountability and taking responsibility for one's actions and family met with a positive response by participating African American men, the larger public reception was mixed. Some commentators attacked the entire project as merely a way of demonizing the American dilemma of race without providing adequate solutions (see Fredrickson 1995). Younger African American women rejected the message of "women as helpmates rather than equals" and being told to be "quiet and prepare food for our warrior kings" (Zook 1995, 86). African American women subsequently formed their own march, and two years later (1997) in Philadelphia, in a similar show of strength, celebrated family unity with demands for social justice (Janofsky 1997).

Although the significance of the men's march remains ambiguous, and the symbolism diffused and unfocused—after all Farrakhan, as leader of the Nation of Islam, was regarded as a bitter anti-Semite and reverse racist—it has become a cauldron within which the ingredients for a new dialogue were being brewed.

In the end it is not a dialogue about race as such, but about conditions of life in America for all people. The growing gulf between rich and poor is certainly not limited to African Americans, but rather the growing income gap over the last fifteen years signals an entirely new dimension, perhaps summarized best in the slogan "meaner is greener" where newly imposed taxes and spending cuts against poor people work out to yield about an additional $10,000 a year for the average upper-income family. By contrast the 20 percent of households at the bottom of the income ladder—those with incomes of less than $13,000—will see a $1,200 reduction for the average low-income household each year (Pearlstein 1995, 6). Clearly, inner-city African American households stand to suffer a stunning blow from such policies.

STRUCTURAL FEATURES OF AFRICAN AMERICAN COMMUNITIES

To understand the social context within which the largest proportion of inner-city African Americans must cope on an everyday basis, we outline

general demographic and structural characteristics that generate profound
social problems for African American families and communities (Taylor
1995; Williams 1995; Goode and Schneider 1994).

As of 1990, only 38 percent of black children lived in two-parent families, compared to 79 percent for whites. At the same time rates for female-
headed households have climbed steadily from 18 percent in the 1950s to
well over 50 percent in 1990. As a result of family breakdown, black illegitimacy skyrocketed, reaching 49 percent in 1975 and in 1995, it stands
close to 70 percent. If current trends continue, black illegitimacy should
rise to 75 percent by the turn of the century.

Median income shows marked disparities between whites and blacks. On
January 15, 1996, CNN reported that the median household income for
white American families was $39,308, versus $21,548 for African American families. Significant worth differences between blacks and whites are
independent of income. In the $2,000–$3,900 monthly income category,
white householder net worth was $50,529, whereas that for blacks was
$15,977. Low rates of home ownership further compound the lack of cu-
mulative assets, which appears to be the result of bank loan discrimination,
as well as the disparity in net worth as a result of historic inequities (Williams 1995, 411).

Because of widespread black migration from the rural South to northern
cities in the period of roughly 1900–1920, and a greater migration surge
into large metropolitan areas after World War II, there has been a heavy
preponderance of African Americans residing in urban areas (Goode and
Schneider 1994). Beginning with a trickle of dissatisfied laborers from barren farmlands the mass of Negro migrants eventually swelled to millions,
as New York, Philadelphia, Detroit, Chicago, Los Angles, and other cities
initially embraced the new immigrants as an energetic and serviceable labor
force. Better jobs, education, and opportunities for community appeared
assured. Discrimination in work, housing, and education soon replaced the
open community, and through "redlining" and other systematic real estate
practices, the African American community soon found itself isolated and
unassimilated. According to the 1990 census, 72 percent of African Americans live in census tracts that are 90 percent or more African Americans
(Goode and Schneider 1994, 4). At the same time, structural barriers served
to keep a disproportionate number of blacks either working in unskilled
jobs or permanently jobless (Mincy 1994).

In the last thirty years, the U.S. economy has gradually shifted from
manufacturing to service jobs. Large factories that had provided relative
security, decent wages, and benefits to many Americans since the 1940s
moved first to the South and then overseas. The jobs that sometimes replace
factory work are either low-end service work or require more education
than did those of earlier decades. Economic shifts have played a significant
role in both the life chances and the diminished expectations of the people

left behind in the urban core. During the 1960s, the federal government moved into the breach with various antipoverty programs that helped mobilize local community development organizations. Yet, in many impoverished and at-risk communities, the new conservative agenda threatens to eradicate these programs.

The combined influx of new middle-class immigrants from Eastern Europe and Asian refugees in the post-Vietnam, post-communist period (1975–1990) coupled with heavy inflow of both legal and illegal Hispanics have generated new competition for African Americans in an already constricted job market. And contrary to expectations, when the black middle-class began to desert the ghetto for suburban living, it proved a mixed blessing. African American movement out of the ghetto reportedly has had a destabilizing effect (W. J. Wilson 1987; Carter 1995; Anderson 1990). Those people left behind were more likely than those leaving to be nonwhite, older and poorer, less educated, less likely to be employed, more likely to be living on welfare, and more likely to be raised in a female-headed household. In 1987, a full third of the African American population lived below the poverty level, with over 50 percent of African American children living in such conditions (Dewart 1989).

Such reduced social circumstances as we have described for contemporary African American communities fits the model of "structural racism" first articulated by Stokeley Carmichael and Charles Hamilton (1967) in their classic definition of the problem:

Racism is both overt and covert. . . . The first consists of overt acts by individuals which cause death, injury or the violent destruction of property. . . . The second type is less overt, far more subtle. . . . But it is no less destructive of human life. The second type originates in the operation of established and respected forces in society, and thus received far less public condemnation than the first type. (p. 4)

It is this dual structure of racism that young ghetto men confront that appears to be the foundation for their rage and increasing visibility as a threatening force in American society.

POVERTY AND CRIME IN THE WAR ZONE

The literal dimension of the African American youth crisis is especially pronounced in the "inner-urban war zones" that have developed within U.S. cities (Garbarino et al. 1992). These "war zones" are the direct outcome of the extended practices of exclusion that have accompanied state policies of denial of access to social and economic opportunities for people of color. These "war zones," permeated by grinding poverty and violence, are the product of the trend to apply military solutions to social problems, a trend that has intensified under the rubric of the "new conservatism."

Structures of inequality and oppression receive their expression in newfound levels of disadvantage. Poverty now reportedly affects nine million U.S. children; indeed, a host of recent reports, given extensive coverage in the national newspaper *USA Today* (11/14/94), attest to the burgeoning numbers of impoverished children living in the United States. Child poverty rose during the 1970s and the 1980s, reaching a peak in 1993. Nearly one in four children and adolescents now lives in poverty. Contributing factors include income inequality, with a widening gap between the earnings of the wealthy and the poor, and family breakdown, with a growing proportion of female-headed households.

The latest data from the 1990 U.S. Census Bureau indicate that approximately half the population of African American children are living below the poverty line. Over 50 percent of African American children living in rural and urban areas are classified as poor, and about 35 percent of these children living in suburban areas are regarded as poor. Over two-thirds of impoverished African American children live with their mother, and over a quarter of African American children spend between eleven and seventeen years in poverty. Further, violence in the home, in the school, or in the street disrupts the daily lives of many African American children, and places them in danger of injury or even death (Garbarino et al. 1992; Kozol 1992; Prothrow-Stith 1993; W. J. Wilson 1987).

The most recent National Crime Victimization Survey (U.S. Department of Justice 1994a) shows that African Americans are subjected to more crimes of violence than any other group in U.S. society. The rate of reported violent victimization among the African American male population is 134.8 per 100,000, compared with a reported rate of 97.5 for the nonblack male population. Households headed by African Americans are also more likely to experience property crime, including burglary and theft. The rate of household crime for African American households is 199.1 per 100,000, whereas the rate for nonblack households is considerably lower at 146 per 100,000.

One of the most notable findings of the latest National Crime Victimization Survey is the very high rates of violent victimization reported by young African American males. This group is much more likely to be the victim of aggravated assault than their white counterparts. This is especially true for the twelve- to fifteen-year-old age group, where the reported victimization rate for African American males is 35.7 per 100,000, compared with the reported victimization rate for while males, which is 17.4 per 100,000. Yet it is in the sixteen- to nineteen-year-old age group, and to a lesser extent the twenty- to twenty-four-year-old age group, that the most pronounced differences are evident. In the case of the sixteen- to nineteen-year-olds, the reported rate of aggravated assault for African American males is 59 per 100,000, and for white males it is 20.2 per 100,000. For the twenty- to twenty-four-year-old age group, African American males are approximately twice as likely to report being the victim of aggravated as-

Table 10.4
Victimization Rates for Persons Age 12 and Over by Race, Sex, Age of Victims, and Type of Crime

Race, Sex & Age	Total Population	Rate per 100,000 in each age group	
		Crimes of Violence	Crimes of Theft
WHITE			
Male			
12-15	5,782,290	91.3	114.6
16-19	5,534,440	88.6	96.4
20-24	7,623,060	83.8	124.6
Female			
12-15	5,522,070	57.9	79.7
16-19	5,362,500	51.9	104.9
20-24	7,508,090	51.0	97.5
BLACK			
Male			
12-15	1,115,770	73.9	90.5
16-19	987,030	158.1	75.9
20-24	1,132,150	131.2	111.4
Female			
12-15	1,103,220	92.7	64.4
16-19	1,052,120	94.8	67.7
20-24	1,314,120	77.7	70.0

Source: Adapted from data included in the report, Criminal Victimization in the United States (U.S. Department of Justice 1994a, 29).

sault than non-African American males of the same age. The extraordinary disparity in reported victimization rates for all crimes of violence reported by sixteen- to twenty-four-year-old males is illustrated in Table 10.4.

Homicide is now the leading cause of death among African American youth (Garbarino et al. 1992). In New York City, the homicide rate is 27.5 per 100,000. In Harlem, the homicide rate is nearly three times this figure at 71.3 per 100,000 persons. This indicates that violent victimization, including homicide, is an interracial phenomenon. This is borne out by findings of the latest National Crime Victimization Survey (U.S. Department of Justice 1994a). These high levels of violence render African American youth especially vulnerable. Inner-city educators and social workers express deep concern, as they observe that under conditions of chronic violence, the problems of children are reaching new levels never before encountered (Edelman 1987).

For African American boys and young men, this crisis is exacerbated; these youth might be said to be confronting a crisis of survival. Hill (1995) portrays this as a crisis that extends across the life course:

African American males continue to experience disproportionate levels of social and economic distress. As preadolescents, they exhibit high rates of suspensions, expulsions, special education placements, foster care placements, dropouts, and push-outs. As adolescents, they are more prone to delinquency, gang participation, and joblessness. As young adults, they are more involved in drug pushing, fathering children out of wedlock, alcohol abuse and drug abuse. . . . Black adult men have high rates of poor physical health, mental illness and homelessness. Moreover, while the life expectancy for white males continued to rise from 71.8 to 72.0 years between 1984 and 1986, the life expectancy for black males fell from 65.6 to 65.2. (p. 333)

POPULAR CULTURE REPRESENTATIONS

To be poor and black in a white supremacist society is everywhere represented—in speech, interpersonal relations, mass media, and social policy—as valueless. The message of capitalism is that money secures strength, intelligence, resources, and futures. For those who cannot escape poverty and victimization, there is no choice but to submerge into a life that is empty and meaningless. The poor learn to be nihilistic (hooks 1994, 168). At the same time, the poor are blamed for their condition. The structural sources of poverty—lack of jobs, low income, inferior education, racial segregation, and unsupported families—are denied or glossed over (Jackson 1991; hooks 1994; MacLeod 1987; Edelman 1987; W. J. Wilson 1987).

African American girls and women do not display the "fixity of boundary relations" in the same way that African American boys and men do (Gunew 1994). Instead, they offer a distinct set of images within the context of black roles. Whereas the stereotype of the young black man centers around his physicality, implicitly laden with violence and sexuality, images of black females are far more complex. The multiple ecologies of black female experience defy a singular definition of "racial category," as history, culture, class, and gender combine to generate diverse representations. For instance, counterpoised to the image of the teenage single mother is the concept of the strong, enduring black woman as an historical type.

African women were an integral part of their communities and were able to maximize their positions with resources gained by their own labor, as highly placed administrators in political systems and as spirit mediums in the religious arena (Vaz 1995, xiii). As part of a cohesive group, African women could band together to redress grievances against men and discipline male offenders, a tradition that has persisted through the slave system and beyond (Vaz 1995).

Enslaved African women passed on their legacy of resilience, resourcefulness, and spirituality to their African-American daughters who adapted these to confront and challenge the slave system. (p. xiii)

This resiliency has given rise to the notion that African-American women have "unique qualifications by virtue of heredity, culture or condition" that enable them to defy racist and sexist attempts to define and constrain them (B. Moss 1995, 19). In the nineteenth century, their anti-abolition efforts, and in the twentieth century, their political activism and wide range of occupational roles have gone largely unnoticed by the dominant society (see, for example, Yee 1995; Pruitt 1995; and Carter 1995).

The mass media, educational system, and popular culture generally blank out critical conditions and developments whose imagery would pose unacceptable challenges to the dominant structures of race and culture power. "Invisible crises," generated by a racist society, advance images of "otherness" that promote contempt, dishonor, and degradation against African Americans. Such attitudes have their source in slavery, Jim Crow practices in Southern states, chronic economic exploitation, and political regimes based on fear and coercion (Adero 1993; Taylor 1995; Tolnay and Beck 1994). In turn, these attitudes, once they are internalized through family socialization, school experience, job failures, and everyday interaction, contribute to the dehumanization and stigma of African American youth. As a result, character formation for many black youth is severely compromised by negative social conditions.

Normal developmental processes occurring in these environments are compromised in chronic stress as youth struggle with developmental tasks in the presence of relentlessly negative stigma. (Spencer 1995, 38)

From a normal developmental perspective, there has been an inclination to view particularly African American adolescents and young adult males as an "endangered species" (Gibbs 1988) and even a "lost generation" (Majors 1994a; 1994b). From another perspective, African American male experiences serve to demonstrate the undiagnosed, unchanged, and untreated fabric of American life (Spencer 1995, 38; hooks 1994).

Lack of appropriate racial male role models is another factor working to the disadvantage of black youth. As successful African Americans abandon the inner city for more-secure suburban neighborhoods, it leaves behind the less resourceful and experienced, especially poor women, children and the elderly. The "invisible crises" grow as low-resourced inner-city residents cope with debilitated and crime-ridden neighborhoods; lack of effective leadership; the demise of an alternative political and social ethos; and the promotion of social practices that kill aspirations, identity, integrity, and autonomy among young black men (MacLeod 1987). The results of pervasive, but denied, institutional classism and racism have produced "cumulative effects" of discrimination. Black Americans, especially boys and young men, continue to represent one of the most disadvantaged groups in the United States regardless of the measure used (W. J. Wilson 1987; Hatchett, Cochran, and Jackson 1995; Majors 1992, 1994b; Taylor 1995).

For example, the control of economic and cultural resources by the dominant society precludes young black men from entering the competitive arena in the first place; but not by choice. A paradoxical persistence of positive academic attitudes prevails among African American adolescents despite low academic achievement (Alexander, Entwisle, and Bedinger 1994). Exclusionary practices are also reflected in the disparity between the willingness to participate in the youth and young adult labor market, and the actual negligible participation rates by inner-city black youth (MacLeod 1987). The availability of local jobs, especially African American–owned-and-operated, has actually declined over the last few decades. African Americans in business face "incremental disadvantages" over a business life span, experiences that merge with that of the collective experience of local residents to produce "a greater enraging and disempowering effect" (Feagin and Sikes 1994, 582).

The streets, gang culture, drugs, and guns offer a seductive alternative for some excluded youth, and allow them to play out the public myth of the gangster (Sheley and Wright 1995). Marginalized by race, class, and gender, young African American men have embraced violence and other high-risk behaviors as normal; simply part of the street lifestyle (Moyers 1995; Majors 1994b). But it is a lifestyle that is no more Afrocentric than poverty. Americans have long had a love affair with violence, which is deeply inculcated in our history and traditions (Davis 1987). Television offers an open season on murder and mayhem resulting in an average child witnessing eight thousand murders by the close of the elementary years (Moyers 1995). Images of violence coupled with the easy availability of handguns in the United States account for the highest rates of murder, aggravated assault, and rape in the Western world (Voigt et al. 1994) (see also Chapter 8).

This normalization of violence in the larger society is the operative framework for the recent "epidemic" of African American youth violence over the last few years (Voigt et al. 1994; Taylor 1995). Violence as a "solution" to the problems of poverty, stigma, and invisibility has the real effect of further undermining vulnerable inner-city communities (Diiulio 1994; Taylor 1995) and decimating the ranks of young black men through death or imprisonment. Homicide is now the leading cause of death for African

American males age sixteen to twenty-four, closely followed by suicide and injuries (Weddle and McHenry 1995).

Whether involved in the street life or not, young black males are aware that they fit the "profile" for expected deviance. The practical consequences of being stopped continuously by police as they move throughout society, their awareness of chronic surveillance by law enforcement, their social perception of being a threatening image to others are everyday features that shape every social and psychological experience (Taylor 1995). Common stereotypes point to all black men as "potential criminals" (Feagin and Sikes 1994). Taylor (1995) says:

Thus, having the attributes of a particular ethnic designation (i.e., African American), belonging to a particular gender group (i.e., male), and occupying a particular status (i.e., being an adolescent, young adult, adult or child assumed to be aggressive) contribute to risk. (p. 53)

Majors (1994a, 33) goes further to emphasize the distinctions between black men and women of terms of public response to cultural representations (see also Majors 1992; 1994b).

We've conditioned our society, that it's hard to love a black man. It's hard to love black youth. It's easier to love women and children, irrespective of color. And it's easier to mobilize our resources around women and children than it is around black men. . . . [Black men] are not inherently bad people. They're only reacting to the lack of opportunities in a marginalized society.

Labeling and stigma act as initial conditions for placing all African American youth at high-risk for counterproductive behaviors that reinforce the racial disadvantage. Such behaviors run the gamut from premature sexuality and early pregnancy for girls to mental health problems, school withdrawal, crime, delinquency, alcohol/drug abuse, victimization, and incarceration for increasing numbers of young black people (see Taylor 1995).

JUSTICE AND STATE POLICY

Contemporary notions of justice are embedded within the hierarchical, competitive, and mechanistic model that has dominated society since the mid-seventeenth century. Within this model, technological control of all life is the norm (Olsen, Lodwick, and Dunlap 1992, 34).

Under conditions of political expediency, justice has lost its philosophical and ethical parameters and has assumed a defensive posture against outsiders. For millions of African American youth, state dependency becomes the operative state principle, channeling female adolescents into the welfare system and male youth into the criminal justice system. Both systems undermine personal autonomy and reinforce a structure of state domination. Social control is played out in a context of a militarized social policy: the war on drugs, war on poverty, war on gangs, war on crime. In practice, it is a war against inner-city residents, especially women and children, as the following sections explore.

State Dependency and Control I: Welfare

The economic well-being of African Americans has actually declined since the 1950s, and today urban poverty is nearly as high as when President Johnson launched his battle against poverty in 1965 (Aponte in W. J. Wilson 1987, 158). Today, over 33 percent of African Americans fall below the poverty line, and in families with single mothers, the poverty rate rises to 50 percent (Taylor 1995). African Americans have long suffered disproportionately throughout history from poverty and family dislocation, including living in a female-headed household and dependence on welfare (Edelman 1987; Adero 1993; Taylor 1995). The so-called "culture of poverty," an intergenerational phenomenon, is a direct outgrowth of welfare policies and pro-family politics, the latter a strategic backlash by New Right groups against feminism and single mother parenting (Acland 1995). For example, the major government program for sustaining poor black, unemployed families is the Aid to Families with Dependent Children (AFDC). In Southern states, the monthly payment runs as low as $42.29 per person or $120.90 for an entire family (Mississippi). But even with payments as high as $372 in the District of Columbia, the living standard is guaranteed destitution. On any dimension considered, the African American family is an imperiled institution.

Mortality rates for poor children in the United States are three times the rate of nonpoor children. The national death rate for black infants under one year actually increased by 6 percent between 1983 and 1984 and has continued to rise throughout the 1990s (Edelman 1987). The steady increase in the infant mortality rates is directly linked to poverty and low access to health care among pregnant women, conditions that are especially pervasive in black communities. These high infant-mortality rates are among the highest of all industrial nations.

In the course of their childhood, more than twice as many black children (86 percent) as white children (42 percent) are likely to spend some time in a single-parent household, and much of it in poverty. Fully 75 percent of black children under the age of eighteen who live in female headed-households in 1985 were poor (Taylor 1985, 9).

Black child poverty is exacerbated by escalating divorce rates and a rapid increase in the incidence of out-of-wedlock births across white and black communities. Among African Americans, one of every three mothers is a teenager; and a third of these go on to have a second child while still in their teens. Since 1965, the incidence of childbearing among unmarried black females, age fifteen to nineteen rose from 57 percent to 83 percent in 1981. By 1985, more than 90 percent of first births to black teenagers were born out of wedlock (Furstenberg, Brooks-Gunn, and Chase-Lansdale 1989). Among single black females who are heads of households, almost 50 percent are below the poverty line (U.S. Census Bureau). Unmarried motherhood among black female teens may be attributed both to the ongoing sex codes among African American men that emphasize marriage-avoidance strategies, and also to a dramatic fall in the number of "marriageable men" due to joblessness, early death, and incarceration (Anderson 1989; W. J. Wilson 1987).

Three-fifths of teenage mothers drop out of school, affecting their lifetime earnings, which are less than half those of women who wait until twenty before bearing their first child. Among black girls, school is often an alienating experience with little reference to their immediate needs and interests. In general, the school resists the culture of subordinate groups; instead it punishes cultural variations in language, style, and behavior differences (Corson 1993). Thus, the young African American mother has few ties to the conventional school, a factor that may contribute to her failure to promote an interest in education for her children.

Because the black population is younger than the general population, with 50 percent less than age twenty-four, the black community is more adversely affected by the disadvantaged states of mothers and their children (Weddle and McKenry 1995). Individuals who live in lower-income environments typically not only experience more stressors, but also stressors that are more disruptive, including excessive crowding, high levels of crime and violence, social isolation from mainstream society, and high levels of social disorganization. "For the poor and especially urban blacks, the fact of greatest significance is the pervasiveness of stressors in their everyday lives" (Weddle and McKenry 1995, 204). In this way, socioeconomic and environmental stressors impact on children and contribute to feelings of powerlessness, despair, and social alienation (Gibbs 1988). And among all age and gender cohorts, young African American males are the most vulnerable and most likely to react in self- and other-destructive ways (Brunswick and Rier 1995; Dembo et al. 1995).

Rather than a system of welfare in the classic sense of income maintenance, health, and well-being for families and their communities, the current structure should be recognized as a punitive, exclusionary system, draining energy, hope, and initiative from those caught within it.

State Dependency and Control 2: Incarceration

Criminalization and incarceration, with their resultant stigmatization and invisibility, are dominant themes in the lives of African American males. In the United States today, African American and Hispanic groups comprise

44 percent of the total jail population, far in excess of their proportion in the larger population. The U.S. Department of Justice (1993) reports that the rate of incarceration within local jails has risen significantly in the last ten years or so. From 1982 to 1992, the rate of incarceration increased from 90 per 100,000 to 174 per 100,000. During this period, the rate of incarceration of white (nonblack) persons rose to 109 per 100,000 white (nonblack) residents, whereas the rate of incarceration for black persons, who comprise about 12 percent of the U.S. population, rose to 619 per 100,000 black residents. Keeping this in perspective, this means that 6 percent of the population (i.e., black males) account for over 40 percent of all the inmates in federal, state, and local lockups.

African American youth are especially vulnerable to arrest, conviction, and incarceration. This is part of the larger pattern of the documented increase in the number of juveniles arrested for violent crimes in the United States during the period of 1982–1991, and the growing contribution by juveniles to the volume of violent crime during this time (U.S. Department of Justice 1993). On any given day, about one in every three African American men is under the jurisdiction of the criminal justice system (Hill 1995). This figure continues to rise as a result of the recent practice of remanding juveniles from the juvenile court to adult court (Bortner 1986). Thus, minority juvenile offenders in certain jurisdictions are more likely to be placed in secure institutions including adult jails (as opposed to diversion and community-based programs) than comparable nonblack juvenile offenders (Diiulio 1994; see also Kratcoski and Kratcoski 1990).

The bitter irony of these social arrangements is that incarceration, although generally a short-term response to a specific crime, has led to increased gang cohesion and membership recruitment in many correctional institutions and has led indirectly to a worsening of the crime problem on the streets (U.S. Department of Justice 1994b).

The criminologist James Messerschmidt attributes this proclivity toward street crime and violence on the part of African American youth to negotiations around masculinity. Messerschmidt (1993) argues that robbery

provides the ideal opportunity to construct an 'essential' toughness and 'maleness,' it provides a means with which to construct that certain type of masculinity— hardman. . . . For marginalized, racial-minority boys, robbery reflects their structural position as the most available resource for constructing a specific type of masculine expression. (pp. 107–8)

These negotiations around gender become particularly critical when African American youth are shut out of legitimate opportunities to establish a masculine identity. In American society today, these opportunities generally revolve around achievement in the labor market—holding down a job, earning a good income, supporting a family, owning a home. Most of these achievements are beyond the reach of large sectors of African American youth. The embrace of illegal options, in order to construct a viable gendered identity and to acquire an income, becomes increasingly likely.

The racial imbalance within the criminal justice process is especially pronounced in the area of sentencing, particularly for those defendants convicted of homicide, sex crimes, robbery, and assault. Spohn's (1994) analysis of racial disparities in sentencing based on race of offender and race of victim reveals that while the rates for offenders convicted of all felonies are remarkably similar—79 percent for blacks who victimized whites, 77 percent for blacks who victimized blacks, and 69 percent for whites who victimized whites—sentencing practices reveal startling racial differences. For example, among African Americans who were convicted of sexually assaulting whites, 86 percent were sent to prison. This compares with only 66 percent of blacks who sexually assaulted blacks, and only 54 percent of whites who sexually assaulted other whites.

Imposing the death penalty on children is a more recent move to severely sanction juvenile violence. Nationally, juveniles (aged seventeen years or under) account for about one-fifth of all weapons arrests, and in 1991 committed a record 2,476 criminal homicides, about 10 percent of the total number. In an overview of the juvenile death penalty, Streib (1995) concluded that race plays a critical role in determining who will be sentenced to death. In a recent study, he found that:

1. Offender profiles among those who received the death penalty indicate that they were most likely to be African American, were between the ages of fifteen and seventeen years at the time of the crime, and had almost always killed a single victim, usually a female. The overwhelming proportion of youthful offenders was male (94 percent).

2. An important feature of the death penalty is that although offenders were typically African American, only 9 percent of their victims were African American. Overwhelmingly, the victims were nonblack (89 percent).

3. The percentage of African American juveniles sentenced to death has increased over time. Prior to 1900, 54 percent of those sentenced to death were black; after 1900, 76 percent of those sentenced to die were black. At the same time, the percentage of white children sentenced to death fell from 36 percent prior to 1900 to 20 percent after 1900.

4. Eighty-one percent of the executions performed have been for crimes of homicide and 15 percent for sexual assault. The sexual assault cases are a more recent phenomenon, with 84 percent occurring since 1900.

5. Regional distinctions show that 79 percent of death sentences were from states in the South. Nationwide, persons under a juvenile death sentence account for less than 2 percent of the total death row population (NAACP 1987, 1).

Streib (1995) concludes that the juvenile death sentence has failed utterly to deter violent crime, and that the imposition of the ultimate sanction upon children is unjustified:

[However] it seems clear that the death penalty for juveniles has been given a long trial period and has been found wanting. Its societal costs are enormous, it tastes terribly foul, and it delays our search for a wise and just means of reducing violent juvenile crime. (p. 158)

When we add the dimension of race, the death penalty for children takes on an ominous note. Indeed, the death penalty may be serving as the contemporary, but now legitimate, substitute for the lynching parties mounted in the former Deep South (see Tolnay and Beck 1994). Both of these strategies punish young African American men for alleged violence against the dominant order, especially infringements of the race-based sexual code.

INDEPENDENCE FROM THE STATE: THE CASE OF THE ILLICIT DRUG ECONOMY

Structured inequality within U.S. society translates into greatly reduced opportunities for African Americans to engage in legitimate occupational activities. In these oppressive social conditions, the illegal drug economy provides employment opportunities for disenfranchised African American youth. Involvement in this illegal economy necessitates the relinquishment of traditional and legitimate routes to social and economic survival (Zimring and Hawkins 1991). The abandonment of these pathways is accompanied by significant risks. As Rosenbaum (1988) points out, the career of the illicit drug user is shaped by particular, predictable patterns of experience. As illicit drug users become more deeply entrenched in the illegal drug economy, their lives become characterized by "risk, chaos and inundation" (Rosenbaum 1988, 48). Laura Fishman's (1992) study of the lives of HIV-positive African American inmates prior to incarceration throws light on this descent into "chaos and inundation."

Fishman (1992, 7) describes how these men adopted a number of styles of "fast living": pronounced drug consumption; a rugged and aggressive demeanor, often involving violence; "unstable relationships" with sexual partners; a highly mobile lifestyle; and engagement in illegal or quasi-illegal activity. In addition, these men reported extended periods of detachment from the legitimate economy of work. High-risk behavior, such as involvement with multiple sex partners, the sharing of drug-using equipment, and use of shooting galleries, characterized these men's lives. Masculinity was defined in terms of "toughness, sexual conquest and thrill seeking" (p. 9). Fishman (1992, 10) concludes that "the picture that emerges is that those men who actively pursue a fast-living lifestyle may also be those who engage in high-risk behavior."

Indeed, high-risk activities, accompanied by the promise of high rewards, contributes to poor youth's involvement in crime and violence and is the basis for the "fast-living lifestyle." Those who are part of the illegal drug distribution network routinely resort to violence to control the behavior of those less powerful than themselves, or those who violate the norms and prescriptions of the illegal drug economy (Johnson, Kaplan, and Schmeidler 1990). These drug distribution networks are assumed to be inherently violent. Goldstein (1989) calls attention to the systemic violence, which permeates the illicit drug economy (see Chapter 7). This systemic violence may occur on the structural or individual level.

We label these different types of violence "*macrosystem violence*" and "*microsystem violence*," respectively. Macrosystem violence involves large-scale disputes or "territorial wars" fought between rival drug cartels or groups operating within the confines of a single area. Microsystem violence—or interpersonal violence—may be sparked by the failure to supply an agreed upon product, adulteration of drugs before sale, or other violations of drug transactions involving two or more people (Goldstein 1989). Hence, the illegal drug economy is saturated with "transactional risks" in the use and sale of drugs, involving "violence, brutality and the presence of firearms" (Arnold et al. 1990, 19).

The dangers posed by involvement in this illicit drug distribution network have been manufactured in large measure by government action—the so-called War on Drugs (see Chapter 8). A militaristic response to the use of drugs has characterized U.S. policy from the mid-1980s onward (see Gardiner and McKinney 1991). Since this time, the "drug problem" has been increasingly incorporated into the "crime problem." Indeed, Christina Johns (1992, 150) has observed, "The war against illegal drug use and drug trafficking has taken on the qualities of a holy war or religious crusade." Anxiety about the sanctity and integrity of society, particularly anxiety regarding danger that emanates from beyond the boundaries of civil society (Hatty 1993), has inspired a militaristic mind-set (see Treback 1994). Skolnick (1990, 75) acknowledges the impact of this militaristic mind-set when he states that under the auspices of the War on Drugs there has been a "vast expansion of the apparatus of social control—particularly law enforcement and prisons—into what begins to resemble a semi-martial state," which has fallen disproportionately on minority groups (see Box 10-A).

The current War on Drugs may be inadvertently serving an additional function, according to Johns (1992). This involves dissipation of the momentum underlying the organized struggle for social and economic reform on the part of African Americans. Johns (1992) claims that deep involvement in drug trafficking and illegal drug use within this community—as a consequence of a lack of viable, alternative means of support—is diverting energy from the reform process. In addition, this involvement may permit the government to demonize this segment of the population by portraying them as "outside the law" (see hooks 1994). Consequently, African Americans can be constructed as the "enemy within" that threatens to unravel the moral fabric of society.

```
┌─────────────────────────────────────────────────────────────────────┐
│                           Box 10-A                                    │
│                   The Racial Politics of Crime                        │
│                                                                       │
│  The National Center on Institutions and Alternatives (NCIA) conducted a sur- │
│  vey of young African American males in Washington, D.C.'s justice system. │
│  The center found that on an average day in 1991, more than four in ten (42 │
│  %) of all the 18–35 year-old African American men who lived in the District │
│  were in jail, in prison, on probation/parole, out on bond, or being sought on │
│  arrest warrants. On the basis of this "one day" count, it was estimated that │
│  approximately 75 percent of all 18-year-old African American males in that │
│  city could look forward to being arrested and jailed at least once before they │
│  reach the age of 35. The lifetime risk hovered even higher; somewhere between │
│  an 80–90 percent likelihood of being arrested. Similar justice supervision rates │
│  exist in other cities, despite the fact that the overwhelming proportion of black │
│  men who were being arrested and jailed were charged on lesser felonies and │
│  misdemeanors. In Baltimore, African Americans of all ages were being arrested │
│  for drug offenses at six times the rate of whites, and over 90 percent of these │
│  arrests were for "possession."                                       │
│                                                                       │
│  Source: Jerome G. Miller. 1996. Search and Destroy: African American Males in the │
│     Criminal Justice System. Cambridge: Cambridge University Press, pp. 7–8. │
└─────────────────────────────────────────────────────────────────────┘
```

In addition to undermining the struggle for civil rights within African American communities, the War on Drugs has seriously affected the legal and health status of members of these communities. It has been said that politicians have given little consideration to the ramifications of the "get-tough" approach to the drug problem (McWilliams 1990, 17). The U.S. prison population now exceeds 1.6 million inmates (1997), and state prisons cannot provide enough new cells to accommodate the flow of drug offenders. Expenditures for correctional facilities have risen to over $30 billion every year (Blomberg and Cohen 1995, 9).

We have already seen that African American males feature disproportionately in these populations. Further, as the political climate in the United States is largely intolerant of harm-reduction approaches to illegal drug use (involving, for example, the provision of needle and syringe exchange services [see Longshore 1992]), the illegal drug-using population is unduly exposed to HIV/AIDS and other transmissible diseases. This has taken a serious toll on the African American community, as large-scale imprisonment and HIV/AIDS threaten the survival of young men.

Poverty and extreme social disadvantage are linked to engagement in the illicit drug economy. The contemporary War on Drugs disproportionately targets the poor and minority groups, especially African Americans. According to estimates by the United States Sentencing Commission, in 1993, fourteen thousand of the ninety thousand federal prison inmates are serving sentences under laws for crack cocaine offenses, with African Americans constituting 88.3 percent of the offenders. Crack cocaine tends to be the drug of choice for many inner-city drug users, because of its availability and low cost. Because of the statutory distinction between crack cocaine and powdered cocaine, penalties are calibrated on a "100–1 ratio." In other words, poor blacks use and deal crack cocaine and go to prison; well-to-do whites use powdered cocaine, and if apprehended, may go to treatment, and far less frequently than crack users, end up in jail (Smothers 1995, A12). Thus, the War on Drugs has criminalized a significant proportion of U.S. youth, and has exacerbated the risk of imprisonment for many of these youth.

Not only prison sentences, but also involvement with intravenous drug use, crack cocaine, alcohol, as well as other illegal substances, combined with an escalation in the War on Drugs, have combined to produce a large population of disenfranchised and marginalized people, who are at serious risk of contracting and transmitting HIV. Social and political circumstances have rendered entire communities vulnerable to illness and death through AIDS or AIDS-related conditions (Cochran and Mays 1995, 436).

SOCIAL JUSTICE AND CHANGE

Clearly, the traditional concept of retributive justice, when applied to the African American communities, must be abandoned. The ecological version of justice proposed earlier resonates with the struggles for change emanating from within African American communities. The philosopher Cornel West (1993b) alludes to similar strategies and approaches when he states,

The time has come for critics and artists of the new cultural politics of difference to cast their nets widely, flex their muscles broadly, and thereby refuse to limit their visions, analyses, and praxis to their particular terrains. The aim is to dare to recast, redefine, and revise the very notions of "modernity," "mainstream," "margins," "difference," "otherness." We have now reached a new stage in the perennial struggle for freedom and dignity. (pp. 216–17)

We join Stephen White (1992, 17) in his call for greater attention to be paid to the "phenomena of *in*justice" as a construct (and experience) of primary importance in its own right, and not merely a derivative of the workings of "justice." We also support his call for an urgent focus on the *fostering* of "otherness," human diversity in all its differences, and not only the *tolerance* of "otherness."

Instead of rejection and punishment of those youth traditionally viewed as outsiders that are marginal to the social enterprise, it is essential that we confront the reality of persons outside our culture set; her or his ways of speaking and being, and determine justice from this perspective. Importantly, this impacts strongly on African American youth, because these young people are caught up to a greater extent in the social control net.

Justice for African American communities posits the necessity to move beyond limited versions of technological justice, reflected in the operations of the criminal justice system and conventional criminological theory. These outmoded discourses offer no satisfactory explanatory schema for the larger array of black youth deviance and alienation. Nor do these discourses generate viable social policies that will confront the widespread mistreatment and injustice directed toward the displaced and disenfranchised members of the African American community.

The general justice principles we have enunciated require a more extensive discussion of their specific application to African American youth. Even so, it is obvious that the effects of the rising incidence of racism in U.S. society, in the wake of the resurgence of conservatism, render the situation one of great urgency. The cultural critic, bell hooks (1990) recognizes the poisonous nature of this "politics of race" in U.S. society; she notes,

To take racism seriously one must consider the plight of underclass people of color, a vast majority of whom are black. For African Americans our collective condition prior to the advent of postmodernism and perhaps more tragically expressed under current postmodern conditions has been and is characterized by continued displacement, profound alienation, and despair. (p. 26)

Clearly, we must search for alternative paradigms of justice. The creation of viable futures for all Americans depends upon it. The attainment of these viable futures is arguably a matter of applying a critical approach to the politicization of the present. Lawrence Grossberg (1992) offers us some guidance here:

How we imagine the future, how we conceptualize the possibilities open to us, depends upon how we interpret our present circumstances. Too many of the stories we are telling ourselves seem to lead nowhere or to some place we would rather not go. Only if we begin to reread our own moment can we begin to rearticulate our future. If you want to change the ending, you have to tell a different story. (p. 11)

For African American youth, this story could well shift from gangsta-rap with its focus of violence to Afrocultural themes that celebrate the rich spiritual heritage, the survival strengths, the capacity for resistance to injustice, and the ability to create indigenous art forms that embody the multiple voices and experiences of African Americans (see *African-Americans: Voices of Triumph—Creative Fire* 1994).

CONCLUSION

This chapter traces the crisis of survival among young African American men, and emphasizes that structural racism in all its manifestations—poor school achievement, joblessness, weakened families and communities, and exposure to deviant activities and lifestyles—reinforce and exacerbate structures of inequality and oppression that characterize the United States in the late 1990s. Today, young black men are more likely to die of homicide, than either illnesses or accidents; and across the life cycle, black men experience disproportionate levels of social and economic distress, including higher rates of physical and mental illness, drug abuse, chronic unemployment, family instability, and death at an early age. Prohibition against drugs, waged so relentlessly by conservative political elements, has created a large, public domain devoted to restriction and punishment (Matza and Morgan 1995). Rather than solve the race problem and related structured inequalities, prohibition and control have exaggerated the racial effects of political oppression. Incarceration serves as an extension of slavery for keeping African Americans under white domination.

The final chapter on "Reconstructing Justice" proposes that we work as a unified community to restore justice in a world that has fallen apart. The chapter exposes the moral indifference that characterizes public life around children's and adolescents' needs and interests, and argues for practicing justice in a wholly different way: creating holistic education models, restorative justice models, and positive welfare programs.

NOTE

1. Another version of this chapter, titled *Revisioning Justice: The Case of Young African-American Men*, is an unpublished manuscript co-authored with Suzanne E. Hatty.

11

Reconstructing Justice: Toward a Healing Paradigm for Youth

For we can do nothing substantial toward changing our course on the planet, a destructive one, without rousing ourselves, individual by individual, and bringing our small imperfect stones [of activism] to the pile.

Alice Walker, *Anything We Love Can Be Saved*

A restructuring of perception is what I am after in this book. I want us to see the child we were, the adult we are, and the children who require us in one way or another, in a light that shifts the valences from curse to blessing, or if not blessing at least symptom of calling.

James Hillman, *The Soul's Code: In Search of Character and Calling*

WHEN THINGS FALL APART

We can no longer continue the "business as usual" social arrangements that contribute to growing numbers of young people's state of loss of identity and direction. We need, as a culture, to collectively admit that the "old ways," limited human lives because of social class, race, gender, and age—and the social exclusion of young people and their families—will not get us where we need to go: toward a humane, morally significant, and just society. The social actions we have considered in this book—from endangered children to various forms of youth reactions—gangs, crime, violence, suicide—are fraught with meaning, and beg for interpretation.

The study of culture, as it has been internalized in the subjective consciousness of individuals, has been an ongoing project in Western thought since the nineteenth century. The rise of individualism was met by early sociological scholars as a mixed blessing. Emile Durkheim was not the first

to point out that industrialization had irrevocably altered our social relations. Marx considered the economic processes as wholly destructive for
the social order, particularly for the poor and downtrodden. Marx's theory
of class struggle and human rights was soon abandoned by those who took
up his ideology. Subsequently, no significant social change has occurred as
a result of systematic revolution from below (because revolutionary leaders,
such as those in China and the former Soviet Union, practiced genocide
against "enemy" civilians).

Durkheim and the French School never attacked capitalism as such, but
emphasized the need for different forms of social control and social justice
to replace those lost by industrialization. The rise of the individual out of
the obscurity of tribal life changes the very nature of what is meant by
"social beings." The task of advanced societies, then, is to create equality
in every arena of human life. Society itself, Durkheim said (1947 [edited
to remove sexist language]):

is a work of justice. . . . Just as the ideal of lower societies was to create or maintain
as intense a common life as possible, in which the individual was absorbed, so our
ideal is to make social relations always more equitable, so as to assure the *free*
development of all our socially useful forces. (pp. 386–87)

Because there are no absolute moral principles, Durkheim reasoned, the
rules of justice must be interpreted, or in postmodern parlance "tested,"
against the constantly changing states of the "collective conscience." Consequently, "the task of most advanced societies is . . . a work of justice."
Not first a work of production; high technology; computer expertise;
money accumulation; individual power; power of the state; social hierarchy; growing inequalities; and entrenched injustices; no, none of these. Under existing rubrics of power, knowledge and resource inequalities, society
cannot endure and is currently falling apart. That is, our children and families and communities cannot endure and prosper. It is the civil society that
is at such intensified risk, despite the stock market's all-time high and the
business editorials lauding our American way of life. Society, as a work of
justice, requires wholly different principles and modes of action.

OBSTRUCTIONS TO RECONSTRUCTING JUSTICE

When we reconstruct justice, we are actually taking up a change in three
entities: the *mind*, the *self*, and the *society*. As G. H. Mead (1934) acknowledged in his efforts to explain the relationship between mind, self,
and society, only an aware mind that recognizes the self as both dependent
upon and independent of others can develop an autonomous enterprise;
that is, change the direction of self (drives, motives, intentions) and influence others. Modern society gave birth to the individual. What that means
is that we can exercise will/free choice, but not always under conditions of

our own making (as Marx so eloquently pointed out). We change ourselves and others fundamentally by changing our significant symbols (language, ritual, gestures, images); by acts of refusals; by statements of affirmation. In this way we exercise choice, either to "get along and go along" with the existing arrangements, or take action against them.

William James (1902/1985; 1974) another early American thinker, recognized through his psychological studies of the religious life that each of us has an inner life that is uniquely our own. James referred to these "reservoirs of consciousness" as psychic structures that individuals can turn to in time of trouble or need for self-understanding. At the same time, this inner pool of knowing and being is not some fixed moral entity. Instead, it, too, reflects the relation between ourselves and our world. James's pragmatic philosophy was both practical and mystical: Practical—he offered a pluralistic worldview; a lifeworld that was always changing, risk-engaged, perpetrated by rules, and transformed by breaks, spontaneities, and freedoms; Mystical—the inner self must be fully engaged in this flow of life. The psychic life is essential for building new conceptions of justice, because without a self (i.e., a self-reflexive, aware being), we are reduced to automatons. This means that we must "feel" our way through the justice-making process, as well as symbolically create new systems of meaning with our language, rituals, gestures, and beliefs.

Severe obstructions to creating justice now prevail and take multiple forms: (1) collective justification of inequalities and cruelties; (2) the "mean world syndrome"; (3) routinized stress and addictions as self-forgetting; and (4) the demise of "calling," or vocation, as self-commitment and passion.

Collective Justifications

Sociologists have always been intrigued with the ordinary contradictions of social life. How can we accept the sheer quantity and depth of our collective inhumanities and cruelties to others, while at the same time pose as defenders of freedom and democracy?

Are we all mere lunatics? David Matza (1990) plays with this idea in listening to (being aware of) juvenile delinquents provide reasons for their hurtful conduct to others through "neutralization techniques." These are rationalizations or supposedly illogical excuses deviants make to account for their violation of values, norms, and laws. Such techniques provide legitimating reasons for misconduct, while saying at the same time, we did nothing wrong.

Some sectors of society are much like Matza's delinquents, who not only drift into moral indifference, but remain ambivalent about living in two quite different lifeworlds: (1) the subterranean world of denial, whereby one exists through rejecting mutual interdependency and commitment to others; and (2) the normative world of awareness, whereby we give an accounting to ourselves and others for our decisions, and often, moral lapses. If we take the "open society" (a short-hand principle of democracy) as the normative world—acceptance of diversity, multiculturalism, open mindedness, tolerance—we confront disadvantaged adolescents, poverty families, victimized children, impoverished schools, and gang disturbances with concern and a sense of injustice: Let's rectify this mess.

But if you are one of the subterranean players for whom adolescence and social disadvantage are equated with deviance, you are likely to need some strong justifications for your hostility and indignation. With the rise of the subterranean principles, especially *ressentiment*, into standard politics, we have become accustomed to project our own social dislocations and psychological unease on to socially defined deviant groups. For subterraneans, who linger in the world of distrust, resentment, and self-consuming anger, the issue of inequalities and hardship, especially of children, is irrelevant, or simply "facts of life" that have nothing to do with them, their community, or their government. Such a posture typically entails no intent to harm; the view is tantamount to non-involvement-on-purpose. Here are five common forms of collective justifications for social inequalities and indifference to human suffering (see Matza 1990).

1. *Denying responsibility*: The morally righteous citizen argues that external forces cause people to "choose" their fate: laziness, alcoholism, spendthriftness, lack of intelligence. "Racism—it's not my fault. Slavery was in the nineteenth century. Why bother me now with that?" "It's not my issue that inner-city kids can't learn. Maybe their parents ought to pay more attention to them." "Leave me alone. I've got my own problems."

2. *Denial of injury*: The justifying citizen writes off the extent of harm suffered, as when the corporate magnate claims that firing half the firm's workers is "good for American industry." After all, frequent job changes are just "part of our American tradition; and besides this practice raises the value of the corporation's stock." The individual worker and his/her family, much less school and community, are simply not part of the corporate equation.

3. *Denying a victim*: The morally upstanding citizen claims that underdogs (e.g., poor children, gang members) deserve to be punished, because they are a blight on American society. Poor parents should be "forced to work, and work hard, because nobody gets something for nothing, and also, because living on welfare undermines the American way of life." Gang members "deserve life in prison without parole to teach them they can't mess around with drugs and crime without paying the price." Empathy rarely enters into the noninvolvement equation.

4. *Condemning the condemners*: Our freedom-loving citizen shifts attention from defending self to attacking liberals and social do-gooders for the "poor state" of society, and the increasing crime and violence of young

people. It is the environmentalists that are "making the world unsafe for business and development," not the other way around. For lawbreaking juveniles, the "best course of action" is either to "let them hang themselves," or "we need to tighten up punishment," and in some instances, offer a "benign neglect" that allows disenfranchised groups to work out their own problems.

5. *Appeal to higher loyalties*: Our citizen rationalizes moral indifference as superior to compassion, "because America was built on hard work and a no-nonsense ethic." "The Constitution guarantees my liberty and freedom, and that means I don't have to be a bleeding heart for all the social problems." As for youth needing intervention? "Send them to adult prison: It's the only way they'll learn the rules."

Such justifications for ignoring human need play out in everyday discourse: radio, television, conversation, political practices, economic choices, and social policy. Rather than counteract such rationalizations, the ordinary citizen tends to agree with them, or tries to ignore the implications. But neutralization techniques that deny the reality of the suffering of others keep the world mean and dangerous.

The "Mean World Syndrome"

How did the world come to be perceived as so dangerous; so noncompassionate; so far removed from our religiously-trained ideologies of faith, hope, redemption, and love? George Grebner (in Stossel 1997) argues that growing up in a violence-laden culture breeds aggressiveness in some and desensitization, insecurity, mistrust, and anger in most. Punitive and vindictive action against dark forces in a mean world is made to look appealing, especially when presented as quick, decisive, and enhancing our sense of control and security.

The media play a critical role here, because they create a culture of fear. Most current news stories and broadcasts about teenagers tend to emphasize violent crime, gangs, teenage pregnancy, and drugs. TV's fictional depiction of the teenager is that of an unprotected, world-weary, insecure lot, who are chronically misunderstood and must take on the insecurities of their elders as well as their own. The monster image surfaces more and more frequently as the media grapple with ratings and teenage entertainment preferences. Rubbing shoulders with vampires (undead beings of dark energy) is all in a day's work for the average television teenage heroine (Hine 1997).

This depicts the world as worse than it is (especially for affluent white suburbanites) but may well mirror the fears of the young. For adults, however, such virtual reality contributes to overreaction: The mind becomes militarized; the culture shifts to one that depends on authorities, strong measures, gated communities, and other proto-police state apparatus.

Box 11-A
System-Wide Neglect of Young People

Just look at the evidence. Of the 57 million children under fifteen years of age living in the United States, more than 14 million are living below the official poverty level. The United States ranks below Iran and Romania in the percentage of low-birth-weight babies. One of every six children is a stepchild, and half a million make their "homes" in residential treatment centers and group and foster homes. More children and adolescents in the United States die from suicide than from cancer, AIDS, birth defects, influenza, heart disease and pneumonia combined. Each day, at least 1 million "latchkey children" go home to where there is a gun. . . . [T]here are [also] those from all economic classes in treatment for attention deficit disorders, hyperactivity, obesity, defiance, bulimia, depression, pregnancy, addiction.

Source: James Hillman. 1996. *The Soul's Code: In Search of Character and Calling.* New York: Random House, p. 84.

Certainly, there is very real and unpredictable danger. The amount of bloodshed in the United States resembles the carnage of an undeclared civil war. During the past two decades, nearly half a million Americans have been murdered, and an additional 2.5 million have been wounded by gunfire. Each day more than ten children die by firearms, usually owned by their parents. The murder statistics exceed the casualties that the U.S. military suffered in World War II. Combining both murders and injuries, the figure rises to more than all the military casualties in all the wars of the past two hundred years. The increase in the U.S. murder rate has also been accompanied by a rising incidence of once-rare crimes. Mass murders, serial murders, and murders by strangers have become more commonplace. For example, estimates place the number of serial killers at large in the United States up to two hundred. Such violent events have also ballooned in the media, where television, film, and news reporting focus on the most gory details of death and destruction (Schlosser 1997b).

The various youth problems and issues raised in this book strongly suggest that Americans have settled for a world where many children and young people are expected to lead impoverished, fearful, anxiety-ridden lives over which they have little control. Disaster is just around the corner—it happens to the best of families, but tends to be concentrated among those in poor neighborhoods, and with weakened families and support groups. Sociologists have sometimes reinforced this view with findings that support the "mean world syndrome"—a world over which evil descends without human pity or remedy (see Box 11-A).

The "happy" brutalization that goes on in the everyday media and films has deadened us to the plight of millions of silenced children, whose constricted and often violent lives are viewed as "not the law's business." Our children and youth are growing up in a cultural environment that is designed to the specifications of a marketing strategy. Accountability is to the system, not to the people affected by the policy. When the world is cruel and people feel overwhelmed, they are told not to whine or bewail their fate, because "that's just how things are." "Take it like a man" is a common phrase. As for women, "they brought it on themselves." Once we indulge, lose ourselves, in the "mean world" imagery, we block out the possibility of compassion and of saving those things and persons we love.

The Stressed Out Society

Every epoch has its distinguishing sign—faith in the Middle Ages; order and rationality in the premodern; and the extension of this worldview in the cult of efficiency and its now-familiar psychic by-product, stress, in our own period. To reiterate from earlier chapters, efficiency is the actualization of what Habermas (1989) refers to as "the ideology of technology": All values concentrate in the system, which is outside personal or collective decision making. The technocratic consciousness pervades government and the economy, education and medicine, political parties and reform organizations. It is a pervasive mentality in which all participate; and all may perish collectively, because it prevents human beings from taking charge of their values, their consciousness, and their lives and from making significant changes. Private persons increasingly feel disengaged from public events, yielding a new form of humanity: the loner, an exile who reflects not the abundance of the technological myth but the ultimate solitariness of an empty life.

Being "stressed out" has become the normal condition of everyday life. From the technocratic perspective, stress simply cannot be avoided; it's part of modern life. But from the spiritual perspective, we can and should work collectively to defeat entropy (Chopra 1993). Chopra points out that three factors contribute to stress:

- Lack of predictability
- Lack of control
- Lack of outlets for frustration

When these are present, everyday events and situations can turn stressful.

Stress afflicts the physical, cognitive, and affective parts of our being. Physically, the stress reaction involves the release of powerful chemicals that damage the liver and undermine the energy system. Additionally, protracted stress involves a host of other destructive processes: muscle wasting, diabetes, fatigue, osteoporosis, thinning of skin, impotence, redistribution of body fat, fragility of blood vessels, hypertension, fluid retention, suppression of immune functions, impaired mental function, and deadened or inappropriate affect (insensitive or overly sensitive). Studies have shown that baby monkeys separated from their mothers and deprived of nurturing (a very high threat situation) exhibit disorientation, hyperactivity, introversion, and various learning disabilities. Other studies have found that stress hastens the spread of cancer and heart attacks (Chopra 1993, 156).

How do people typically handle stress? Consider your own case: With your favorite addiction (medically prescribed drugs, contraband drugs, alcohol, relationship dependency, food dependency, overwork [producing delayed stress symptoms], sex, credit cards, cleaning rituals, spectator sports, you name it)? Or with exercise and a health regime as the answer to your sense of ennui and disconnection? Or the use of anger and irritation as a way of letting other people know that you're having a bad day/life? What few people in our technocratic social order do is to stop, pay attention to what is happening to them, and make positive changes that will transform their hyperstress condition to one of self-care and heightened awareness. People may fear that if they stop their present activities, their "house of cards" (illusions) will collapse, and with that the death of personal identity. Our denial and obliviousness to others' suffering requires that we first become aware of our own pain. This may explain the strength of the current "New Age" movement and its emphasis on self-healing. We cannot change the world, until we have worked on ourselves first. It is impossible to achieve clarity about social issues until we have reached a degree of spiritual clarity within ourselves (Chopra 1997).

The Neglect of "Calling"

The sense of "calling," or behaving according to one's life purpose, is itself a conundrum, a puzzle that cannot be completed until the individual acquires an awareness that *this* activity, career, occupation, or way of life is right. James Hillman (1996) personifies this as a double image. One is the image of an "acorn," the innate talent, ability, gift, knowingness that all humans possess, albeit to different degrees. As an organic metaphor it reminds us that seeds must be planted in the earth, must develop roots, and must be nurtured to reach their fruition. The other image is our divine "helper" or "fate," which attaches itself to us, or may be part of the acorn itself. A person is said to be in touch with or connected with her "genius," "destiny," "angel," "daimon," "fate," or "guide." There is no mistaking the "call," as it is relentless and remorseless, and you ignore it at your peril. Among the Eskimo people and others who follow shamanistic practices, Hillman (1996, 9) says, "it is your spirit, your free-soul, your animal-soul, your breath-soul" that accompanies you on your earthly journey. There is simply no exit from its demands. Native Americans initiated their warriors by engaging them in vision quests, whereby the individual would receive both his spirit animal for protection and his calling for a purposeful life after a period of prayer and fasting.

Does the culture honor the unique qualities—special gifts and talents—of our young people? Do we cherish the acorn, or do we stomp on it? Do we listen to the stories, the biographies, that young people tell us as they try to make sense of their lives? Do we help them sort out their personal destiny away from the incessant chatter of the television, the computer, or the street? Do we respect who they authentically are, instead of who we want them to be? If you have been reading this book at all carefully, you will have to answer these questions in the negative.

The culture fails to develop strong minds because it does little to prevent the young mind from wasting itself on trivia: sit-coms, shopping, action movies, spectator sports, routines of niceness, and vacuous politeness. Conversely, the emergent self grows up in a context where race, class, and gender dominate relationships, and where parents and teachers are often passive, evasive, insensitive, indifferent, harsh, or overwhelmed. Under the existing market paradigm, the society has effectively canceled out both the call for character and habits of the heart.

UNDOING THE UNJUST SOCIETY

Obstacles to doing justice need our attention so that we can effectively confront them and begin to deconstruct the unjust society in favor of building a just society. Proposals for reconstructing *mind, self,* and *society* toward a just society for youth have been circulating among reformers since the development of the American Republic. We are currently on the cusp of changing global paradigms with social, scientific, and moral consciousness moving from an objectivist/causal/positivistic perspective to one that is subjectivist/interpretive/hermeneutic. Grounded in notions of social construction (Foucault 1978; 1979; 1980), social interactionism (Mead 1934; Vygotsky 1978), cultural analysis (Douglas 1970, 1978; Douglas and Wildavsky 1982), and social reconstruction (Berger and Luckmann 1966), theorists emphasize the constructed nature of reality and moral order.

Unsustainable cultural patterns can be changed; and indeed are being modified throughout a number of institutions (schools, families, juvenile justice system). But the process remains inchoate and fails to meet the challenge for radical change. Now there is a felt urgency among growing numbers of reformers and citizens to move from talk to action. What I propose here is to outline an initial strategy for healing youth and the community through a three-part approach to doing justice.

Mind: Development of character and spirituality

Self: Development of a holistic educational model

Society: Development of a restorative justice model and a "positive welfare" agenda

Character and Justice

In modern culture, "care of the soul" (T. Moore 1996) has been assigned to a professional class of soulkeepers: priests, ministers, rabbis, and the psychiatric profession. The results are understandably less than admirable. The overly scripted religious agenda too often teaches obedience instead of creativity, bigotry instead of love, and guilt instead of hope. In its contemporary medical mode, psychiatry is ill equipped to work with the human soul. It must divest itself first of the pathology model of the human mind/spirit, and reconsider healing at levels other than pharmaceutical intervention (the Prozac solution).

What is character, and how can it be developed toward realizing a just world? Character is the visible outcome of acting on the basis of our unique, natural attributes, or "acorn." As Hillman argues, acorn is an organic concept derived from the Sanskrit, via the Greek *ago*, *agein*, which means basically to push, to direct toward, to lead or guide. The acorn theory of biography relates to the archetype of the "eternal youth," or genius, who embodies a timeless, eternal, yet fragile connection with invisible worlds. Acorns represent a primordial food, which is a way of saying that you feed off your inner kernel. Parents can nurture the inner self of their child, but only if they too feed off their own acorn.

Soul, as another metaphor for the invisible, is not measurable—not a substance, not a force, not corporeal. Physical means will not arouse it. Instead "only curious thought, devotional feeling, suggestive intuition, and daring imagination, each a way of [inner] knowing" (Hillman, 1996, 286). Acorn or soul, whichever metaphor you prefer, is at the mercy of the social environment and socialization. Additionally, we should admit a larger array of influences to the creation of character, including the metaphysical: heredity, early conditioning, group norms, personal choices, cosmic patterns (karma, zeitgeist), our shadow (the dark part of the soul), personality traits, and our calling. If any of these are tainted, suffer defeat, or are ignored, our sense of justice is diminished or lost. M. Scott Peck observes that some of his patients are "evil," as in a diagnostic condition: Evil basically consists in arrogant, selfish narcissism or supreme willfulness (Peck 1983).

To reconstruct a damaged soul requires effective rituals, including a rejection of innocence, self-acknowledgement of evil, felt remorse and mourning, a moral net to support the reforming soul, and a willingness to recognize that care of the soul is a lifetime effort. As such, it can never be turned over to professionals. It remains an inside task. For example, personal growth typically involves "shadow" work, work on unconscious patterns that are difficult to face but must be confronted as a condition of achieving intimacy with ourselves.

Justice, then, begins with the soul-making capacity of the human mind that recognizes an inner state and is willing to take up the healing process. It may also necessitate the cultivation of "virtues," long associated with classical theories and practices of social justice. Names such as Socrates, Plato, Aristotle, Seneca, Thomas Aquinas, Martin Luther King, Jr., Mother Teresa, The Dalai Lama, and other luminaries have provided spiritual guidance over the centuries. They embody the virtues that are at the basis of social justice—compassion, faith, love, hope, forgiveness, fortitude, perseverance, courage, patience, humility, and generosity—that has denoted character development throughout Western thought. The self-evolved human character is the basis for the new justice. Richard Moss (1995) says

We are each the authors of our own lives, and to be one's own author, to exercise authorship over ourselves, is true authority. (p. 91)

Holistic Education and Justice

The purpose of education is to provide the experiences that develop and unfold the capacities for inner activity: music and art, literature, physical movement, imaginative play, encounters with nature. Here we leave the domain where curriculum is explicit, numbers have authority, and higher educational careers are determined by scores on the Scholastic Aptitude Tests. Enter a world where different values—self-development within the context of community—are promoted; values that are now antithetical to the individualistic, scientific-rational worldview that dominates the educational system. These values are love and compassion (see Box 11-B).

Above all, justice is profoundly relational. Even as the mind is an outcome of the soul's inner work, self is a creation of interaction with others in community. As we develop positive attributes, we understand that their essential quality is to serve as a lifeline to others— to connect us more intimately and lovingly. Social justice is not about rules disseminated by external authority that is isolated from the context of social relations. Rather, it is about a new community of relationships: collaborative, co-creative, and mutually reverent. Holistic education is foremost the reclaiming of the sacred in everyday life.

The story is told of a remarkable documentary called "The Transformation of Allen School" (in Palmer 1997). Allen School is an inner-city school in Dayton, Ohio, which for many years was at the bottom on all educational criteria (attendance, test scores, dropout rates), and with stu-

---

Box 11-B
Extolling the Values of Love and Compassion

His Holiness, the Dalai Lama, winner of the Peace Prize in 1989, questions Western education's emphasis on the intellect and the expectation that all problems can be solved through technology. At the Conference on Education and Spirituality, held on June 1, 1997, he called for love and compassion as ordinary conditions for operating a society.

> [I]n order to eliminate ignorance [which causes pain and suffering] education, no doubt, becomes very important. But even as education is very helpful, I think a good heart, a warm heart, can expel the short-sightedness. If one looks at a very limited area, and says, "I'm in here" and does not bother with the consequences of one's action in a larger arena, that is very often where problems begin. By keeping the larger community in mind, we can eliminate the problems resulting from narrow-mindedness . . . or extreme selfishness. . . . [W]hat we call love and compassion is not necessarily a religious matter. They are basic necessities of life not only for society but also for the individual.

Source: The Dalai Lama, "Education and the Human Heart," *Holistic Education Review* 10(3):

---

dents deeply involved in the juvenile justice system. Administrators, however creative, failed to alter the educational milieu, until a new principal came along, a principal who, the documentary takes pains to show, came from the Philippines. The Philippines is a culture that has an inherent respect for spirituality in a way that American culture does not. Bringing the teachers together, the new principal addressed them saying:

We have to start to understand that the young people we are working with have nothing of external substance or support. They have dangerous neighborhoods. They have poor places to live. They have little food to eat. They have parents who are on the ropes and barely able to pay attention to them. The externals with which American education is obsessed will not work in this situation.

But these students have one thing that no one can take away from them. They have their souls. And from this day forth in this school, we are going to lift those souls up. We are going to make those souls visible to the young people themselves and to their parents and to the community. We are going to celebrate their souls, and we are going to reground their lives in the power of their souls, remembering that we, too, are soul-driven, soul-animated creatures. (Quoted in Palmer 1997, 8–9)

In a five-year period, that school, the Allen School in Dayton, Ohio, rose to the top of every attribute for which it had been on the bottom—hard work, discipline, attentiveness to the inward factors, all were developed in a spirit of co-creation, collaboration, and compassion.

Holistic education is not a panacea for social justice. Rather, it is a foundation on which justice depends. For example, it embraces humanistic, affective learning that focuses on self-esteem, values clarification, and community consciousness. The teaching presence is one of "open-hearted responsiveness." Consider the four basic principles of holistic education (R. Miller 1997).

1. The human being is a complex existential entity made up of many layers of meaning—biological, ecological, psychological, emotional. We live in an ideological environment, a social and cultural environment, and we have a spiritual core. Holism is a point of view that recognizes this multifaceted dimension. Thus, any educational method—rational, academic, child-centered—is a "partial vision" only (Neville 1989). Just as an overrational education stifles imagination, a romantic or child-centered vision shuts off the possibility of having the young person confront his or her shadow.

2. Human development occurs in two spheres. One is personal—each child develops at a different rate, and with his/her special attributes. The other is universal—human consciousness appears to be engaged in a very long historic process of unfolding. And both processes must be supported.

3. The spirituality of holistic education is not an other-worldly phenomenon. It represents an integral part of Western spirituality that has created democracy, works to heal hatred and racial and class oppression, and teaches young people universal moral rules. Today, it stands for confronting mechanization and standardization of children's souls. Ron Miller (1997) calls for a national movement of civil disobedience toward a mass refusal against required national standards. Such imposed standards fail to honor the spirit of the child.

4. Holistic education cannot be reduced to any one technique; in fact, there is no particular technique. Rather holistic education is "the art of cultivating meaningful human relationships" (R. Miller 1997, 29). This entails a dialogue between teacher and student in a community of learners. Invariably, proponents embrace the notions of transformation and the development of the whole person or an emotional/cognitive unity (Kaufman 1994). The transformative position can be linked to social constructivists' views of mind and learning that stem from a theory of cognition as a socially mediated process (Astington and Pelletier 1996).

From this perspective the child can be viewed as a "connected knower," who comes to share and manage what is referred to as "objective knowledge." The focus is on the intersubjective understanding of self and others by means of problem-solving, intuition, wisdom, reflection-in-action, and critical consciousness, where activities promote the negotiation of intentions (Wells and Chang-Wells 1992). The transformative approach further envisions the classroom as a culture or a community of inquiry that provides the opportunity for a variety of voices (students, teachers, parents, community members) to engage in discourse with one another, resulting in the co-instruction of knowledge. Thus, knowledge is viewed as the integration between personal and public (Berlak and Berlak 1983), and between cognitive and spirit-based processes (Wilber 1997). Social justice is the outcome of this integrative educational process.

Restorative Justice Model as Peacemaking

Crime was originally viewed as an offense against the victim and the victim's family (Hoebel 1973). In a broader sense, the ancient pattern— Code of Hammurabi (1700 B.C.E.), Roman Law of the Twelve Tables (440 B.C.E.), and the Germanic tribal laws in Old Europe—responded to crime by requiring offenders and their families to make amends to victims and their families. Injured persons were expected to receive restitution, but the larger effort was aimed to restore community peace.

Ancient Hebrew justice also aimed to restore wholeness. In the language of the Hebrew Scriptures, *shalom* describes the ideal state in which the community should function. This entails

much more than absence of conflict; it signified completeness, fulfillment, wholeness—the existence of right relationships among individuals, the community, and God. Crime was understood to break *shalom*, destroying right relationships within a community and creating harmful ones. Along with restitution came the notion of vindication of the victim and of the law itself. . . . In short, the purpose of the justice process was through vindication and reparation, to restore a community that had been sundered by crime. (Van Ness and Strong 1997, 8–9)

The Norman invasion of Britain signified a turning away from this community justice perspective, and the rise of a formal state apparatus for determining crime and punishment. Informal justice, in which ordinary members of the community could determine definitions of crime and justice, was abandoned in favor of official systems of control.

The invention of the juvenile justice system in Chicago in 1899 was predicated on the belief that children of immigrants, lower working class, and sons of former slaves were dangerous and out of control, but invariably, also in need of help (see Whitehead and Lab 1996). Waves of delinquency, however, are not products of the "dangerous classes," as sociologists have been saying for over a century, but represent occurrences related to the larger social conditions associated with modernization, urbanization, and industrialization (T. Bernard 1992). Unlike adult criminals, though, whose offenses were believed to be caused from willful violation of laws, juveniles were perceived as deficient in *socialization*.

The court solution to young offenders' special claims was to offer individualized justice in a bureaucratic context. David Matza (1990) argues that such a combination generates opposing criteria for judgment: demands for severity from intolerant and victimized publics, and pleas for mercy from social workers and child advocates. The upshot is a system riddled in mystification and "blatant injustice." Matza takes special aim at the principle of "individualized treatment" as an "aimless guide to action."

The principle of individualized treatment is a mystification. Indeed, it is one of the very best examples of mystification in current society. To the extent that it prevails, its function is to obscure the process of decision and disposition rather than to enlighten it. The principle of individualized justice results in a frame of relevance that is so large, so all-inclusive, that any relation between the criteria of judgment and the disposition remains obscure. (p. 115)

In the context of an all-inclusive criteria (class and race background; relationships with parents and other authority; school achievement; type of offense—drugs, gangs, crime; employment; proximity to criminal opportunity; and a host of others), the would-be enlightened professionals are expected to carry out treatment that will change the life course of the youthful miscreant. This usually boils down to two choices—prison or probation—often made in a wholly discretionary manner, depending upon public reaction, bureaucratic pressures on the court, the juvenile's attitude, and a host of other inchoate considerations.

Today, scholars and the public have attacked the juvenile justice system as a misinformed, poorly managed structure that reproduces the crises it was aimed to prevent. As juvenile crime becomes more serious, goals of rehabilitation have been abandoned in favor of punishment, deterrence, and/or incapacitation. Today, over six thousand juvenile offenders have been sentenced to adult prisons, many for life terms. And juvenile detention centers hold nearly a half million other young people. It is a system that is blatantly ineffective and inhumane. This imprisonment trend also represents the end of juvenile justice as we have known it (T. Bernard 1992; Krisberg and Austin 1993).

Restorative justice represents a movement to replace the existing defunct juvenile justice system with a less formal, more community- and victim-centered intervention for youth. A number of movements predates the current restorative justice movement:

1. General liberation movements—the African American, Native American, and other racial/ethnic movements; the women's movement; the peace and justice movement; the social justice movement (e.g., prisoners' rights, farmworkers' movement); and youth rights—have all contributed a part to the emerging mosaic that forms the restorative justice model. These movements aim to expand the arena of individual rights within a community context.

2. Informal justice emphasizes increased participation, more access to law, deprofessionalization, delegalization, and the minimization of stigma and coercion. The discretionary routines in juvenile justice that contributed to such a sense of inconsistency and injustice do not play a role in this approach. This is especially important for restoring young offenders' lives (see Youth Bill of Rights, Appendix).

3. Participatory justice, as a response to crime, is characterized by direct communication between those injured by crime and the perpetrators of the conflict. Compensation and the avoidance of state infliction of pain are dual goals.

4. Restitution movement, which pays attention to victims' claims, as well as the rehabilitative value for the offender of paying the victim, also emphasizes the reduction in retributive sanctions. Restitution constitutes a new paradigm of justice, insofar as it explores the rights of the victim, not the behavior of the offender.

5. Victims' movements have had a remarkable impact on the justice system. Whether victims' families of drunk drivers (i.e., MADD), or of violent crime or property offenses, victims have rallied and demanded participation throughout the criminal justice process. In many jurisdictions, the system response entails increasing services to victims in the aftermath of the crime; increasing the likelihood of financial reimbursement for harm done; and expanding victims' opportunities to intervene during the criminal justice process.

6. Reconciliation/conferencing movement has two major strands. The first, victim-offender reconciliation/mediation brings together victims and offenders to discuss the harm that has resulted from crime. Working with a mediator/facilitator, they formulate a course of future action that permits the offender to "make things right." Family group conferences differ from victim-offender reconciliation and mediation in several ways. Groups are larger, and include family members and community representatives. Outcomes are focused at not only giving aid to victims but also promoting reintegration of the offender.

7. Social justice movement was initiated by the Quakers and has evolved as a reaction to abuses in prison, as well as the belief that criminal justice could not be achieved in an unjust society. Feminist scholars have also criticized the values of control and punishment, and have called for restructuring of criminal justice and transformative justice that will increase safety in the community.

Restorative justice incorporates elements of all these justice movements, building upon the widespread dissatisfaction with the current criminal/juvenile justice. Restorative justice is justice that promotes healing. Van Ness and Strong (1997) answer four questions about restorative justice (see Box 11-C). The basic assumption of restorative justice is reconciliation (Van Ness and Strong 1997; Galaway and Hudson 1996), which may be ex-

Box 11-C
Four Questions about Restorative Justice

1. What Is Restorative Justice?
- It is a *different* way of thinking about crime and our social response to it.
- It focuses on the *harm caused by crime:* repairing the harm victims experience and reducing future harm by preventing crime.
- It requires offenders to *take responsibility* for their actions, and confront the harm they have caused.
- It aims for *redress* for victims, *compensation* by offenders, and *reintegration* of both in the community.
- Restorative justice is achieved through cooperative efforts by communities and the government (relevant social agencies).

2. How is Restorative Justice Different From What Is Done Now?
- It offers a distinctly *comprehensive approach to crime and injustice,* rather than limiting definitions of crime to lawbreaking, inasmuch as offenders bring harm to victims, communities, society and themselves.
- It involves *more parties* to the justice process. Once restricted to the offender and law enforcement, it now adds the victim, the community, and other interested parties (family members).
- It *measures success in a different way* rather than measuring how much punishment has been inflicted, it measures how much harm has been repaired or prevented.
- Restorative justice stresses the importance of *community involvement and initiative* in responding to and reducing crime. It rejects the government monopoly over crime definition and control.

3. How Does Restorative Justice Respond to Crime?
- It stresses *victim recovery* through compensation, vindication, and healing.
- It emphasizes *recompense by the offender* through reparation, fair treatment and habilitation.
- It establishes processes through which victims can *uncover the truth* about what happened and the resultant harms, *to identify the injustices,* and *to agree on future actions* for *rectifying the harms.*
- Restorative justice develops *evaluation procedures* for monitoring the new processes, and creates *new strategies* for preventing crime.

4. How Does Restorative Justice Seek to Prevent Crime?
- It builds on the *strengths of the community and the government.* The community can build peace through "strong, inclusive and righteous relationships"; the government builds order through fair, effective, limited, and minimal force.
- It places the repair of *past harms* as the priority action toward building a peaceful future.
- It solicits cooperation of the offender in *reconciling* with victims that have been harmed.
- Restorative justice helps communities learn to reintegrate victims and offenders alike.

Source: Daniel Van Ness and Karen Heetderks Strong, 1997.

pressed as follows: *Justice requires that we work to restore victims, offenders, and communities who have been injured by crime.* To promote healing, society must respond appropriately, considering the needs and responsibilities of each party. For example, being victimized through a physical injury, monetary loss, or emotional suffering is by definition an experience of powerlessness. Both compensation and vindication should be a part of the process. Accepting and working with victims in crisis are essential (Andrews 1990).

Persons in crisis tend to be emotionally aroused and highly anxious; often they are weepy. Occasionally they will act extremely controlled and noncommunicative as a way of coping with high anxiety, but most often they will express despair, grief, embarrassment, and anger. . . . People in crisis act in ways similar to people with certain forms of mental illness, but it must be emphasized that the crisis state is time limited, usually lasting no more than a few days to six weeks.

Responding to the "needs" of the community that have been harmed by crime necessitates that we address what "community" is. Is the "community" a geographic unit (e.g., a town, neighborhood, district), or a "community of interest"? Or does it refer to society as a whole? Regardless of which community reference, it is important to address what has been injured: order, safety, common values, public property, private property, public morale, and so forth. When youths vandalize shopkeepers, they destroy not only the monetary value of those stores that have been damaged, but in addition they have undermined the sense of safety and order for the entire neighborhood and community.

The offenders' injuries must be acknowledged as well. Social justice requires that the offender confront not only the loss of reciprocity but also violation of community or organizational trust. Where is the offender's sense of belonging, and has that changed in any way? The offender may have been wounded during the crime, or incarcerated as a result of it, leading to loss of status and emotional distress. Harming others contributes to moral and spiritual injury to self, loss of family support, community alienation, and long-term employment disadvantages. The "habilitation" goal requires the offender to confront injuries done to others as a response to crime.

The four-sided model: offender, victim, community, and social agencies (government and private groups) are engaging in a reciprocal pattern; that is, redressing wrongs, healing, fairness, and other positive justice actions that restore order and reintegrate both victims and offenders (see Figure 11.1).

John Braithwaite (1989) proposes that the family conference offers the greatest likelihood of reintegrating the youthful offender. Borrowed from the New Zealand model of the native Maori extended family conference,

Figure 11.1
Four-sided Model of Justice

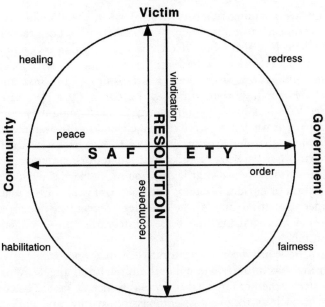

Source: Daniel Van Ness and Karen Heetderks Strong. 1997. *Restoring Justice.* Cincinnati, OH: Anderson Publishing, p. 40.

the approach uses shame as a reintegrative strategy. "Reintegrative shaming" works on the assumption that there is a correlation between low crime rates and the high social power of shaming. He argues that internal control is more effective than external control in restraining crime; that internal control—the conscience—is acquired (usually during childhood); and that families are best able to build consciences when society supports them through reintegrative shaming. The idea is simple: People who are shamed feel personal remorse for what they have done, as well as feel concerned about the disapproval of significant people in their lives. Reintegrative shaming works because it does not involve stigmatization and is followed by "gestures of reacceptance." Braithwaite (1989) says:

Shaming has a great advantage over formal punishment. Shaming is more pregnant with symbolic content than punishment. Punishment is a denial of confidence in the morality of the offender by reducing norm compliance to a crude cost-benefit calculation; shaming can be a reaffirmation of the morality of the offender.... Punishment erects barriers between the offender and punisher through transforming the relationship into one of power assertion and injury; shaming produces a greater interconnectedness between the parties . . . [with] the establishment of a potentially more positive relationship following reintegration. (p. 1)

Reintegrative shaming is most effective when the shaming is done by someone significant to the offender—someone with whom the offender is interdependent. It is also more effective in a society that is *communitarian*, one with dense networks of interdependencies and with strong devotion to the mutual obligations from these relationships (Van Ness and Strong 1997, 118). For many urban youth who are either too fragmented or alienated and who lack a strong community base, shaming may not have the desired impact. If we can preserve certain elements of the reintegrative concept *without* the shaming feature, the approach can be retrieved: (1) mutual respect must occur between offender and facilitators/conference group; (2) mutual commitment between at least some of the parties must prevail; (3) group rejection of deviant behavior must be firm, while also understanding the offender's situation; and (4) the offender's repentance and group/victim forgiveness is a crucial ingredient for reintegrating the offender into the family/community.

We have only just begun a restorative justice approach for youth, an approach that has an international and multicultural appeal. Whatever direction it goes, whether informal or formal justice, it should be compatible with virtues such as forgiveness, compassion, mercy, and understanding. What is antithetical is an insistence on punishment, whose sole justification is to cause pain and isolation (Galaway and Hudson 1996; Bayatpour and Umbreit 1995).

Positive Welfare

The idea of institutional reform on behalf of youth—education and justice systems—is predicated upon providing people and communities with the necessary resources to generate changes. Reform essentially requires that we change the risk structure inherited from early modernity to enable citizens to overcome the crisis of motivation that characterizes our late modern epoch. To repeat, our current epoch has generated a high-risk society as a result of racism, job instability, massive social and economic inequalities, lack of a family wage, underemployment, workaholism, and ecological devastation. This requires that we address the welfare system, as it was, and as it can be.

I turn to the British sociologist Anthony Giddens (1973; 1982) whose trenchant analysis of class structure in capitalist societies qualifies him as perhaps the foremost analyst of what politics and the state should be in a globalized, postmodern world. In a recent *New Yorker* magazine article, Giddens explained his position regarding the current arrangement of wealth and income distributions. He concludes that the welfare system, as we know it, is virtually over. It is the wrong kind of risk system, because modernization yields a system "fraught with risks of high consequence."

The welfare state is a passive-risk system—it isn't designed to encourage people to make active investment decisions with their lives. It only reacts to things when they go wrong: It takes care of you when you are ill, puts you on the dole when you're unemployed. But it has been ineffective in actually countering poverty or redistributing wealth in the long term. (Giddens in Boynton 1997, 69)

Giddens proposes that instead of living in a world of "manufactured risk"—a world that makes us extremely self-conscious, and where life becomes a series of complex calculations in which we "establish a portfolio of risk assessment" for a viable identity—we move "beyond left and right" solutions. Think of welfare as a kind of insurance policy, Giddens explains, that allows people to take risks as part of personal responsibility.

We must provide people with the resources they require to be active investors, as it were, but at the same time we must provide security mechanisms which protect them. (Quoted in Boynton 1997, 71)

Giddens calls this concept of welfare-as-social-insurance "positive welfare," a scheme that involves the state in a proactive yet less intrusive role in its citizens' lives. By emphasizing job stability over increased income, for example, the state might broaden its concern to encompass the psychological, and not just the economic well-being of people. Tax restructuring and greater equality will be essentials of the "positive welfare" scheme. Because

the possession of wealth doesn't necessarily make one happy, any more than poverty as such is a source of misery, why not, therefore, attempt to bring the conditions of life of rich and poor closer together? (Giddens in Boynton 1997, 70)

Giddens rejects the standard wealth and income transfers that diminish recipients' personal responsibility, as well as their dignity and creativity, now so entrenched in the current system. Instead, he recommends tax incentives for corporations that "gear recruitment and job stability to wider social needs" or to those who break down the division between "men's and women's jobs," thereby helping to modernize the family. Under positive welfare, Giddens sees the possibility of diminishing social inequality while simultaneously enhancing personal responsibility. Giddens' version of a radical ideology in the context of a global market society boils down to two values: "social justice and individualism."

Along with such "positive welfare" schemes should be added the need for a "safety net" for all children (Berwick 1997). This net should cover psychological and social, as well as economic, needs. The qualities of social justice—individualism, equality, fairness, protection, and others that Giddens and this book detail—will be important features of the safety net and should not be dismissed as either utopian or visionary. Rather, these qualities are foundational for a reconstructed society. Because our youth problems revolve around "manufactured risk" rather than inherent biological or social properties, we can consciously reorganize our political and economic strategies to accommodate individualism and social justice, beginning with those populations least able to protect themselves and most at passive risk under current conditions. Surely, the world we save will be our own and that of all our beloved children.

CONCLUSION

This chapter takes up the issue of social justice, a theme that prevails throughout the book. We recounted how, as a high-risk society, we have failed to confront the growing inequality among youth, because we have either anesthetized ourselves or have found a variety of rationalizations that neutralize our sense of personal responsibility for change. Everyday stress plays havoc with us all, and contributes to our collective "forgetting" that we all have a part to play in making this a better world.

The suffering of the young that I have described throughout this book should be a call to action. Cultural patterns that will not sustain us into the new millennium need to be changed. We seek a change of mind that takes into account the qualities of character and spirituality. We require a transformation of self that can be nourished within a holistic educational system. And we demand wholly different approaches to remedy misbehaving and alienated youth. Both the restorative justice model and positive welfare are quite practical justice endeavors. They can be implemented both from below—through local community efforts—and from above—with federal government initiation and direction.

In the case of holistic education as a justice practice, this can be accomplished at the public school district level. Of course, old bureaucratic practices and their practitioners—the beneficiaries of the current system—may have to be retired, demoted, or fired. The idea of public schooling as simply a technical activity (i.e., "mass education") without heart or soul has dominated education for most of this century. As an idea, it has long outlived its usefulness.

Doing justice for children and youth is a daily task for everyone; it cannot be restricted to experts and professionals. The work essentially requires that we all pitch in to save the children, bringing whatever positive life skills and love we have to bear on the considerably difficult mission that lies ahead.

As we have said repeatedly, the social task in front of us entails "working the systemic," developing different priorities and working within the interrelated, grounded level of our mutual relationships. We cannot emphasize enough that justice cannot be restricted to institutional or agency mandates, because little social justice occurs in these all adult-centered sites. The ecological conception of justice proposed in this book emphasizes that we respect and celebrate diversity; that we recognize the mutual interdependence between young people and adults throughout our political and social system; and that we take into account the social and legal rights of young people in both public and private spheres: home, school, work, street, and genuine "correctional" institutions (the latter of which must aim for transforming selves).

Honoring the young demands that we pay attention to their specialness: to respect their age-related habits of the heart and to delight in their dreams. Respect for and delight in the young could be a first step toward social transformation.

Appendix

Youth Bill of Rights

The National Child Rights Alliance believes that civil rights apply to all people—including children and youth. NCRA works to establish these rights for children:

THE RIGHT TO LIBERTY

No children shall be forced to live in any household against their will—this includes biologic as well as foster and adoptive households. No children shall be forced into marriage. No children shall be institutionalized against their will without due process rights.

THE RIGHT TO SAFETY

All children shall have the right to safe haven on request, without fear of criminal charges. NCRA supports Sanctuary for Children, and is establishing a fund in defense of this right.

THE RIGHT TO SURVIVAL

All children have the right to adequate food, shelter, medical care, and a healthy environment. NCRA supports a free national health care system for children which is not dependent on parent income nor parental permission, and living wage rights for workers, and a guaranteed income for those unable to work, so that families need not be torn apart by poverty.

THE RIGHT TO EDUCATION

All children shall have the right to a free education—including college and technical schools—at public expense. Programs must be free of cultural, racial, or gender bias in all respects.

THE RIGHT OF FREE SPEECH

All children shall have the right of free speech. This includes both in personal expression and in school-based and public media.

THE RIGHT OF NON-DISCRIMINATION

NCRA supports all efforts to end curtailment of a child's potential and self-esteem based on age, race, gender, language, country of origin, the economic or marital status of parents, religious or sexual preference, and physical or mental limitations or differences.

THE RIGHT OF FREE CHOICE

No child shall be either forced or forbidden to choose a religious or political affiliation, philosophy, or creed.

THE RIGHT TO AN ATTORNEY

All children shall have the right to legal representation whereby the attorneys act as an attorney for—not guardian of—their clients.

Source: National Child Rights Alliance, Washington, D.C.

Bibliography

Abadinsky, H. 1990. *Organized Crime*. 3d ed. Chicago: Nelson-Hall, Inc.

Abbott, Mary. 1993. *Family Ties: English Families 1540–1920*. London and New York: Routledge.

Accampo, Elinor. 1989. *Industrialization, Family Life, and Class Relations*. Berkeley: The University of California Press.

Acland, Charles R. 1995. *Youth, Murder, Spectacle: The Cultural Politics of Youth in Crisis*. Boulder, CO: Westview Press.

Adero, Malaika, ed. 1993. *Up South: Stories, Studies and Letters of This Century's Black Migrations*. New York: The New Press.

African-Americans: Voices of Triumph—Leadership. 1993. Alexandria, VA: Time-Life Books.

African-Americans: Voices of Triumph—Perseverance. 1993. Alexandria, VA: Time-Life Books.

African-Americans: Voices of Triumph—Creative Fire. 1994. Alexandria, VA: Time-Life Books.

Agee, Vicki L. 1990. "Treatment of the Violent Incorrigible Adolescent." Pp. 183–200 in *Juvenile Delinquency: A Justice Perspective*, 2d ed, edited by R. A. Weisheit and R. G. Culbertson. Prospect Heights, IL: Waveland Press.

Akers, Ronald L. 1990. "Scary Drug of the Year: Myths and Realities in the Changing Drug Problem." Paper presented at the Annual Meeting of the American Society of Criminology, Baltimore, MD, November 7–10.

Alan Guttmacher Institute. 1993. "Abortion in the United States: Facts in Brief." New York: The Alan Guttmacher Institute (January).

———. 1994. *Sex and America's Teenagers*. New York: The Alan Guttmacher Institute.

Alder, Christine. 1991a. "Victims of Violence: The Case of Homeless Youth." *Australian and New Zealand Journal of Criminology* (March) 24: 1–14.

———. 1991b. "Explaining Violence: Socioeconomics and Masculinity." Chapter in *Australian Violence: Contemporary Perspectives*, by Duncan Chappell,

Peter Grabosky, and Heather Strong. Canberra, Australia: Australian Institute of Criminology.

Alexander, Karl F., D. R. Entwisle, and S. D. Bedinger. 1994. "When Expectations Work: Race and Socioeconomic Differences in School Performance." *School Psychology Quarterly* 57, no. 4, (December): 283–99.

Altschuler, David M. 1995. "Juveniles and Violence: Is There an Epidemic and What Can Be Done?" Paper presented to the Annual Meeting of the American Society of Criminology, Boston, MA.

Altschuler, David M., and T. L. Armstrong. November 1990. *Intensive Community-Based Aftercare Programs: Assessment Report.* Office of Juvenile Justice and Delinquency Prevention, Washington, DC.

American Association of University Women (AAUW). 1993. *Hostile Hallways: The AAUW Survey on Sexual Harassment in America's Schools.* Washington, DC: AAUW Educational Foundation Research.

———. 1995. *The AAUW Report: How Schools Shortchange Girls.* Washington, DC: AAUW Educational Foundation Research.

———. 1996. *Girls in the Middle: Working to Succeed in School.* Washington, DC: AAUW Educational Foundation Research.

American Psychiatric Association. 1987. *Diagnostic and Statistical Manual.* Washington, DC: American Psychiatric Association.

Anderson, Elizah. 1989. "Sex Codes and Family Life among Poor Inner-City Youths." *The Annals of the American Academy of Political and Social Science* 501 (Jan.).

———. 1990. *Streetwise: Race, Class, and Change in an Urban Community.* Chicago: University of Chicago Press.

———. 1994. "The Code of the Street." *Atlantic Monthly* (May): 81–94.

Andrews, Arlene B. 1990. "Crisis and Recovery Services for Family Violence Survivors." In *Victims of Crime: Problems, Policies, and Programs,* edited by Arthur Lurigio et al. Newbury Park, CA: Sage.

Ansley, L. 1997. "It Just Keeps Getting Worse." *USA Weekend* (August 13–15): 5.

Anslinger, Harvey J., and Courtney Ryley Cooper. 1937. "Marijuana: Assassin of Youth." *American Magazine* (July).

Aos, Steve, Roxanne Lieb, and Robert Barnoski. 1996. "Trends in At-Risk Behaviors of Youth in Washington." A Report to the Washington State Legislature. Washington State Institute for Public Policy. Olympia: The Evergreen State College.

Aponte, Robert. 1987. "Urban Poverty: A State-of-the-Art Review of the Literature." Appendix in *The Truly Disadvantaged: The Inner City, the Underclass, and Public Policy,* by William Julius Wilson. Chicago: The University of Chicago Press.

Apple, Michael W. 1993. *Official Knowledge: Democratic Education in a Conservative Age.* Brandon, VT: Great Ideas in Education.

Archer, J., ed. 1994. *Male Violence.* London/New York: Routledge.

Arendt, Hannah. 1963. *On Revolution.* New York: Viking.

———. 1990. "Reflections on Violence." Pp. 35–76 in *Anthology, Selected Essays from Thirty Years of* The New York Review of Books. New York: The New York Review of Books.

Aries, Phillippe. 1965. *Centuries of Childhood: A Social History of Family Life*. New York: Random House.

Arnold, R. A., P. J. Goldstein, H. H. Brownstein, and P. J. Ryan. 1990. "Suggestive Trends in 1988 Homicide Data Involving Female Victims: The Drugs-Violence Nexus." Paper presented at the Annual Meeting of the American Society of Criminology, Baltimore, MD, November 7–10.

Aronowitz, Stanley, and Henry Giroux. 1991. *Postmodern Education: Politics, Culture, and Social Criticism*. Minneapolis: University of Minnesota Press.

Astington, J., and J. Pelletier. 1996. "The Language of Mind: Its Role in Teaching and Learning." Pp. 593–620 in *Handbook of Education and Human Development: New Models of Learning, Teaching, and Schooling*, edited by D. Olson and N. Torrance. Oxford, UK: Blackwell.

Baggett, G., and B. Donough. 1988. *Oregon Runaway and Homeless Youth Project*. Portland, OR: Tri-County Youth Services Consortium.

Bailyn, Bernard. 1960. *Education in the Forming of American Society*. New York: Random House.

Ball, Richard A., and G. David Curry. 1995. "The Logic of Definition in Criminology: Purposes and Methods for Defining Gangs." *Criminology* 33(2): 225–46.

Ball-Rokeach, Sandra. 1980. "Normative and Deviant Violence from a Conflict Perspective." *Social Problems* 28: 45–62.

Ballantine, Jeanne. 1997. *The Sociology of Education*. 4th ed. Upper Saddle River, NJ: Prentice Hall.

Banner-Haley, Charles T. 1995. *The Fruits of Integration: Black Middle-Class Ideology and Culture*, 1, 960–1990. Jackson, MS: University Press of Mississippi.

Bayatpour, M., and M. S. Umbreit. 1995. "Rethinking the Sanctioning Function in Juvenile Court: Retributive or Restorative Responses to Youth Crime." *Crime and Delinquency* 41(3): 296–316.

Bayatpour, M., R. D. Wells, and S. Holford. 1992. "Physical and Sexual Abuse as Predictors of Substance Use and Suicide among Pregnant Teenagers." *Journal of Adolescent Health* 13: 128–32.

Beaglehole, E. 1940. "Psychic Stress in a Tongan Village." Pacific Science Association 139: 43–54.

Beauvais, Fred. 1992a. "Trends in Indian Adolescent Drug and Alcohol Use." *American Indian and Alaska Native Mental Health Research* 5(1): 1–12.

———. 1992b. "The Consequences of Drug and Alcohol Use for Indian Youth." *American Indian and Alaska Native Mental Health Research* 5(1): 32–37.

Beck, Ulrich. 1992. *Risk Society: Towards a New Modernity*. Thousand Oaks, CA: Sage.

Becker, Howard S. 1967. "History, Culture and Subjective Experiences: An Exploration of the Social Bases of Drug-Induced Experiences." *Journal of Health and Social Behavior* 8(September): 163–76.

Belenky, Mary Field, Blythe McVicker Clinchy, Nancy Rule Goldberger, and Jill Mattuck Tarule. 1986. *Women's Way of Knowing*. New York: Basic Books.

Bell, A., and M. Weinberg. 1978. *Homosexualities: A Study of Diversity among Men and Women*. New York: Simon and Schuster.

Bell, Nancy J., and Robert W. Bell, eds. 1993. *Adolescent Risk Taking*. Newbury Park, CA: Sage.

Bellah, Robert N., ed., Richard Madsen, William M. Sullivan, Steven M. Tipton, and Ann Swidler. 1996 (updated ed.). *Habits of the Heart: Individualism and Commitment in American Life*. Berkeley: University of California Press.

Berger, P., and T. Luckmann. 1966. *The Social Construction of Reality: A Treatment in the Sociology of Knowledge*. Garden City, NY: Anchor.

Berlak, A., and H. Berlak. 1983. "Toward a Nonhierarchical Approach to School Inquiry and Leadership." *Curriculum Inquiry* 13: 268–94.

Berliner, David C., and Bruce J. Biddle. 1995. *The Manufactured Crisis: Myths, Fraud, and the Attack on Public Schools*. Reading, MA: Addison-Wesley.

Bernard, Jessie. 1981. *The Female World*. New York: The Free Press.

Bernard, Thomas J. 1992. *The Cycle of Juvenile Justice*. New York: Oxford University Press.

———. 1996. "What Stays the Same in History?" Pp. 3–9 in *Exploring Delinquency: Causes and Consequences*, edited by Dean G. Rojek and Gary F. Jensen. Los Angeles: Roxbury Publishing.

Bernstein, Basil. 1977. *Class, Codes and Control*. 3 volumes. New York: Methuen.

Bernstein, Ellen. 1997. "Child Beauty Pageants Pushed into Limelight." *Caller-Times Interactive*, January 19.

Berwick, Patricia. 1997. "A Safety Net for All Children." Paper presented to the Second Congress of Family Law and the Rights of the Child and Youth. San Francisco (June).

Bessant, Judith. 1993. "Young People and the Discovery of the Australian 'New Underclass.' " Paper presented to the American Society of Criminology, October.

Best, Joel, ed. 1994. *Troubling Children: Studies of Children and Social Problems*. New York: Aldine De Gruyter.

Beyette, B. 1988. "Hollywood's Teen-Age Prostitutes Turn Tricks for Shelter, Food." *Las Vegas Review Journal* (August 21).

Binder, Arnold, Gilbert Geis, and Dickson D. Bruce, Jr. 1997. *Juvenile Delinquency: Historical, Cultural and Legal Perspectives*. 2d ed. Cincinnati, OH: Anderson Publishing Co.

Black, Donald. 1998. *The Social Structure of Right and Wrong*. Revised ed. San Diego: Academic Press.

Blau, Judith, and Peter Blau. 1982. "The Cost of Inequality: Metropolitan Structure and Violent Crime." *American Sociological Review* 47: 114–29.

Block, Carolyn Rebecca, and Richard Block. 1993. "Street Gang Crime in Chicago." *National Institute of Justice: Research in Brief*. Washington, DC: U.S. Department of Justice.

Blomberg, Thomas G., and Stanley Cohen, eds. 1995. *Punishment and Social Control*. New York: Aldine De Gruyter.

Blumstein, Alfred. 1995. "Violence by Young People: Why the Deadly Nexus?" *National Institute of Justice Journal*. Issue No. 229. Washington, DC: U.S. Department of Justice.

Bly, Robert. 1996. "New Dimensions." Interview. Seattle KUOW, National Public Radio (December 1).

Blyth, Dale A., and Nancy Leffert. 1995. "Communities as Contexts for Adolescent

Development: An Empirical Analysis." *Journal of Adolescent Research* 10 (1): 64–87.

Boethius, Ulf. 1995. "The History of High and Low Culture." In *Youth Culture in Late Modernity*, by J. Fornas and G. Bolin. Thousand Oaks, CA: Sage.

Bohannan, Paul. 1960. *African Homicide and Suicide.* Princeton, NJ: Princeton University Press.

Bookchin, Murray. 1991. *The Ecology of Freedom: The Emergence and Dissolution of Hierarchy.* Montreal: Black Rose Books.

Bordo, S. 1993. *Unbearable Weight: Feminism, Western Culture and the Body.* Los Angeles: University of California Press.

Bortner, M. A. 1986. "Traditional Rhetoric, Organizational Realities: Remand of Juveniles to Adult Court." *Crime and Delinquency*, 32(1): 55–73.

Boswell, John. 1988. *Kindness of Strangers: The Abandonment of Children in Western Europe from Late Antiquity to the Renaissance.* New York: Pantheon Books.

Botvin, Gilbert J. 1990. "Substance Abuse Prevention: Theory, Practice, and Effectiveness." Pp. 461–520 in *Drugs and Crime*, edited by Michael Tonry and James Q. Wilson. Chicago: University of Chicago Press.

Bourdieu, Pierre. 1977. "Cultural Reproduction and Social Reproduction." In *Power and Ideology in Education*, edited by J. Karabel and A. H. Halsey. New York: Oxford University Press.

Bourdieu, Pierre, and J.C. Passeron. 1977. *Reproduction in Education, Society, and Culture.* Beverly Hills, CA: Sage.

Bourgois, Philippe. 1996. "In Search of Masculinity: Violence, Respect and Sexuality among Puerto Rican Crack Dealers in East Harlem." *The British Journal of Criminology* 36(3): 412–27.

Bowers, C. A. 1993. *Education, Cultural Myths, and the Ecological Crisis.* Albany, NY: State University of New York Press.

Bowles, Samuel, and Herbert Gintis. 1977. *Schooling in Capitalist America: Educational Reform and the Contradictions of Economic Life.* New York: Basic Books.

Boyer, Debra et al. 1988. *In and Out of Street Life.* Tri-County Youth Project. Portland, OR: Tri-County Youth Services Consortium.

Boynton, Robert S. 1997. "The Two Tonys." *New Yorker* (October 6).

Braithwaite, John. 1989. *Crime, Shame, and Reintegration.* New York: Cambridge University Press.

Braithwaite, John, and V. Braithwaite. 1980. "The Effects of Income Inequality and Social Democracy on Homicide." *The British Journal of Criminology* 20: 473–97.

Brake, M. 1980. *The Sociology of Youth Culture and Youth Subcultures.* London and Boston: Routledge.

———. 1985. *Comparative Youth Culture: The Sociology of Youth Cultures and Youth Subcultures in America, Britain and Canada.* London: Routledge.

Braswell, Michael C., Reid H. Montgomery, and Lucien X. Lombardo, eds. 1994. *Prison Violence in America.* 2d ed. Cincinnati, OH: Anderson Publishing.

Bridges, George S., and Martha A. Myers, eds. 1994. *Inequality, Crime, and Social Control.* Boulder, CO: Westview Press.

Broder, David S. 1996. "Replacing a Bad Ending with a Promising Start." *Seattle Post Intelligencer* (July 28): 14.

Brooks, J. S., M. Whiteman, and E. B. Balka. 1997. "Drug Use and Delinquency: Shared and Unshared Risk Factors in African American and Puerto Rican Adolescents." *The Journal of Genetic Psychology* 158(1): 25–39.

Brown, B. 1996. *Trends in the Well-Being of America's Children and Youth, 1996.* Washington, DC: Office of the Assistant Secretary for Planning and Evaluation, U.S. Department of Health and Human Services.

Brown, L. M. 1991. "Telling a Girl's Life: Self Authorization as a Form of Resistance." Pp. 71–86 in *Women, Girls and Psychotherapy*, edited by C. Gilligan, A. Rogers, and D. Toman. Binghamton, NY: Harrington Park Press.

Brown, L., and C. Gilligan. 1992. *Meeting at the Crossroads.* Cambridge, MA: Harvard University Press.

Brownmiller, S. 1975. *Against Our Will: Men, Women and Rape.* New York: Simon and Schuster.

Brunswick, Ann F., and David A. Rier. 1995. "Structural Strain: Drug Use among African American Youth." In *African American Youth: Their Social and Economic Status in the United States*, edited by Ronald L. Taylor. Westport, CT: Praeger.

Bryant, A. T. 1949. *The Zulu People as They Were before the White Man Came.* Petermaritzburg: Shuter and Shooter.

Bullington, Bruce. 1990. "All About Eve: The Many Faces of United States Drug Policy." Paper presented at the Annual Meeting of the American Society of Criminology, Baltimore, MD, November 7–10.

Burdekin, B. 1989. *Report of the National Inquiry into Homeless Children.* Human Rights and Equal Opportunity Commission. Canberra: Australian Government Publishing Service.

Bureau of Justice Statistics. 1996. *Sourcebook of Criminal Justice Statistics 1995*, edited by K. Maguire and A. L. Pastore. Washington, DC: U.S. Department of Justice.

Bursik, Robert J., Jr., and Harold G. Grasmick. 1993. *The Dimensions of Effective Community Control.* Lexington, MA: Lexington Books.

Burt, Martha. 1997. "Causes of the Growth of Homelessness during the 1980s." *Understanding Homelessness: New Policy and Research Perspectives.* Washington, DC: Fannie Mae Foundation.

Buss, D. M. 1994. "Mate Preferences in 37 Countries." Pp. 197–201 in *Psychology and Culture*, edited by W. J. Lonner and R. S. Malpass. Boston: Allyn and Bacon.

Butterfield, Fox. 1996a. "Experts on Crime Warn of a 'Ticking Time Bomb.' " *New York Times* (January 6).

———. 1996b. "Crimes of Violence among Juveniles Decline Slightly." *New York Times* (August 9): 1A.

———. 1997a. "Study Links Violence Rate to Cohesion of Community." *New York Times* (August 17): A11.

———. 1997b. "Few Options or Safeguards in a City's Juvenile Courts." *New York Times* (July 22): A1–A10.

———. 1997c. "Drop in Homicide Rate Linked to Crack's Decline." *New York Times* (October 27): A10.

Butts, J. 1996. *Offenders in Juvenile Court, 1994*. Washington, DC: Office of Juvenile Justice Delinquency Prevention.

Buxton, T. F. 1968. *The African Slave Trade*. 2d ed. London: Dawsons.

Campagna, Daniel S., and Donald L. Poffenberger. 1988. *The Sexual Trafficking in Children: An Investigation of the Child Sex Trade*. New York: Auburn House Publishing.

Campbell, Anne. 1991. *The Girls in the Gang*. 2d ed. Cambridge, MA: Basil Blackwell.

———. 1995. "Female Participation in Gangs." Pp. 70–77 in *The Modern Gang Reader*, edited by Malcolm W. Klein, Cheryl L. Maxson, and Jody Miller. Los Angeles: Roxbury Publishing Co.

Campbell, Anne, and Steven Muncer. 1994. "Men and the Meaning of Violence." Chapter in *Male Violence*, edited by J. Archer. London/New York: Routledge.

Carmichael, Stokely, and Charles Hamilton. 1967. *The Politics of Liberation*. New York: Vintage Books.

Carnegie Council on Adolescent Development. 1995. *Great Transitions: Preparing Adolescents for a New Century*. Concluding Report. Carnegie Corporation of New York.

Carnegie Institute. 1994. "Starting Points: Meeting the Needs of Our Youngest Children." New York: Carnegie.

Carpenter, G., B. Glassner, B. D. Johnson, and J. Loughlin. 1988. *Kids, Drugs and Crime*. Lexington, MA: Lexington Books.

Carter, Deborah Brown. 1995. "The Impact of the Civil Rights Movement on the Unionization of African American Women: Local 282-Furniture Division-IUE, 1960–1988." Pp. 96–109 in *Black Women in America*, edited by Kim Marie Vaz. Thousand Oaks, CA: Sage.

Cass, B. 1991. "The Housing Needs of Women and Children." *The National Housing Strategy*. Canberra: Commonwealth of Australia.

Chadwick, Bruce A., and Tim B. Heaton. eds. 1996. *Statistical Handbook on Adolescents in America*. Phoenix, AZ: The Oryx Press.

Chamberlain, C., and D. MacKenzie. 1993. "Temporal Dimensions of Youth Homelessness." Paper presented at the Conference on "Rethinking Policies for Young People: Towards a National Perspective." Melbourne, Australia, April 14–16.

Chesney-Lind, Meda. 1993. *Humanity and Society* 17(3): 321–44.

Chesney-Lind, M., and R. G. Shelden. 1993. *Girls' Delinquency and Juvenile Justice*. Belmont, CA: Brooks/Cole Publishing Co.

Chin, Ko-lin. 1990. *Chinese Subculture and Criminality*. Westport, CT.: Greenwood Press.

———. 1992. "Gang Violence in Chinatown." Paper presented at the Annual Meeting of the American Society of Criminology, New Orleans (November).

———. 1995. "Chinese Gangs and Extortion." Pp. 46–52 in *The Modern Gang Reader*, edited by Malcolm W. Klein, Cheryl L. Maxson and Jody Miller. Los Angeles: Roxbury Publishing Co.

Chin, Ko-lin, Robert J. Kelly, and Jeffrey A. Fagan. 1993. "Methodological Issues in Studying Chinese Gang Extortion." *The Gang Journal* 1(2): 25–36.

Chopra, Deepak. 1993. *Ageless Body, Timeless Mind*. New York: Harmony Books.

———. 1997. *The Path to Love: Renewing the Power of Spirit in Your Life*. New York: Harmony Books.

Clement, Mary. 1996. Crimes against children. Ch. 6 in *Juvenile Justice System: Law and Process*. Woburn, MA: Butterworth-Heinemann.

Cloward, R. A., and L. E. Ohlin. 1960. *Delinquency and Opportunity: A Theory of Delinquent Gangs*. New York: Free Press.

Cochran, Susan D., and Vickie M. Mays. 1995. "Sociocultural Facets of the Black Gay Male Experience." Pp. 432–40 in *Men's Lives*, by Michael S. Kimmel and Michael A. Messner. Boston: Allyn & Bacon.

Coffey, M., and D. Wadelton. 1991. "Shelter and the Streets: A Statistical Survey of Homeless Youth in New South Wales." Youth Accommodation Association, NSW.

Cohen, Albert K. 1990. "Foreword and Overview." Pp. 7–21 in *Gangs in America*, edited by C. Ronald Huff. Newbury Park, CA: Sage.

Cohen, L. E., and M. Felson. 1979. "Social Changes and Crime Rate Trends: A Routine Activities Approach." *American Sociological Review* 44: 558–608.

Coleman, James S. 1990. *Equality and Achievement in Education*. Boulder, CO: Westview Press.

Collins, James J., and Marianne W. Zawitz. 1990. *Federal Drug Data for National Policy*. Drugs and Crime Data, U.S. Department of Justice: Office of Justice Programs, Bureau of Justice Statistics.

Commission on Behavioral and Social Sciences and Education, National Research Council. 1993. *Losing Generations: Adolescents in High Risk Settings*. Washington, DC: National Academy Press.

Congress of the United States 1991. "Children and Youth: The Crisis at Home for American Families." Hearing before the Committee on Labor and Human Resources. United States Senate. Washington, DC: U.S. Government Printing Office.

Connell, Robert W. 1987. *Gender and Power*. Sydney: George Allen and Unwin.

Coordinating Council on Juvenile Justice and Delinquency Prevention. 1996. "Combating Violence and Delinquency: The National Juvenile Justice Action Plan." Washington, DC: Department of Justice.

Corson, David. 1993. *Language, Minority Education, and Gender*. Toronto: Ontario Institute for Studies in Education.

Costello, L. 1991. "We Are the Children Our Parents Warned Us About." Thesis. Department of Geography, The University of Newcastle, Newcastle, NSW, Australia.

Cotten, N. U. et al. 1994. "Aggression and Fighting Behavior among African-American Adolescents: Individual and Family Factors." *American Journal of Public Health* 84: 618–22.

Courtois, Christine A. 1988. *Healing the Incest Wound: Adult Survivors in Therapy*. New York: W. W. Norton & Company.

Craig, Conna. 1995. "What I Need Is a Mom: The Welfare State Denies Homes to Thousands of Foster Children." *Policy Review* 73 (Summer): 41–49.

Cremin, Lawrence. 1961. *The Transformation of the School*. New York: Alfred A. Knopf.

The Criminologist: Special Issue. 1995. Newsletter of the American Society of Criminology. Vol. 20(6) (November/December).

Cullen, Francis T., and Karen E. Gilbert. 1992. "Reaffirming Rehabilitation." Chapter in *Corrections: An Issues Approach*, 3d ed, by Lawrence F. Travis, Martin D. Schwartz, and Todd R. Clear. Cincinnati: Anderson.

Cunningham, M. R. et al. 1995. "Their Ideas of Beauty Are, on the Whole, the Same as Ours: Consistency and Variability in the Cross-Cultural Perception of Female Attractiveness." *Journal of Personality and Social Psychology* 68: 261–79.

Currie, Elliot. 1985. *Confronting Crime*. New York: Pantheon.

Curry, G. David, Richard A. Ball, and Robert J. Fox. 1994. *Gang Crime and Law Enforcement Recordkeeping*. Washington, DC: Office of Justice Programs.

Curry, G. David, and Scott H. Decker. 1998. *Confronting Gang: Crime and Community*. Los Angeles: Roxbury Publishing Co.

Curry, G. David, and Irving A. Spergel. 1992. "Gang Involvement and Delinquency among Hispanic and African-American Adolescent Males." *Journal of Research in Crime and Delinquency* 29(3): 273–91.

Curry, G. David, Mary Jo Ullom, and Christa Foster. 1993. "Social Correlates of Adolescence and Subsequent Gang-Related Crime." Paper prepared for the Administration for Youth and Families, U.S. Department of Health and Human Services, Washington, DC.

Curtis, Lynn A. 1985. *American Violence and Public Policy*. New Haven, CT: Yale University Press.

———. 1992. "Youth Investment and Community Reconstruction: Street Lessons on Drugs and Crime for the Nineties." Paper presented to the American Sociological Association, Chicago (August).

Dahrendorf, R. 1978. *Life Chances*. Chicago: University of Chicago Press.

The Dalai Lama (His Holiness). 1997. "Education and the Human Heart." *Holistic Education Review* 10(3): 5–8.

Davidson, Basil. 1980. *The African Slave Trade* (rev. and expanded ed.). Boston: Little, Brown.

Davidson, Joe. 1996. "Clinton, Dole Getting Tough on Juvenile Crime." *Wall Street Journal* (August 22): A16.

Davis, Nanette J. 1980. *Sociological Constructions of Deviance: Issues and Perspectives in the Field*. 2d ed. Dubuque, IA: Wm. C. Brown.

———. 1987. "The Politics of Violence: A Reassessment." *The Journal of Violence, Aggression and Terrorism* 1: 69–98.

———, ed. 1993a. *Prostitution: An International Handbook on Trends, Problems, and Policies*. Westport, CT: Greenwood Press.

———. 1993b. "Assessing Risk Factors, Networks, and Intervention among Homeless Female Youth in Sydney, Australia." *Final Report*. Submitted to the Australian-American Educational Foundation (Fulbright Commission). Canberra: Australian National University.

———. 1993c. "Systemic Gender Control and Victimization Among Homeless Female Youth." *Socio-Legal Bulletin* (Summer): 8.

Davis, Nanette J., and Bo Anderson. 1983. *Social Control: The Production of Deviance in the Modern State*. New York: Irvington Publishers.

Davis, Nanette J., S. E. Hatty, and Stuart Burke. 1994. "Rough Justice." In *Ways of Resistance: Social Control and Young People in Australia*, edited by Richard Hil and Cheryl Simpson. Sydney: Hale & Iremonger.

Davis, Nanette J., J. James, and P. Vitaliano. 1982. "Female Sexual Deviance: A Theoretical and Empirical Analysis." *Deviant Behavior* Vol. 3: 175–95.

Davis, Nanette J., and Clarice Stasz. 1990. *Social Control of Deviance: A Critical Perspective.* New York: McGraw-Hill.

Dean, Alan. 1990. "Culture and Community: Drink and Soft Drugs in Hebridean Youth Culture." *Sociological Review* 38(3): 517–63.

Dean, Christian. 1994. "Strengthening Families: From 'Deficit' to 'Empowerment.' " *Journal of Emotional and Behavioral Problems* 2(4): 8–11.

Decker, Scott H. 1994. "Gangs and Violence: The Expressive Character of Collective Involvement." Unpublished paper. University of Missouri-St. Louis.

del Olmo, Rosa. 1991. "The Hidden Face of Drugs." *Social Justice* 18(4): 10–48.

deMause, Lloyd, ed. 1974. *The History of Childhood.* London: Souvenir Press.

Dembo, Richard et al. 1995. "Delinquency and Drug Use among High Risk Youths over Time." In *African American Youth: Their Social and Economic Status in the United States*, edited by Ronald L. Taylor. Westport, CT: Praeger.

Demos, John. 1986. *Past, Present, and Personal: The Family and the Life Course in American History.* New York: Oxford University Press.

Denning, P. 1997. "Clinical Psychology and Substance Use Management." *First National Harm Reduction Conference. Special Edition.* New York: Harm Reduction Coalition.

Destro, Robert A. 1993. "Gangs and Civil Rights." Chapter in *Gangs: The Origins and Impact of Contemporary Youth Gangs in the United States*, edited by Scott Cummings and David J. Monti. Albany: State University of New York Press.

Dewart, Janet. 1989. *The State of Black America.* New York: National Urban League.

Diiulio, John J., Jr. 1994. "The Question of Black Crime." *The Public Interest, V.* 117 (Fall): 3–32.

Donzelot, Jacques. 1979. *The Policing of Families.* New York: Pantheon Books.

Dorney, J. A. 1995. "Educating toward Resistance: A Task for Women Teaching Girls." *Youth and Society* 27(1): 55–72.

Douglas, Mary. 1970. *Natural Symbols: Explorations in Cosmology.* New York: Pantheon Books.

———. 1978. *Implicit Meanings.* London: Routledge & Kegan Paul.

Douglas, Mary, and Aaron Wildavsky. 1982. *Risk and Culture.* Berkeley: University of California Press.

Downey, Ann M. 1990–91. "The Impact of Drug Abuse upon Adolescent Suicide." *Omega* 22(1): 261–75.

Doyle, Larry. 1987. "Violence Is Top Teen Killer, Studies Say." *Philadelphia Inquirer* (June 26): A-3.

Drucker, Ernest. 1992. "Addiction, Treatment, and AIDS Prevention in the U.S.: Low Enrollment, Retention and Therapeutic Efficacy Limit Population Impact." Paper presented to the VIII International Conference on AIDS, Amsterdam, The Netherlands, July 19–24, 1992.

Dryfoos, Joy G. 1993. "Common Components of Successful Interventions with High Risk Youth." Pp. 131–47 in *Adolescent Risk Taking*, edited by Nancy J. Bell and Robert W. Bell. Newbury Park, CA: Sage.

Dugger, Celia W. 1996. "Immigrant Cultures Raising Issues of Child Punishment." *New York Times* (February 29): A1, A12.

Duran, Eduardo, and Bonnie Duran. 1995. *Native American PostColonial Psychology*. Albany, NY: State University of New York Press.

Durkheim, Emile. 1947. *The Division of Labor in Society*. Glencoe, IL: Free Press.

———. 1956. *Education and Sociology*. Glencoe, IL: Free Press.

———. 1973. *Moral Education*. New York: Free Press.

Duster, T. 1988. "Crime, Youth Unemployment and the Black Urban Underclass." *Crime and Delinquency* 30: 300–16.

Dye, Thomas R. 1978. *Understanding Public Policy*. Englewood Cliffs, NJ: Prentice-Hall.

Echols, Alice. 1989. *Daring to Be Bad: Radical Feminism in America 1967–1975*. Minneapolis: University of Minnesota Press.

Edelman, Marian Wright. 1987. *Families in Peril: An Agenda for Social Change*. Cambridge, MA: Harvard University Press.

Edelman, Peter, and Joyce Ladner, eds. 1991. *Adolescence and Poverty*. Washington, DC: Center for National Policy Press.

Ehrenreich, B., and D. English. 1973. *Witches, Midwives and Nurses: A History of Women Healers*. Old Westbury, New York: The Feminist Press.

Ehrlich, Paul R., and Anne H. Ehrlich. 1990. *The Population Explosion*. New York: Simon and Schuster.

Eisler, Riane, and Rob Koegel. 1996. "A Partnership Model: A Signpost of Hope." *Holistic Education Review* 9(1): 5–15.

Elliott, Delbert S. 1994. "Serious Violent Offenders: Onset, Developmental Course and Termination." *Criminology* 32(1): 1–21.

Emans, S. Jean and Astrid H. Heger, eds. 1992. *Evaluation of the Sexually Abused Child: A Medical Textbook and Photographic Atlas*. New York: Oxford University Press.

Encyclopedia of World Problems and Human Potential. www.uia.org

Engels, Friedrich. 1884/1985. *The Origin of the Family, Private Property and the State*. (Introduction by Michele Barrett). Middlesex, England: Penguin Books.

Erikson, E. H. 1963. *Childhood and Society*. 2d ed. New York: Norton.

Esbensen, Finn-Aage, and David Huizinga. 1993. "Gangs, Drugs, and Delinquency in a Survey of Urban Youth." *Criminology* 31(4): 565–89.

Esman, Aaron. 1990. *Adolescence and Culture*. New York: Columbia University Press.

Estroff, T. W., R. H. Schwartz, and N. G. Hoffmann. 1989. "Adolescent Cocaine Abuse." *Clinical Pediatrics* 28(12): 550–555.

Fagan, Jeffrey. 1990. "Intoxication and Aggression." Pp. 241–320 in *Drugs and Crime*, edited by Michael Tonry and James Q. Wilson. Chicago: University of Chicago Press.

———. 1996. "What Do We Know About Gun Use Among Adolescents?" Boulder, CO: Center for the Study and Prevention of Violence, University of Colorado.

Faller, Kathleen Coulborn. 1993. *Child Sexual Abuse: Intervention and Treatment*

Issues. National Center on Child Abuse and Neglect. McLean, VA: The Circle, Inc.

Fanon, Frantz. 1968. *The Wretched of the Earth*. New York: Grove Press.

Feagin, Joe R., and Melvin P. Sikes. 1994. *Living with Racism: The Black Middle-class Experience*. Boston: Beacon Press.

Featherstone, Mike. 1995. *Undoing Culture: Globalization, Postmodernism and Identity*. Thousand Oaks, CA: Sage.

Federal Bureau of Investigation. 1996. "Supplementary Homicide Reports." Washington, D.C.: Department of Justice.

Felson, Richard B. 1996. "Big People Hit Little People: Sex Differences in Physical Power and Interpersonal Violence." *Criminology* 34(3): 433–52.

Ferrell, Jeff. 1995a. "Adrenalin, Pleasure, and Criminological Verstehen." Paper presented to the Annual Meeting of the American Society of Criminology (November), Boston, MA.

———. 1995b. "Urban Graffiti: Crime, Control, and Resistance." *Youth and Society* 27(1): 73–92.

Fessler, L. W., ed. 1983. *Chinese in America: Stereotyped Past, Changing Present*. New York: Vantage.

Fine, M. 1991. *Framing Dropouts*. Albany: State University of New York Press.

Finkelman, Paul. 1991. "The Latest Front in the War on Drugs: The First Amendment." *Drug Law Report* 2(20): 229–36.

Finklehor, David. 1979. *Sexually Abused Children*. New York: Free Press.

———. 1988. "The Trauma of Child Sexual Abuse: Two Models." Pp. 61–82 in *Lasting Effects of Child Sexual Abuse*, edited by G. E. Wyatt and G. J. Powell. Newbury Park, CA: Sage.

Finklehor, David, and Larry Baron. 1990. "High-Risk Children." Pp. 136–47 in *Violence: Patterns, Causes, Public Policy*, edited by N. A. Weiner, M. A. Zahn, and R. J. Sagi. New York: Harcourt Brace Jovanovich.

Finklehor, David, and A. Browne. 1985. "The Traumatic Impact of Child Sexual Abuse." *American Journal of Orthopsychiatry* 55: 530–41.

Finklehor, David, and J. Dziuba-Leatherman. 1994. "Children as Victims of Violence: A National Survey." *Pediatrics* 94: 413–420.

———. 1995. *The Victimization of Children*. Family Research Library.

Finklehor, David, D. G. Hotaling, I. A. Lewis, and C. Smith. 1990. "Sexual Abuse in a National Survey of Adult Men and Women: Prevalence, Characteristics, and Risk Factors." *Child Abuse and Neglect* 14(1): 19–28.

Finnegan, William. 1997. "The Unwanted." *New Yorker* (December 1): 60–78.

Fishman, L. T. 1992. "I've Got the Monster! The Responses of African American and Latino Prisoners to a Diagnosis of HIV/AIDS." Paper presented at the Annual Meetings of the American Society of Criminology. New Orleans, November 4–7.

———. 1995. "The Vice-Queens: An Ethnographic Study of Black Female Gang Behavior." Pp. 83–92 in *The Modern Gang Reader*, edited by Malcolm W. Klein, Cheryl L. Maxson, and Jody Miller. Los Angeles: Roxbury Publishing Co.

Fitch, Robert. 1994. *The Assassination of New York*. New York: Verso Publishers.

Fleisher, Mark S. 1995. *Beggars and Thieves: Lives of Urban Street Criminals*. Madison, WI: The University of Wisconsin Press.

Flores, Ike. 1996. "Heroin Has Its Deadly Hooks in Teens across the Nation." *USA Today* (October 9): 4A.

Forbes, David. 1994. *False Fixes: The Cultural Politics of Drugs, Alcohol, and Addictive Relations.* Albany, NY: State University of New York.

Forst, Martin L. 1991. "Sexual Risk Profiles of Delinquent and Homeless Youth." *Journal of Community Health* 19(2): 101–14.

Forst, Stuart W., and Dean G. Rojek. 1991. "A Comparison of Drug Involvement between Runaways and School Youths." *Journal of Drug Education* 21(1): 13–25.

Forsyth, Alasdair J. 1996. "Places and Patterns of Drug Use in the Scottish Dance Scene." *Addiction* 91(1): 511–21.

Foucault, Michel. 1978. *The History of Sexuality.* New York: Pantheon.

———. 1979. *Discipline and Punish: The Birth of the Prison.* Translated by A. Sheridan. New York: Pantheon.

———. 1980. *Power/Knowledge.* New York: Pantheon.

———. 1990. "Two Lectures." Pp. 200–21 in *A Reader in Contemporary Social Theory,* edited by N. B. Dirks, G. Eley, and S. B. Ortner. Princeton, NJ: Princeton University Press.

Fox, Matthew. 1988. *The Coming of the Cosmic Christ.* San Francisco: Harper & Row.

Frankel, Glenn. 1997. "The Longest War." *Washington Post National Weekly Edition* (July 7): 6–8.

Fraser, Antonia. 1984. *The Weaker Vessel.* New York: Alfred A. Knopf.

Fredrickson, George M. 1995. "Demonizing the American Dilemma." *New York Review of Books* (October 19): 10–16.

Freeman, Richard B. 1992. "Crime and the Employment of Disadvantaged Youths." In *Urban Labor Markets and Job Opportunity,* edited by George E. Peterson and Wayne Vroman. Washington, DC: Urban Institute Press.

French, Howard W. 1997. "Africa's Culture War: Old Customs, New Values." *New York Times,* February 2.

Freud, Sigmund. 1977 ed. *Civilization and Its Discontents.* New York: W. W. Norton and Co., Inc.

Furlong, Andy and Fred Cartmel. 1997. *Young People and Social Change: Individualization and Risk in Late Modernity.* Buckingham, England: Open University Press.

Furstenberg, F. F., J. Brooks-Gunn, and L. Chase-Lansdale. 1989. "Teenage Pregnancy and Childbearing." *American Psychologist* 44: 313–20.

Gagnon, Paul. 1995. "What Should Children Learn?" *Atlantic Monthly* 276(6): 65–79.

Gaines, Donna. 1992. *Teenage Wasteland: Suburbia's Dead End Kids.* New York: HarperPerennial.

Galaway, Burt, and Joe Hudson, eds. 1996. *Restorative Justice: International Perspectives.* Monsey, NY: Criminal Justice Press.

Garbarino, James. 1991. "Before Dreams Disappear: Preventing Youth Violence." Testimony before the Subcommittee on Children, Family, Drugs and Alcoholism, Committee on Labor and Human Resources, United States Senate, One Hundred and Third Congress, Second Session.

Garbarino, James, Nancy Dbrow, Kathleen Kostelny, and Carole Pardo. 1992.

Children in Danger: Coping with the Consequences of Community Violence. San Francisco: Jossey-Bass Publishers.

Garber, J., N. S. Robinsonk, and D. Valentiner. 1997. "The Relation between Parenting and Adolescent Depression: Self-Worth as a Mediator." *Journal of Adolescent Research* 12(1): 12–33.

Gardiner, Gareth S., and Richard N. McKinney. 1991. "The Great American War on Drugs: Another Failure of Tough-Guy Management." *The Journal of Drug Issues* 21(3): 605–661.

Garofalo, J., and M. J. Hindelang. 1977. *An Introduction to the National Crime Survey.* U.S. Department of Justice, Law Enforcement Assistance Administration, National Criminal Justice Information and Statistics Service, SD-VAD-4 1977. Washington, DC: U.S. Government Printing Office.

Gerbner, George, Hamid Mowlana, and Herbert I. Schiller, eds. 1996. *Invisible Crises: What Conglomerate Control of Media Means for America and the World.* Boulder, CO: Westview Press.

Giamo, B. 1992. "Making Dust: The Symbolic Landscape of Homelessness." *Journal of Social Distress and the Homeless.* Vol. 1 (January): 23–36.

Gibbs, J. T. 1988. "The New Morbidity: Homicide, Suicide, Accidents and Life-Threatening Behaviors." In *Young, Black, and Male in America: An Endangered Species,* edited by J. T. Gibbs. Dover, MA: Auburn House.

Gibson, P. 1996. "Gay Male and Lesbian Suicide." *Report of the Secretary's Task Force on Youth Suicide.* U.S. Department of Health and Human Services.

Giddens, Anthony. 1973. *The Class Structure of the Advanced Societies.* New York: Harper Torchbooks.

———. 1982. *Profiles and Critiques in Social Theory.* Berkeley and Los Angeles: University of California Press.

———. 1991. "Education, Power, and Society." *Introduction to Sociology.* New York: W. W. Norton.

Gilligan, C. 1982. *In a Different Voice: Psychological Theory and Women's Development.* Cambridge, MA: Harvard University Press.

Gilligan, James. 1996. *Violence: Our Deadly Epidemic and Its Causes.* New York: G. P. Putnam's Sons.

Gillis, John R. 1974. *Youth in History.* New York: Academic Press.

Giroux, Henry. 1992. *Border Crossing: Cultural Workers and the Politics of Education.* New York and London: Routledge.

Goldberg, Carey. 1996. "Survey Reports More Drug Use by Teen-Agers." *New York Times* (August 21): A9.

Goldstein, P. J. 1989. "Drugs and Violent Crime." In *Pathways to Criminal Violence,* edited by N. A. Weiner and M. E. Wolfgang. Newbury Park, CA: Sage.

———. 1995. "The Drugs/Violence Nexus: A Tripartite Conceptual Framework." Pp. 255–64 in *The American Drug Scene,* edited by James A. Inciardi and Karen McElrath. Los Angeles: Roxbury Publishing Co.

Gonsiorek, J. C., W. H. Bera, and D. LeTourneau. 1994. *Male Sexual Abuse: A Trilogy of Intervention Strategies.* Thousand Oaks, CA: Sage.

Goode, Erich. 1993; 1984. *Drugs in American Society* (4th ed.; 2nd ed.) New York: McGraw-Hill.

———. 1990. "The American Drug Panic of the 1980s: Social Construction or

Objective Threat?" *The International Journal of the Addictions* 25(9): 1083–98.

Goode, Erich, and Nachman Ben-Yehuda. 1994. *Moral Panics: The Social Construction of Deviance.* Cambridge, MA: Blackwell.

Goode, Judith, and Jo Anne Schneider. 1994. *Reshaping Ethnic and Racial Relations in Philadelphia.* Philadelphia: Temple University Press.

Gordon, Linda. 1988. *Heroes of Their Own Lives: The Politics and History of Family Violence.* New York: Penguin.

Greene, Marcia S. 1996. "The Street Rules the Cellblock." *Washington Post National Weekly Edition* (October 7–13).

Greenfeld, Lawrence A. 1993. "Cultural Studies and/or New Worlds." Pp. 89–105 in *Race, Identity, and Representation in Education,* edited by C. McCarthy and W. Crichlow. New York: Routledge & Kegan Paul.

Greenfeld, Lawrence A., and Marianne W. Zawitz. 1995. "Weapons Offenses and Offenders: Firearms, Crime and Criminal Justice." Annapolis Junction, MD: Bureau of Justice Statistics Clearinghouse.

Grossberg, Lawrence. 1992. *We Gotta Get Out of This Place: Popular Conservation and Postmodern Culture.* New York: Routledge.

Gunew, Sneja. 1994. "Play Centre Field: Representation and Cultural Difference." In *Representation, Discourse and Desire,* edited by P. Fuery. Melbourne: Longman Cheshire.

Gusfield, Joseph R. 1963. *Symbolic Crusade: Status Politics and the American Temperance Movement.* Urbana: University of Illinois Press.

Habermas, Jurgen. 1975. *Legitimation Crisis.* Boston: Beacon Press.

———. 1979. *Communication and the Evolution of Society.* Boston: Beacon Press.

———. 1989. *The Structural Transformation of the Public Sphere.* T. Burger and F. Lawrence (trans.). Cambridge: Polity Press.

Hagan, John. 1991. "Destiny and Drift: Subcultural Preferences, Status Attainments, and the Risks and Rewards of Youth. *American Sociological Review* 56: 567–82.

———. 1993. "Structural and Cultural Disinvestment and the New Ethnographies of Poverty and Crime." *Contemporary Sociology,* 327–32.

Hagedorn, John M. 1988. *People and Folks: Gangs, Crime and the Underclass in a Rustbelt City.* Chicago: Lakeview.

———. 1990. "How Do Gangs Get Organized." Pp. 85–103 in *Juvenile Delinquency: A Justice Perspective.* 2d ed, edited by R. A. Weisheit and R. G. Culbertson. Prospect Heights, IL: Waveland.

———. 1991. "Gangs, Neighborhoods, and Public Policy." *Social Problems* 38(4): 529–42.

Haggerty, R. J., L. R. Sherrod, N. Garmezy, and M. Rutter. 1994. *Stress, Risk and Resilience in Children and Adolescents: Process, Mechanisms and Interventions.* New York: Cambridge University Press.

Hamburg, D. A. 1992. *Today's Children: Creating a Future for a Generation in Crisis.* New York: Times Books.

Hamm, Mark S. 1993. *American Skinheads.* Westport, CT.: Greenwood Publishing Group.

Hammarstrom, Anne. 1991. "Health Consequences of Youth Unemployment: Review from a Gender Perspective." *Social Science and Medicine* 38(5): 699–709.

Hatchett, Shirley J., Donna L. Cochran, and James S. Jackson. 1995. "Family Life." Pp. 46–83 in *Life in Black America*. Newbury Park, CA: Sage.

Hatty, S. E. 1993. "Methadone and the War on Drugs: The Australian Experience." *Journal for Social Justice Studies* 5: 20–33.

Hauser, S. T. 1991. *Families and Their Adolescents*. New York: Free Press.

Hawkins, Darnell F., ed. 1995. *Ethnicity, Race and Crime*. Albany, NY: State University of New York Press.

Hawkins, Gordon, and Franklin E. Zimring. 1991. *Pornography in a Free Society*. New York: McGraw-Hill.

Hawkins, J. David. 1995. "Controlling Crime before It Happens: Risk-Focused Prevention." *NIJ Journal* #229, August.

Hawkins, J. David, R. F. Catalano, and J. Y. Miller. 1992. "Risk and Protective Factors for Alcohol and Other Drug Problems in Adolescence and Early Adulthood: Implications for Substance Abuse Prevention." *Psychological Bulletin* 112: 64–105.

Hawkins, J. David, and James J. Fitzgibbon. 1993. "Risk Factors and Risk Behaviors in Prevention of Adolescent Substance Abuse." *Adolescent Medicine: State of the Art Reviews* 4(2): 249–62.

Hawkins, J. David, J. M. Jenson, R. F. Catalano, and D. M. Lishner. 1988. "Delinquency and Drug Abuse: Implications for Social Services." *Social Service Review* 62: 258–284.

Hawley, Chandra. 1996. "Violence in Our Schools." Center for Adolescent Studies, Indiana University.

Heath, D. B. 1983. "Alcohol and Aggression: A 'Missing Link' in Worldwide Perspective." In *Alcohol, Drug Abuse and Aggression*, edited by E. Gottheil et al. Springfield, IL: Thomas.

Heide, Kathleen M. 1992. *Why Kids Kill Parents: Child Abuse and Adolescent Homicide*. Columbus, OH: Ohio State University Press.

———. 1993. "Parents Who Get Killed and the Children Who Kill Them." *Journal of Interpersonal Violence* 8(4): 531–44.

Heimer, C. A. 1988. "Social Structure, Psychology and the Estimation of Risk." *American Review of Sociology* 14: 491–519.

Henry, Mary E. 1996. Review of *Compulsory Schooling and Human Learning: The Moral Failure of Public Education in America and Japan*. San Francisco: Caddo Gap Press, 1994. Review published in *Holistic Education Review* 9(1): 66–67.

Herbert, Bob. 1994. "Who Will Help the Black Man?" *New York Times Magazine* (December 4): 73–110.

———. 1995a. "Buying Clothes without Exploiting Children." *New York Times* (August 4): A19.

———. 1995b. "Don't Call It Welfare Reform." *New York Times* (September 25): A11.

Hill, Robert B. 1995. "Breaking the Cycle of Disadvantage: Toward a Comprehensive National Policy for Social Intervention." In *African American Youth: Their Social and Economic Status in the United States*, edited by Ronald L. Taylor. Westport, CT: Praeger.

Hillman, James. 1996. *The Soul's Code: In Search of Character and Calling*. New York: Random House.

Hine, Thomas. 1997. "TV's Teen-Agers: An Insecure, World-Weary Lot." *New York Times* (October 26): Section 2, 1–38.

Hirst, C. 1989. "Forced Exit: A Profile of the Young and Homeless in Inner Urban Melbourne." Report of the Salvation Army Youth Homelessness Policy Development Project. Melbourne, Australia.

Hochschild, A. 1989. *The Second Shift: Working Parents and the Revolution at Home.* New York: Viking.

———. 1997. *The Time Bind: When Work Becomes Home and Home Becomes Work.* New York: Metropolitan Books.

Hoebel, E. Adamson. 1973. *The Law of Primitive Man: A Study in Comparative Legal Dynamics.* New York: Atheneum.

Hofstadter, Richard. 1955. *The Age of Reform.* New York: Knopf.

Hollinger, Robert. 1994. *Postmodernism and the Social Sciences.* Vol. 4. Thousand Oaks, CA: Sage.

Homes for the Homeless. 1998. "Ten Cities: A Snapshot of Family Homelessness Across America." New York City. Internet: hn-4061@handsnet.org.

Homonoff, Emeline et al. 1994. "It Takes a Village to Raise a Child: A Model of Training for Prevention of Youth Abuse of Alcohol and Other Drugs." *Child and Adolescent Social Work Journal* 11(1): 53–61.

hooks, bell. 1990. *Yearning: Race, Gender, and Cultural Politics.* Boston: South End Press.

———. 1994. *Outlaw Culture: Resisting Representations.* New York: Routledge.

Horowitz, Ruth. 1990. "Sociological Perspectives on Gangs: Conflicting Definitions and Concepts." Pp. 37–54 in *Gangs in America*, edited by C. R. Huff. Newbury Park, CA: Sage.

Horsley, W., and R. Buckley. 1991. *Nippon—New Superpower.* London: BBC Books.

Howard, J. 1991. "Taking a Chance on Love? Change in HIV Risk Behaviours of Sydney Street Youth." Paper presented to the Ninth National Behavioural Medicine Conference. The University of Sydney, Sydney, Australia.

Howe, Neil, and Bill Strauss. 1993. *13th Generation.* New York: Vintage Books.

Hughes, Gordon. 1996. "Strategies of Multi-Agency Crime Prevention and Community Safety in Contemporary Britain." *Studies on Crime and Crime Prevention* 5(2): 221–44.

Hughes, Robert, Jr., and Dalauna Sutton. 1996. "Adolescent Pregnancy Prevention: A Practitioner's Guide." Department of Family Relations and Human Development, Ohio State University, Columbus, Ohio.

Huston, A. C., E. Donnerstein, N. Feshback, P. Katz, and H. H. Fairchild. 1993. *Big World Small Screen: The Role of Television in American Society.* Lincoln, NE: University of Nebraska Press.

Ice-T. 1995. "The Killing Fields." Pp. 147–54 in *The Modern Gang Reader*, edited by Malcolm W. Klein, Cheryl L. Maxson, and Jody Miller. Los Angeles: Roxbury Publishing Co.

Illick, Joseph E. 1974. *Colonial Pennsylvania: A History.* Millwood, NY: Kraus.

Inciardi, James A. 1992. *The War on Drugs II: The Continuing Epic of Heroin, Cocaine, Crack, Crime, AIDS, and Public Policy.* Mountain View, CA: Mayfield.

Inciardi, James A., R. Horowitz, and A. E. Pottieger. 1993. *Street Kids, Street Drugs, Street Crime*. Belmont, MA: Heath.

Inciardi, James A., and Karen McElrath, eds. 1995. *The American Drug Scene*. Los Angeles: Roxbury Publishing Co.

Inciardi, James A., and Anne E. Pottieger. 1991. "Kids, Crack, and Crime." *Journal of Social Issues* 21(Spring): 257–70.

Ingersoll, Sarah, and Donni LeBoeuf. 1997. "Reaching Out to Youth out of the Education Mainstream." *Juvenile Justice Bulletin* (February). Washington, DC: Office of Juvenile Justice and Delinquency Prevention.

Irwin, Charles E., Jr. 1993. "Adolescence and Risk Taking, How Are They Related?" Pp. 7–28 in *Adolescent Risk Taking*, edited by Nancy J. Bell and Robert W. Bell. Newbury Park, CA: Sage.

Irwin, John. 1970. *The Felon*. Englewood Cliffs, NJ: Prentice-Hall.

Irwin, John, and James Austin. 1997. *It's About Time: America's Imprisonment Binge*. 2d ed. Belmont, CA: Wadsworth.

Jackson, James S., ed. 1991. *Life in Black America*. Newbury Park, CA: Sage.

Jackson, John S., and William Crotty. 1996. *The Politics of Presidential Selection*. New York: HarperCollins.

James, Allison, and Alan Prout, eds. 1990. *Constructing and Reconstructing Childhood: Contemporary Issues in the Sociological Study of Childhood*. London and New York: The Falmer Press.

James, William. 1902/1985. *The Varieties of Religious Experience*. Cambridge, MA: Harvard University Press.

———. 1974 (originally published in 1907). *Essays in Pragmatism*. Glencoe, IL: The Free Press.

Janofsky, Michael. 1997. "At Million Woman March, Focus Is on Family." *New York Times* (October 26): A1, A18.

Janus, M. D. et al. 1987. *Adolescent Runaways: Causes and Consequences*. Lexington, MA: Heath.

Jarrett, Robin L. 1995. "Growing Up Poor: The Family Experiences of Socially Mobile Youth in Low-Income African American Neighborhoods." *Journal of Adolescent Research* 10(1): 111–35.

Jefferson, Tony. 1996. "Introduction: Masculinities, Social Relations and Crime." Special Issue. *The British Journal of Criminology* 36(3): 337–47.

Jenks, C. 1994. *The Homeless*. Cambridge, MA: Harvard University Press.

Jessor, R., and S. L. Jessor. 1977. *Problem Behavior and Psychosocial Development: A Longitudinal Study of Youth*. New York: Academic Press.

Joe, Karen. 1994. "The New Criminal Conspiracy? Asian Gangs and Organized Crime in San Francisco." *Journal of Research in Crime and Delinquency* 31(4): 390–415.

Johns, Christina. 1992. *Power, Ideology, and the War on Drugs*. New York: Praeger.

Johns, Christina, and Jose Maria Borrero. 1991. "The War on Drugs: Nothing Succeeds Like Failure." In *Crimes by the Capitalist State*, edited by Gregg Barak. New York: State University of New York Press.

Johnson, B. D., M. A. Kaplan, and J. Schmeidler. 1990. "Days with Drug Distribution: Which Drugs? How Many Transactions? With What Returns?" In

Drugs, Crime, and the Criminal Justice System, edited by Ralph A. Weisheit. Cinncinnati, OH: Anderson Publishing.

Johnson, B. D., T. Williams, K. A. Dei, and H. Sanabria. 1990. "Drug Users in the Inner City: Impact on Hard-Drug Users and the Community." Pp. 9–68 in *Drugs and Crime*, edited by Michael Tonry and James Q. Wilson. Chicago: University of Chicago Press.

Johnston, L. D., P. M. O'Malley, and J. C. Backman. 1995. *Drug Use among American High School Students, College Students, and Other Young Adults*. Washington, DC: U.S. Government Printing Office.

Jordon, W. J. 1991. "AIDS and Adolescence: A Challenge to Both Treatment and Prevention." Journal of Adolescent Health 12(8): 611–18.

Jordon, W. J., J. Lara, and J. M. McPartland. 1996. "Exploring the Causes of Early Dropout among Race-Ethnic and Gender Groups." *Youth and Society* 28(1): 62–94.

Journal of Adolescent Research. 1995. "Special Issue: Creating Supportive Communities for Adolescent Development: Challenges to Scholars." Volume 10.

Kane, Jeffrey. 1995. "Adolescence: A Time without Place." *Holistic Education Review* 8(1): 2–4.

———. 1996. "Personal Reflections on Sources of Illusion and Hope." *Holistic Education Review* (3): 24.

Katz, J. 1988. *Seductions of Crime*. New York: Basic Books.

Katz, Michael, ed. 1971. *School Reform Past and Present*. Boston: Little Brown and Company.

Kaufman, J. 1994. "The Wedge between Emotion and Cognition: Feminism, Knowledge and Power." *Holistic Education Review* 7: 43–49.

Kaufmann, Walter Arnold. 1950. *Nietzsche: Philosopher, Psychologist, Antichrist*. Princeton, NJ: Princeton University Press.

Kendig, H. 1984. "Gentrification in the City." Chapter in *Gentrification, Displacement and Neighborhood Revitalization*, edited by J. Palen and B. Ondon. New York: State University of New York Press.

Kercher, G., and M. McShane. 1984. "The Prevalence of Child Sexual Abuse Victimization in an Adult Sample of Texas Residents." *Child Abuse and Neglect* 8: 495–502.

Kersten, Joachim. 1996. "Culture, Masculinities and Violence against Women." *The British Journal of Criminology* 36(3): 381–95.

Kilias, Martin, and Ambros Uchtenhagen. 1996. "Does Medical Heroin Prescription Reduce Delinquency among Drug Addicts? On the Evaluation of the Swiss Heroin Prescription Projects and Its Methodology." *Studies on Crime & Crime Prevention* 5(2): 245–256.

King, I. 1991. "Disadvantaged Youth Project: Final Report." Commonwealth AIDS Prevention and Education & King's Cross Youth Resources, 234 Liverpool St., Sydney, NSW, Australia.

Kipke, Michele D. et al. 1997. "Homeless Youth and Their Exposure to and Involvement in Violence While Living on the Streets." *Journal of Adolescent Health* 20: 360–67.

Klein, Malcolm W. 1971. *Street Gangs and Street Workers*. Englewood Cliffs, NJ: Prentice-Hall.

———. 1995. *The American Street Gang: Its Nature, Prevalence, and Control.* New York: Oxford.

Klein, Tanna. 1996. "Dropping Out of School." *Office of Social and Economic Data Analysis* 7(1). University of Missouri System, Lincoln University.

Knudsen, Dean D., and JoAnn L. Miller, eds. 1991. *Abused and Battered: Social and Legal Responses to Family Violence.* New York: Aldine De Gruyter.

Kobler, John. 1973. *Ardent Spirits: The Rise and Fall of Prohibition.* New York: G.P. Putnam.

Koch, G. 1955. "The South Seas—Yesterday and Today: Cultural Change Among Tongans and an Attempt to Interpret this Development." Braunschweig: Albert Limback Verlag.

Koper, Christopher S., and Peter Reuter. 1996. "Suppressing Illegal Gun Markets: Lessons from Drug Enforcement." *Law and Contemporary Problems* 59(1): 119–43.

Kopperud, Gunnar. 1994. "Angola's Unending Anguish." *Sydney Herald* (April 2).

Korf, Dirk J. 1990. "Cannabis Retail Markets in Amsterdam." *The International Journal on Drug Policy* 2 (July/August): 23–27.

Kozol, Jonathan. 1992. *Savage Inequalities: Children in America's Schools.* New York: HarperPerennial.

Kral, A. H. et al. 1997. "Prevalence of Sexual Risk Behaviour and Substance Use among Runaway and Homeless Adolescents in San Francisco, Denver and New York City." *International Journal of STD & AIDS* 8: 109–17.

Kratcoski, Peter C., and Lucille Dunn Kratcoski. 1990. *Juvenile Delinquency.* 3d ed. Englewood Cliffs, NJ: Prentice-Hall.

Krauss, Clifford. 1996. "Decoding Crimes in Graffiti." *New York Times* (October 4): A8.

Krisberg, Barry, and James F. Austin. 1993. *Reinventing Juvenile Justice.* Newbury Park, CA: Sage.

Lab, Steven P., and R. D. Clark. 1994. "Gauging Crime and Control in the Schools." Paper presented at the American Society of Criminology Meeting, Miami, FL (November).

Lareau, Annette. 1987. "Social Class Differences in Family-School Relationships." *Sociology of Education* 60(April): 73–85.

Larkin St. Youth Center. 1984. Client Statistics. San Francisco.

Lasch, Christopher. 1977. *Haven in a Heartless World: The Family Beseiged.* New York: W. W. Norton.

Laslett, Peter. 1977. *Family Life and Illicit Love in Earlier Generations.* New York: Cambridge University Press.

Laszlo, Ervin. 1994. *The Choice: Evolution or Extinction?* New York: G. P. Putnam's Sons.

Law Enforcement News. 1996. Vol. 22, No. 445 (May 15).

Lawson, Hal A. 1996. "Expanding the Goodlad Agenda: Interprofessional Education and Community Collaboration in Service of Vulnerable Children, Youth, and Families." *Holistic Education Review* 9(1): 20–34.

LeBoeuf, Donni, and Robin V. Delany-Shabazz. 1997. "Conflict Resolution." Office of Juvenile Justice and Delinquency Prevention. Washington, DC: U.S. Department of Justice.

Lee, Gary. 1993. "A New Frontier of Violence: Drugs and Gangs Transform Heartland Cities." *Washington Post National Weekly Edition* (June 28–July 4, 8).

Lender, M. E. and J. K. Martin. 1987. *Drinking in America*. New York: Free Press.

Leone, Peter E., ed. 1990. *Understanding Troubled and Troubling Youth*. Newbury Park, CA: Sage.

Lerman, Paul. 1970. "Beyond Gault: Injustice and the Child." In *Delinquency and Social Policy*, edited by Paul Lerman. New York: Praeger.

————. 1990. "Delinquency and Social Policy: A Historical Perspective." Pp. 5–16 in *Juvenile Delinquency*, 2d. ed, edited by Ralph A. Weisheit and Robert G. Culbertson. Prospect Heights, IL: Waveland Press.

————. 1995. "Delinquency and Social Policy: A Historical Perspective." In *Juvenile Delinquency: A Justice Perspective*, 3rd ed., edited by R. A. Weisheit and R. G. Culbertson. Prospect Heights, IL: Waveland Press.

Levine, H. G. 1984. "The Alcohol Problem in America: From Temperance to Alcoholism." *British Journal of Addiction* 79: 109–19.

Lewin, Tamar. 1997. "Teen-Agers Alter Sexual Practices, Thinking Risks Will Be Avoided." *New York Times* (April 5): A7.

Lewis, David Levering. 1993. *W. E. B. DuBois: Biography of a Race 1868–1919*. New York: Henry Holt & Co.

The Lindesmith Center for Research on Drugs. 1997. "The Case for Legalization." The Lindesmith Center Home Page (www.lindesmith.org/lindesmith/tlewe.html).

Lipsitz, George. 1995. "Toxic Racism." *American Quarterly* 47(3): 416–426.

London, Scott. 1996. "Global Villager: An Interview with Pico Iyer." *The Sun* (January): 7–13.

Longshore, D. (1992). "AIDS Education and Drug Users: Existing Research and New Directions." *The Journal of Drug Issues* 22(1): 1–16.

Lopez, Jose, and Alfredo Mirande. 1992. "Chicano Urban Youth Gangs: A Critical Analysis of a Social Problem?" *Latino Studies Journal* 3(3): 15.

Los Angeles County Sheriff's Department. 1994. "A Street Gang Manual." *Operation Safe Streets, Street Gang Detail*. Los Angeles, CA.

Los Angeles Police Department. 1990a. "Asian Gangs." Gang Activities Section; Asian Gang Unit. Los Angeles, CA.

————. 1990b. "Hispanic Street Gangs." Gang Activities Section. Los Angeles, CA.

Luckenbill, David F., and Daniel P. Doyle. 1996. "Structural Position and Violence: Developing a Cultural Explanation." Pp. 176–86 in *Exploring Delinquency: Causes and Consequences*, edited by D. G. Rojek and G. F. Jensen. Los Angeles: Roxbury Publishing Co.

Lyman, Michael D. 1989. *Gangland: Drug Trafficking by Organized Criminals*. Springfield, IL: Charles C. Thomas.

Lyng, Stephen. 1993. "Dysfunctional Risk Taking: Criminal Behavior as Edgework." Pp. 107–130 in *Adolescent Risk Taking*, edited by Nancy J. Bell and Robert W. Bell. Newbury Park, CA: Sage.

Lyotard, Jean-François. 1992. *The Postmodern Condition: A Report on Knowledge*. Manchester, England: Manchester University Press.

Maccoby, E. 1980. *Social Development: Psychological Growth and the Parent-Child Relationship*. New York: Harcourt Brace Jovanovich.

Macedo, Donald. 1994. *Literacies of Power: What Americans Are Not Allowed to Know*. Boulder: Westview.

MacIntyre, Alasdair. 1981. *After Virtue*. Notre Dame, IN: University of Notre Dame Press.

MacLeod, Jay. 1987. *Ain't No Makin' It: Leveled Aspirations in a Low-Income Neighborhood*. Boulder, CO: Westview.

Maguire, K., A. L. Pastore, and T. J. Flanagan, eds. 1993. *Sourcebook of Criminal Justice Statistics 1992*. U.S. Department of Justice, Bureau of Justice Statistics. Washington, DC: U.S. Government Printing Office.

Mahan, Sue. 1996. *Crack Cocaine, Crime, and Women*. Thousand Oaks, CA: Sage.

Majors, Richard. 1992. *Cool Pose: The Dilemmas of Black Manhood in America*. Lexington, MA: Lexington.

————. 1994a. "The Dilemma of the Black American Male." *The Crisis*. 101(4): 8–11; 32–33.

————. 1994b. *The American Black Male: His Present Status and His Future*. Chicago: University of Chicago Press.

Malcolm X. 1966. *The Autobiography of Malcolm X*. New York: Grove Press.

Males, Mike A. 1996. *The Scapegoat Generation*. Monroe, ME: Common Courage Press.

Mandle, Jay. 1978. *The Roots of Black Poverty: The Plantation Economy after the Civil War*. Durham, NC: Duke University Press.

Mannix, Daniel Pratt. 1962. *Black Cargoes: A History of the Atlantic Slave Trade: 1518–1865* (with Malcolm Crowley). New York: Viking Press.

Marable, Manning. 1981. *Race, Reform, and Rebellion*. Jackson: University Press of Mississippi.

Mason, Mary Ann, and Eileen Gambrill, eds. 1994. *Debating Children's Lives: Current Controversies on Children and Adolescents*. Thousand Oaks, CA: Sage.

Matza, David. 1990. *Delinquency and Drift*. 2d ed. (Originally published in 1964.) New Brunswick, NJ: Transaction.

Matza, David, and Patricia Morgan. 1995. "Controlling Drug Use: The Great Prohibition." Pp. 229–58 in *Punishment and Social Control*, edited by T. G. Blomberg and S. Cohen. New York: Aldine De Gruyter.

Maxfield, Michael G., and Cathy Spatz Widom. 1995. "Childhood Victimization and Patterns of Offending through the Life Cycle: Early Onset and Continuation." Paper presented at the Annual Meeting of the American Society of Criminology, Phoenix (November).

Maxson, Cheryl L. 1995. "Research in Brief: Street Gangs and Drug Sales in Two Suburban Cities." Pp. 228–35 in *The Modern Gang Reader*, edited by Malcolm W. Klein, Cheryl L. Maxson, and Jody Miller. Los Angeles: Roxbury Publishing Co.

Maxson, Cheryl L., Kristi J. Woods, and Malcolm W. Klein. 1996. "Street Gang Migration: How Big a Threat?" *National Institute of Justice Journal* (February): 26–31.

McCarthy, B., and J. Hagan. 1991. "Homelessness: A Criminogenic Situation?" *British Journal of Criminology* 31(4): 393–410.

McCoy, H. Virginia, Christine Miles, and James A. Inciardi. 1995. "Survival Sex: Inner-City Women and Crack-Cocaine." Pp. 172–77 in *The American Drug*

Scene, edited by James A. Inciardi and Karen McElrath. Los Angeles: Roxbury Publishing Co..

McCuen, Gary E. 1985. *Pornography and Sexual Violence*. Hudson: Gary E. McCuen Publications, Inc.

McElrath, Karen. 1995. "Alcoholics Anonymous." Pp. 314–17 in *The American Drug Scene*. edited by James A. Inciardi and Karen McElrath. Los Angeles: Roxbury Publishing Co.

McIntyre, Lisa J. 1994. *Law in the Sociological Enterprise*. Boulder, CO: Westview Press.

McLaren, Peter. 1993. *Schooling as a Ritual Performance*. 2d ed. London and New York: Routledge.

McMillen, M. M., P. Kaufman, and S. D. Whitener. 1994. *Dropout Rates in the United States, 1993*. Washington, DC: U.S. Department of Education, Office of Research and Improvement.

McNall, Scott G., and Sally A. McNall. 1992. *Sociology*. Englewood Cliffs, NJ: Prentice Hall.

McWilliams, John C. 1990. "The Futility of the War on Drugs." Paper presented at the Annual Meeting of the American Society on Criminology, Baltimore, MD, November 7–10.

Mead, George Herbert. 1934. *Mind, Self and Society*. Chicago: University of Chicago Press.

Mead, Lawrence M. 1992. *The New Politics of Poverty*. New York: Basic Books.

Meade, Michael. 1996. Conference on Youth. Bellingham, WA.

Mendez, Deborah. 1996. "More and More Girls Joining Violent Male Gangs." *The Seattle Times* (October 27): A7.

Merchant, Carolyn. 1983. *The Death of Nature*. New York: Basic Books.

———. 1992. *Radical Ecology: The Search for a Livable World*. New York: Basic Books.

Messerschmidt, J. 1993. *Masculinities and Crime*. Baltimore, MD: Rowman and Littlefield.

Miller, Alice. 1984. *For Your Own Good: Hidden Cruelty in Child-Rearing and the Roots of Violence*. Translated by Hildegarde and Hunter Hannum. New York: Farrar, Straus & Giroux.

———. 1986. *Thou Shalt Not Be Aware: Society's Betrayal of the Child*. New York: A Meridian Book.

———. 1990. *Banished Knowledge*. New York: Anchor Books.

———. 1993. *Breaking Down the Wall of Silence*. New York: A Meridian Book.

Miller, Jerome G. 1996. *Search and Destroy: African-American Males in the Criminal Justice System*. Cambridge: Cambridge University Press.

Miller, J. Mitchell, and Albert Cohen. 1996. "Gang Theories and Their Policy Implications." Pp. 3–16 in *Gangs: A Criminal Justice Approach*, edited by J. Mitchell Miller and Jeffrey P. Rush. Cincinnati, OH: Anderson.

Miller, J. Mitchell, and Jeffrey P. Rush, eds. 1996. *Gangs: A Criminal Justice Approach*. Cincinnati, OH: Anderson.

Miller, Ron. 1993. *The Renewal of Meaning in Education: Responses to the Cultural and Ecological Crisis of Our Times*. Brandon, VT: Holistic Education Press.

————. 1997. "Holistic Education for an Emerging Culture." *Holistic Education Review* 10(3): 26–31.

Miller, Walter B. 1981. "American Youth Gangs: Past and Present." In *Current Perspectives on Criminal Behavior*, 2d ed, edited by A. S. Blumberg. New York: Knopf.

————. 1990. "Why the United States Has Failed to Solve Its Youth Gang Problem." Pp. 263–87 in *Gangs in America*, edited by C. R. Huff. Newbury Park, CA: Sage.

Mincy, Ronald B., ed. 1994. *Nurturing Young Black Males*. Washington, DC: The Urban Institute Press.

Minton, Lynn. 1996. "I Live in a War Zone in America." *Parade Magazine*. (August 18): 11.

Mintz, Steven. 1985. *A Prison of Expectations: The Family in Victorian Culture*. New York: New York University Press.

Mintz, Steven, and Susan Kellogg. 1988. *Domestic Revolutions: A Social History of American Family Life*. New York: The Free Press.

Miron, L. F., and M. Lauria. 1995. "Identity Politics and Student Resistance to Inner-City Public Schooling." *Youth and Society* 27(1): 29–54.

Mock, Lois Felson. 1996. "Young People, Violence and Guns." Chapter in *Criminal Justice: Concepts and Issues*, edited by Chris W. Eskridge. Los Angeles: Roxbury Publishing Co.

Moore, Joan W. 1978. *Homeboys: Gangs, Drugs and Prison in the Barrios of Los Angeles*. Philadelphia: Temple University Press.

————. 1992. *Going Down to the Barrio: Homeboys and Homegirls in Change*. Philadelphia: Temple University Press.

Moore, Thomas. 1996. *The Reenchantment of Everyday Life*. New York: HarperCollins.

Morgan, Harry. 1995. "Drug Use in High School: Race and Gender Issues." *Journal of Educational Research* 88(5): 301–08.

Morin, Richard. 1995. "It Ain't Easy Being Young: Surveys Find That Teenagers of the 1990s Are Facing Tougher Challenges Than Their Parents Did." *Washington Post National Weekly Edition* (December 18–24).

Morrow, Raymond Allan and Carlos Alberto Torres. 1995. *Social Theory and Education*. Albany: State University of New York Press.

Moss, Barbara A. 1995. "African Women's Legacy: Ambiguity, Autonomy, and Empowerment." Pp. 19–37 in *Black Women in America*, edited by Kim Marie Vaz. Thousand Oaks, CA: Sage.

Moss, Richard, M. D. 1995. *The Second Miracle: Intimacy, Spirituality, and Conscious Relationships*. Berkeley, CA: Celestial Arts.

Mouffe, C. 1988. *Radical Democracy: Modern or Postmodern?* Pp. 31–45 in *Universal Abandon: The Politics of Postmodernism*, edited by A. Ross. Minneapolis: University of Minnesota Press.

Moyers, Bill. 1995. "What Can We Do about Violence?" A Bill Moyers Special, Public Broadcasting System, January 9, 11.

Murphy, Sheila, and Dan Waldorf. 1991. "Kickin' Down to the Street Doc: Shooting Galleries in the San Francisco Bay Area." *Contemporary Drug Problems* 18: 9–29.

Musto, David F. 1987. *The American Disease: Origins of Narcotic Control.* New York: Oxford University Press.

Nadelmann, Ethan A. 1989. "Drug Prohibition in the United States: Costs, Consequences, and Alternatives." *Science* 245 (September): 939–47.

National Association of Anorexia Nervosa and Associated Disorders (ANAD). 1996. "Compelling Reasons for Intensifying and Expanding Education/Prevention Programs in the Eating Disorders Field and for Providing Additional Support Programs for Victims and Their Families." Ten Year/Abuse Study.

National Association for the Advancement of Colored People (NAACP). 1919/ 1969. *Thirty Years of Lynching in the United States.* Reprint. New York: Arno Press.

———. 1987. Legal Defense and Educational Fund, Inc. *Death Row, U.S.A.* (March).

National Child Rights Alliance. 1989. P.O. Box 61125, Durham, NC 27705 (see Web site: http://www.ai.mit.edu/people/ellens/NCRA/rights.htm112/2/97).

National Coalition for the Homeless. 1998. "How Many People Experience Homelessness?" NCH Fact Sheet #2. Internet: http://nch.ari.net/numbers.html

National Commission on Adolescent Sexual Health. 1995. "Facing Facts: Sexual Health for America's Adolescents." Sexuality Information and Education Council. Washington, DC.

National Council for Children's Rights. 1996. "Crisis in Family Law: Children as Victims of Divorce." Report #R101. Washington, DC.

National Institute of Justice. 1996. *Research Preview.* Washington, DC: NIJ.

———. 1997. *Drug Use Forecasting: Annual Report on Adult and Juvenile Arrestees.* Washington, DC: U.S. Department of Justice.

National Organization of Women. 1995. *Legal Defense and Education Fund Report.* Washington, DC: NOW.

National School Boards Association. *Report.* 1993. Washington, D.C.

National Victim Center. 1992. *Rape in America.* Arlington, VA.

Nava, Mica. 1992. *Changing Cultures: Feminism, Youth and Consumerism.* Newbury Park, CA: Sage.

Neville, B. 1989. *Educating Psyche: Emotion, Imagination and the Unconscious in Learning.* Blackburn, Australia: Collins Dove.

Nietzsche, Friedrich. 1969. *On the Genealogy of Morals.* New York: Vintage.

Noddings, Nel. 1995. *Philosophy of Education.* Boulder, CO: Westview Press.

Novacek, J., R. Raskin, and R. Hogan. 1991. "Why do Adolescents Use Drugs? Age, Sex, and User Differences." *Journal of Youth and Adolescence.* 20(5): 175–192.

O'Connor, I. 1989. *Our Homeless Children: Their Experiences.* Report to the Human Rights and Equal Opportunity Commission, Australia.

Office of Juvenile Justice and Delinquency Prevention. 1993. *Urban Delinquency and Substance Abuse: Technical Report.* Washington, DC: Department of Justice.

———. 1995. *Program Report on Youth Gun Violence.* Washington, DC: Department of Justice.

———. August 1996a. *Juvenile Offenders and Victims: A National Report.* Washington, DC: Department of Justice.

—— 1996b. *Reducing Youth Gun Violence: An Overview of Programs and Initiatives.* Washington, DC: U.S. Department of Justice.

—— 1996c. *Juvenile Detention Training Needs Assessment.* Washington, DC: U.S. Department of Justice.

Office of the National Drug Control Policy. 1989. *The National Drug Control Strategy.* Washington, DC: U.S. Government Printing Office.

——. 1994. "Fact Sheet: Drug-Related Crime." Drugs and Crime Clearinghouse (September). Rockville, MD: National Criminal Justice Reference Service.

——. 1995. "Fact Sheet: Drug Use Trends." Drugs and Crime Clearinghouse (June). Rockville, MD: National Criminal Justice Reference Service.

Ohlin, Lloyd, and Michael Tonry, eds. 1987. "Justice and Gender." *Philosophy and Public Affairs* 16: 42–72.

——. 1989. *Family Violence.* Chicago: University of Chicago Press.

Okin, Susan Moller. 1989. *Justice, Gender and the Family.* New York: Basic Books.

Olsen, M. E., D. G. Lodwick, and R. E. Dunlap. 1992. *Viewing the World Ecologically.* Boulder, CO: Westview Press.

Oppenheimer, Todd. 1997. "The Computer Delusion." *The Atlantic Monthly* (July): 45–62.

Orr, David W. 1992. *Ecological Literacy: Education and the Transition to a Postmodern World.* Brandon, VT: Great Ideas in Education.

Orvis, Gregory P. 1996. "Treating Youth Gangs Like Organized Crime Groups: An Innovative Strategy for Prosecuting Youth Gangs." Pp. 93–104 in *Gangs: A Criminal Justice Approach*, edited by J. Mitchell Miller and Jeffrey P. Rush. Cincinnati, OH: Anderson.

Ozment, Steven. 1983. *When Fathers Ruled: Family Life in Reformation Europe.* Cambridge, MA: Harvard University Press.

Padilla, Felix. 1995. "The Working Gang." Pp. 53–61 in *The Modern Gang Reader*, edited by Malcolm W. Klein, Cheryl L. Maxson, and Jody Miller. Los Angeles: Roxbury Publishing Co.

Pagelow, Mildred Daley. 1984. *Family Violence.* New York: Praeger Publishers.

——. 1989. "The Incidence and Prevalence of Criminal Abuse of Other Family Members." Pp. 263–314 in *Family Violence.* Crime and Justice: A Review of Research, Vol. 11, edited by Lloyd Ohlin and Michael Tonry. Chicago and London: The University of Chicago Press.

Palmer, Parker J. 1997. "The Grace of Great Things: Reclaiming the Sacred in Knowing, Teaching and Learning." *Holistic Education Review* 10(3): 8–16.

Parker, Howard. 1996. "Young Adult Offenders, Alcohol, and Criminological Cul-De-Sacs." *British Journal of Criminology* 36(2): 282–98.

Parker, Howard, T. C. Harford, and I. M. Rosenstock. 1991. "Alcohol, Other Drugs, and Sexual Risk-Taking among Young Adults." *Journal of Substance Abuse* 6(1): 87–93.

Parker, Howard, and Linda-Anne Rebhun. 1995. *Alcohol and Homicide.* Albany, NY: State University of New York Press.

Parks, Carolyn P. 1995. "Gang Behavior in the Schools: Reality or Myth?" *Educational Psychology Review* 7(1): 41–69.

Pear, Robert. 1997. "New Estimate Doubles Rate of H.I.V. Spread." *New York Times* (December 3).

Pearlstein, Steven. 1995. "The Growing Income Gap." *Washington Post National Weekly Edition* (June 12–18).

Peck, M. Scott. 1983. *People of the Lie: The Hope for Healing Human Evil.* New York: Simon and Schuster.

———. 1993. *A World Waiting to Be Born: Civility Rediscovered.* New York: Bantam Books.

Perreault, Joe. 1991. "Society as Extended Family: Giving a Childhood to Every Child." *Dimensions* 19(4): 3–8, 31.

Peterson, Peggy L., and John B. Lowe. 1992. "Preventing Fetal Alcohol Exposure: A Cognitive Behavior Approach." *The International Journal of the Addictions* 27(5): 613–26.

Pfeffer, Cynthia R. 1996. "Childhood Suicidal Behavior." American Foundation for Suicide Prevention.

Pfeffer, C. R., G. L. Klerman, S. W. Hurt, T. Kakuma, J. R. Peskin, and C. A. Siefker. 1993. "Suicidal Children Grow Up: Rates and Psychosocial Risk Factors for Suicide Attempts during Follow-Up." *Journal of the American Academy of Child and Adolescent Psychiatry* 32: 106–13.

Pipher, Mary. 1994. *Reviving Ophelia: Saving the Lives of Adolescent Girls.* New York: Ballantine Books.

Platt, Anthony. 1969. *The Child Savers.* Chicago: University of Chicago Press.

Pleck, Elizabeth. 1987. *Domestic Tyranny: The Making of Social Policy against Family Violence from Colonial Times to the Present.* New York: Oxford University Press.

Pogrebin, Letty C. 1983. *Family Politics.* New York: McGraw-Hill.

Polk, Ken. 1988. "Education, Youth Unemployment and School Resistance." Chapter in *Discipline and Schools*, edited by Roger Slee. Melbourne: Macmillan Publishers.

———. 1994. *When Men Kill: Scenarios of Masculine Violence.* Cambridge, UK/New York/Melbourne: Cambridge University Press.

Pollan, Michael. 1995. "How Pot Has Grown." *New York Times Magazine* (February 19): 31–57.

———. 1997. "Living with Medical Marijuana." *New York Times Magazine* (July 20): 22–56.

Pollock, Linda. 1983. *Forgotten Children: Parent/Child Relations from 1500 to 1800.* Cambridge, England: University of Cambridge Press.

Pope, Carl, and William Feyerherm. 1996. "Minorities and the Juvenile Justice System: A Research Summary." In *Exploring Delinquency: Causes and Control*, edited by Dean G. Rojek and Gary E. Jensen. Los Angeles: Roxbury Publishing Co.

Popenoe, David. 1988. *Disturbing the Nest: Family Change and Decline in Modern Societies.* New York: Aldine De Gruyter.

———. 1991. "Breakup of the Family: Can We Reverse the Trend?" *USA Today Magazine* (May): 50–53.

Poulin, John E. 1991. "Racial Differences in the Use of Drugs and Alcohol among Low Income Youth and Young Adults." *Journal of Sociology and Social Welfare* 18(3): 159–66.

Prothrow-Stith, Deborah. 1993. *Deadly Violence.* New York: Harper Perennial.

———. 1995. "The Epidemic of Youth Violence in America: Using Public Health

Prevention Strategies to Prevent Violence." *Journal of Health Care for the Poor and Underserved* 6(2): 95–101.

Pruitt, Mary C. 1995. "Racial Justice in Minnesota: The Activism of Mary Toliver Jones and Josie Robinson Johnson." Pp. 71–95 in *Black Women in America*, edited by Kim Marie Vaz. Thousand Oaks, CA: Sage.

Quimby, Ernest. 1990. "Drug Trafficking and the Caribbean Connection: Survival Mechanisms, Entrepreneurship and Social Symptoms." *Urban League Review 1990–1991* 14(2): 61–70.

Quinney, Richard and Wildeman, John. 1991. *The Problem of Crime: A Peace and Social Justice Perspective*. Mountain View, CA: Mayfield Publishing Company.

Regoli, R. M., and J. D. Hewitt, 1991. *Delinquency in Society: A Child-Centered Approach*. New York: McGraw-Hill.

Reiss, Albert J., Jr. 1986. "Why Are Communities Important in Understanding Crime?" Pp. 1–33 in *Communities and Crime. Crime and Justice: A Review of Research*, Vol. 8, edited by Albert J., Reiss, Jr., and Michael Tonry. Chicago and London: The University of Chicago Press.

Reiss, Albert J., Jr. and Jeffrey A. Roth, eds. 1993. *Understanding and Preventing Violence*. Washington, DC: National Academy Press.

Richardson, John G. 1994. "Common, Delinquent, and Special: On the Formalization of Common Schooling in the American States." *American Educational Research Journal* (Winter), 31(4): 695–723.

Richardson, Lynda. 1995. "To Sleep, Perchance to Stay Awake in Class." *The New York Times* (December 27): A1, B9.

Riley, Pamela L. 1995. "School Violence: Let's Get It Out of Our System." Raleigh, NC: North Carolina Center for the Prevention of School Violence.

Riley, Richard W. 1994. "State of American Education: Remarks Prepared for the Congress of the United States." Washington, DC: Department of Education.

Robins, L. N., and K. S. Ratcliff. 1979. "Risk Factors in the Continuation of Childhood Antisocial Behavior into Adulthood." *International Journal of Mental Health* 7: 76–116.

Robson, B. 1992. *Rough Justice: A Report on Sexual Assault, Homelessness and the Law*. Melbourne: North Easte Centre Against Sexual Assault.

Rojek, Dean G., and Gary F. Jensen, eds. 1996. *Exploring Delinquency: Causes and Consequences*. Los Angeles: Roxbury Publishing Co.

Rose, Phyllis. 1984. *Parallel Lives: Five Victorian Marriages*. New York: Alfred A. Knopf.

Rosenbaum, Marsha. 1988. *Women on Heroin*. 3d ed. New Brunswick, NJ: Rutgers University Press.

Rosenberg, Mark L. 1995. "Violence in America: An Integrated Approach to Understanding and Prevention." *Journal of Health Care for the Poor and Underserved* 6(2): 102–12.

Rotheram-Borus, M. J. et al. 1991. "Sexual and Substance Use Acts of Gay and Bisexual Male Adolescents in New York City." *Journal of Sex Research* 31(1): 17–57.

Rothman, David J. 1990. *The Discovery of the Asylum*. 2d ed. Boston: Little Brown.

Russell, H. 1948. *Human Cargoes: A Short History of the African Slave Trade*.

Ryan, Alan, ed. 1993. *Justice.* New York: Oxford University Press.

Sampson, R. J., and J. H. Laub. 1993. *Crime in the Making: Pathways and Turning Points through Life.* Cambridge, MA: Harvard University Press.

Sanders, William B. 1994. *Gangbangs and Drive-bys: Grounded Culture and Juvenile Gang Violence.* New York: Aldine De Gruyter.

Schlesinger, Arthur M. 1963. *The Politics of Hope.* Boston: Houghton Mifflin.

Schlosser, Eric. 1994a. "Reefer Madness." *Atlantic Monthly* (August): 45–64.

———. 1994b. "Marijuana and the Law." *Atlantic Monthly* (Sept.): 82–94.

———. 1997a. "More Reefer Madness." *Atlantic Monthly* (April): 90–102.

———. 1997b. "A Grief Like No Other." *Atlantic Monthly* (Sept.): 37–76.

Schneider, Hans Joachim. 1996. "Violence in the Institution." *International Journal of Offender Therapy and Comparative Criminology* 40(1): 5–18.

Schneider, K. S. 1996. "Mission Impossible." *People* 45(22): 64–74.

Schuckit, Marc A. 1990. "Are There Dangers to Marijuana?" *Drug Abuse and Alcoholism Newsletter* 19: 1–4.

Schuerman, John R., Tina L. Rzepnicki, and Julia H. Littell. 1994. *Putting Families First: An Experiment in Family Preservation.* New York: Aldine De Gruyter.

Schwartz, Ira. 1989. *(In) Justice for Juveniles: Rethinking the Best Interests of the Child.* Lexington, MA: Lexington Books.

Schwartz, Ira, and William H. Barton, eds. 1994. *Reforming Juvenile Detention: No More Hidden Closets.* Columbus, OH: Ohio State University Press.

Schwartz, Wendy. 1994. "School Dropouts: New Information about an Old Problem." New York: ERIC Clearinghouse on Urban Education.

Sealock, M. D., D. C. Gottfredson, and C.A. Gallagher. 1995. "Addressing Drug Use and Recidivism in Delinquent Youth: An Examination of Residential and Aftercare Treatment Programs." Paper presented at the Annual Meeting of the American Society of Criminology. November 15. Boston, MA.

Sedlak, Andrea J., and Diane D. Broadhurst. 1996. "Executive Summary." *The Third National Incidence Study of Child Abuse and Neglect.* U.S. Department of Health and Human Services Administration for Children and Families.

Seng, Magnus J. 1989. "Child Abuse and Adolescent Prostitution: A Comparative Analysis." *Adolescence* 24(95): 665–75.

Sennett, Richard, and Jonathan Cobb. 1973. *The Hidden Injuries of Class.* New York: Vintage.

Sereny, G. 1985. *The Invisible Children: Child Prostitution in America, West Germany, and Great Britain.* New York: Alfred A. Knopf.

Shaffer, D. et al. 1990. "Adolescent Suicide Attempters: Response to Suicide Prevention Programs." *Journal of the American Medical Association* 264: 3151–55.

Shahar, Shulamith. 1990. *Childhood in the Middle Ages.* London and New York: Routledge.

Shapiro, Andrew L. 1993. "Children in Court: The New Crusade." *Nation* 257, no. 9 (September 27): 301–19.

Shaw, Amy E., and Cynthia Dickinson. 1996. "Preventing Teen Pregnancy." Sonoma County Medical Association.

Sheley, Joseph F., and James D. Wright. 1995. *In the Line of Fire: Youth, Guns, and Violence in Urban America.* New York: Aldine De Gruyter.

Short, James. 1984. "The Social Fabric at Risk: Toward the Social Transformation of Risk Analysis." *American Review of Sociology* 49: 711–25.

———. 1990. "Gangs, Neighborhoods, and Youth Crime." *Criminal Justice Research Bulletin* 5(4).

Shorter, Edward. 1976. *The Making of the Modern Family.* New York: Basic Books.

Siegel, Harvey A., and James A. Inciardi. 1995. "A Brief History of Alcohol." Pp. 45–49 in *The American Drug Scene*, edited by James A. Inciardi and Karen McElrath. Los Angeles: Roxbury Publishing Co.

Sigmon, Scott B. 1994. "Youth Violence Syndrome (YVS) and American Society." *Viewpoints.* Educational Resources Information Center (ERIC). Washington, DC: U.S. Department of Education.

Silvers, Jonathan. 1996. "Child Labor in Pakistan." *Atlantic Monthly* (February): 79–92.

Skolnick, Jerome H. 1990. "A Critical Look at the National Drug Control Strategy." *Yale Law and Policy Review* 8(1): 75–116.

———. 1995. "Gangs and Crime Old as Time; But Drugs Change Gang Culture." Pp. 222–27 in *The Modern Gang Reader*, edited by Malcolm W. Klein, Cheryl L. Maxson, and Jody Miller. Los Angeles: Roxbury Publishing Co.

Smith, M. P. 1992. "Postmodernism, Urban Ethnography, and the New Social Space of Ethnic Identity." *Theory and Society* 21: 493–531.

Smothers, Ronald. 1995. "Wave of Prison Uprisings Provokes Debate on Crack." *New York Times* (October 24): A12.

Smrekar, Claire. 1996. *The Impact of School Choice and Community.* Albany: State University of New York.

Snow, D., S. Baker, and L. Anderson. 1989. Criminality and Homeless Men: An Empirical Assessment." *Social Problems* 36: 532–549.

Snyder, H. N., and M. Sickmund. 1994. "Are Juveniles Driving the Violent Crime Trend." *Office of Juvenile Justice Delinquency Prevention Fact Sheet #16.* Washington, DC: Office of Juvenile Justice and Delinquency Prevention.

———. 1995. *Juvenile Offenders and Victims: A National Report.* Washington, DC: Office of Juvenile Justice and Delinquency Prevention.

Snyder, H. N., Melissa Sickmund, and Eileen Poe-Yamagata. 1996. "Juvenile Offenders and Victims: 1996 Update on Violence." Washington, DC: Office of Juvenile Justice and Delinquency Prevention.

Snyder, James, and Debra Huntley. 1990. "Troubled Families and Troubled Youth." Pp. 194–225 in *Understanding Troubled and Troubling Youth*, edited by Peter E. Leone. Newbury Park, CA: Sage.

Solomon, Robert. 1990. *A Passion for Justice.* Reading, MA: Addison-Wesley.

Sommerville, John. 1982. *The Rise and Fall of Childhood.* Beverly Hills, CA: Sage.

Speigel, D. 1986. "Disassociation, Double Binds, and Posttraumatic Stress in Multiple Personality Disorder." In *Treatment of Multiple Personality Disorder*, edited by B. G. Braun. Washington, DC: American Psychiatric Press, Inc.

Spencer, Margaret Beale. 1995. "Old Issues and New Theorizing about African American Youth: A Phenomenological Variant of Ecological Systems Theory." Pp. 37–71 in *African American Youth: Their Social and Economic Status in the United States*, edited by Ronald L. Taylor. Westport, CT: Praeger.

Spergel, Irving A., and G. David Curry. 1995. "The National Youth Gang Survey:

A Research and Development Process." Pp. 254–75 in *The Modern Gang Reader*, edited by Malcolm W. Klein, Cheryl L. Maxson, and Jody Miller. Los Angeles: Roxbury Publishing Co.

Spohn, Cassia. 1994. "Crime and the Social Control of Blacks: Offender/Victim Race and the Sentencing of Violent Offenders." In *Inequality, Crime, and Social Control*, edited by George S. Budge and Martha A. Myers. Boulder, CO: Westview.

Stallard, K., B. Ehrenreich, and H. Sklar. 1983. *Poverty in the American Dream: Women and Children First*. New York: South End Press.

Stanley, Barbara, and Joan E. Sieber. 1992. *Social Research on Children and Adolescents*. Newbury Park, CA: Sage.

Steele, B. F. 1986. "Notes on the Lasting Effects of Early Child Abuse throughout the Life Cycle." *Child Abuse and Neglect* 10: 283–91.

Sterber, James P. et al. 1995. *Morality & Social Justice: Point/Counterpoint*. London: Rowman & Littlefield.

Stevens, M. M., L. A. Mott, and F. Youells. 1996. "Rural Adolescent Drinking Behavior: Three Year Follow-Up in the New Hampshire Substance Abuse Prevention Study." *Adolescence* 31(Spring): 159–66.

Stolz, Barbara Ann. 1990. "Congress and the War on Drugs: An Exercise in Symbolic Politics." Paper presented at the Annual Meeting of the American Society of Criminology, Baltimore, MD, November 7–10.

Stone, Lawrence. 1980. *The Family, Sex and Marriage in England, 1500–1800*. New York: Harper and Row.

Stossel, Scott. 1997. "The Man Who Counts the Killings." *The Atlantic Monthly* (May): 86–104.

Strasburger, V. C. 1995. *Adolescents and the Media: Medical and Psychological Consequences*. Newbury Park, CA: Sage.

Straus, Murray A. 1991. "Physical Violence in American Families: Incidence Rates, Causes and Trends." Pp. 17–34 in *Abused and Battered: Social and Legal Responses to Family Violence*, edited by Dean D. Knudsen and JoAnn L. Miller. New York: Aldine De Gruyter.

———. 1993. "Identifying Offenders in Criminal Justice Research on Domestic Assault." *American Behavioral Scientist* 36(5): 587–600.

Straus, Murray A., and Carrie L. Yodanis. 1993. "Corporal Punishment, Normative Approval of Violence, and Assaults on Spouses." Paper presented at the American Society of Criminology Meeting (October).

Strauss, William and Neil Howe. 1998. *The Fourth Turning: An American Prophecy*. New York: Broadway Books.

Streib, Victor L. 1995. "Imposing the Death Penalty on Children." Pp. 145–60 in *Juvenile Delinquency: A Justice Perspective*, 2d ed, edited by R. A. Weisheit and R. G. Culbertson. Prospect Heights, IL: Waveland Press.

Suransky, Valerie P. 1982. *The Erosion of Childhood*. Chicago and London: The University of Chicago Press.

Swart, William J. 1995. "Female Gang Delinquency: A Search for 'Acceptably Deviant Behavior.' " Pp. 78–92 in *The Modern Gang Reader*, edited by Malcolm W. Klein, Cheryl L. Maxson, and Jody Miller. Los Angeles: Roxbury Publishing Co.

Sweeney, P. et al. 1995. "Teenagers At Risk of Human Immunodeficiency Virus

Type 1 Infection." *Archives of Pediatric and Adolescent Medicine* 149 (May): 521–28.

Sykes, Gresham. 1958. *A Society of Captives: A Study of a Maximum Security Prison.* Princeton, NJ: Princeton University Press.

Takanishi, R., ed. 1993. *Adolescence in the 1990s: Risk and Opportunity.* New York: Teachers College Press.

Taylor, R. B., and J. Covington. 1988. "Neighborhood Changes in Ecology and Violence." *Criminology* 26: 553–90.

Taylor, Ronald L. 1992. "Poverty and Adolescent Black Males: The Subculture of Disengagement." Pp. 139–62 in *Adolescence and Poverty*, edited by Peter Edelman and Joyce Ladner. Washington, DC: Center for National Policy Press.

———. 1994. "Black Inner-City Youth and the Subculture of Disengagement." In *Teenage Pregnancy: Developing Strategies for Change in the Twenty-First Century*, edited by D. J. Jones and S. F. Battle. New Brunswick, NJ: Transaction.

———. ed. 1995. *African American Youth: Their Social and Economic Status in the United States.* Westport, CT: Praeger.

Terrell, N. E. 1997. "Aggravated and Sexual Assaults among Homeless and Runaway Adolescents." *Youth and Society* 28(3): 267–90.

Thomas, Keith. 1971. *Religion and the Decline of Magic.* New York: Penguin.

Thomas, Melvin E., C. Herring, and H. D. Horton. 1994. "Discrimination over the Life Course: A Synthetic Cohort. Analysis of Earnings Differences between White and Black Men, 1940–1990." *Social Problems* 41, no. 4 (November): 608–28.

Thomas, Melvin E., and Horton, H. D. 1992. "Race, Class, and Family Structures: The Case of Family Income, 1968–1988." *Sociological Perspectives.* 35: 433–50.

Thompson, S. 1995. *Going All the Way.* New York: Hill and Wang.

Thrasher, F. M. 1927. *The Gang: A Study of 1,313 Gangs in Chicago.* Chicago: University of Chicago Press.

Thurow, Lester C. 1995. "Companies Merge; Families Break Up." *New York Times* (September 3): A11.

Tiefer, Leonore. 1995. *Sex Is Not a Natural Act.* Boulder, CO: Westview Press.

Tifft, Larry L. 1993. *Battering of Women: The Failure of Intervention and the Care for Prevention.* Boulder, CO: Westview Press.

Tolnay, Stewart E. 1994. *A Festival of Violence: An Analysis of the Lynching of African Americans in the American South, 1882–1930.* Urbana, IL: University of Illinois Press.

Tolnay, Stewart E., and E. M. Beck. 1994. "Lethal Social Control in the South: Lynchings and Executions Between 1880 and 1930." In *Inequality, Crime, and Social Control*, edited by George S. Bridges and Martha A. Myers. Boulder, CO: Westview Press.

Tonry, Michael, and James Q. Wilson, eds. 1990. *Drugs and Crime.* Chicago: University of Chicago Press.

Treback, Arnold S. 1994. "Thinking Through Models of Drug Legalization." *The Drug Policy Letter* 23: 10–15.

Treback, Arnold S., and James A. Inciardi. 1993. *Legalize It: Debating American Drug Policy.* Washington, DC: The American University Press.

Tromanhauser, Edward. 1995. "A Descriptive Survey of Selected Characteristics of Street Gang Members in the United States." Paper presented at the 1995 Meeting of the American Society of Criminology. November 16, Boston.

Uehara, Edwina S. et al. 1996. "African American Youth Encounters with Violence: Results from the Community Mental Health Council Violence Screening Project." *Journal of Black Studies* 26(6): 768–81.

Uniform Crime Reports (UCR). 1994. *Crime in the United States.* Washington, DC: Government Printing Office.

United Nations on the Prevention of Crime and the Treatment of Offenders (Ninth Congress). 1990. *United Nations Crime Prevention and Criminal Justice Newsletter* 28–29: 19–20.

U.S. Centers for Disease Control. 1991. "Attempted Suicide among High School Students—United States, 1990." *Morbidity and Mortality Weekly Report* 40 (September 20): 633–35.

———. 1991–92. "State-Specific Pregnancy and Birth Rates among Teenagers." CDC Document 451011.

U.S. Department of Health and Human Services. 1996. *The Relationship between Family Structure and Adolescent Substance Use.* Rockville, MD: National Clearinghouse for Alcohol and Drug Information (NCADI).

U.S. Department of Justice, Bureau of Crime Statistics. 1989. *Criminal Victimization in the United States, 1987.* National Crime Survey Report NCJ-115524, August.

U.S. Department of Justice. 1993. *Comprehensive Strategy for Serious, Violent, and Chronic Juvenile Offenders.* Washington, DC: Office of Justice Programs, Bureau of Justice Statistics.

———. 1994a. *Criminal Victimization in the United States, 1992.* Washington, DC: Office of Justice Programs, Bureau of Justice Statistics.

———. 1994b. *Juvenile Justice and Delinquency Prevention.* Washington, DC: Office of Justice Programs, Bureau of Justice Statistics.

———. 1994c. "Drugs, Delinquency, and Other Data." *Juvenile Justice.* Washington, DC: Office of Juvenile Justice and Delinquency Prevention.

———. 1995a. "Drug Use Forecasting: 1994 Annual Report on Adult and Juvenile Arrestees." Washington, DC: National Institute of Justice.

———. 1995b. "Juvenile Offenders and Victims: A Focus on Violence." Statistics Summary. Washington, DC: Office of Juvenile Justice and Delinquency Prevention.

———. 1995c. "Prosecuting Gangs: A National Assessment" (February). Washington, DC: National Institute of Justice.

———. 1996. "Estimating the National Scope of Gang Crime from Law Enforcement Data" (August). Washington, DC: National Institute of Justice.

———. 1997. "Expert Panel Issues Report on Serious and Violent Juvenile Offenders" (October). Washington, DC: Office of Juvenile Justice and Delinquency Prevention.

U.S. Department of Labor, Bureau of Labor Statistics, 1994. *Employment of School-Age Youth, Graduates, and Dropouts.* Washington, DC.

van der Kolk, B. 1984. *Psychological Trauma*. Washington, DC: American Psychiatric Association.

Vanderschmidt, H. F. et al. 1993. "Risks among Inner-City Young Teens: The Prevalence of Sexual Activity, Violence, Drugs, and Smoking." *Journal of Adolescent Health* 14(4): 282–288.

Vanderstaay, Steven. 1992. *Street Lives*. Philadelphia: New Society.

Van Dyke, Anne. 1995. "All Things Considered" (April 4). National Public Radio.

Van Mastright, Hans. 1990. "The Abolition of Drug Policy: Toward Strategic Alternatives." *The Journal of Drug Issues* 20(4): 647–57.

Van Ness, Daniel, and Karen Heetderks Strong. 1997. *Restoring Justice*. Cincinnati, OH: Anderson Publishing.

Vaz, Kim, ed. 1995. *Black Women in America*. Thousand Oaks, CA: Sage.

Verhovek, Sam Howe. 1995. "States Are Already Providing Glimpse at Welfare's Future." *New York Times* (September 21): A1/A10.

———. 1997. "Pentagon Halts Drug Patrols after Border Killing." *New York Times* (July 31): A1, A9.

Vigil, James Diego. 1990. "Cholos and Gangs: Culture Change and Street Youth in Los Angeles." Pp. 116–28 in *Gangs in America*, edited by C. Ronald Huff. Newbury Park, CA: Sage.

Vigil, James, and John M. Long. 1990. "Emic and Etic Perspectives on Gang Culture: The Chicano Case." Pp. 37–55 in *Gangs in America*, edited by C. Ronald Huff. Newbury Park, CA: Sage.

Vigil, James, and Steve Chong Yun. 1990. "Vietnamese Youth Gangs in Southern California." Pp. 146–62 in *Gangs in America*, edited by C. Ronald Huff. Newbury Park, CA: Sage.

Vilakazi, A. 1962. *Zulu Transformations: A Study of the Dynamics of Social Change*. Pietermaritzburg: University of Natal Press.

Voigt, Lydia, William E. Thornton, Leo Barrile, and Jerrol M. Seaman. 1994. *Criminology and Justice*. New York: McGraw-Hill.

Vygotsky, L. 1978. *Mind in Society*. Cambridge, MA: Harvard University Press.

Walker, Alice. 1997. *Anything We Love Can Be Saved: A Writer's Activism*. New York: Random House.

Walker, Dean. 1995. "Violence in Schools: How to Build a Prevention Program from the Ground Up." *OSSC Bulletin* 38(5).

Walzer, Michael. 1983. *Spheres of Justice*. New York: Basic Books.

Warren, K. R., and R. J. Bast. 1988. "Alcohol-Related Birth Defects: An Update." *Public Health Report* 103: 638–43.

Weber, Max. 1977. *The Protestant Ethic and the Spirit of Capitalism*. New York: Macmillan.

Weddle, K. D., and P. C. McKenry. 1995. "Self-Destructive Behaviors among Black Youth: Suicide and Homicide." In *African American Youth: Their Social and Economic Status in the United States*, edited by R. L. Taylor. Westport, CT: Praeger.

Weil, Andrew. 1995. "Why People Take Drugs." Pp. 3–11 in *The American Drug Scene*, edited by James A. Inciardi and Karen McElrath. Los Angeles: Roxbury Publishing Co.

Weiner, Neil Alan, Margaret A. Zahn, and Rita J. Sagi. 1990. *Violence: Patterns, Causes, Public Policy*. San Diego: Harcourt Brace Jovanovich.

Weisberg, D. K. 1985. *Children of the Night: A Study of Adolescent Prostitution.* Lexington, MA: Lexington Books.

Weisheit, Ralph A., and Robert G. Culbertson. 1995. *Juvenile Delinquency: A Justice Perspective.* 3d ed. Prospect Heights, IL: Waveland Press.

Wells, G., and G. Chang-Wells. 1992. *Constructing Knowledge Together: Classrooms as Centers of Inquiry and Literacy.* Portsmouth, NH: Heinemann Educational Books.

West, Cornel. 1993a. *Race Matters.* Boston: Beacon Press.

———. 1993b. "The New Cultural Politics of Difference." In *The Cultural Studies Reader,* edited by S. During. London: Routledge.

Wheatley School Home Page. 1997. (Internet), http://www.ewsd.k12.ny.us/wheatley/wheatley.html

Whitcomb, Debra, Gail S. Goodman, Desmond K. Runyan, and Shirley Hoak. 1994. "The Emotional Effects of Testifying on Sexually Abused Children." National Institute of Justice, *Research in Brief.* U.S. Government Printing Office.

White, Joseph L. 1989. *The Troubled Adolescent.* New York: Pergamon Press.

White, R., R. Underwood, and S. Omelczuk. 1991. "Victims of Violence: The View from the Youth Services." *Australian-New Zealand Journal of Criminology* 24: 5–39.

White, Stephen. 1992. *Political Theory and Postmodernism.* New York: Cambridge University Press.

Whitehead, John T., and Steven P. Lab. 1996. *Juvenile Justice.* 2d ed. Cincinnati: Anderson.

Widom, Cathy Spatz. 1989. "Child Abuse, Neglect, and Violent Criminal Behavior." Criminology 27(2): 251–71.

Widom, Cathy Spatz, and Suzanne Morris. 1995. "Accuracy of Adult Recollections of Childhood Victimization." Paper presented at the American Society of Criminology (November), Phoenix, AZ.

Wiesel, Elie. 1995. Commencement address to Sacred Heart University. Reprinted in the *New York Times* (May 29), p. 9.

Wilber, K. 1997. *The Eye of Spirit: An Integral Vision for a World Gone Slightly Mad.* Boston: Shambhala.

Wilczynski, Ania. 1995. "Risk Factors for Parental Child Homicide: Results of an English Study." *Criminal Justice* 7(2): 193–222.

Williams, Walter E. 1995. "A Tragic Vision of Black Problems." *American Quarterly* 47(3): 409–27.

Wilson, Edward O. 1994. *Naturalist.* New York: Shearwater Books/Island Press.

Wilson, James Q. 1975. *Thinking about Crime.* New York: Basic Books.

———. 1990. "Against the Legalization of Drugs." *Commentary* (February).

———. 1992. *American Government: Institutions and Policies.* 5th ed. Lexington, MA: D.C. Heath.

Wilson, Margo, and Martin Daly. 1993. "Lethal Confrontational Violence among Young Men." Pp. 84–106 in *Adolescent Risk Taking,* edited by Nancy J. Bell and Robert W. Bell. Newbury Park, CA: Sage.

Wilson, W. J. 1987. *The Truly Disadvantaged: The Inner City, The Underclass and Public Policy.* Chicago: University of Chicago Press.

——. 1996. *When Work Disappears: The World of the New Urban Poor.* New York: Knopf.

Winn, Marie. 1984. *Children without Childhood.* New York: Penguin Books.

Wolf, N. 1991. *The Beauty Myth: How Images of Beauty Are Used against Women.* New York: William Morrow.

Wolfe, David A., Christine Wekerle, and Katreena Scott. 1997. *Alternatives to Violence: Empowering Youth to Develop Healthy Relationships.* Thousand Oaks, CA: Sage.

Women's Educational Equity Act (WEEA). 1995. *Gendered Violence: Examining Education's Role.* Newton, MA: WEEA Publishing Center.

World Health Organization. 1993; 1996 (updated). "A One-Way Street?" *A Report on Phase I of the Street Children Project. Program on Substance Abuse, WHO.* Geneva: Regional Office of the Western Pacific, P.O. Box 2932, Manila (updated 1996).

Wren, Christopher S. 1997a. "Marijuana Use by Youths Rebounding after Decline." *New York Times* (February 20): A10.

——. 1997b. "A Seductive Drug Culture Flourishes on the Internet." *New York Times* (February 20): A10.

Wright, Robert. 1995. "The Biology of Violence." *The New Yorker* (March 13): 67–77.

Wyatt, Gail E. and Gloria Powell. 1988. *Lasting Effects of Child Sexual Abuse.* Newbury Park, CA: Sage.

Yee, Shirley J. 1995. "Organizing for Racial Justice: Black Women and the Dynamics of Race and Sex in Female Antislavery Societies, 1832–1860." Pp. 38–53 in *Black Women in America*, edited by Kim Marie Vaz. Thousand Oaks, CA: Sage.

Ylikahri, R. H. et al. 1978. "Acute Effects of Alcohol and Anterior Pituitary Secretion of the Tropic Hormones." *Journal of Clinical Endocrinology and Metabolism* 46: 715–20.

Young, G. M. 1953. *Victorian England: Portrait of an Age.* New York: Doubleday Anchor Books.

"Young Hispanic Adolescents in South Florida." *Women and Health* 24(1): 21–40.

Youth Justice Project. 1990. *Kids in Justice.* A project of the Youth Justice Coalition, NSW. Funded by the Law Foundation of the NSW.

Zaluar, A., and A. I. Ribeiro. 1995. "The Drug Trade, Crime and Policies of Repression in Brazil." *Dialectical Anthropology* 20(1): 95–108.

Zeldin, Theodore. 1994. *An Intimate History of Humanity.* New York: Harper-Collins.

Zimring, Franklin E., and Gordon J. Hawkins. 1973. *Deterrence: The Legal Threat in Crime Control.* Chicago, University of Chicago Press.

——. 1991. "What Kind of Drug War?" *Social Justice* 18(4): 104–21.

Zingraff, Matthew T., Jeffrey Leiter, Kristen A. Myers, and Matthew C. Johnsen. 1993. "Child Maltreatment and Youthful Problem Behavior." *Criminology* 31(2): 173–202.

Zook, Kristal Brent. 1995. "A Manifesto of Sorts for a Black Feminist Movement." *New York Times Magazine* (November 12): 86–89.

Index